BRITISH COLUMBIA IN THE BALANCE

Jean Barman

BRITISH COLUMBIA

in the Balance

1846–1871

HARBOUR
PUBLISHING

Copyright © 2022 Jean Barman

1 2 3 4 5 — 26 25 24 23 22

All rights reserved. No part of this publication may be reproduced, stored in a retrieval system or transmitted, in any form or by any means, without prior permission of the publisher or, in the case of photocopying or other reprographic copying, a licence from Access Copyright, www.accesscopyright.ca, 1-800-893-5777, info@accesscopyright.ca.

Harbour Publishing Co. Ltd.
P.O. Box 219, Madeira Park, BC, VON 2H0
www.harbourpublishing.com

Edited and indexed by Audrey McClellan
Text design by Carleton Wilson
Map by Roger Handling / Terra Firma Digital Arts
Printed and bound in Canada

Harbour Publishing acknowledges the support of the Canada Council for the Arts, the Government of Canada, and the Province of British Columbia through the BC Arts Council.

LIBRARY AND ARCHIVES CANADA CATALOGUING IN PUBLICATION

Title: British Columbia in the balance : 1846-1871 / Jean Barman.
Names: Barman, Jean, 1939- author.
Description: Includes index.
Identifiers: Canadiana (print) 20220249679 | Canadiana (ebook) 20220249709 | ISBN 9781550179880 (hardcover) | ISBN 9781550179897 (EPUB)
Subjects: CSH: British Columbia—History—1849-1871. | CSH: British Columbia—Politics and government—1849-1871.
Classification: LCC FC3822 .B37 2022 | DDC 971.1/02—dc23

British Columbia in the Balance is dedicated to Donna Sweet,
with whom I have spent more years than I can count searching out
the history of British Columbia—Donna to recover her family's story,
myself its general complement.

TABLE OF CONTENTS

MAP	9
PREAMBLE: Sensing the Past	11
CHAPTER 1: Today's British Columbia Coming into View	18
CHAPTER 2: The Year That Changed Everything (1858)	41
CHAPTER 3: James Douglas and the Colonial Office (1859–64)	85
CHAPTER 4: The Colonial Office in Action (1864–67)	138
CHAPTER 5: The Moderating Influence of Bishop Hills (1860–63)	166
CHAPTER 6: Taking Gold Miners Seriously (1858–71)	208
CHAPTER 7: Crediting Indigenous Women	236
CHAPTER 8: Along the Pathway to Canada (1866–71)	253
APPENDIX	295
INDEX	303

PREAMBLE

Sensing the Past

For as long as I can remember, I have viewed British Columbia as a kind of promised land. Growing up in northwest Minnesota a few miles south of the Canadian border, I would, while waiting in the car for the school bus to arrive a half mile from my parents' farm, listen to the weather forecast on Winnipeg radio, interspersed with my father once again musing on why, in emigrating from Sweden as a young man, he had not continued farther west to Saskatchewan or, better yet, to British Columbia. What deterred him, I came to realize, were the charms of my mother, who he had wooed during her holidays from teaching school, spent on her family's farm, half a mile from where my father had taken up land. It would be many years later, in a twist of fate, that my father had the opportunity to live out his dream of spending time in British Columbia after my husband accepted an academic position at the University of British Columbia in Vancouver, where I later also taught.

My father's dream has never left me. When our children were young, I conceived the idea of a popular history of British Columbia to appeal to newcomer families like our own, only to be summarily informed, on approaching a local historian for advice, that it was best for me as an outsider not to meddle in the history of British Columbians. Despite subsequently doing so time and again, I only recently came to realize the full extent to which I had, in my writing, possibly due to that earlier admonition as to whose history it was, ignored the province's beginnings as a non-Indigenous place. Hence, I am only now so turning my attention.

To understand the critical quarter of a century between 1846, when Great Britain acquired the land base that would become today's British Columbia, and 1871, when that land base joined a newly formed Canadian Confederation, I not only probed known and recorded happenings but also peered beneath the surface of events. It was my good fortune to do so just as the primary source closest to the ground—namely, the private correspondence exchanged between the Colonial Office in London, which had charge of British colonies around the world (including what would become British Columbia) and those overseeing them on site—became accessible online thanks to University of Victoria historian James Hendrickson.

Reading the Colonial Office correspondence turned my attention to the formative role played by a gold rush that began on the British Columbia mainland in 1858—a time when the future Canadian province's non-Indigenous population was almost wholly linked to a trade in animal pelts. I quickly became aware that among the reasons British Columbia became a Canadian province—rather than an American state or states, despite its proximity to an expansive United States—none was more important from the top down than the leadership of long-time fur trader James Douglas on site and of the Colonial Office in faraway London. While the gold rush as such mattered to the course of events, so did miners sticking around rather than moving on once gold lost its lustre, due very possibly to their having partnered with local Indigenous women at a time when non-Indigenous women were a rarity. Just as James Douglas and the Colonial Office affected the course of events from the top down, such unions were fundamental in the years during which the future of British Columbia hung in the balance.

Those of us who peer beneath the surface of events have our own instances of happenchance. One of my most consequential originated with the head of the Anglican Archives at the University of British Columbia having some years earlier generously offered me, while I was researching another topic, a transcribed copy of the private journal kept by George Hills, founding bishop of the Church of England in British Columbia, from the time of his arrival in the colony in 1860. There, Hills jotted down on an almost daily basis what mattered to him in the everyday, giving us a perspective from the bottom up that might otherwise have been lost from view.

Reading through the journal, my search for understanding took on a life of its own. As one example among the many that intrigued me, on May 20, 1862, Bishop Hills described a recent event in the small gold rush town of Douglas, now Port Douglas:

> Almost every man in Douglas lives with an Indian woman. The Magistrate Mr. Gaggin is not an exception from the immorality. Recently the constable Humphreys was ordered to a distance by the Magistrate. The Indian woman he lived with was named Lucy, by whom he had a child. He proposed to take her with him. The

magistrate was for some reason opposed. [The constable asked,] May I depend upon your honour that she shall be safe during my absence. The magistrate promised such should be the case. He violated the promise & induced the woman to come to him. The constable was highly incensed on his return ... & at length quitted the situation.

What can we expect when the representatives of England thus deport themselves.[1]

My response to this entry might have gone no further except for a chance encounter some years earlier. While researching another topic, I was introduced to a descendant of the child born to Humphreys and Lucy who, on learning of my interest in British Columbia's history, and believing the time had come to do so, shared with me her family's version of the story, which I included in *Invisible Generations: Living between Indigenous and White in the Fraser Valley*, published in 2019.[2]

Such occurrences are not ordinary but, on the other hand, not that unusual. As historians we learn from each other's stories, from what is written down, from what we and others share, and from the happenchance in the everyday of our lives.[3] We each in our own way come to sense the past, as I have had the good fortune to do thanks to both the many people who have shared stories with me and the array of fine historians who have gone before me.

Sensing the past

Our living in the present day, with all its twists and turns, does not preclude us also sensing the past. Doing so, I have come to understand to my satisfaction how it was that British Columbia, following a quarter of a century in the balance, was saved for Canada as opposed to falling into eager American hands.

---

1   May 20, 1862, entry in "The Journal of George Hills," 50, typescript in Anglican Church, Ecclesiastical Province of British Columbia, Archives.

2   Jean Barman, *Invisible Generations: Living between Indigenous and White in the Fraser Valley* (Halfmoon Bay, BC: Caitlin Press, 2019). The Humphreys story is interwoven on pages 56–61, 74–79, and 101–5.

3   Two excellent examples of what was written down are Hubert Howe Bancroft, *History of British Columbia* (San Francisco: History Company, 1887), and Margaret Ormsby, *British Columbia: A History* (Toronto: Macmillan, 1958).

The sequence of events began on June 15, 1846, when Great Britain and the United States divided between them the huge mass of the Pacific Northwest extending from the boundaries of California north to Russian America, now Alaska, and from the Rocky Mountains to the Pacific Ocean, which had been up to then unclaimed by any other non-Indigenous nation. Dividing the region along the forty-ninth parallel of latitude, with a jog south around Vancouver Island, the United States got the southern half and Britain the northern half, which, a quarter of a century later in 1871, would become today's Canadian province of British Columbia.

The intervening years had several stages. In 1849 the London-based Hudson's Bay Company (HBC), which had control of the fur trade, moved its headquarters from Fort Vancouver on the Columbia River, now in American territory, north to Vancouver Island, which was in the same year declared a British colony, to be governed from 1851 to 1864 by long-time HBC employee James Douglas.

The adjacent mainland was, for its part, largely left to its own devices until 1858, when a gold rush in the pattern of California a decade earlier transformed the territory into a destination for men from around the world hoping to get rich quick and be on their way. Named British Columbia by Queen Victoria, the mainland was, like its Vancouver Island counterpart, put under the charge of James Douglas.

Six years later, in 1864, the Colonial Office dismissed Douglas from his governorships, replacing him with two appointees, one for each colony. Two years after that, the two colonies of Vancouver Island and British Columbia were, for administrative efficiency, joined into a single colony named British Columbia, which was in 1871 made a province of the recently formed Dominion of Canada. So it remains to the present day.

A remarkable quarter of a century

Reflecting on this sequence of events, I have many times asked myself how such a fundamental outcome of these years during which British Columbia hung in the balance could have occurred in such a short period of time. It is not as if the province is tiny in size and easily bandied about. At 944,735 square kilometres (364,764 square miles), British Columbia is almost four times the size of its one-time mother country of Great Britain (242,495 square kilometres or 93,628 square miles).

The rapidity of the metamorphosis is unusual. Whereas most political entities around the world have emerged relatively slowly, it took British Columbia just a quarter of a century, 1846 to 1871, to be transformed from the almost wholly

Indigenous place it had been since time immemorial into a province of a newly formed Canada.

Those of us who are fortunate enough to live in British Columbia and Canada know the end of the story. We know that British Columbia did become a Canadian province, but we are mostly unaware, as I long had been, of precisely who was responsible for that outcome and how it was accomplished. Here I seek to explain to my own satisfaction, and I hope to that of others, what seems to be on the surface an implausible, impossibly rapid sequence of events.

Two complementary approaches

A distinct physical entity since 1846, British Columbia became a Canadian province twenty-five years later, in 1871, because people like you and me, Indigenous and non-Indigenous, made it so.

Reading and reflecting on the writing of others, I have come to realize more than ever that viewing the past from the top down, as has been most often the case, provides a perspective that is often quite different from what is seen from the bottom up, by peering beneath the surface of events as they occur. These two complementary approaches inform *British Columbia in the Balance*.

In going about the task, I returned time and again to accounts written by insiders. For a political and cultural perspective, I read and reread, among other sources, the published reminiscences of John Sebastian Helmcken, an English medical doctor who arrived in Victoria from England in 1850, and whose insights are heightened by his becoming James Douglas's son-in-law.[4] For a religious and cultural perspective, I had fortuitously shared with me, as noted above, the daily journal of George Hills, who came from England a decade later as the founding bishop of the Church of England on both Vancouver Island and the mainland.

Peering at the past from the top down, my attention almost inevitably turned to colonial fur trader and politician James Douglas, about whom I had written in snatches over the years but had never taken as seriously as I might have or probably should have. Employed across the Pacific Northwest by the Hudson's Bay Company and then as governor of the British colonies of Vancouver Island and British Columbia in 1851–64 and 1858–64, respectively, James Douglas was at the centre of events, but at whose behest?

---

4   Dorothy Blakey Smith, ed., *The Reminiscences of Doctor John Sebastian Helmcken* (Vancouver: UBC Press, 1975).

I needed to know more and had the good fortune to seek this information at the time James Douglas's correspondence with the Colonial Office in London, responsible for British colonies around the world, became accessible online, thanks, as noted above, to the initiative of long-time University of Victoria history professor James Hendrickson and his successor, John Lutz. Reading through the voluminous transcribed correspondence, I came to see that had it not been for Douglas and the Colonial Office acting in tandem and separately, British Columbia would almost certainly not have become a Canadian province, but rather passed into the hands of the United States.

What also soon became clear to me was that the Colonial Office's management of its myriad possessions around the world was a critical complement to the actions of Douglas on site at the time British Columbia hung in the balance. The decisions those in charge made in past time affected not only everyday life but also a colony's long-term direction. Each time a Colonial Office official—uniformly highly educated, most likely in an elite private school followed by a private university—read a letter arrived from some faraway colony, he assessed its content in a note known as a "minute," intended to be shared with the others who similarly read the letter on its way to a composite response by their superior. Thus was British Columbia crafted.

Turning to gold miners

The two remote British colonies that would become British Columbia were not alike in their transformations from Indigenous to non-Indigenous places. While Vancouver Island adopted the patina of a British possession early on, the sprawling mainland north of the forty-ninth parallel remained more an Indigenous place until gold finds from 1858 onward enticed there, as noted earlier, thousands of men from around the world intent on bettering themselves. Given that they almost always arrived on their own, intending to get rich quick and be on their way, and that white women were few and far between, it was almost always with an Indigenous woman that a man who tarried long enough to do so partnered.

By their everyday actions, gold miners and Indigenous women tipped the balance from the bottom up, even as James Douglas and the Colonial Office were doing so from the top down in the face of American determination to acquire the remaining hunk of the North American west coast that was not yet theirs. The two approaches, the one top down and the other bottom up, are interwoven here, just as they were during the quarter century from 1846 to 1871 that was British Columbia in the making.

Surfacing the past thanks to many others

Surfacing the past, as I do here, is possible due only to those who have gone before me. More than any other source, my perceptions, understandings, and writing are grounded in family stories generously shared with me or otherwise available. To the many descendants and others doing so, I am enormously grateful. The Colonial Office records that recently became publicly accessible validate these family stories.

We learn from each other, and I thank everyone from students to friends to fellow historians to interested others whose insights and queries have over the course of many years enriched my understanding of British Columbia. The eminent historian Margaret Ormsby early on privately validated to me the formative role played by Indigenous women and their families by non-Indigenous men, both in her principal area of research, the Okanagan Valley, and across the province for which I am especially grateful. Bruce Watson's research and writing on early British Columbia has been fundamental to my thinking, as have conversations over many years with my husband, Roderick, and children, Rod and Emily. Harbour Publishing and Audrey McClellan anchored *British Columbia in the Balance* in important ways as it was being readied for press. Thanks also to Anna Comfort O'Keeffe, Luke Inglis, Rebecca MacKenney, Lynn Rafferty, Caroline Skelton, Carleton Wilson, and Coralie Worsley at Harbour for their assistance. I am especially grateful to the many historians who have painstakingly contributed biographies to the *Dictionary of Canadian Biography*, now online and generally accessible to readers.

CHAPTER 1

Today's British Columbia Coming into View

The origins of British Columbia as an Indigenous place go back to time immemorial. Its location on the western edge of a continent, North America, and an ocean away from the adjacent continent of Asia, long protected the region's inhabitants from protracted non-Indigenous incursions, permitting them to develop distinct and complex ways of life best suited to their diverse physical settings.

Among the earliest non-Indigenous intruders into the future British Columbia was the Hudson's Bay Company, a private fur-trading company based in London and operating in North America out of Montreal. The HBC's search for beaver pelts, valued in Europe for trimming garments, was legitimized by the British government, which in 1670 granted it a trading monopoly over the entirety of the vast region known as Rupert's Land, defined as everywhere watered by rivers flowing from the Rocky Mountains into Hudson Bay.[1] On Decem-

---

1   Following a meeting with HBC head Sir John Henry Pelly on September 23, 1846, Colonial Office permanent under-secretary Sir James Stephen minuted: "It appeared by his answers to the questions posed to him that the Hudson's Bay Company are not able to define their Territory otherwise than by stating it to comprise all the Lands watered by the Rivers falling into Hudson Bay." Minute by JS [Stephen] to Benjamin Hawes, under-secretary of state for the colonies, September 24, 1846, on Pelly to Henry George Grey, Earl Grey, secretary of state for the colonies, September 7, 1846, 1074, CO 305:1, *The Colonial Despatches of Vancouver Island and British Columbia 1846–1871*, Edition 2.2, ed. James Hendrickson and the Colonial Despatches project (Victoria, BC: University of Victoria), https://bcgenesis.uvic.ca/V465HB01.html. Colonial Office dispatches relating to Vancouver Island and British Columbia, 1846–1863, including the letters cited here, are accessible online at https://bcgenesis.uvic.ca/search.html. All letters cited here are available on the Colonial Despatches website unless otherwise noted. For tables giving information on names and initials that appear on the letters, see the Appendix.

ber 5, 1821, the British government granted the HBC another exclusive trading licence, this one extending from the Rocky Mountains west to the Pacific Ocean. This grant was renewed in 1838 for another twenty-one years.

It was at about the same point in time that the HBC expanded into what was to become British Columbia.[2] The Company hired both officers in charge and fixed-term employees on individual contracts that provided round-trip transportation from their place of recruitment and back again, with an agreed wage paid on returning there. In practice, numerous HBC employees opted, on their contract's expiration, to remain where they had been last employed, due very possibly to their having along the way settled down with an Indigenous woman by whom they had a family—many with descendants into the present day.[3]

Dividing the Pacific Northwest

The fur trade was not the only factor shaping the course of events in the Pacific Northwest—the area lying between the Rocky Mountains and the Pacific Ocean, and extending from today's Alaska south through the American state of Oregon. While almost wholly fought elsewhere, the War of 1812 between Britain and the young United States also had an impact, with the two countries agreeing in its aftermath to joint possession of the Pacific Northwest.

This arrangement broke down in the 1840s due to westward migration from the eastern states. An expanding United States wanted it all, Britain resisted, and the result was a compromise. By the terms of a treaty signed on June 15, 1846, the two countries divided between them the vast, still almost wholly Indigenous Pacific Northwest along the forty-ninth parallel of latitude, with a jog south around the tip of Vancouver Island. The United States acquired the southern half to become the American states of Washington and Oregon and parts of

---

[2] Harold Adam Innis, *The Fur Trade in Canada: An Introduction to Canadian Economic History* (New Haven, CT: Yale University Press, 1930), 115–16. On the terms of the licence, see Pelly to Earl Grey, September 7, 1846, 1074, CO 305:1. The HBC's licence for exclusive trading with Indigenous people would be revoked on November 3, 1858, as noted in a letter from the secretary of state for the colonies, Edward George Earle Dulwer Lytton, to James Douglas, February 11, 1859, LAC RG7:G8C/7, 107.

[3] The fur trade during this time period is detailed in Jean Barman, *French Canadians, Furs, and Indigenous Women in the Making of the Pacific Northwest* (Vancouver, UBC Press, 2014).

neighbouring states, Britain the northern half to become the Canadian province of British Columbia.

Enter the Colonial Office

Britain's new acquisition was, as a matter of course, turned over for administration to the Colonial Office in London, which minded territory around the world that Britain deemed expedient to colonize for its own economic and political purposes. The Colonial Office was a complex bureaucracy whose employees vetted incoming letters, both from those having charge of British possessions and from others with an interest in them. At the end of each letter he had read, the employee doing so would add a note, known as a "minute," assessing its content to guide the response to the letter by the secretary of state for the colonies, who had overall charge of the Colonial Office and thereby of Britain's colonial policy.

By the time of the 1846 boundary settlement, the Hudson's Bay Company had for a quarter of a century operated a profitable fur trade across today's Pacific Northwest, with half of its trading posts now in American territory.[4] In anticipation of the 1846 agreement, the HBC had established a post on Vancouver Island, and in 1849 moved its Pacific Northwest headquarters from today's American state of Oregon north to Vancouver Island. Not unexpectedly, in the settlement's aftermath the HBC sought to acquire trading rights not just to Vancouver Island, but also to the entirety of newly acquired British territory north of the forty-ninth parallel.

Just three months after the signing of the June 1846 boundary agreement, the London governor of the Hudson's Bay Company, Sir John Henry Pelly, queried the British secretary of state for the colonies, Earl Grey, about "the intentions of Her Majesty's Government as to the acquisition of lands, or formation of Settlements, to the North of Lat. 49." Pelly reminded the secretary that "the Company, by a grant from the Crown, dated May 13, 1838, have the exclusive right of trading with the natives of the Countries west of the Rocky Mountains for 21 years from that date," or to 1859.[5] As Grey minuted on the end of this letter from Pelly, it

---

4   For details and maps, see Bruce Watson, *Lives Lived West of the Divide: A Biographical Dictionary of Fur Traders Working West of the Rockies, 1793–1858* (Kelowna, BC: University of British Columbia Okanagan, 2010), 996–1004.

5   Pelly to Earl Grey, September 7, 1846, 1074, CO 305:1.

seemed that unless the British government acted promptly to "consider what is to be done as to colonize the territory," it might well slide into the HBC's hands.[6]

Six weeks later, in October 1846, Pelly proposed to the Colonial Office, almost as a matter of course, that the HBC acquire "in perpetuity" Britain's newly acquired territory:

> If Her Majesty be graciously pleased to grant the Company in perpetuity, any portion of the territory westward of the Rocky Mountains, now under the dominion of the British Crown, such grant will be perfectly valid [given] the Company may legally hold any portion of the territories belonging to the Crown, westward of the Rocky Mountains.[7]

Following up in March 1847, Pelly was even more straightforward respecting the HBC's acquiring "the Queen's Dominions westward of the Rocky Mountains in North America" so as to permanently extend its reach across what was, by then, Canada:

> I beg leave to say that if Her Majesty's Ministers should be of opinion that the Territory in question would be more conveniently governed and colonized (as far as may be practicable) through the Hudson's Bay Company, the Company are willing to undertake it, and will be ready to receive a Grant of all the Territories belonging to the Crown which are situated to the North and West of Rupert's Land.[8]

The Colonial Office was, to its credit, incensed by how "without a word of preliminary discussion" the HBC had sent not only the letter, but also "the d^{ft} of

---

6   Minute by G [Grey], September 25, 1846, on Pelly to Earl Grey, September 7, 1846, 1074, CO 305:1. This file contains the Colonial Office's extensive internal correspondence seeking to sort out its position respecting the HBC.

7   Pelly to Hawes, October 14, 1846, 1301, CO 305:1. Like the September 7, 1846, file, this file contains extensive internal correspondence, including conversations with Pelly and a detailed physical description of Vancouver Island by James Douglas from 1842.

8   Pelly to Earl Grey, March 5, 1847, 333, CO 305:1.

CHAPTER 1

a Charter to accomplish this object."[9] Written in traditional language and script echoing the original 1670 parchment charter granting Rupert's Land to the HBC, the draft charter addressed to "Her Majesty Queen Victoria" detailed the history of "The Governor & Company of Adventurers of England heading into Hudson's Bay," before requesting, almost as a given, this additional "Grant of Territory in North America."[10]

Vancouver Island becoming a British colony

While the British government rejected out of hand the HBC's colonization proposal for the entirety of present-day British Columbia, stating it was "too extensive for Her Majesty's Government to entertain," a year later, in March 1848, Secretary of State for the Colonies Earl Grey invited the HBC governor Sir John Pelly to submit a scheme "more limited and definite in its object...for the Colonization of Vancouver's Island."[11] The consequence was a ten-year HBC grant or lease.

To ensure Britain's hold over Vancouver Island, on January 13, 1849, the island was declared a British colony overseen by the Colonial Office, becoming one more of an array of comparable entities around the world. Indicative of these British colonies' multiplicity and uniformity during this period are the responses of officials in the Colonial Office to an 1864 request from the governor of Vancouver Island for information on fees charged by the colony's attorney general. The officials compared fees charged for a similar purpose in New Zealand, Sierra Leone, Ceylon (now Sri Lanka), Hong Kong, Mauritius, four colonies in today's Australia, and six colonies in the West Indies, as well as Ontario, Quebec, Nova Scotia, New Brunswick, and Newfoundland.[12]

---

9   Minute by JS [Stephen], March 8, 1847, on Pelly to Earl Grey, March 5, 1847, 333, CO 305:1.

10 Crowder & Maynard, the HBC's solicitors in London, to Queen Victoria, "Grant of Territory in North America," enclosed in Pelly to Earl Grey, March 5, 1847, CO 305:1.

11 Minute by JS [Stephen] to Hawes, March 8, 1848, on Pelly to Earl Grey, March 4, 1848, 471, CO 305:1; also Pelly to Earl Grey, Private, March 4, 1848, 475, CO 305:1, detailing the logic of the rejected proposal and its importance owing to American proximity; and for the Colonial Office's thinking, the extensive minutes on Pelly to Earl Grey, September 7, 1846, CO 305:1.

12 Minutes by various clerks in the Colonial Office, including VJ [Vane Jadis], November 12; WD [William Dealtry], November 14; WR [William Robinson], November 16; HCN

James Douglas in charge

The Hudson's Bay Company had centred itself around its Fort Victoria trading post, founded in 1843 on the southern tip of Vancouver Island, which meant that no other location was considered for the capital of the new British colony.

The selection of a colonial governor to take charge should have been equally obvious.

Not so fast.

Rather than turning to experienced HBC officer James Douglas, who had overseen the construction of Fort Victoria and on whose behalf Governor Pelly lobbied, the Colonial Office in July 1849 offered the governorship of the colony of Vancouver Island to Cambridge University–educated Richard Blanshard.[13] Dallying along the way, Blanshard did not arrive until March 1850, and was said to be "rather startled by the wild aspect of the country," so that not unexpectedly, as summed up by historian James Hendrickson, his "tenure was both brief and unhappy."[14] Indicative of Blanshard's outlook was his reporting to the Colonial Office four months after finally making it to Vancouver Island that "nothing of importance has since occurred in the colony, no settlers or immigrants have arrived nor have any land sales been effected."[15]

Blanshard's replacement on May 16, 1851, by the HBC's choice of James Douglas was not unexpected. As one Colonial Office official minuted to the others on an arriving letter, "It will be regarded as a complete surrender to the Company," to which came the response, "I fear this is true," and from a third only: "I will submit Mr Douglas' name to the Queen."[16]

[Henry Charles Norris], November 16; SJB [Samuel Jasper Blunt], November 17, 1864, on Arthur Kennedy, governor of Vancouver Island, to Edward Cardwell, secretary of state for the colonies, No. 64, August 31, 1864, CO 305:23.

13   See Pelly to Earl Grey, September 13, 1848, CO 305:1, and April 16, 1851, CO 305:3.

14   James E. Hendrickson, "Richard Blanshard," in *Dictionary of Canadian Biography*, vol. 12 (University of Toronto/Université Laval, 2003–), http://www.biographi.ca/en/bio/blanshard_richard_12E.html. The characterization of Blanshard, quoted by Hendrickson, was from HBC chief factor James Douglas, who would be Blanshard's successor.

15   Richard Blanshard, governor of Vancouver Island, to Earl Grey, June 15, 1850, 7370, CO 305:2.

16   Minutes by HM [Herman Merivale], BH [Hawes], and G [Grey] on Pelly to Earl Grey, April 16, 1851, 3118, CO 305:3.

CHAPTER 1

Born in 1803 in British Guiana to a Scots merchant and a local "creole" woman—meaning she had some Black ancestry—James Douglas was early on sent to a private boys' school in Scotland and likely studied with a French tutor prior to being apprenticed at age sixteen into the fur trade.[17] Douglas's Black heritage would shadow him to the present day. Even in 2003, a book about "the dark-skinned, dour Douglas" opened with a chapter cheekily entitled "Idylls of a Mulatto King."[18] Posted in 1826 to Fort St. James in today's central British Columbia, then known as New Caledonia, Douglas partnered with Amelia Connolly, the daughter of the post's chief trader and of a Cree woman, and brought her with him to Fort Victoria, along with their children.

Following the 1846 boundary settlement, Fort Victoria—including nearby Esquimalt with, in Douglas's words, its "magnificent harbor" making it accessible to seagoing vessels—took on a new role.[19] As well as being the HBC's headquarters of its ongoing trade west of the Rocky Mountains, Fort Victoria became the preferred site for retiring HBC officers and employees from across the Pacific Northwest.

The good news is that, as historians Adele Perry and John Adams describe in their fine biographies, James Douglas understood power, and while as governor he sought to protect the interests of the HBC, he did so within the larger British colonial framework in which Vancouver Island was enmeshed.[20] Earlier, when Douglas had been stationed at other posts in the Pacific Northwest, he had arranged a boundary with the Russian American Company then in charge of today's Alaska, traded with Mexican authorities in control of California, and checked out trading possibilities with the Hawaiian Islands, then a monarchy. He was a skilled negotiator comfortable in new situations.

The length of time it took for letters to travel from London to the west coast of North America, and for their responses to return to London, put the onus

---

17   Biographical information is taken from Margaret A. Ormsby, "Sir James Douglas," *Dictionary of Canadian Biography*, vol. 10, http://www.biographi.ca/en/bio/douglas_james_10E.html.

18   Donald J. Hauka, *McGowan's War* (Vancouver: New Star, 2003).

19   Douglas to Henry Pelham Fiennes Pelham-Clinton, Duke of Newcastle, secretary of state for the colonies, July 28, 1853, CO 305:4, No. 9499.

20   Adele Perry, *Colonial Relations: The Douglas-Connolly Family and the Nineteenth-Century Imperial World* (Cambridge: Cambridge University Press, 2015); John Adams, *Old Square Toes and His Lady: The Life of James and Amelia Douglas* (Victoria, BC: Horsdal & Schubart, 2001).

James Douglas, shown ca. 1861, was governor of the colony of Vancouver Island from 1851 to 1864, and governor of the mainland colony of British Columbia from 1858 to 1864. He married Amelia Connolly, shown ca. 1865, in 1828. *Image A-01227 and A-02834 courtesy of the Royal BC Museum.*

on James Douglas in the everyday and also in relation to the unexpected. The Colonial Office's letter of May 19, 1851, informing Douglas of his appointment as governor, did not reach him in Vancouver Island's capital of Victoria until October 3, with his letter of acceptance arriving in London on February 4, 1852.[21] It was nonetheless the case that every letter received, whatever its origin, was given individual consideration by several officials when it arrived at the Colonial Office in London, each of them minuting on it his response. Nothing much slipped by them.

Colonizing Vancouver Island

James Douglas's task as governor was to attend to Vancouver Island as a British colonial possession under Hudson's Bay Company oversight. He was the Colonial Office's conduit to this far corner of the world, about which no one knew

---

21   Earl Grey to Douglas, May 19, 1851, CO 410:1; Douglas to Earl Grey, October 31, 1851, 484, CO 305:3; date of response noted on the letter and also in Earl Grey to Douglas, February 4, 1852, LAC RG71G8C/1.

more than he did. His detailed reports were intended to placate the Colonial Office as much as to effect change.

As acknowledged by Sir John Pelly early on, "one of the main objects of the Company is to civilize the native tribes by fixing settlers among them, who will find employment for them, and shew them the advantages to be derived from cultivating the Soil."[22] Douglas repeatedly emphasized the positive, as in a letter of 1852 evoking Indigenous peoples' "many large and well kept fields of potatoes...and fine cucumbers."[23] Rather than non-Indigenous people taking Indigenous land by force, Douglas negotiated fourteen separate land purchases on Vancouver Island in the form of treaties between 1850 and 1854.

It was white folk, or rather the lack of them, who were the problem. The ongoing concern, in line with Colonial Office priorities, was "what the H.B.C^y intended to do about Colonizing the Island."[24] In fact, colonization was hampered by the HBC having agreed in January 1849 to the Colonial Office's proviso that "no grant of land shall contain less than twenty acres," and that it must be acquired at a cost of "one [English] pound per acre."[25]

Given that the terms of colonization also required the introduction of suitably British settlers, it is unsurprising that nothing much happened. Dispatched to assess "the Colonization of the Southern part of Vancouver [Island]," visiting British admiral Fairfax Moresby observed in the summer of 1851 how, for all of Douglas's "energy & intelligence,...the attempt to Colonize Vancouver [Island] by a Company with exclusive rights of Trade is incompatible with the free & liberal reception of an Emigrant Community." The few settlers with whom Fairfax Moresby conversed were dissatisfied. "There is a general complaint that no Title deeds are granted, that the price of Land & the condition of bringing out Labourers, render the formation of a Colony hopeless."[26] It was, one Colonial

---

22 Pelly to Hawes, November 22, 1849, 9816, CO 305:2.

23 Douglas to Sir John Pakington, secretary of state for war and the colonies, No. 7, August 27, 1852, 10199, CO 305:3.

24 BH [Hawes] to Earl Grey on Pelly to Earl Grey, April 16, 1851, 3118, CO 305:3; also Douglas to Newcastle, July 28, 1853, 9499, CO 305:4.

25 "Vancouver's Island" and "Resolutions of the Hudson's Bay Company: Colonization of Vancouver Island," both attached to John Jervis and John Romilly to Earl Grey, July 10, 1849, CO 305:2. For the arrangement's complexities, see Pelly to Hawes, October 24, 1846, 1301, CO 305:1, and November 22, 1849, 9816, CO 305:2.

26 Fairfax Moresby to the Admiralty, July 7, 1851, enclosed in J. Parker on behalf of the

Office employee minuted respecting the admiral's report, "a very unsatisfactory state of affairs."[27] As calculated by historian Stephen Royle, 343 men, 119 women, and 179 children—a total of 641 persons—travelled to Vancouver Island on HBC vessels between 1848 and 1854.[28]

Proximity to the United States was from early on a mitigating factor, as it would continue to be. Anglican schoolmaster and chaplain Robert John Staines, who arrived in Victoria with his wife in 1849 to take up his dual position, was incensed when he learned that potential settlers, "by just crossing the straits & stating before a magistrate their intention to become Citizens of the U.S.,... will become entitled to 160 acres of land gratis & if they marry, to 320 any time they choose to settle." By comparison, settlers in Victoria were faced with "land at £1 an acre, tied down as it is by conditions, which do not allow a man more than 20 acres except he import English labourers at the rate of 1 man for every 20 acres."[29]

Writing a year later, in July 1853, Douglas was similarly focused on complaints from the handful of settlers over the price of land.[30] What Douglas did not mention was that he was himself buying up land. By 1858, according to historian Margaret Ormsby, his holdings had grown from 400-plus acres in 1853 to 1,200 acres.[31]

Admiralty to Frederick Peel, under-secretary of state for the colonies, November 28, 1851, 10075, CO 305:3. Respecting the requisite introduction of settlers, see among other Colonial Office correspondence T.W.C. Murdoch and C. Alexander Wood, of the Colonial Land and Emigration Office, to Herman Merivale, permanent under-secretary for the colonies, January 19, 1853, 535, CO 305:4.

27 Minute by VJ [Jadis], December 4, 1851, to Merivale on Parker to Peel, November 28, 1851, 10075, CO 305:3.

28 Stephen Royle, *Company, Crown and Colony: The Hudson's Bay Company and Territorial Endeavour in Western Canada* (London: I.B. Tauris, 2011), 247.

29 Robert John Staines to Thomas Boys, July 6, 1852, enclosed in Boys to John Otway O'Connor Cuffe, 3rd Earl of Desart, under-secretary of state to the colonies, October 11, 1852, CO 305:3; see also "Robert John Staines," *Dictionary of Canadian Biography*, vol. 8, http://www.biographi.ca/en/bio/staines_robert_john_8E.html.

30 Douglas to Newcastle, July 28, 1853, CO 305:4, No. 9499.

31 Ormsby, "Sir James Douglas."

CHAPTER 1

Turning to the mainland

It was not only the Colonial Office that Douglas had to manage. The Hudson's Bay Company brought with it to Vancouver Island its exclusive licence to trade for animal pelts with Indigenous people everywhere west of the Rocky Mountains, which had been agreed by the British government in 1821 and renewed in 1838 for twenty-one years.[32] This gave the HBC charge not only of Vancouver Island but also, nominally, of the mainland north of the forty-ninth parallel, known within the fur trade as New Caledonia. There and on Vancouver Island, as of 1849, the HBC operated fifteen trading posts that stretched across the future province of British Columbia: Connolly Post, Fort Alexandria, Fort Babine, Fort George, Fort Hope, Fort Langley, Fort Okanogan, Fort St. James, Fort Simpson, Fort Stikine, Fort Victoria, Fraser Lake, Kootenay Post, McLeod Lake, and the Thompson River/Kamloops Post.[33]

The HBC's efforts to "colonize" Vancouver Island were, as set out in 1849, to be assessed every two years as to the number of settlers and amount of land sold, with the possibility for termination of the grant by the British government after five years. The terms were straightforward:

> The condition of the grant is declared to be the colonization of the island. With this object the Company is bound to dispose of the land in question at a reasonable price, and to expend all the sums they may receive for land or minerals (after the deduction of not more than 10 per cent, for profit) on the colonization of the island.

At the end of ten years, "the Government may repurchase the land on repayment of the sums expended by the Company on the island and the value of their establishments."[34]

---

32 See, among other sources, Hubert Howe Bancroft, *History of British Columbia*, vol. 32 of *The Works of Hubert Howe Bancroft* (San Francisco: The History Company, 1887), 218.

33 For information on individual posts, including years of operation, see Watson, *Lives Lived West of the Divide*, 996–1095.

34 "Vancouver's Island" and "Resolutions of the Hudson's Bay Company: Colonization of Vancouver Island," both attached to Jervis and Romilly to Earl Grey, July 10, 1849, CO 305:2. For the arrangement's complexities, see Pelly to Hawes, October 24, 1846, 1301, CO 305:1, and November 22, 1849, 9816, CO 305:2. Respecting the negotiations that ensued

28

Encouraging non-Indigenous settlement

Between 1848 and 1852, the HBC brought a total of "270 males with 80 females and 84 children" to Vancouver Island as its own employees. The men, "chiefly agricultural labourers," were promised that "if they perform their contracts of service in a satisfactory manner, they shall receive a reward of £25 over and above their wages, to be paid to them in land at the price of 20/- per acre, so that it may be expected that many of them will become settlers."[35] Eighty of these employee settlers, nearly all of them men, and including medical doctor John Sebastian Helmcken, arrived in March 1850 after a six-month voyage from England on the HBC's vessel the *Norman Morison*. The ship returned in 1852 with twenty-five more arrivals, again almost all men, and the next year with 115, ranging from couples with children to single men contracted by the HBC for five years, to be rewarded with 25 acres of land if hired as labourers, 50 acres if as tradesmen.[36] A grid of streets was laid out in Victoria in 1852, and "town lots" were offered for sale.

According to a census taken in the summer of 1855 and reported to the Colonial Office, Vancouver Island's "native Indian" population was "about 22,000," raised in a closer count a year later to 25,873.[37] The Island's "white" population, which had "not much increased for the last twelve months by spontaneous emigration," stood in 1855 at 774. Of these, 232 lived in Victoria proper; 150 in Nanaimo, a hundred kilometres to the north, where the HBC was mining recently discovered coal deposits; and the other 400 or so were scattered among a variety of locations. The 1855 count of the white population turned up 1,418 acres of improved land with 243 dwelling houses and 39 shops. There were 284 horses,

---

at the end of the ten years, see, among other correspondence, S. Walcott, secretary to the colonial land and emigration commissioners, to T.F. Elliot, assistant under-secretary in the Colonial Office, October 14, 1861, CO 60:12; H.H. Berens, HBC governor, to Newcastle, November 7, 1861, CO 60:12.

35 Andrew Colvile, deputy governor of the HBC, to Pakington, November 24, 1852, CO 305:3.

36 "Ships List of Passengers for the 'Norman Morison' 1852" is available on the Vancouver Island GenWeb Project website, part of the British Columbia GenWeb database, at http://sites.rootsweb.com/%7Ecbcvancou/ships/nmor33.htm

37 Douglas to Lord John Russell, secretary of state for the colonies, August 21, 1855, 10048, CO 305:6; attachment to Douglas to Henry Labouchere, secretary of state for the colonies, October 20, 1856, 11582, CO 305:7.

240 milch cows, 206 oxen, 560 other cattle, 6,214 sheep, and 1,010 swine.[38] This "distant Dependency," to use the Colonial Office's description, was in the larger scheme of things among the tiniest of British possessions.[39]

Another of James Douglas's responsibilities was to create governing structures consistent with Colonial Office practice around the world. Writing in October 1851, Douglas noted that he had appointed someone to fill the position he previously held on the existing three-man "Council of this Island," left vacant by his appointment as governor, but there things came to a halt.[40] It was, he explained a year later, inexpedient to do more "until the population increases, and there be a sufficient number of persons of education and intelligence in the Colony."[41] Douglas acknowledged in July 1853 that "we have done nothing of any importance in the way of legislating for the Colony."[42]

Indicative of the slow increase in white male British residents, only in the spring of 1855 could the Hudson's Bay Company report that there were "more than Forty Freeholders possessed of twenty acres of land, and upwards, which the Regulations have declared to be the qualification of voters for Members of [the House of] Assembly."[43] Colonial Office officials were not so sure about the numbers, being well aware of Douglas's tendency to conflate retired and present HBC employees with "colonists" in the usual sense of that word. One of the officials said as much in a minute on another letter. "I confess that I think the establishment of [a] representative System under the circumstances of the Island w^d be little better than a parody, especially if true as sometimes asserted that very nearly the whole of the occupiers [of land] are Servants of the C^y living on its pay."[44]

---

38   Douglas to Russell, August 21, 1855, 10048, CO 305:6.

39   Minute by AB^d [Arthur Blackwood] on Douglas to Russell, August 21, 1855, 10048, CO 305:6.

40   Douglas to Earl Grey, October 31, 1851, 484, CO 305:3.

41   Douglas to Pakington, November 11, 1852, 933, CO 305:3.

42   Indicative was Douglas "appointing a resident Magistrate for each district of the Colony, except Soke [Sooke near Victoria], where none of the Colonists are qualified in points of character or education to perform the duties of that responsible office." See Douglas to Newcastle, July 28, 1853, 9499, CO 305:4.

43   Colvile to Merivale, April 16, 1855, CO 305:6.

44   Minute by JB [John Ball] to Sir William Molesworth, secretary of state for the colonies, August 3, 1855, on Colvile to Russell, June 9, 1855, 5599, CO 305:6.

However, Douglas's looser approach to settlement won out over the alternative, seriously considered within the Colonial Office, of removing Vancouver Island from HBC oversight because the Company had not fulfilled the conditions of the grant by 1854, which was five years after the agreement was signed. From its perspective, the decision to leave the colony under HBC control had less to do with Douglas than with American influence:

> It is difficult to say whether the more serious risk of collision with the American population of Oregon is greater or less than it w^d be if the Island were resumed [by Britain] from the C^y. Recent despatches show that there are inflammable Materials on both sides especially the American. In my opinion the only real strength for such a community is to be sought in increasing population & if the Island were resumed [to Britain] I sh^d think it wise to give small lots—of 5 or 10 acres to a reasonable number of actual occupants at a mere nominal price—resumable if not brought fully into cultivation.[45]

The Colonial Office's solution was the establishment on Vancouver Island of a "legislative authority," independent of the Hudson's Bay Company. This was enacted in 1856 in the form of an eight-member elected Legislative Assembly.[46]

Writing to the Colonial Office in June 1856, Douglas's mind was more immediately on "a large arrival of" Indigenous people from the Queen Charlotte Islands, located on the northwest coast of Vancouver Island and known today as Haida Gwaii.[47] Six weeks later Douglas reported, alongside a brief mention of "a smouldering volcano" in the form of "great numbers of northern [Indigenous

---

45 Minute by JB [Ball], August 3, 1855, on Colvile to Russell, June 9, 1855, 5599, CO 305:6; for detail, see Arthur Johnstone Blackwood, senior clerk in the Colonial Office, to Newcastle, May 18, 1854, CO 305:5.

46 Minute by JB [Ball], August 3, 1855, on Colvile to Russell, June 9, 1855, 5599, CO 305:6; also Labouchere to Douglas, No. 5, February 28, 1856, LAC RG7:G8C/1; Douglas to Labouchere, No. 12, May 22, 1856, 1790, CO 305:7; Douglas to Labouchere, No. 14, June 7, 1856, CO 305:7; No. 23, July 22, 1856, CO 305:7; No. 29, October 31, 1856, 319, CO 305:7; No. 20, June 30, 1857, 8655, CO 305:8; and Frederic Rogers to Merivale, October 5, 1857, 9208, CO 305:8.

47 Douglas to Labouchere, No. 14, June 7, 1856, CO 305:7.

CHAPTER 1

people]," the good news that "the propositions in respect to the convening and constitution of the Assembly were approved and passed without alteration, at the meeting of the 9th of June." However, "in order to suit the circumstances of the Colony, the property qualification of Members [of the Assembly]" had been reduced, given that "a higher standard of qualification would have disqualified all the present representatives."[48]

Over half of these qualified to vote had arrived with the fur trade, being one-time officers or employees grateful for the opportunity to settle down with their families, almost always with Indigenous or part Indigenous women, in this remote British colony.[49] As to why it was not possible also to secure independent settlers in numbers, Andrew Colvile, deputy governor of the Hudson's Bay Company, pointed out to the Colonial Office in 1855 four "peculiar difficulties," namely:

> The great distance of the Island from this country, and consequent length of the voyage, the high rate of wages given in the Gold districts of California which unsettles the minds of the labouring population, the system of free grants of land that prevails on the opposite shore of the Straits of De Fuca, and the distance from any market, except for those on American territory where the Import duties are almost prohibitory.[50]

As for Vancouver Island's inaugural Legislative Assembly meeting in August 1856, "the affair passed off quietly, and did not appear to excite much interest among the lower orders," in Douglas's words.[51] Among the seven men comprising the first House of Assembly was Thomas Skinner, an English gentleman enticed to manage an HBC subsidiary and arriving with his family in time to do so.[52]

The Assembly's election as Speaker of John Sebastian Helmcken, by now married to Douglas's eldest daughter, Cecilia, was, whether intended or not, a conciliatory gesture to Douglas, who had initially opposed the idea of a Legislative Assembly that might hamper his actions as governor and HBC officer. On his

---

48   Douglas to Labouchere, No. 15, July 22, 1856, CO 305:7.

49   The list is attached to Colvile to Merivale, April 16, 1855, 3578, CO 305:6.

50   Colvile to Russell, June 9, 1855, CO 305:6.

51   Douglas to Labouchere, No. 19, August 20, 1856, CO 305:7.

52   The Skinner family is tracked in Jean Barman, *Constance Lindsay Skinner: Writing on the Frontier* (Toronto: University of Toronto Press, 2003).

arrival in 1850, the resourceful Helmcken had been dispatched to Prince Rupert on the north coast, but he was soon transferred to Vancouver Island, where he continued to practise medicine while engaging in colonial politics. He would hold the Speaker's position until a united British Columbia joined Canada a decade and a half later in 1871.

Managing the economy

Douglas's management of the Vancouver Island economy was no easy matter, hemmed in as it was by the HBC and the fur trade, and to the south by the United States. Mindful of his double masters of the HBC and the Colonial Office, Douglas early on marked out for the former the boundaries of twenty-five square miles on the southeast corner of Vancouver Island which the HBC had "held as their exclusive property" since the founding of Fort Victoria in 1843. Douglas pointed out defensively to the Colonial Office in 1852 that the Company had "expended large sums of money in bringing the land into cultivation." It also used the land as a cattle range and "as a protection from the intrusion of American citizens," who were at this point in time daily expected on Vancouvers Island.[53] In spite of the "large sums" spent on cultivation, Douglas also acknowledged "a deficiency of bread stuffs for the consumption of the Colony" due to so few farms, just thirty-one by his count.[54]

Another of Douglas's tasks as governor was to educate the mother country respecting the geography and economy of Vancouver Island. Douglas pointed out, in the summer of 1852, the island's "most unfortunate position for Trade; at the distance of more than 4000 miles from the nearest British possession and separated from the Mother Country by half the circumference of the Globe." In consequence, "it has no available outlet for its productions, consisting of Saltfish, Deals, Limestone and Spars for Masts, which with the exception of the last will do little more than defray the expensive transport to Great Britain."[55] Three years later, in 1855, the island's limited "foreign trade" was "confined to the Sandwich Islands [Hawaiian Islands] and the Ports of California."[56]

Douglas took particular pleasure in confirming reports of "the existence of

---

53   Douglas to Earl Grey, No. 5, June 15, 1852, 9099, CO 305:3
54   Douglas to Newcastle, No. 9, Miscellaneous, October 24, 1853, 12345, CO 305:4.
55   Douglas to Pakington, No. 6, August 2, 1852, 9399, CO 305:3.
56   Douglas to Russell, No. 16, August 21, 1855, 10048, CO 305:6

coal" at a place "named 'Nanymo' after the Tribe" of the same name. Douglas's initial letter of August 1852 had sent Colonial Office officials into a veritable tizzy of relief and anticipation that maybe this faraway place was not as useless as it seemed to be, as the under-secretary of state for the colonies described at length:

> I do not think the attention of the Gov^t of this country has been sufficiently directed to the fact of the very great importance, of which the possession of Queen Charlottes & Vancouver islands may have to this country. Whatever the event of the rumoured and partially proved discovery of gold in the former—the possession of coal in Vancouvers Island—a solitary instance along the long line of coast of the two Americas (as far as we have yet discovered), together with its favorable position as regard St Francisco & the whole Western coast of N America ought to make it the centre of the Pacific commerce.[57]

The HBC exploited the find to its own gain. "Twenty three Coal Miners with their families forming collectively about 109 persons sent from England, by the Hudson's Bay Company, for their coal works at Nanaimo," was "the largest accession of white inhabitants the Colony" received in 1855, Douglas informed the Colonial Office.[58]

Minding the United States and Russia

It was not only the Colonial Office, the Hudson's Bay Company, Indigenous peoples, and a handful of settlers that Douglas had to mind, but also Vancouver Island's neighbour to the south. One of the most persistent irritants over his dozen years in charge was American unwillingness to accept the forty-ninth parallel as a forever border—and the less willing they were to accept the border, the more uncertain the colony's future became.

Far more rapid white settlement to the south exacerbated the determination

---

57 Minute by D [John Otway O'Connor Cuffe, 3d Earl of Desart] November 16, 1952, on Douglas to Pakington, No. 7, August 27, 1852, 10199, CO 305:3. A copy of the letter was immediately sent "to Admiralty and Geographical Society; and Land B^d," and an extract "PRINTED FOR PARLIAMENT 'Gold'—Queen Charlotte's Island' 18/53."

58 Douglas to Russell, No. 16, August 21, 1855, 10048, CO 305:6.

of both the United States government and individual Americans to fill in the remainder of the North American west coast. The pressure intensified after the 1846 boundary agreement, when the United States acquired the large hunk of land that became the American states of Oregon and Washington, as well as small parts of neighbouring states. As well, California, which had been taken from Mexico by force, became an American territory in 1848, and in 1850 a state.

For a short time in the 1850s Russia, to the north and west, was also a concern. The Crimean War was underway in Europe, and in the winter of 1854–1855 there were skirmishes between Anglo-French and Russian forces on the Kamchatka Peninsula lying west of Alaska. The British Navy established a base at Esquimalt to service its ships and provide medical care for battle casualties.

Indicative of the swirling course of events are three 1854 letters to the Colonial Office, two from Douglas describing Vancouver Islanders' fear of "a descent by the Russians"; the other containing a minute that asks whether "it is desirable the present state of things should longer continue, with Russia on one side of the little settlement & the U.S. on the other."[59] Among Douglas's ongoing responsibilities as governor, the foremost was to keep an acquisitive United States at bay. Not only were many Americans in and out of the political realm convinced they should have acquired the entirety of the Pacific Northwest in 1846, and better late than never, but a gold rush to California beginning in 1848 grew interest in similar locales where riches might be had.

The tension was ever present. Douglas's letter of October 31, 1851, accepting the position of governor, described in its final paragraphs how "the natives have discovered Gold in Englefield Bay, on the West Coast of Queen Charlottes Island," in conditions similar to those unleashing the California gold rush. Not only that, but "several American vessels are fitting out in the Columbia [River in American territory] for Queen Charlottes Island for the purpose of digging Gold."[60]

Douglas sought the Colonial Office's advice respecting Queen Charlotte's Island, today known as Haida Gwaii, only to be sidelined on the grounds that it "is not within the government of Vancouver's Island," with no apparent interest

---

59   Douglas to Newcastle, No. 35, August 17, 1854, CO 305:5; and minute by HM [Merivale], January 8, 1855, on A.E. Cockburn (UK attorney general) and Richard Bethell (UK solicitor general) to Sir George Grey, secretary of state for the colonies, December 28, 1854, CO 305:5.

60   Douglas to Earl Grey, October 31, 1851, 484, CO 305:3.

being expressed by the Colonial Office as to which country's territory it was.[61] Douglas's follow-up letter, written before he received a response to its predecessor, reported on vessels "chartered by large bodies of American Adventurers" who, if they found gold, intended "to colonize the Island, and establish an independent Government until by force or fraud they become annexed by the United States." While one of these ships was wrecked and the other "intimidated by the hostile appearance of the Natives,"[62] Douglas remained uneasy as to what might ensue the next time around—and his fears were not allayed on receipt of a return letter from the Colonial Office stating:

> With regard to the discovery of Gold on the West Coast of Queen Charlotte's Island, I do not consider that it would be expedient to issue any prohibitions against the resort thither of Foreign Vessels. Were there no other objection to such a step it would be a sufficient reason against it that Her Majesty's Government are not prepared to send there a force to give effect to the prohibition.[63]

However, the Colonial Office had a change of heart. Even before Douglas reported in April 1852 that two American vessels calling at "Gold Harbour" on Queen Charlotte's Island had "been beaten off by the Natives; though the American force was considerable, and well armed,"[64] the Office had "directed the attention of the Lords Commissioners of the Admiralty to the necessity which appears to exist for stationing a Vessel of War off Queen Charlotte's Island."[65] This situation was resolved, at least for the moment, but others were in the offing.

Describing three years later in 1855 "the deplorable state of American Oregon, which is now involved in a disastrous war, with the native Tribes of that country, which appear to be animated with a rancorous hatred of American domination," Douglas expressed relief as to how their northern counterparts "entertain a high degree of respect for the British name." In a follow-up letter he reported "no change

---

61   Minute by HM [Merivale], January 22, 1852, to Peel on Douglas to Earl Grey, October 31, 1851, 484, CO 305:3.
62   Douglas to Earl Grey, January 29, 1852, 3742, CO 305:3.
63   Earl Grey to Douglas, February 4, 1852, LAC RG7:G8C/1, 41.
64   Douglas to Earl Grey, April 15, 1852, 6485, CO 305:3.
65   Pakington to Douglas, March 18, 1852, LAC RG7:G8C/1, 62.

observable in their demeanour towards the British settlements."[66] Respecting Vancouver Island, a realistic Colonial Office official minuted on the earlier letter, "I regret to say that the Settlement is totally destitute of a military force," to which another added with a verbal sigh of relief how "one can have little doubt that the Yankees are really the aggressors."[67] The Colonial Office grew so concerned over "the disturbed state of relations between Indian and American Settlers in Oregon and the North West generally... in the vicinity of the British Territory," it gave Douglas authority in early 1856 to act on his own volition as he thought best so as not "to endanger the peace of the community of Vancouver's Island."[68]

Come 1857, Douglas was caught up in another dispute with the United States. This time it was over San Juan and neighbouring islands, which had up to then been assumed to be British possessions by virtue of their proximity to Victoria, despite their being marked on maps of the day as crossing the agreed international boundary of the forty-ninth parallel. The dispute would fester, eventually going to international arbitration that in 1871 handed the San Juans to the United States.

A waiting game, with British Columbia in the balance

American proximity, alongside James Douglas's apparent disinclination to grow Vancouver Island's non-Indigenous population—the result of his dual mandates to sustain the HBC and to govern—were not lost on the Colonial Office. One official stated them baldly in a minute to the others in July 1856:

> It is time to consider what position the British Gov^t sh^d take with regard to this Dependency having in view the probable extension of population on the American frontier... it may be doubted whether this island will remain British if there is not an influx of British population & it does not appear that the practical effect of the present system is to attract population.[69]

---

66 Douglas to Molesworth, No. 23, November 8, 1855, 380, CO 305:6; and Douglas to Sir George Grey, March 1, 1856, CO 305:7.

67 Minutes by AB^d [Blackwood], July 16, 1856, and HM [Merivale] January 17, 1856, on Douglas to Molesworth, No. 23, November 8, 1855, 380, CO 305:6.

68 Labouchere to Douglas, Confidential, February 28, 1856, CO 410:1.

69 Minute by JB [Ball], July 21, 1856, on John Shepherd, deputy governor of the HBC, to Labouchere, July 14, 1856, 6281, CO 305:7.

From the Colonial Office's perspective, Vancouver Island had become a waiting game, as one official almost gleefully reminded the others in the fall of 1857 respecting the upcoming termination of the HBC's grant of Vancouver Island, along with the expiry in 1859 of its exclusive right to trade with Indigenous peoples: "Yes—we must soon give a formal notice to the H.B. Company that we mean to disconnect Van Couvers Island with them & the whole question of its establishment will have to be considered."[70]

It was in this uneasy set of circumstances, with no perceived best outcome with respect to the isolated and fragile British colony of Vancouver Island, that the unexpected intervened.

Responding to gold finds

James Douglas's oversight of Vancouver Island took a different turn, as did the history of British Columbia, on the discovery in 1856 of gold on the mainland just across the Strait of Georgia from Vancouver Island. That a gold rush in the pattern of California in 1848 and Australia in 1851—which each attracted many thousands of prospective miners from around the world—would directly challenge the assumed authority of the HBC and of the Colonial Office had been in the back of James Douglas's mind from the day he was appointed governor in 1851.

Douglas reported in April 1856 that "Gold has been found in considerable quantities within the British Territory on the Upper Columbia," the location being on the mainland of the future British Columbia. Douglas had also been informed that "valuable deposits of Gold will be found in other parts of that country," and so what, if anything, should he do about it?[71] The Colonial Office's return letter was, as earlier in respect to the Queen Charlottes, equivocal at best:

> In the absence of all effective machinery of Government, I conceive that it would be quite abortive to attempt to raise a Revenue from licenses to dig for Gold in that region. Indeed as Her Majesty's Government do not at present look for a revenue from this distant quarter of the British dominions, so neither are they

---

70   Minute by HL [Labouchere] October 10, 1857, on Rogers to Merivale, October 5, 1857, 9208, CO 305:8.

71   Douglas to Labouchere, No. 10, April 16, 1856, 5815, CO 305:7.

prepared to incur any expense on account of it. I must therefore leave it to your discretion to determine the best means of preserving order in the event of any considerable increase of population flocking into this new gold district."[72]

Douglas updated the Colonial Office a year later, July 15, 1857, "corroborating the former accounts" respecting the mainland, while acknowledging "yet a degree of uncertainty respecting the productiveness of those gold fields, for reports vary so much on that point, some parties representing the deposits as exceedingly rich, while others are of opinion, that they will not repay the labor and outlay of working, that I feel it would be premature for me to give a decided opinion on the subject." Douglas described industrious local Indigenous peoples "expelling all the parties of gold diggers, composed chiefly of persons from the American Territories, who had forced an entrance into their country."[73] Longtime Colonial Office official and permanent under-secretary Herman Merivale minuted on the letter on September 21, 1857, as if foreseeing the future, that "if any interference is to take place" respecting the HBC's exclusive right to trade west of the Rocky Mountains, "I believe it will be necessary to...form it into a colony."[74]

Before receiving a response to his letters, Douglas wrote again at the end of December 1857 respecting "gold found in its natural place of deposit within the limits of Fraser's River and Thompson's River Districts" on the largely unknown mainland, over which he had no authority. Douglas once again pointed out "the exertions of the native Indian Tribes who having tasted the sweets of gold finding, are devoting much of their time and attention to the pursuit," and also "much excitement among the population of the United States Territories of Washington and Oregon," who he had no doubt would be "attracted thither with the return of the fine weather in spring." Douglas was aware that his authority to act as needed in "Continental America...may perhaps be called into question," even though he was, he pointed out to the Colonial Office, "invested with the authority, over the premises, of the Hudson's Bay Company."[75]

---

72 Labouchere to Douglas, No. 14, August 4, 1856, LAC RG7:G8C/1.
73 Douglas to Labouchere, No. 22, July 15, 1857, 8657, CO 305:8.
74 Minute by HM [Merivale], September 21, 1857, on Douglas to Labouchere, No. 22, July 15, 1857, 8657, CO 305:8.
75 Douglas to Labouchere, No. 35, December 29, 1857, 2084, CO 305:8.

CHAPTER 1

The Colonial Office in action

What to do, Douglas pointed out in his late December 1857 letter, was up to the Colonial Office. He enclosed a draft proclamation "declaring the rights of the crown in respect to gold ... and forbidding all persons to dig or disturb the soil in search of Gold until authorized on that behalf by Her Majesty's Colonial Government." He continued, "Should Her Majesty's Government not deem it advisable to enforce the rights of the Crown as set forth in the Proclamation, it may be allowed to fall to the ground, and to become a mere dead letter."[76] The future province of British Columbia hung in the balance.

By now the faraway Colonial Office had realized the importance of the situation, as Douglas hoped it would. The minutes on his letter of July 15, 1857, respecting forming the area of the reported gold finds into a colony, indicate that it had been decided "this question should be postponed until we receive more definite information," which came in Douglas's December letter.[77] After that letter's arrival in London on March 2, 1858, a warrant was drafted appointing Douglas to be "Lieutenant Governor of HM's Territories and Possessions in North America which are bounded on the North by the 54^h Degree of North Latitude, on the East by the Rocky Mountains and on the South by the 49^h Degree of North Latitude."[78] The appointment as head of state would formally be offered to Douglas four months later in July 1858, whereas the decision to retain control of the future province with Douglas in charge had already been taken.

So it is that today's British Columbia comes into view. It would do so politically with the creation, in 1858, of a second British colony encompassing the mainland, and it would do so spatially when the boundary between the United States and British territory extending from the Rocky Mountains to the Pacific Ocean, running along the forty-ninth parallel, was surveyed.[79] Looking ahead a decade and a half in time, it would be in 1871, a quarter of a century after the 1846 division of the Pacific Northwest, that British Columbia, by then including Vancouver Island, became the Canadian province it is today.

---

76 Douglas to Labouchere, No. 35, December 29, 1857, 2084, CO 305:8.

77 Minute by AB^d [Blackwood], September 30, 1857, following on that of HM [Merivale], September 21, 1857, on Douglas to Labouchere, No. 22, July 15, 1857, 8657, CO 305:8.

78 Minute by AB^d [Blackwood], February 3, 1858, in Douglas to Labouchere, No. 35, December 29, 1857, 2084, CO 305:8.

79 Edmund Hammond, Foreign Office, to Merivale, January 18, 1858, 635 NA, CO 6:2.

CHAPTER 2

The Year That Changed Everything (1858)

James Douglas's governorship of Vancouver Island, following its acquisition by Britain in 1846, was one thing; to be landed with a gold rush on the mainland thirty times that island's size was a wholly different matter.[1] That Douglas, overseen by the Colonial Office in faraway London, managed the feat during 1858, the year that changed everything, is remarkable.

Enter the 1858 gold rush

As 1858 came into view, so did the possibility of a gold rush.[2] Unlike Vancouver Island, over which the fur-trading Hudson's Bay Company had requested and received a ten-year lease extending to May 1859, the mainland of today's British Columbia was, except for a handful of HBC trading posts, an Indigenous place.[3]

In a letter of March 22, 1858, to the Hudson's Bay Company that was shared with the Colonial Office, James Douglas previewed what might ensue. Having experienced the gold rush in small doses, he envisaged the arrival on the largely unknown mainland of "a great number of Americans," some of them veterans of the California gold rush where miners had had ongoing confrontations with civil authority.

Douglas offered to do what was wanted: "I should be glad to keep these

---

1 The relative sizes are 31,285 square kilometres (12,079 square miles) and 913,450 square kilometres (352,685 square miles).

2 Among accounts of the gold rush from a British Columbia perspective is George Fetherling, *River of Gold: The Fraser & Cariboo Gold Rushes* (Vancouver: Subway, 2009).

3 Useful on this point is the long minute by HM [Merivale], September 2, 1859, on T.W.C. Murdoch, chairman of the Colonial Land and Emigration Commission, to Merivale, August 29, 1859, CO 60:5.

parties out of the British Territory, and would undertake with a very moderate force to accomplish that object, as the avenues to the country are few, and might be easily guarded." He had already "written to Her Majesty's Government on the subject and shall not fail to communicate with you as soon as I receive their reply." Three days later Douglas followed up with the HBC once he had been informed by "an experienced miner" that "the bedrock and other geological features" of "the principal diggings" on the banks of the Fraser River "are all characteristics of the gold Districts of California and other countries."[4]

Indigenous miners initially in charge

Indigenous people had been a priority for Douglas during his many years in the fur trade and continued to be so. Writing shortly thereafter to the secretary of state for the colonies, Henry Labouchere, Douglas described "the search for gold" as being "carried on almost exclusively by the native Indian population, who have discovered the productive beds, and put out almost all the gold, about eight hundred ounces, which has been hitherto exported from the country; and who are moreover extremely jealous of the whites and strongly opposed to their digging the soil for gold." Douglas explained how "the few white men who passed the winter at the diggings, chiefly retired Servants [employees] of the Hudson's Bay Company, though well acquainted with Indian character, were obstructed by the natives,... who having, by that means, obtained possession of the spot, then proceeded to reap the fruits of their labors." Douglas considered it "worthy of remark and a circumstance highly honorable to the character of these [Indigenous people] that they have on all occasions scrupulously respected the persons and property of the white visitors, at the same time that they have expressed a determination to reserve the gold for their own benefit."[5]

As the search for gold expanded, Douglas's sense of obligation to the Indigenous population vied with his sympathy for growing numbers of newcomers unaware of what might befall them.[6] Hopes for "a second California or Australia" were, he wrote to the Colonial Office in May, being "sustained by the false and exaggerated statements of steamboat operators, and other interested

---

4   Douglas to W.G. Smith, HBC secretary, March 25, 1858, enclosed in Shepherd to Lytton, June 3, 1858, 5419, CO 305:9.

5   Douglas to Labouchere, No. 15, April 6, 1858, 5180, CO 305:9.

6   Douglas to Labouchere, No. 15, April 6, 1858, 5180, CO 305:9.

parties, who benefit by the current of emigration, which is now setting strongly toward this quarter."[7] Douglas's task was to persuade the Colonial Office that the mainland existed and that, with or without a gold rush, it mattered.

Non-Indigenous gold miners' arrival at Victoria

In what would be the first of numerous such occurrences, Douglas reported from Victoria how on April 25, 1858, "the American Steamer 'Commodore' arrived in this Port, direct from San Francisco with 450 passengers on board, the chief part of whom were gold miners," who "have since left in boats and canoes for Frasers River." Douglas counted among them about sixty British subjects, with an equal number of native-born Americans, the rest being chiefly Germans, with a small proportion of Frenchmen and Italians.[8] Throughout the next months the story would be much the same: "Crowds of people coming in from all quarters. The American Steamer 'Commodore' arrived on the 13th of Instant [June] with 450 passengers and the Steamer 'Panama' came in yesterday from the same Port with 740 passengers, and other vessels are reported to be on the way."[9]

Black arrivals from California

Indicative of the gold rush's many understories, Douglas did not mention to the Colonial Office then or subsequently, it seems, the inclusion among the passengers who arrived April 25, 1858, on the *Commodore* of sixty-five free Black people, one of whom had negotiated with Douglas in advance to ensure their equitable treatment should they leave California. Slavery had been abolished in British colonies in 1834, whereas the United States was characterized by a mixture of slave and free states and territories prior to the abolition of slavery in 1865 consequent on the American Civil War. The arrivals had every reason to fear for their future, given the United States Supreme Court had a year earlier denied citizenship both to enslaved Black people and to their descendants.

The April arrivals would be the nucleus of the arrival of several hundred free Black people, many with their families, who crossed the border to make their

---

7   Douglas to Labouchere, No. 19, May 8, 1858, 6113, CO 60:1.
8   Douglas to Labouchere, No. 19, May 8, 1858, 6113, CO 60:1.
9   Douglas to Lord Edward Henry Stanley, secretary of state for the colonies, No. 28, June 19, 1858, CO 305:9.

homes in Victoria and elsewhere on Vancouver Island and nearby islands.[10] Douglas would keep an eye on their well-being, noting approvingly at the beginning of 1861 how "a Volunteer Rifle Corps has been formed amongst the coloured population, which I have fostered to the best of my ability" given the lack of any other means for Vancouver Island to defend itself if need be.[11]

Douglas's May 8, 1858, query to the Colonial Office

By the beginning of May 1858, James Douglas realized he was in need of advice respecting the growing numbers of gold rush arrivals and so informed the Colonial Office. With the exception of the Black arrivals, Douglas had expected to find the newcomers, based on how they had been described to him by others, as "being, with some exceptions, a specimen of the worst of the population of San Francisco; the very dregs, in fact, of society," but he repeatedly came in for a surprise. Despite there being in Victoria "a temporary scarcity of food, and dearth of house accommodations; the Police few in number; and many temptations to excess in the way of drink, yet quiet and order prevailed, and there was not a single committal for rioting, drunkenness or other offenses, during their stay here," which was only as long as it took for arrivals to find transportation from Victoria across the water to the gold fields.[12]

In his May 8 letter to the Colonial Office, Douglas described how "boats, canoes, and every species of small craft, are continually employed in pouring their cargoes of human beings into Fraser's River" on the way to gold fields along the river. Envisaging these persons' possible fates, Douglas reflected on "canoes having been dashed to pieces and their cargoes swept away by the impetuous

---

10 Crawford Kilian, *Go Do Some Great Thing: The Black Pioneers of British Columbia* (Madeira Park, BC: Harbour Publishing, 2020); James William Pilton, "Negro Settlement in British Columbia, 1858–1871" (master's thesis, Department of History, University of British Columbia, 1951), 30–36; Jean Barman, "What a Difference a Border Makes: Putting Perspective on Blacks' Experiences in Early British Columbia and Alberta," forthcoming in Handel Wright and Afua Cooper, eds., *Black British Columbia, Past and Present* (Black Point, NS: Fernwood, in press).

11 Douglas to Newcastle, No. 19, February 19, and No. 51, Military, August 8, 1861, both CO 305:17; also C. Paget, Admiralty, to Frederic Rogers, permanent under-secretary of state for the colonies, June 17, 1861, CO 305:18.

12 Douglas to Labouchere, No. 19, May 8, 1858, 6113, CO 60:1.

stream, while of the ill fated adventurers who accompanied them, many have been swept into eternity."

Putting on his hat as governor of Vancouver Island, Douglas described how "the merchants and other business classes of Victoria are rejoicing at the advent of so large a body of people in the Colony." These residents became, and would continue to be, along with the nearby port of Esquimalt, which was already being used by the Royal Navy as a base for minding the Pacific, the immediate beneficiaries of the unexpected turn of events.

Douglas came to realize more generally that, because he had no authority over the mainland, nor did anyone else in a formal sense, he needed guidance so as to act as best he could with respect to an escalating situation. In his May 8 letter, Douglas queried his Colonial Office superiors at length respecting the management of a gold rush that was officially none of his business. Who among the arrivals belonged? Who should be encouraged to stay? What about the ever-present American factor? What to do?

> If the country be thrown open to indiscriminate immigration the interests of the [British] empire may suffer, from the introduction of a foreign population, whose sympathies may be decidedly anti-British, and if the majority be Americans, strongly attached to their own country and peculiar institutions.
>
> Taking that view of the question it assumes an alarming aspect and suggests a doubt as to the policy permitting the free entrance of foreigners into the British Territory for residence, under any circumstances whatever, without in the first place requiring them to take the oath of allegiance, and otherwise to give such security, for their conduct, as the government of the country may deem it proper and necessary to require at their hands.
>
> It is easy, in fact, to foresee the dangerous consequences that may grow out of the unrestricted immigration of foreigners into the interior of Fraser's River. If the majority of the immigrants be American, there will always be a hankering in their minds after annexation to the United States, and with the aid of their countrymen in Oregon and California, at hand, they will never cordially submit to British rule, nor possess the loyal feelings of British subjects.[13]

---

13   Douglas to Labouchere, No. 19, May 8, 1858, 6113, CO 60:1.

Douglas thereupon posed a fundamental query to the Colonial Office in London respecting the future, which is just as appropriate for us to ask each other in the present day: how best to respond to newcomers in our midst.

> Out of the considerations thus briefly reviewed, arises the question which I beg to submit for your consideration, as to the course of policy that ought, in the present circumstances to be taken, that is whether it be advisable to restrain immigration, or to allow it to take its course.

Douglas closed his letter respectfully, as he was wont to do. "I shall be most happy to receive your instructions on the subjects in this letter."[14]

Douglas's May 8 letter speaks not only to the character of newcomers as Douglas perceived them, but also to his assumptions respecting the unexpected turn of events. During his years in the fur trade and then as governor of Vancouver Island, with its white population almost wholly linked to the fur trade, Douglas's authority had been taken for granted by both current and former HBC employees.

Not so in the gold rush, as Douglas was already finding out and would continue to do so.[15] Gold miners had no reason beyond immediate convenience to respect British colonial authority. Nor did Douglas have reason to respect uninvited newcomers given their wide range of backgrounds and outlooks unfamiliar to him and so almost by definition not to his liking.

Maintaining everyday control over cascading events

Even while awaiting a response from the Colonial Office to his May 8, 1858, letter, which would not reach Douglas until September 30, four and a half months later, when the mining season was winding down due to the colder weather, he almost certainly marshalled in his mind the three influences that had guided, and would continue to guide, his outlook and actions.

The first influence that would assist Douglas in maintaining control was confidence in himself and in the decisions that he made as a matter of course in the

---

14   Douglas to Labouchere, No. 19, May 8, 1858, 6113, CO 60:1.

15   For a general description of tensions respecting Douglas's actions on Vancouver Island in 1858–59, see Margaret A. Ormsby, "Sir James Douglas," *Dictionary of Canadian Biography*, vol. 10, http://www.biographi.ca/en/bio/douglas_james_10E.html.

everyday, be it in the fur trade or now, unexpectedly, a gold rush. The second was the everyday comfort of his family with Amelia, which by 1858 comprised a seven-year-old son and five daughters between the ages of four and twenty-four. The third influence guiding his outlook and actions was the long-distance relationship he had forged on paper over the past half-dozen years with the distant Colonial Office.

While awaiting a response, Douglas regularly updated London respecting actions taken perforce on his own volition. Among those initiatives, he on May 8 wrote at length to the Colonial Office and issued a proclamation "asserting the rights of the Crown to all gold in its natural place of deposit," which he had published in the newspapers of the Oregon and Washington Territories.[16]

Given "boats and other small craft from the American Shore were continually entering Fraser's River, with passengers and goods, especially Spirits, Arms, Ammunition, and other prohibited and noxious Articles," Douglas also "took immediate steps to seek to put a stop to those lawless practices by issuing a Proclamation" warning of the consequences of doing so, to be distributed by the British Royal Navy ship *Satellite* that had arrived at the Vancouver Island port of Esquimalt to assist in marking out an international boundary with the United States. Douglas was by now convinced that "it is utterly impossible, through any means within our power, to close the gold districts against the entrance of foreigners, as long as gold is found in abundance."[17]

Douglas experiencing the gold rush first-hand

It is not surprising, given his travels in the future British Columbia over the previous three decades, while employed in the fur trade, that Douglas early on determined to experience the gold rush first-hand. In letters of June 10 and 15, 1858, to the Colonial Office, and in a letter to the Hudson's Bay Company of June 7, he described his trip. The fifty-five year old Douglas boarded *Satellite*, "anchored off the mouth of Fraser's River," and headed up the river to the longtime HBC post of Fort Langley. From there he travelled four days upriver "in canoes manned chiefly by native Indians" to gold diggings extending from the small post of Fort Hope as far as it was possible to go given "the present high state of the River." In one twenty-mile stretch Douglas counted "about 190 men,

---

16   Douglas to Labouchere, No. 19, May 8, 1858, 6113, CO 60:1.
17   Douglas to Stanley, May 19, 1858, 6667, CO 305:9.

and there was probably double that number of native Indians, promiscuously engaged with the whites in the same exciting pursuit."[18]

Gold's appeal lay, Douglas came to appreciate, in the precious metal's combination of easy accessibility, at this point being "taken entirely from the surface," and in its assured high value. He observed "six parties of Miners, successfully engaged in digging for Gold, on as many partially uncovered River Bars" containing gold in the form of flecks, "there being no excavation on any of them deeper than two feet." The leader of the most successful party Douglas encountered "produced for my inspection the product of his morning's (6 hours) work, with a rocker [not unlike a child's sand sifter on the beach] and three hands besides himself, nearly 6 ozs. of clean float gold, worth one hundred dollars in money, being at the rate of 50 dollars a day for each man employed." Other miners with whom Douglas talked "were making from two and a half to 25 dollars to the man for the day." Yet others "had found 'flour gold,' that is, gold in powder floating on the water of Fraser's River during the freshet," the note referring to fast-flowing water resulting from melting snow. Douglas's references to American currency speak to these and other miners' identities, as also does Douglas's description of one of those with whom he spoke as "an old California miner."[19]

Minding gold miners

Douglas also witnessed what would be the first of numerous disagreements between Indigenous peoples and miners, the former perceived to be trespassing on what miners considered to be their territory. He described "white Miners… in a state of great alarm on account of a serious affray which had just occurred with the native Indians, who mustered under arms, in a tumultuous manner, and threatened to make a clean sweep of miners assembled there."[20]

Every disagreement has two sides, and this one Douglas resolved for the interim by taking "the leader in the affray, an Indian, highly connected in their way, and of great influence, resolution, and energy of character, into the Government service, and found him exceedingly useful in settling other Indian difficulties." Douglas described how he "spoke with great plainness of speech to the white miners, who were nearly all foreigners, representing almost every nation

---

18   Douglas to Smith, June 7, 1858, enclosed in Berens to Lytton, August 12, 1858, CO 6:26.

19   Douglas to Smith, June 7, 1858, enclosed in Berens to Lytton, August 12, 1858, CO 6:26.

20   Douglas to Stanley, June 15, 1858, No. 26, 7830, CO 60:1.

THE YEAR THAT CHANGED EVERYTHING (1858)

Miners pan for gold near Yale in the 1870s. Though the Fraser River gold rush was long over, some men still tried their luck in the waters. *Image A-01958 courtesy of the Royal BC Museum.*

of Europe," as to how "they were permitted to remain there merely on sufferance; that no abuses would be tolerated, and that the Laws would protect the rights of the Indian, no less than those of the white man."[21]

---

21   Douglas to Stanley, June 15, 1858, No. 26, 7830, CO 60:1.

CHAPTER 2

Douglas informed the miners that the land was "not open for the purpose of settlement," although, he confided in a letter to the HBC, "the whole district of Fraser's River should be immediately thrown open." He was taking steps to have it surveyed so as "to lay it out in convenient allotments for sale."[22] Fundamental change was on the way.

Douglas also sought to ease the situation generally during what would be the first of numerous such visits. He wrote that he appointed "a British Subject, as Justice of the Peace for the District of 'Hill's Bar,' and directed the Indians to apply to him for redress, whenever any of them suffer wrong, at the hands of white men, and also cautioned them against taking the Law into their own hands, and seeking justice according to their own barbarous customs." Douglas appointed "Indian Magistrates, who are to bring forward when required any man of their several Tribes, who may be charged with offences against the Laws of the country, an arrangement which will prevent much evil." Douglas feared that, except for "the exercise of unceasing vigilance on the part of the Government, Indian troubles will sooner or later occur." He noted that the recent defeat in Oregon Territory of American troops headed by Colonel Edward Steptoe, after whom the event is known, had "greatly increased the natural audacity of" Indigenous peoples. From Douglas's perspective, "it will require I fear the nicest tact to avoid a disastrous Indian war."[23]

Attending to the mainland

His spring 1858 trip up the Fraser River had another outcome in Douglas's fuller realization, set forth initially in his May 8 letter and followed up in a long letter of early June, that the mainland, whose non-Indigenous population prior to the gold rush was 150 or so persons and over which he had no authority, mattered greatly over the longer term:

> My own opinion is that the stream of immigration is setting so powerfully towards Fraser's River, that it is impossible to arrest its course, and that the population will occupy the land as squatters, if they cannot obtain a title by legal means. I think it is a measure of obvious necessity, that the whole country be immediately

---

22   Douglas to Smith, June 9, 1858, enclosed in Berens to Lytton, August 12, 1858, CO 6:26.
23   Douglas to Stanley, June 15, 1858, No. 26, 7830, CO 60:1.

thrown open for settlement, and that the land be surveyed and sold at a fixed rate not to exceed twenty shillings an acre... Either that plan or some other better calculated to maintain the rights of the Crown, and the authority of the Laws, should, in my opinion, be adopted with as little delay as possible, otherwise the country will be filled with lawless crowds, the public lands occupied by squatters of every description, and the authority of Government will ultimately be set at naught.[24]

On the trip's completion, the captain of the *Satellite*, the Royal Navy ship which had provided Douglas with water transportation, was ambivalent respecting its outcome. He described to the Colonial Office how "Mr. Douglas the Governor of Vancouver's Island appears to have acted with exceeding ability & judgement, so far as he is able, but he has no staff whatever to support or assist him & his position at the present time is one of immense difficulty, & anxiety."[25]

What almost certainly sustained Douglas during the gold rush's first heady months were his decades minding fur trade employees not that different in backgrounds than many of the miners, or so he thought. Just as the fur trade was hierarchical, so Douglas similarly viewed the gold rush and sought with middling success to make it so.

Enter Sir Edward Bulwer Lytton

During these same weeks and months that the gold rush was exploding, the query in James Douglas's letter of May 8 to the Colonial Office in faraway London as to "whether it is advisable to restrain immigration, or to allow it to take its course" hung over the decisions Douglas made. His uncertainty as to how to proceed, given he had no authority beyond Vancouver Island, caused him to return to his query in a letter written to the Colonial Office on July 26, two and a half months after the original letter to which he had as yet had no reply:

> I am, not without cause, looking forward most anxiously to receiving your instructions, respecting the plan of Government

---

24 Douglas to Smith, June 7, 1858, enclosed in Berens to Lytton, August 12, 1858, CO 6:26.
25 James C. Prevost, captain of HMS *Satellite*, to W.G. Romaine, Admiralty, June 7, 1858, enclosed in Romaine to Merivale, August 16, 1858, 8219 NA, CO 6.25.

CHAPTER 2

for Fraser's River. The torrent of immigration is setting in with impetuous force, and to keep pace with the extraordinary circumstances of the times; and to maintain the authority of the Laws, I have been compelled to assume an unusual amount of responsibility.[26]

Douglas's May 8 letter would, on its arrival in London on June 25, be referred to the incoming secretary of state for the colonies. Douglas had written to Henry Labouchere, who had held that position since 1855, but now the prolific novelist, playwright, poet, and sometime Member of Parliament Sir Edward Bulwer Lytton was in charge:[27] Sir Edward Bulwer Lytton, as he was named in the Colonial Office and in Parliament, Sir Edward, as he was termed within the Colonial Office, and Lytton, as he was known to outsiders and is mostly used here.[28] Due to his dislike of Eton's headmaster, Lytton had rejected attendance at England's elite boys' boarding school. Instead he had been privately schooled before, in the usual upper-class practice, attending Cambridge University.[29] Lytton's background was a world away from the Scottish private school to which James Douglas, his contemporary in age, had been dispatched from British Guiana, but on the other hand not that different given both men came of age in the shadow of the British Empire.

Even as Douglas was worrying himself through the summer of 1858, Lytton twice responded thoughtfully and respectfully to his May 8 letter. The two letters asking for advice, both written on July 1, reached Victoria in early September. It would, in other words, take virtually the entire 1858 mining season for Douglas's key question respecting the Colonial Office's policy toward unrestrained immigration occasioned by the gold rush to get a response. In the interim Douglas continued to be on his own, trusting his resources, such as they were, and common sense.

The first of Lytton's two July 1 letters referenced the new colony's defences, being for that reason written in "Confidence." Douglas was informed that "the

---

26 Douglas to Stanley, No. 31, July 26, 1858, 9253, CO 305:9.

27 In the view of Lytton's biographer, "during his lifetime Bulwer may have been the most widely read novelist next to [Charles] Dickens." James Campbell Sr., *Edward Bulwer Lytton* (Boston: Twayne Publishers, 1986), 21.

28 As an example of the use of "Sir Edward," alongside "Sir. E. Lytton," see the minute by HM [Merivale], January 30, 1859, on Douglas to Lytton, No. 37, November 27, 1858, CO 60:1.

29 Leslie Mitchell, *Bulwer Lytton: The Rise and Fall of a Victorian Man of Letters* (London and New York: Hambledon and London, 2003), 8–10.

Officers commanding Her Majesty's Vessel at Vancouver's Island will be directed to give you all the support in their power... if the Civil Government should require a force to maintain order among the adventurers resorting to the Gold Fields." Lytton expressed his confidence in Douglas so far as possible acting peaceably:

> Her Majesty's Government feeling the difficulties and critical nature of your present circumstances have not hesitated to place these considerable powers in your hands, but they rely upon your forbearance, judgment and conciliation to avoid all resort to Military or Naval force, which may lead to conflict and loss of life, except under the pressure of extreme necessity.

Lytton reminded Douglas of the differing goals of his long-term employer, the profit-based Hudson's Bay Company, and the British government and Colonial Office. Douglas's loyalty must now be, and must be seen to be, solely to the latter:

> Still less need I impress upon you the importance of avoiding any act which directly or indirectly might be construed into an application of imperial resources to the objects of the Hudson's Bay Company in whose service you have so long been engaged. Even the suspicion of this, however unfounded, would be eminently prejudicial to the Establishment of civil government in the Country lying near the Fraser's River, and would multiply existing difficulties and dangers.[30]

Thus, rather than relying on HBC employees, Douglas was to encourage "the leading men amongst the American Immigrants...to co-operate with you in preserving order amongst their countrymen." Looking to the future, "all claims and interests must be subordinated to that policy which is to be found in the peopling and opening up of the new country with the intention of consolidating it as an integral part of the British Empire."[31]

Lytton's second letter of July 1, also responding to Douglas's May 8 letter, approved on behalf of Her Majesty's Government "the course which you have

---

[30] Lytton to Douglas, Confidential, July 1, 1858, CO 410:1. Lytton reiterated this point in his letter to Douglas, No. 4, of July 16, 1858, CO 410:1.

[31] Lytton to Douglas, Confidential, July 1, 1858, CO 410:1.

adopted in asserting both the dominion of the Crown over this region and the right of the Crown over the precious metals," and expressed the wish that Douglas would "continue [his] vigilance" in doing so. Lytton responded at length to Douglas's specific query respecting policy toward gold miners:

> It is in no part of their [Her Majesty's Government's] policy to exclude Americans and other foreigners from the Gold fields. On the contrary you are <u>distinctly instructed</u> to <u>expose no obstacle whatever</u> [underlining in original] to their resort thither for the purpose of digging in those fields, so long as they submit themselves, in common with the subjects of Her Majesty, to the recognition of Her Authority, and conform to such rules of Police as you may have thought proper to establish.
>
> Under the circumstances of so large an immigration of Americans into English Territory, I need hardly impress upon you the importance of caution and delicacy in dealing with those manifest cases of international relationship and feeling which are certain to arise, and which but for the exercise of temper and discretion might easily lead to serious complications between two neighbouring and powerful States...
>
> Her Majesty's Government must leave much to your discretion on this most important Subject; and they rely upon your exercising whatever influence and powers you may possess in the manner which from local knowledge and experience you conceive to be best calculated to give development to the new Country and to advance Imperial interests.[32]

As the two letters attest, the adjacent United States was ever on the Colonial Office's mind.

Lytton looking ahead in time

Lytton, for his part, even as the two letters were making their way to North America, was not playing for small change with respect to British Columbia, but for the jackpot. He was committed in principle and in practice to the

---

32   Lytton to Douglas, No. 2, July 1, 1858, CO 410:1.

Imperial project in which Britain was engaged around the world.[33] Two decades earlier Lytton had, as a Member of Parliament, so declared himself to his constituents:

> England is essentially a colonizing country—long may she be so!—to colonize is to civilise. Be not led away by vague declamations on the expense and inutility of colonies. When you are told to give up your dependent possessions—consider first whether you wish this island, meagre in its population, sterile in its soil, limited in its extent, to hold a first rate empire, or to constitute a third rate nation... But would I maintain a colony by force of arms when that colony desires to be free, *and can support itself*? No![34]

Implementing British Columbia's colonization

The roadmap to British Columbia's colonization was firmly in place by the time Lytton had, a month earlier on June 5, 1858, been named secretary of state for the colonies. Parts of North America and of the Caribbean had been colonized from the early 1600s onward, parts of Europe and Asia from the eighteenth century, and parts of sub-Saharan Africa from the early nineteenth century. More recently, the Falkland Islands were made a British colony in 1841, Hong Kong in 1843, Sarawak and North Borneo in 1846, Vancouver Island in 1849, Victoria in today's Australia in 1851, and the Cocos Islands in the Indian Ocean in 1857. Now it was British Columbia's turn.

So it was that Lytton, consistent with his view on Britain's role in the world, virtually overnight transformed a still almost wholly unknown place into a

---

33 On Lytton, see James Campbell Sr., *Edward Bulwer Lytton* (Boston: Twayne Publishers, 1986), 16–19, esp. 17; Alan Conrad Christensen, *Edward Bulwer Lytton: The Fiction of New Regions* (Athens: University of Georgia Press, 1976), 228–29; Alan Conrad Christensen, ed., *The Subverting Vision of Bulwer Lytton: Bicentenary Reflections* (Newark: University of Delaware Press, 2004), especially Charles W. Snyder, "Bulwer Lytton and 'The Cult of the Colonies,'" 174–83, and Lillian Nayder, "Bulwer Lytton and Imperial Gothic: Defending the Empire in The Coming Race," 212–21; Leslie Mitchell, *Bulwer Lytton: The Rise and Fall of a Victorian Man of Letters* (London and New York: Hambledon and London, 2003), 207–19.

34 Report of the Proceedings of the Lincoln Dinner, 1838, quoted in Mitchell, *Bulwer Lytton*, 210–11.

CHAPTER 2

second Pacific coast British colony complementing Vancouver Island. He put his plan into place almost immediately.

A "Bill to provide, until the Thirty-first Day of December (One thousand eight hundred and sixty two), for Government of New Caledonia," as the mainland had been called during the fur trade, was introduced into the House of Commons in London on July 1, the same day Lytton wrote the two letters to Douglas. The bill was to be debated in the House on July 8, 12, and 13. Drawing on Douglas's letters, to which he added some literary flourishes, Lytton made his case to the House of Commons at the beginning of the bill's second reading on July 8. He began by describing how unusual the situation was, as compared to "other colonies which have gone forth from these islands" where "something is known of the character of the colonists." Hence his goal:

> Among settlers so wild, so miscellaneous, perhaps so transitory, and in a form of society so crude...the immediate object is to establish temporary law and order amidst a motley inundation of immigrant diggers, of whose antecedents we are wholly ignorant, and of whom perhaps few, if any, have any intention to become resident colonists and British subjects...with the avowed and unmistakable intention of yielding its sway at the earliest possible period to those free institutions for which it prepares the way.
>
> [Given] the discovery of goldfields, the belief that those goldfields will be eminently productive, the number of persons of foreign nations and unknown character already impelled to the place by that belief, I need say no more to show the imperative necessity of establishing a Government wherever the hope of gold—to be had for the digging—attracts all adventurers and excites all passions...Thus, the discovery of gold compels us to do at once, what otherwise we should very soon have done—erect into a colony a district that appears, in great part, eminently suited for civilized habitation and culture.[35]

---

35 Speech by Sir Edward Bulwer Lytton, July 8, 1858, House of Commons, *Hansard's Parliamentary Debates*, vol. 151, 1090–121.

As for governance, the legislation would empower the Crown, for a limited period, till December 1862, to make laws for the district by Orders in Council.

In making the case for immediate action "to secure this promising and noble territory from becoming the scene of turbulent disorder, and to place over the fierce passions which spring from the hunger for gold the restraints of established law," Lytton foresaw a future "in that new world" that he could not have imagined would come to pass in a mere dozen years. In respect to the much smaller nine-year-old British colony of Vancouver Island, he proposed "to leave the question of annexation open to further experience, and the Act will empower the Crown to annex Vancouver to New Caledonia, if the Legislature of the island intimate that desire by an Address to the Crown."

Looking eastward across the continent, Lytton astutely anticipated the next quarter century:

> I do believe that the day will come, and that many present will live to see it, when, a portion at least of the lands on the other side of the Rocky Mountains being also brought into colonization and guarded by free institutions, one direct line of railway communication will unite the Pacific to the Atlantic."[36]

The House of Commons debate

Following Lytton's July 8, 1858, speech in the House of Commons, his Colonial Office predecessor, Henry Labouchere, opened debate respecting the proposed British colony of New Caledonia by paying "a humble tribute to the excellent qualities of Governor Douglas" and remarking on the relative lack of conflict with Indigenous peoples as compared with the adjacent United States. Labouchere proposed that the new colony be renamed, given "a large island in the neighbourhood of Australia belonging to France bore the name already."[37]

None of the speakers following Labouchere opposed the bill, but rather touched on topics linked to their own expertise and interests. In order of speaking, they foresaw how "the Indians must disappear, and the more rapidly the better." They applauded how the bill would "create a counterpoise to the power

---

36 Speech by Lytton, July 8, 1858, House of Commons.

37 Remarks by Henry Labouchere, July 8, 1858, House of Commons.

of the United States in these regions," over which Douglas was "most fitted" to have charge. They emphasized that the HBC monopoly must end and the boundary must be fixed so as to prevent "a repetition of previous difficulties with the United States." They advised the new colony to avoid the Vancouver Island experience, where the high price of land "prevented colonization from being carried on to any great extent," but rather to make land "more easily obtainable, so that out of the shifting population who might be attracted to the colony a deposit of good settlers should be left," in consequence to "fix such a price upon the land as would stimulate population." Coming full circle, a lone speaker dismissed Douglas as "a very incompetent man" for "the duties proposed to be entrusted to him" because "he had never been accustomed to deal with white men; all his dealings were with Indians."[38] No one disagreed with another speaker who rose to "congratulate the right hon. Baronet on this good commencement of his Colonial administration."[39]

The question of the new colony's name surfaced at least twice. In the initial debate one speaker suggested a "native name," another "the colony of Lytton Bulwer." The names Pacifica and New Albion, as the long-ago explorer Sir Francis Drake had termed the area, were considered without enthusiasm.[40] On the bill reaching the House of Lords, "after no opposition had been offered to the principles of the Bill in the other house," it was read for the first time on July 21 and for the second time on July 26, when "New Caledonia" was replaced by "British Columbia," being the name proposed by Queen Victoria. The bill passed the next day. Returned to the House of Commons, the amended bill passed on July 30 and was given royal assent on August 2, 1858. Within a month the deed was done without contention or controversy.

Now not one but two British colonies shared the North American Pacific Northwest between them.

---

38 In order of speaking, John Arthur Roebuck who had lived in Lower Canada; Edward Ellice, with ties to the HBC; manufacturer Samuel Christy; Viscount Sandon, who had been private secretary to Henry Labouchere; Robert Lowe, who had lived in the future Australia, with whom James White, a London merchant chiefly engaged in trade with China, and Francis Crossley, a Yorkshire manufacturer, agreed; Charles William Wentworth-Fitzwilliam. All House of Commons, *Hansard's Parliamentary Debates*, vol. 151, 1090–121.

39 This was James Wyld, who owned a large map-making company.

40 Sittings of July 8 and 12, 1858, House of Commons, *Hansard's Parliamentary Debates*, vol. 151.

Enter the Royal Engineers

A confidential letter from Lytton dated July 16, 1858, alerted Douglas that it was "the desire of Her Majesty's Government" to appoint him as governor of British Columbia for a six-year term "in conjunction with your present Commission as Governor of Vancouver's Island." The new appointment was on the condition he "entirely unconnected" himself as employee or shareholder from the HBC, whose legal rights to both Vancouver Island and the mainland would in any case shortly terminate.[41]

Initially all seemed to be well. One of Lytton's two letters shared with Douglas the news of "an act passed by the Imperial Parliament authorizing the establishment of a regular Government in the Territory West of the Rocky Mountains," which had been without a formal status since its acquisition a dozen years earlier after the 1846 boundary settlement. Queen Victoria had herself named her newest possession, whose future Lytton evoked in glowing terms:

> I need hardly observe that British Columbia, for by that name the Queen has been graciously pleased that the country should be known, stands on a very different footing from many of our early Colonial settlements. They possessed the Chief elements of success in lands which afforded safe, though no very immediate sources of prosperity. This territory combines in a remarkable degree the advantages of fertile lands, fine Timber, adjacent Harbors, rivers, together with rich mineral products. These last, which have led to the large immigration of which all accounts speak, furnish the Government with the means of raising a revenue which will at once defray the necessary expenses of an Establishment.[42]

---

41   Lytton to Douglas, Confidential, July 16, 1858, CO 410:1. Lytton to Douglas, No. 3, September 2, 1858, LAC RG7:G8C/6, 8, reported the HBC grant's revocation; on October 4, 1858, Douglas informed Lytton that he would "take early measures for withdrawing from the Hudson's Bay Company," which was so acknowledged in Lytton to Douglas, Private, December 16, 1858, CO 398:1. On the complexities respecting remuneration requested by the HBC, see among other correspondence Murdoch and Rogers, Colonial Land and Emigration Office, to Merivale, May 7, 1859, CO 305:12.

42   Lytton to Douglas, No. 6, July 31, 1858, CO 410:1.

CHAPTER 2

Lytton's July 31 letter put the onus on Douglas to determine the best way forward within the constraints emanating from the Colonial Office, which included that its newest colony become self-supporting:

> The question of how a revenue can best be raised in this new country depends so much on local circumstances upon which you possess such superior means of forming a judgment to myself, that I necessarily, but, at the same time willingly, leave the decision upon it to you, with the remark that it will be prudent on your part, and expedient to ascertain the general sense of the Immigrants upon a matter of so much importance. Before I leave this part of the subject I must state that whilst the Imperial Parliament will cheerfully lend its assistance in the early establishment of this new Colony, it will expect that the Colony shall be self supporting as soon as possible. You will Keep steadily in view that it is the desire of this Country that representative Institutions, and self Government should prevail in British Columbia when by growth of the fixed population the material for those Institutions shall be shown to exist; and that to that object you must from the commencement aim and shape all your policy.[43]

Lytton's letter to Douglas written a day earlier, on July 30, 1858, the day the bill creating the British colony of British Columbia passed into law, introduced another element into the Colonial Office's relationship with its newest colony that would initially be welcomed, but later become contentious from Douglas's perspective. Lytton's letter read in its entirety:

> I have to inform you that Her Majesty's Government propose sending to British Columbia by the earliest possible opportunity an Officer of Royal Engineers (probably a Field officer, with two or three Subalterns) and a Company of Sappers and Miners made up to One hundred and fifty non-Commissioned Officers and men.
>
> I must trust to you to make such arrangements in the colony for the reception of this party as you may deem necessary or suitable.

---

43   Lytton to Douglas, No. 6, July 31, 1858, CO 410:1.

I shall provide the Officer in command with general instructions for his guidance of which you shall have a copy.[44]

Lytton's letter of July 31 tied his vision for the new colony to the Royal Engineers, who he had a day earlier, without forewarning, informed Douglas were on the way. At the end of enumerating their tasks, the letter slid into the hard reality that the new colony would in due course be paying for their services.

> It will devolve upon them to survey those parts of the Country which may be considered most suitable for settlement, to mark out allotments of land for public purposes, to suggest a site for the seat of Government, to point out where Roads should be made, and to render you such assistance as may be in their power on the distinct understanding however, that this force is to be maintained at the Imperial cost for only a limited period; and that if required afterwards, the Colony will have to defray the expense thereof.[45]

Lytton's July 31 letter respecting the Royal Engineers comes across as duplicitous, given it would either soon be, or already had been, decided within the Colonial Office that virtually the whole cost of the Royal Engineers would be downloaded onto British Columbia. Writing two weeks later, the permanent under-secretary for the colonies, Herman Merivale, recounted that decision to the secretary of state for war:

> It will be necessary that an account should be kept of all the expenses incurred for this expedition, it being intended that the new Colony shall ultimately defray the entire cost of its establishment. In the meanwhile arrangements are being made with the Lord Commissioners of the Treasury to advance funds, on the requisition of the Governor, sufficient to cover the expense

---

44 Lytton to Douglas, No. 5, July 30, 1858, CO 410:1. On background to Lytton's letter, see H.K. Storks, secretary for military correspondence, War Office, to Merivale, July 27, 1858, CO 6:26; and J.R. Godley, assistant under-secretary, War Office, to Lytton, July 29, 1858, CO 6:26.

45 Lytton to Douglas, No. 6, July 31, 1858, CO 410:1.

CHAPTER 2

which this Party of Engineers shall occasion in case there should be no Colonial resources immediately available for that purpose.[46]

Merivale had, to his credit, sought to get part of the cost "paid from Army Funds," only to have the proposal rejected by the War Office given that the "men are required for Colonial and Surveying purposes."[47]

The difference in opinion between the Colonial Office and the War Office respecting costs would be decided at the highest level. Writing on October 18, 1858, respecting the "difference, which has arisen between the War Office and yourself," Benjamin Disraeli, then Chancellor of the Exchequer and a future prime minister, informed Lytton that "it was understood that the regimental pay of the detachment of Royal Engineers, sent to British Columbia, should be paid by the War Office, and that the working, or extra, [all underlining in original] pay, although advanced from imperial funds, should be repaid by the Colony," which "is in accordance with previous practice."[48]

What British Columbia gained by this decision was a small part, but at least a part, of the Royal Engineers' cost.

Lytton's expectations for Douglas

Embedded in Lytton's letters to Douglas of July 30 and 31, 1858, welcoming him to the inner workings of the Colonial Office were five expectations and obligations respecting his oversight of British Columbia's new status as a British colony. In summary:

---

46 Draft of Herman Merivale to secretary of state for war, Immediate, August 18, 1858, enclosed in J.R. Godley, assistant under-secretary, War Office, to Merivale, August 17, 1858, CO 6:26.

47 Storks to Merivale, August 20, 1858, CO 6:26, which resulted in a flurry of minutes from within the Colonial Office and lengthy letters, which were attached to the file, from the Colonial Office to the Chancellor of the Exchequer on October 14 and to the under-secretary of state for war on November 10, 1858, seeking a compromise respecting funding, but to no avail.

48 B. Disraeli, Chancellor of the Exchequer, to Lytton, October 18, 1858, CO 60:2; Newcastle to Douglas, No. 4, September 23, 1859, CO 398:1.

1. **Cut HBC ties.** The first obligation, if personally troubling given Douglas's long career in the fur trade, was doable. Lytton's second letter of July 31, which was confidential, reiterated the necessity for him, should he accept the appointment, to relinquish his ties with the Hudson's Bay Company and related entities.[49]
2. **Deal respectfully with Indigenous peoples.** A second obligation, also not unexpected, was for Douglas to pursue a benign policy toward Indigenous peoples:

> I have to enjoin upon you to consider the best and most humane means of dealing with the Native Indians. The feelings of this country would be strongly opposed to the adoption of any arbitrary or oppressive measures towards them…This question is of so local a character that it must be solved by your Knowledge and experience, and I commit it to you in the full persuasion that you will pay every regard to the interests of the Native which an enlightened humanity can suggest. Let me not omit to observe that it should be an invariable condition in all bargains or treaties with the Natives for the cession of Lands possessed by them, that subsistence should be supplied to them in some other shape, and above all that it is the earnest desire of Her Majesty's Government that your early attention should be given to the best means of diffusing the blessings of the Christian Religion and of civilization among the Natives.[50]

3. **Conciliate newcomers.** A third obligation put on Douglas was to "appease the mixed population which will be collected in British Columbia," to seek "by all legitimate means to secure the confidence and good will of the Immigrants," and in doing so to "exhibit no jealousy whatever of Americans or other foreigners who may enter the country."[51] It seems Lytton could already foresee the eventual makeup of the non-Indigenous population of the new colony.
4. and 5. **Be self-supporting while also funding the Royal Engineers.** The fourth and fifth obligations would be in combination the most

---

49 Lytton to Douglas, Confidential, July 31, 1858, CO 410:1.
50 Lytton to Douglas, No. 6, July 31, 1858, CO 410:1.
51 Lytton to Douglas, No. 6, July 31, 1858, CO 410:1.

difficult, indeed impossible, for Douglas to realize. As put by Lytton in his July 31 letter respecting the fourth obligation, "I must state that whilst the Imperial Parliament will cheerfully lend its assistance in the early establishment of this new Colony, it will expect that the Colony shall be self supporting as soon as possible."[52]

Running counter to Lytton's fourth obligation was his hardening position respecting the funding of the Royal Engineers. The fifth obligation, as set out on July 31, stated "that this force is to be maintained at the Imperial cost for only a limited period; and that if required afterwards, the Colony will have to defray the expenses thereof."[53]

Within the month, even before the Royal Engineers left England on what would be a four-month voyage to British Columbia, Lytton informed Douglas, in line with an earlier letter from the permanent under-secretary of state for the colonies to the War Office, that "any expenditure which the British Treasury shall have incurred on this account will have to be reimbursed by the Colony, as soon as its circumstances permit."[54] British Columbia was thereby commanded to fund not only itself, but also the cost of a quasi-military contingent over which Douglas had had no say as to whether it was wanted or needed.

From Douglas's May 8 query to the instructions he received for a colony in the making was the longest of distances and tallest of orders. Should Douglas accept the invitation, the weight of newly proclaimed British Columbia was on his shoulders, alongside his continuing governorship of Vancouver Island.

Douglas updating the Colonial Office

In the interim, unaware of what was happening in London, Douglas kept updating the Colonial Office respecting gold miners, even though they were not on his turf, living as he did in Victoria on Vancouver Island. On July 1, 1858, Douglas reported how, based on numbers of arriving passengers, "this country and Fraser's River have gained an increase of 10,000 inhabitants within the last six weeks…who have been quiet and submissive to the Laws of the country."

---

52 Lytton to Douglas, No. 6, July 31, 1858, CO 410:1.
53 Lytton to Douglas, No. 6, July 31, 1858, CO 410:1.
54 Lytton to Douglas, No. 8, September 2, 1858, CO 398:1; on the Royal Engineers still being in England, Lytton to Douglas, No. 7, September 2, 1858, CO 398:1.

From what he had been told, much as with his earlier report, "about two thirds of the emigrants from California are supposed to be English and French, the other one third are Germans and native citizens from the United States."[55] A minute added on the letter by Herman Merivale gave a nearly audible sigh of relief: "This conveys the very important information that only a very small proportion of the immigrants are Americans—only part of a third."[56] Recognition of the danger of American intervention extended to the Colonial Office in far-away London.

Four letters later, Douglas reported on August 19, 1858, there were "about 10,000 foreign miners, in Fraser's River," with upward of three thousand of them "profitably engaged in gold mining." Among the others, Douglas applauded five hundred gold miners "composed of many nations, British subjects, Americans, French, Germans, Danes, Africans and Chinese who volunteered their services immediately on our wish to open a practicable route into the interior of the Fraser's River District." Not only did the men volunteer to build a road, but each of them "on being enrolled into the corps, paid into our hands, the sum of 25 dollars, as security for good conduct." As to their conditions,

> They receive no remuneration in the form of pay, the Government having merely to supply them with food while employed on the road, and to transport them free of expense, to the commencement of the road on Harrison's Lake [on a tributary of the Fraser River]; where the money deposit of 25 dollars is to be repaid to them in provisions, at Victoria prices, when the road is finished.[57]

The construction of roads across the vast place that is today's British Columbia would be a continuing priority for Douglas.

Douglas's next letter, dated August 27, related the killing of two miners "by Indigenous peoples of Fraser's River," a total initially reported erroneously as "42 gold miners." Douglas described the acquisition from the *Satellite* and from another vessel of "a force of 33 officers and men to proceed with me to the scene of the disaster." Douglas's goals in so acting, he explained to the Colonial Office,

---

55 Douglas to Stanley, No. 29, July 1, 1858, 7833, CO 60:1.

56 Minute by HM [Merivale], August 10, 1858, on Douglas to Stanley, No. 29, July 1, 1858, 7833, CO 60:1.

57 Douglas to Stanley, No. 34, August 19, 1858, 10342, CO 60:1.

were twofold: "the enforcement of such laws as may be found necessary for the maintenance of peace and good order among the motley population of foreigners, now assembled in Frasers River, and also practically to assert the rights of the Crown, by introducing the levying of a Licence duty on persons digging for gold, in order to raise a revenue for the defence and protection of the Country."[58] As would continue to be his practice, Douglas from time to time took aim at persons not as suitably British as he preferred them to be.

The new order of things

In the new order of things in London, which was yet unknown to Douglas, British Columbia was officially proclaimed a British colony on August 2, 1858. Doing so caused Lytton as secretary of state for the colonies to attend more closely to this distant corner of the vast British Empire than the Colonial Office might otherwise have done, given the recent proliferation of colonies around the world.

The months between letters being dispatched from the Colonial Office and responses received from Douglas, which only began to be remedied at year's end by a more expeditious mail route, made the precision of this sole means of communication essential.[59] That arriving letters were passed between Colonial Office officials for individual comments in the form of minutes contributed to more nuanced responses than would otherwise have been the case.

Douglas's August 19 letter describing miners volunteering for road construction was, like the others, repeatedly minuted on its arrival in London on October 11. In the perspective of one official, "this is an interesting dispatch—and speaks well for Governor Douglas's management of his miscellaneous population."[60] Another minute referenced Colonial Office policy generally:

---

58 Douglas to Stanley, No. 35, August 27, 1858, 10343, CO 60:1; also James C. Prevost, captain of HMS *Satellite*, to R. Lambert Baynes, captain of HMS *Ganges*, No. 20, August 31, 1858, CO 60:2.

59 See Douglas to Lytton, No. 16, November 5, 1858, CO 60:1. As of the beginning of 1858, and perhaps also thereafter, "mail for Vancouvers Island" was dispatched in roughly two-week intervals, being January 1 and January 16. Minute by VJ [Jadis], December 30, 1857, on Hawes to Merivale, December 30, 1857, CO 305:8.

60 Minute by HTI [Henry Turner Irving], October 11, on Douglas to Stanley, No. 34, August 19, 1858, 10342, CO 60:1.

Write in reply...that Sir E. Lytton has seen with very great satisfaction the ability, the resource, and tact & conciliation w^h Govr Douglas has displayed under circumstances so difficult & unexpected as to task the highest powers of administration...I think that as yet we have abstained from praising and that now we ought in justice to Govr Douglas to give him credit for great capacity under trying circumstances. Approval especially when discriminately given is not only just in his case but is good policy.[61]

Upping the demands on British Columbia

What had initially especially resonated for Lytton respecting incoming letters was his conviction based on what Douglas wrote that "the affairs of Government might be carried on smoothly with even a single company of infantry," and "under proper management, that the country will produce a large revenue for the Crown." Indicative of how rapidly Lytton's perspective had shifted, it was now British Columbia's profitability for the mother country as opposed to its well-being that, even in the infant colony's first months of existence, took priority. Colonies were intended to benefit the mother country.

The key to British Columbia's future as Lytton envisaged it lay, not unexpectedly given he had sent them, in "the superior intelligence & discipline of the Sappers & Miners, & their capacity at...expediting the work of civilization."[62] As to their funding, Lytton had already reminded Douglas in a letter dispatched on September 2, 1858, not yet received, that it now lay wholly with the new colony to provide it:

> Her Majesty's Government expect that British Columbia shall be self supporting, and that the first charge upon the Land Sales must be that of defraying all the expenses which this Engineer party shall occasion. Any expenditure which the British Treasury shall have incurred on his account will have to be reimbursed by the

---

61 Minute by C [Earl Carnarvon], October 12, on Douglas to Stanley, August 19, 1858, 10342, CO 60:1.

62 Minute by EBL [Lytton], undated, on Douglas to Stanley, No. 34, August 19, 1858, 10342, CO 60:1.

Colony, as soon as its circumstances permit, and for which I have now to instruct you to make suitable provision.[63]

Lytton's minute on Douglas's August 19 letter instructed Colonial Office staff as to how the new colony should be viewed in light of Douglas's description of miners volunteering for roadbuilding:

> The laudable cooperation in the construction of the road which his energy has found in the good sense & public spirit of the Miners... bears out the principle of policy on which I desired to construct a Colony that was intended to perpetuate the great qualities of the Anglo-Saxon race.

Perceiving British Columbia much as Douglas did, and never one to pass over an opportunity for a literary flourish, Lytton minuted on the letter how "from England we send skill & discipline—the raw material (that is the mere men) a Colony intended for free institutions & on the borders of so powerful a Neighbour as the United States of America, should learn, betimes, of itself to supply."[64]

The draft of Lytton's letter to Douglas was vetted by Colonial Office staff, causing the final version to have a sentence added respecting the Indigenous factor. This was almost certainly in response to the arrival of Douglas's August 27 letter describing Indigenous people's killing of two miners.[65]

It is small wonder Lytton confided to an acquaintance at precisely this point in time, "I feel as if the Colonial Empire would go smash if I were out of reach of the mails and messengers two days together."[66]

Lytton and Douglas jointly in charge of the gold rush

Douglas and Lytton's correspondence during the latter's tenure as secretary of

---

[63] Lytton to Douglas, No. 8, September 2, 1858, par. 11, CO 398:1.
[64] Minute by EBL [Lytton], undated, on Douglas to Stanley, No. 34, August 19, 1858, 10342, CO 60:1.
[65] Lytton to Douglas, No. 30, October 16, 1858, LAC RG7:G8C/6.
[66] Lytton to Miss Johnes, October 1858, National Library of Wales, Dolaucothi MSS, 8099, quoted in Mitchell, *Bulwer Lytton*.

state for the colonies from June 5, 1858, to June 11, 1859, would sometimes push the boundaries, as when the Royal Engineers were dispatched solely at Lytton's behest. Both strong-willed men, they each believed that they had charge of the gold rush, while in practice they held it jointly.

On September 9, 1858, Douglas wrote from "Fort Hope, Fraser's River." Having just received Lytton's letter of July 1, answering his much earlier query respecting policy toward gold miners, Douglas expressed his "indescribable satisfaction that Her Majesty's Government approve of the measures which I conceived it necessary to resort to, in order to assert the dominion of the Crown over the gold Districts of Fraser's River, and the rights of the Crown over the precious metals." In his letter, Douglas reviewed the policy he had effected so as to display strength even while persuading some miners to stay longer and possibly settle down:

> I have to observe for the information of Her Majesty's Government that all foreigners and especially American citizens who have visited Fraser's River since the commencement of the gold excitement, have been treated with kindness, and protected by the laws. The rights of the Crown as well as the trading rights secured by statute to the Hudson's Bay Company, have been broadly asserted in my several proclamations, with the object of maintaining British supremacy, by establishing a moral control over the masses of foreigners, who, under the false impression that the country was free and open to all nations, and that we had no military force at our disposal, were rushing defiantly, and without ceremony into Her Majesty's Possessions, and we succeeded by that means, in securing respect and obedience to the Laws, at a time when a policy of concession would have been mistaken for weakness and have proved injurious to British interests.[67]

Responding on December 30 to Douglas's September 9 letter, Lytton was pleased and even more so, it would seem, relieved. "I can but repeat (and I do so with great pleasure) the testimony which I have already borne to your energy and promptitude amidst circumstances so extraordinary as those in which you found yourself placed." The letter concluded with "cordial approval of the

---

67   Douglas to Lytton, No. 39, September 9, 1858, 12177, CO 60.1.

manner in which you appear to have carried out the two objects which at the onset of such a Colony should be steadfastly borne in view—vizt a liberal and kindly welcome to all honest immigrants, and the unquestionable supremacy of British Sovereignty and Law."[68]

Douglas's reply of September 29 to Lytton's confidential letter of July 1 acknowledged his awareness that he should not be seen to favour the HBC. In respect to conciliating "the American population," Douglas observed confidently their "general feeling is in favor of English rule in Fraser's River, the people having a degree of confidence in the sterling uprightness and integrity of Englishmen, which they do not entertain for their own countrymen."[69] A Colonial Office official was so taken by "Govr Douglas' remark upon the general preference for English over American rule," he recommended it be forwarded to the Admiralty.[70]

To a confidential letter of July 16 alerting Douglas to the mainland's governance and to his being invited to take charge of British Columbia for "six years at least," being 1864 or longer, Douglas responded to Lytton on its October arrival with the expected appreciation, as he also did to his trio of letters written at the end of July notifying Douglas of the legislation's passage and instructing him accordingly.[71]

Douglas reporting on gold miners

Douglas for his part continued to give priority to the task at hand. To monitor the situation on the ground, he travelled in early October 1858 to the gold fields accompanied by "a force of Thirty-five non-commissioned officers and men" furnished by the Royal Navy ship *Satellite*, which had also supported his earlier travels. Finding "the Indian population" at Fort Hope "much incensed against the miners; [Douglas] heard all their complaints, and was irresistibly led to the conclusion that the improper use of spirituous liquors had caused much of the evils they complained of," and so declared "the sale or gift of spirituous liquors to Indians, a penal offence," which it would remain.[72]

---

68   Lytton to Douglas, No. 60, December 30, 1858, CO 398:1.

69   Douglas to Lytton, No. 40, September 29, 1858, 12178, CO 60:1.

70   Minute by C [Carnarvon], November 30, 1858, on Douglas to Lytton, No. 40, September 29, 1858, 12178, CO 60:1.

71   Douglas to Lytton, Private, October 4, 1858, 12643, CO 60:1; October 11, 1858, 12180, CO 60:1; No. 6, October 26, 1858.

72   Douglas to Lytton, No. 3, October 12, 1858, 12721, CO 60:1; also No. 1, same date, CO 60:1.

In reporting on his travels, Douglas repeatedly sought to engage the Colonial Office in the everyday of the gold rush. Fort Hope's now three hundred-strong "white population" was, he reported from there, "engaged in trade, and other pursuits," living in tents and huts, and "all desirous of settling in the country." While there, Douglas appointed a justice of the peace and chief constable. He then headed to Fort Yale, whose population he estimated as two thousand, and similarly appointed officials. In the fifteen-mile distance, he and the others counted three thousand gold miners along the Fraser River's banks, with some of whom Douglas stopped and talked. "I was much struck with the healthy robust appearance of the miners...all seemingly in good health, pleased with the country, and abundantly supplied with wholesome food." From Douglas's perspective, "the whole course of the river exhibited a wonderful scene of enterprise and industry."[73] In his minute on Douglas's letter, Lytton complimented "the ability and power of organization w^h he possesses."[74]

Writing two weeks later, on October 29, Douglas was more realistic, by virtue of his recent trip, about the obligations incurred by his having accepted the governorship.

> The class of men who are mining in Fraser's River are composed of all nations, some of them no doubt respectable, but when I landed at Fort Yale in my late journey to Fraser's River, it struck me that I had never before seen a crowd of more ruffianly looking men, than were assembled on that occasion.
>
> About 3000 were present, and to add to the horror of the scene, many of them were drunk; things, however, wore a better appearance next day, and after saying a few kind words to them, they were profuse in acclamations, and did, at my command, give three cheers for the Queen, but evidently with a bad grace. There is a strong American feeling among them, and they will require constant watching, until the English element preponderates in the Country.[75]

---

73   Douglas to Lytton, No. 3, October 12, 1858, 12/21, CO 60:1.

74   Minute by EBL [Lytton], December 15, on Douglas to Lytton, No. 3, October 12, 1858, 12721, CO 60:1.

75   Douglas to Merivale, Private, October 29, 1858, 506, CO 60:1.

Douglas nonetheless enthused how "the Town site of 'Lytton' was laid out, and now contains 50 houses and a population of 900 persons," with a land route to the site, which had been strategically named in Lytton's honour, completed at a cost of £10,000. "The Revenue collected already in the country is to defray the whole expense" of the road, by which provisions and other supplies were now able to be brought by mule train to Lytton, similar to how mules were also being used elsewhere across the mainland to transport goods.[76] Port Douglas, named for Douglas, was now served by river steamers. Douglas estimated "the mining population along Fraser's River" as 10,600.[77]

Writing a month later, at the end of November, Douglas noted how "a great number of miners have left Fraser's River and returned to California and Oregon."[78] Among the departures of "100 persons a week," some reported "having families to visit and business to settle in California, others dreading the supposed severity of the climate, others alleging the scarcity, and high price of provisions, none of them assigning as a reason for their departure the want of gold."[79] So British Columbia's first gold-mining season drew to a close.

In the matter of finances

The two men in charge of British Columbia's first gold rush season, one on the ground, the other in faraway London, sometimes but not necessarily had the same goals with respect to the critical issue of funding the new colony. As indicated by the tone and content of their ongoing correspondence, James Douglas was not always his own person to act as he would, whereas Sir Edward Bulwer Lytton's flattering and cajoling did not necessarily get him his way.

One unresolvable tension, from Douglas's perspective, given his dual role as governor also of Vancouver Island, had to do with displaced Hudson's Bay Company employees, about whom "a sense of justice leads me to exert the little influence I possess, in protecting from injustice, men who have served their country

---

[76] Douglas to Lytton, No. 30, November 9, 1858, CO 60:1; Douglas to Lytton, No. 3, October 12, 1858, CO 60:1.

[77] Douglas to Lytton, No. 30, November 9, 1858, CO 60:1.

[78] Douglas to Lytton, No. 30, November 9, 1858, CO 60:1; Douglas to Lytton, No. 52, December 24, 1858, CO 60:1.

[79] Douglas to Lytton, No. 40, November 30, 1858, CO 60:1.

Lytton, named to honour Secretary of State for the Colonies Sir Edward Bulwer Lytton, was established at the height of the Fraser River gold rush in 1858. This photo is ca. 1867. *Image A-03551 courtesy of the Royal BC Museum.*

so faithfully and so well."[80] A minute on the resultant letter reminded others in the Colonial Office respecting the HBC how "the establishment of the new Colony w^d have been very different from what it was and is had we not had the service and support of the organization w^h they had previously created."[81] Lytton assured Douglas that, although "no regulations giving the slightest preference to the Hudson's Bay Company will be in future admissible," in respect to "the Indian trade,...the Company's private property will be protected in common with that of all Her Majesty's subjects," which it was.[82]

The far more important and immediate topic was financing the new colony. It was in this respect that Douglas and Lytton drew apart. Douglas approved in

---

80   Douglas to Lytton, No. 6, October 26, 1858, 12724, CO 60:1.

81   Minute by C [Carnarvon], December 15, 1858, on Douglas to Lytton, No. 6, October 26, 1858, 12724, CO 60:1.

82   Lytton to Douglas, No. 8, August 14, 1858, CO 410:1.

principle of Lytton's various proposals for raising revenue "to meet the unavoidable increasing expenditure of Government," including "opening the country to permanent settlement." Even as Douglas agreed, though, he raised and would repeatedly do so over the half dozen years of his governorship the need for financial assistance to get the new colony up and running.

Managerial assistance for British Columbia

The October 1858 trip to the gold fields heightened Douglas's awareness of the need for managerial, along with financial, assistance to meet his obligations. He could not do it all, as he had been wont to do of necessity in respect to British Columbia, which unlike Vancouver Island did not have capable one-time fur trade officers and others at hand:

> I am at present in great perplexity for want of efficient help...to perform the duties that now devolve upon me alone, a misfortune for myself and the Country, as both suffer in consequence of that want...
> Let me therefore have the assistance of Officers, capable of managing the subordinate departments, of drafting dispatches and so forth, so as to leave me time for the executive functions of Government which are more than enough to occupy my attention.[83]

While Douglas was not yet so aware, help was on the way. In a letter written on August 14, 1858, Lytton enthused how British Columbia's "immense resources...will at once free the Mother Country from those expenses which are adverse to the policy of all healthful colonization." To assist, Lytton committed in respect to this "Country hitherto so wild" to have "sent from home" to fill key positions qualified men "freed from every suspicion of local partialities, prejudices and interests."[84]

Matthew Begbie, appointed chief justice of the mainland colony, was already en route and Douglas's letter spurred more action.[85] As minuted on Douglas's

---

83   Douglas to Merivale, Private, October 29, 1858, 586, CO 60:1.

84   Lytton to Douglas, No. 8, August 14, 1858, CO 410:1.

85   Lytton to Douglas, No. 4, September 2, 1858, CO 398:1, respecting Begbie; and minute by VJ [Jadis], January 17, 1859, on Douglas to Merivale, Private, October 29, 1858, 586, CO

September 29 letter: "The Govr asks that an Attorney General, Colonial Secretary & Treasurer may be appointed."[86] What Douglas sought, Lytton was prepared to grant, including a private secretary.[87] As well, the new colony needed its capital to have a name, and the original choice of Queensborough having been rejected as "not only prosaic—it is the quintessence of vulgarity," the name chosen was "New Westminster."[88]

The need for roads

In thanking Lytton for sending personnel, Douglas raised the stakes respecting the mainland colony. In his response he emphasized the need for roads, and he would continue to do so. He noted that his hopes for sustaining the economy over the long term hinged on roadbuilding. Given "Fraser's River is the only great artery of the Country," Douglas explained to Lytton in October 1858, he looked to a system of roads "providing access to the remote settlements of British Columbia." That the colony was almost four times the size of Britain meant, in and of itself, that Douglas faced a daunting task:

> The Government will have to grapple vigorously with the arduous and expensive operation of opening a great system of roads, and providing access to the remote settlements of British Columbia,

---

60:1, including a note on the transcript of the letter. See also David Ricardo Williams, "Sir Matthew Baillie Begbie," *Dictionary of Canadian Biography*, vol. 12, http://www.biographi.ca/en/bio/begbie_matthew_baillie_12E.html; and Williams, "... *The Man for a New Country*": *Sir Matthew Baillie Begbie* (Sidney, BC: Gray's Publishing, 1977). Respecting other necessary appointments, Lytton to Douglas, No. 11, September 2, 1858, RG7:G8C/6, respecting Chartres Brew as chief inspector of police; Lytton to Douglas, No. 21, September 23, 1858, re Wymond Hanley as collector of customs; and Lytton to Douglas, No. 22, September 23, 1858, re James Cooper as harbour master at Esquimalt.

86 Minute by VJ [Jadis], January 17, 1859, on Douglas to Merivale, Private, October 29, 1858, 12724, CO 60:1.

87 Minute by HM [Merivale], January 20, 1859, on Douglas to Lytton, No. 25, November 8, 1858, CO 60:1; Douglas to Lytton, No. 31[a], November 13, 1858, CO 60:1, recommending the appointment of William A.G. Young of the Royal Navy as colonial secretary.

88 Minutes by HM [Merivale], March 30; C [Carnarvon], March 31; EBL [Lytton], April 1; and by ABd [Blackwood], May 2, 1859, on Douglas to Lytton, No. 93, January 58, 1859, CO 60:4.

before its mineral resources can be developed, and become a fruitful source of revenue...

To accomplish that great object of opening up a very inaccessible Country for settlement, by the formation of roads and bridges, immediately and pressingly wanted... in a wilderness of forest and mountains, is a Herculean task, even with all the appliances of wealth and skill, and it must necessarily involve in the first place, a large expenditure, much beyond the means of the Country to defray... My own opinion of the matter is that Parliament should at once grant the sum of £200,000, either as a free gift, or a loan to be repaid hereafter, in order to give the new Colony a fair start, in a manner becoming the great nation, of whose empire it forms a part.[89]

The minutes on Douglas's letter dissected his request at length. The under-secretary of state for the colonies, the Earl of Carnarvon, considered the letter with its request for funding no surprise:

It is very satisfactory in many respects as showing the energy and capacity with w^h Govr Douglas is creating a completely new system in the Colony and he deserves I think for it the highest praise...

This is evidence of the probable cost of the Colony w^h we may expect. I have always believed that the charge next year will not fall much short of £100,000. The amount of pecuniary assistance to be given next Session to the Colony is a serious question. Where everything from the jail to the Gov$^{r's}$ house has to be created and wages exceed 13 shillings a day the expenses must & will be very heavy.[90]

Lytton's minute, written the same day, got to the heart of the matter from the government's perspective:

---

89 Douglas to Lytton, No. 6, October 26, 1858, CO 60:1.
90 Minute by C [Carnarvon], December 15, 1858, on Douglas to Lytton, No. 6, October 26, 1858, CO 60:1.

> It will be necessary to give the most anxious consideration to the question raised of expenditure by the Mother Country. What proposition will Parl^t least unwillingly receive. Parl^t which is prepared, as the Public is, to suppose the Col^y at once self-supporting... The idea of a gift to any amount seems to me impossible. What occurs to me as best is a loan... rather than a guarantee, to be repaid by the Colony from Crown Lands & other revenues.[91]

Following up on Lytton's minute, the permanent under-secretary for the colonies, Herman Merivale, astutely put the matter in a larger context:

> I have thought that, with so able a man there, it is better simply to tell him that he must pinch than to indicate where [both underlining in original] he is to pinch.
>
> But I own I see very little prospect from his financial returns of his being at all able to meet his expenses. The winter has arrived, when receipts will be next to nothing, and, a host of pioneers & employés thrown on his hands.
>
> As to the general question, to which Sir E. Lytton adverts, about self supporting colonies, I am afraid it is one of the many on which facts broadly contradict popular opinion.
>
> No successful colony, founded by Englishmen in modern times, has been self supporting; or with one exception only. Upper Canada, Nova Scotia, N.S. Wales, South Australia, New Zealand, all cost this country very large sums at the outset in one form or the other, & all those with, and upon, a large English expenditure. The smaller colonies of Nth America had no such aid, or little; and their progress was very slow.
>
> The only exception is Victoria [in Australia, originating in gold discoveries], and this scarcely a complete one; for the original "Port Phillip" was an offshoot of the very costly colony of New South Wales.
>
> In truth we are driven back for instances to the old Nth Am[erican] Colonies, now States. They cost this country nothing, but

---

91   Minute by EBL [Lytton], December 15, 1858, on Douglas to Lytton, No. 6, October 26, 1858, CO 60:1.

their progress was very slow indeed, according to our impatient ideas.[92]

From early on, Douglas governed on a financial tightrope and would continue to do so.

The Royal Engineers' cost coming into view

The other ongoing tension complicating matters further was Lytton's demand that British Columbia be not only self-supporting but also fund the Royal Engineers. Writing at length on December 14, 1858, as the year that changed everything was coming to a close, Douglas was cautiously optimistic respecting what was and was not feasible, even as he foresaw the very large cost of the Royal Engineers:

> The American Steamer "Pacific" left this place on the 4th of Instant with 400 passengers principally returning miners, for the Port of San Francisco. The export of Gold dust by that vessel was reported to be ten thousand ounces, exclusive of a large amount in private hands. An export duty on gold would now yield a respectable amount of revenue, and together with the duties levied on imports, would probably yield an income of £100,000 per annum.
>
> With some assistance from Parliament in the outset, either by way of loan or as a free grant, the Colony will soon emerge from its early difficulties, and defray all its own expenses. This has hitherto been accomplished without assistance from any quarter, as I have not yet drawn upon you for any expenditure incurred in the Colony; which have all, nevertheless, been paid.
>
> I cannot however undertake immediately to defray the cost of the detachment of Royal Engineers appointed for the protection of the country; as a large sum must, this year, be provided for the erection of the many public buildings so much needed, in British Columbia. I propose building a small Church and Parsonage, a Court house, and Goal [jail] immediately at Langley and to defray

---

92 Minute by HM [Merivale], December 15, 1858, on Douglas to Lytton, No. 6, October 26, 1858, CO 60:1.

the expense out of the proceeds arising from the sale of Town Lands there.[93]

The minutes on Douglas's December letter were generally complimentary. "Edward Lytton will doubtless regard this dispatch as very satisfactory: especially as Gov.[r] Douglas is not a man to express exaggerated opinions."[94]

Ongoing unease with the United States

Something else was also happening: Americans were shadowing the course of events. Douglas was very aware from the outset of the large proportion of miners who were American, which caused him to be more attentive than he might otherwise have been. It was likely common knowledge among interested Americans that, as Douglas reported to the Colonial Office at the end of November 1858, out of a hundred thousand plus ounces of gold dust produced that year, well over half had been exported to the United States.[95]

Douglas was also aware from early on that Americans were not unwilling to take advantage of events, and he had constantly to be on guard. When a physician at Port Townsend, just across the international boundary, complained to the Colonial Office, in a letter forwarded to Douglas, that incoming miners bringing their own tools were nonetheless compelled to purchase them from the HBC in Victoria, Douglas responded that the HBC at that point in time had no mining tools for sale and generally that,

> from the first period of the gold discoveries in Fraser's River much petty jealously has been exhibited by the inhabitants of Port Townsend...which thought proper to feel aggrieved at the

---

93   Douglas to Lytton, No. 51, December 14, 1858, CO 60:1

94   Minute by AB[d] [Blackwood], January 29, 1859, on Douglas to Lytton, No. 51, December 14, 1858, CO 60:1.

95   Out of 106,395 ounces of gold dust produced in 1858, 16,593 ounces were exported by San Francisco–based Wells Fargo, which had in the summer of 1858 opened an office in Victoria; 15,712 ounces by two Wells Fargo–linked companies, and 30,000 ounces by private parties, likely mostly to the United States. Four thousand ounces were exported by the HBC, with 40,000 ounces by Douglas's estimate in the hands of miners. Douglas to Lytton, No. 40, November 30, 1858, CO 60:1.

prosperity of Victoria, and commenced a crusade against British interests in general, and against the Hudson's Bay Company in particular, and the American press in that quarter, has teemed with Articles of the most absurdly fabulous character."[96]

The ongoing border dispute over the San Juan Islands located between Vancouver Island and American territory was also on Douglas's mind, as he had been requested by Lytton in August 1858 to monitor the situation.[97]

Funding the Royal Engineers

From Lytton's perspective, which mattered the most, it was the Royal Engineers that were the answer, the magic bullet if you will. Writing in October 1858, Lytton ramped up his enthusiasm for them. There was seemingly nothing they could not accomplish, he informed Douglas, "as pioneers in the work of civilization, in opening up the resources of the Country by the construction of Roads and Bridges, in laying the foundations of a future City or Sea Port, and in carrying out the numerous Engineering Works, which in the earlier Stages of Colonization are so essential to the progress and welfare of a Community."[98]

Along with the arrival in April 1859 of the main body of 121 Royal Engineers, accompanied by thirty-one wives and thirty-four children, came an ever wider gulf as to their funding.[99] Even as the detachment was on its way to British Columbia, the War Office in London informed the Colonial Office that, given these "officers and men are required for Colonial and Surveying purposes," it was up to Lytton to "make arrangements with the Treasury for the payment of the whole of the expenses involved."[100]

To protect his own bottom line, Lytton had already, almost as a matter of course and without consultation, downloaded the Royal Engineers' costs to

---

96   Douglas to Lytton, No. 13, November 3, 1858, 53, CO 60:1.

97   Douglas to Lytton, No. 47, November 12, 1858, CO 305:9, responding to Lytton to Douglas, Confidential, August 21, 1858; and No. 46, November 12, 1858, CO 305:9.

98   Lytton to Douglas, No. 30, October 16, 1858, CO 398:1.

99   For the Engineers' arrival by date between the end of October 1858 and end of June 1859, see Frances Woodward, "The Influence of the Royal Engineers on the Development of British Columbia," BC Studies 24 (Winter 1974–75): 12.

100 Storks to Merivale, August 20, 1858, 8503 NA, CO 6:26.

British Columbia. His doing so even before their arrival ran counter to the practical reality of an infant colony just four months of age that was, in Douglas's words to Lytton in his letter of November 4, 1858, not "entertaining much hope of being immediately able to meet the expense of the military establishments of the country." Douglas pointed to "other indispensable outlay, which must be incurred before the country can possibly become a fruitful source of revenue; like a nurseling it must for a time be fed and clothed, yet I trust it will before many years re-imburse the outlay and re-pay the kind care of the mother country, with interest."[101] In a follow-up letter written the same day, Douglas was even blunter as to how "the revenues of the country will not be immediately capable of defraying the expenses of this detachment and I shall be under the necessity of drawing upon the Lords Commissioners of the Treasury...until the new Colony is in a position to meet that expenditure."[102]

Douglas had by now come to realize that if he did not stick up for the mainland colony, nobody else was going to do it for him. Colonial Office minutes on his letters make clear Douglas's November 4 response was no surprise. "This is the answer w^h might be expected," Carnarvon wrote.[103] The long-experienced Arthur Blackwood made explicit the logic, or lack of it, behind the Colonial Office's thinking:

> We have relied or pretended to rely upon the gold being produced in such quantities as would be sufficient to render B. Columbia self supporting in all respects save the salary of the Governor... In this hope we have indulged ourselves that the Colony would also have the means of defraying the expense of the detachment of Royal Engineers, and therefore, the Governor having himself given us such cheering accounts of the prospects of the place, we have never distinctly authorized him to draw upon the British Treasury for Engineers or for any other service... [His now doing so] is really no more nor less than we have expected.[104]

---

101   Douglas to Lytton, No. 14, November 4, 1858, CO 60:1.

102   Douglas to Lytton, No. 15, November 4, 1858, CO 60:1.

103   Minute by C [Carnarvon], January 18, 1859, on Douglas to Lytton, No. 15, November 4, 1858, CO 60:1.

104   Minute by AB^d [Blackwood], January 25, 1859, on Douglas to Lytton, No. 15, November 4, 1858, CO 60:1.

Douglas had been, to borrow a cliché, led down a verbal garden path with no other recourse than to put the new colony in debt for a service he had not requested in the form imposed on him.

Concluding the year that changed everything

On November 27, 1858, Douglas reaped the rewards, such as they were, of the year that changed everything, proclaiming at the long-time HBC post of Fort Langley "the Act of Parliament providing for the Government of British Columbia." Incoming Chief Justice of British Columbia, Matthew Begbie, arrived just in time, via San Francisco, to take part in the ceremony.[105]

Come year's end, Douglas thanked Lytton for "the effective steps you have taken to support my authority and the various measures which you have adopted to aid me in the arduous task of organizing the government of the Colony."[106] As for the management of the gold rush:

> I was sensible from the outset, of the arduous nature of the task of framing regulations so perfectly adapted for a comparatively unknown country, as to be unobjectionable, especially for a country situated as is British Columbia, in the close vicinity of a powerful state whose inhabitants would for a time at least form the great bulk of the population. It was to establish a legal control over the adventurers who were rushing, from all sides, into the country, to anticipate their own attempts at legislation and to accustom them to the restraints of lawful authority, that I prepared and issued the gold regulations.[107]

Carnarvon astutely minuted: "This desp.[despatch] shows how easy it is to theorise in England & how difficult it is sometimes to give effect to those theories in a new Colony."[108]

Douglas's and Lytton's messages exchanged at year's end point out how

---

105 Douglas to Lytton, No. 34, November 27, 1858, CO 60:1.
106 Douglas to Lytton, No. 56, December 27, 1858, CO 60:1.
107 Douglas to Lytton, No. 63, December 30, 1858, CO 60:1.
108 Minute by C [Carnarvon], March 3, 1859, on Douglas to Lytton, No. 63, December 30, 1858, CO 60:1.

transformative 1858 had been. Even as they each pushed their favourites, the two men were cordial.

Douglas not unexpectedly put his emphasis on Vancouver Island, where he lived and of which he was also governor. Indicative of his ongoing preference for it, Douglas had earlier let slip respecting the location of "a sea-port Town for the Colony of British Columbia" that "should Vancouver's Island be incorporated with British Columbia, ... the safe and accessible harbour of Esquimalt Vancouver's Island should be made the Port of Entry to sea going vessels for both Colonies."[109] Douglas also used his year-end message to point out how Victoria in particular had benefited from the newer colony of British Columbia:

> There has been a remarkable increase this year in the population of this Colony, in consequence of the discovery of Gold in Fraser's River. Victoria from a village has grown up into a town of considerable extent, and become the seat of a large and growing trade, being still the only Port of Entry for ships bound to British Columbia.[110]

Lytton's year-end letter to Douglas was similarly respectful: "I cannot conclude without expressing my cordial approval of the manner in which you appear to have carried out the two objects which at the onset of such a Colony should be steadfastly borne in view—vizt a liberal and kindly welcome to all honest Immigrants, and the unquestionable supremacy of British Sovereignty and Law."[111] As did Douglas, Lytton voiced his preferences, emphasizing one more time how his chosen Royal Engineers "will at once assist in the construction of roads and bridges, the want of which is so sensibly felt." Lytton had no doubt that all would work out well. "I look to the Royal Engineers under Colonel Moody and the able Officers at his Command for the opening of the readiest and speediest means of access and communication."[112]

As 1858 drew to a close, James Douglas had yet to receive either Lytton's just-written letter congratulating him as "a Governor who has shewn himself so provident and sagacious," or a letter dispatched in early December notifying him

---

109   Douglas to Lytton, No. 9, November 3, 1858, CO 60:1.
110   Douglas to Lytton, No. 50, December 11, 1858, CO 305:9.
111   Lytton to Douglas, No. 60, December 30, 1858, CO 398:1.
112   Lytton to Douglas, No. 61, December 30, 1858, CO 398:1.

that "the Queen has been graciously pleased to confer upon you the distinction of a Companion of the Order of the Bath."[113] From Douglas's perspective on doing so, all of the challenges of the tumultuous year that changed everything almost certainly fell by the way, at least for the moment.

---

[113] Lytton to Douglas, No. 61, December 30, 1858, CO 398:1; and Lytton to Douglas, Private, December 7, 1858, CO 398:1.

CHAPTER 3

James Douglas and the Colonial Office (1859–64)

James Douglas had singlehandedly—or rather doublehandedly along with the Colonial Office in faraway London headed by Sir Edward Bulwer Lytton—managed the 1858 gold rush across the vast, then almost wholly Indigenous space that is today's British Columbia. Events during the year that changed everything went relatively peacefully, and almost certainly led to Douglas being kept on as governor of the two distant British colonies of Vancouver Island and British Columbia, even following Lytton's departure in June 1859 after a change of government in Britain. Douglas stayed on even though it was evident that with the passage of time the Colonial Office was losing interest in the future province.[1]

It was not until the spring of 1864—a good dozen years since Douglas's 1851 Colonial Office appointment to govern Vancouver Island, where he continued to make his home, and half a dozen years since also taking on the mainland colony of British Columbia in 1858—that Douglas was replaced by separate governors for the two colonies.

James Douglas's governorship

That the Colonial Office, headed by the new secretary of state for the colonies, Henry Pelham Clinton, 5th Duke of Newcastle, kept James Douglas on as governor of the two distant colonies for as long as it did is to his credit. The mainland colony fell out of favour early on, or, more realistically, was never in favour compared to its island counterpart.

One of all governors' responsibilities was to sum up annually the place they oversaw in a compilation of facts and numbers known as a Blue Book, owing

---

1   Douglas to Newcastle, No. 84, Financial, August 28, 1860, CO 60.8.

CHAPTER 3

to the colour of the books they were to use in a British practice going back a century and more. On reading Vancouver Island's inaugural Blue Book in 1865, Douglas's successor as governor, Arthur Kennedy, considered "substantially correct...the European, Negro, and Chinese together numbering about 8000 and the Aboriginal Indians about 10,000."[2]

What James Douglas did not mention in his ongoing correspondence with the Colonial Office was that his governance was being buttressed by the presence of Bishop George Hills, who arrived from England in January 1860 as the appointed head in the two colonies of the Church of England, today's Anglican Church. The two men socialized in everyday life due in part to their living in proximity to each other in Victoria. Hills's private journal, which forms the basis of Chapter 5, makes clear his awareness of the ways in which Douglas, while an acquaintance, did not in his view quite measure up:

> The Governor is a self made man...He has not been to England for many years...Hence makes mistakes in dealing with those who repeat here English society. Yet he is anxious to do the right thing. He has been accustomed to be absolute in the Hudson's B.C. & secret in his plans, & to deal with inferiors. His position is difficult when in contact with accomplished men of the world as our Naval & Military people & where a Legislature & Council are concerned. He is resolute in his own view.[3]

Douglas having charge did not, in Hills's view, signify his being necessarily respected and admired.

Judge Begbie's perspective

While Bishop Hills's observations were for his eyes only and would continue to be so virtually into the present day, those of British Columbia's chief justice Matthew Baillie Begbie, a Cambridge University graduate dispatched from Britain in 1858 who routinely travelled large areas of the mainland colony in order

---

2 Arthur Kennedy, governor of Vancouver Island, to Cardwell, No. 74, Separate, August 24, 1865, CO 305:26.

3 March 21, 1860, entry in "The Journal of George Hills," 1860: 53, typescript in Anglican Church, Ecclesiastical Province of British Columbia, Archives.

to hold court, were routinely shared with Douglas.[4] Begbie made his first trip in the spring of 1859 accompanied by "Mr [Charles] Nicol the High Sheriff of British Columbia and by Mr [Arthur] Bushby the Registrar and assize clerk" and by "an Indian body servant, and 7 other Indians carrying our tent, blankets, and provisions." Along the way Begbie noted the lay of the land, potential for agriculture, feasibility for grazing of animals, water and other natural resources, ease of communication, gold mining and access to foodstuffs. His descriptions were so comprehensive as to include on his inaugural trip "restaurants on the road, one at Spuzzum, one at the top of the hill immediately above Yale, one at Quayome [Boston Bar], and another about 18 miles from Lytton." The "chief points" striking Begbie were:

1. The ready submission of a foreign population to the declaration of the will of the executive, when expressed clearly and discreetly, however contrary to their wishes.
2. The great preponderance of the California, or Californicized element of the population, and the paucity of British Subjects.
3. The great riches, both auriferous [being rocks or minerals containing gold] and agricultural, of the country.
4. The great want of some fixity of tenure for agricultural purposes.
5. The absence of all means of communication except by foaming torrents in canoes or over goat tracks on foot, which renders all productions of the country except such as like gold can be carried with great care in small weight [5]

Colonial Office uncertainty

The Colonial Office, for its part, continued to wax hot and cold—or more accurately warm and lukewarm—respecting a governor over whom it did not have the immediate control it would have possessed had he been immersed in its

---

4   On Begbie see David R. Williams, "... *The Man for a New Country*"; *Sir Matthew Baillie Begbie* (Sidney, BC: Gray's Publishing Ltd, 1977), and Williams, "Sir Matthew Baillie Begbie," *Dictionary of Canadian Biography*, vol. 12, http://www.biographi.ca/en/bio/begbie_matthew_baillie_12E.html.

5   "Report of M.B. Begbie 25/4/59," enclosed in Douglas to Lytton, No. 167, June 8, 1859, CO 60:4.

expectations prior to his appointment (as opposed to being an independent-minded outsider). Douglas was from time to time commended, as with a Colonial Office minute of 1860 by Assistant Under-Secretary Thomas Elliot, who noted that "his views seem to me broad and commanding, and to afford fresh evidence of that practical ability which I always think apparent in Mʳ Douglas!"[6]

Douglas's complaints respecting the Royal Engineers, to which we shall soon turn, were not, however, to the Colonial Office's liking.[7] Looking ahead in time, Douglas's replacements in 1864 would be handpicked for their acquiescence to the status quo, serving only a year, until the two colonies were joined into a single colony of British Columbia that would five years later, in 1871, be hustled into the new Dominion of Canada.

Minding the Fraser River gold rush

Prominent among Douglas's obligations alongside his separate governance of the two colonies was minding British Columbia's ongoing gold rush centred on the Fraser River. While some arrivals spent their first winter in Victoria, others headed south to California, and some few stayed put. Come January 1859, Douglas reported to Lytton how miners in his namesake community of Lytton had "generally suspended work in consequence of the coldness of the weather."[8]

From Douglas's perspective as an Englishman, it was taken for granted that miners were, with some exceptions, not equal to himself. Douglas was, and would continue to be, suspicious of non-Englishmen almost as a matter of course. Faced during the slack winter months of 1858–59 with a cluster of bored gold miners, he reduced them in his mind to "reckless desperadoes requiring the strong arm to curb them." Douglas generalized to the Colonial Office as to how "we cannot rely on a force raised from the mining population."[9]

In Douglas's reports on the gold rush's second year he wrote, "The miners are full of confidence in the resources of the country, and look forward to

---

6   Minute by TFE [Thomas Frederick Elliot], May 18, 1860, on Douglas to Newcastle, No. 33, Miscellaneous, March 22, 1860, CO 60:7.

7   On items of a military character being charged to British Columbia, Douglas to Newcastle, No. 6, Financial, January 10, 1863, CO 60:15.

8   Douglas to Lytton, No. 79, January 21, 1859, CO 60:4.

9   Douglas to Lytton, No. 68, January 8, 1859, CO 60:4.

great discoveries." By evoking recently arrived Chinese men conveying soil in wheelbarrows to a nearby river for washing, a hundred mules weekly packing in foodstuffs for miners, Port Douglas's "white population" of about 150 contributing three hundred dollars toward the construction of a needed bridge, and a detachment of Royal Engineers making a road from Hope to Boston Bar, Douglas sought to hold the attention and the confidence of the faraway Colonial Office.[10]

The dilemma posed by the Royal Engineers

Of all the issues that muddied Douglas's governorship of the mainland colony of British Columbia, none would be more time-consuming than the Royal Engineers. Their presence was fundamental to the roadbuilding, which was necessary to cohere the far-flung colony, and at the same time frustrating since Douglas was not able to exercise the control he sought over them.

From the Colonial Office's perspective, British Columbia was, despite its gold rushes, not unlike some sixty other British possessions around the world, each intended to become self-sustaining. Even when the Royal Engineers dispatched to British Columbia in the summer of 1858 were still in England, the secretary of state for the colonies, Sir Edward Bulwer Lytton, assured Douglas, "They will relieve you of much anxiety," given "they will immediately on their arrival, proceed to survey and lay out lands for sale and occupation," hence covering their cost." What was not taken into account, Douglas pointed out, was that the 170-some men were outside his control, so he could not direct how they might best serve the colony of which he had charge.

Despite Lytton's written instructions to their head, Colonel Richard Clement Moody, that the Royal Engineers "incur no unnecessary expenses," and despite Moody's awareness even before he left England that all items would be "chargeable eventually to the Colony," Moody's demands were seemingly endless. Not only did he insist that he and "two Servants" travel together to British Columbia "in a manner befitting... the position of honour and trust" accorded him; he also ordered to be taken with him from England two years of mainly food supplies, by

---

10   Douglas to Lytton, No. 185, July 4, 1859, CO 60:4.
11   Lytton to Douglas, No. 20, September 16, 1858, CO 398:1.

one estimate totalling 250 to 300 tons.[12] An increasingly exasperated Governor Douglas explained to the Colonial Office in July 1859:

> The Colony is most anxious to acquit herself of every obligation conferred upon her, and she is quite capable of meeting all her civil expenditures in a befitting and proper manner, but the cost of the maintenance of the Military Force, with the heavy charge for [the men's] Colonial Pay, is at present more than her Finances can bear...
>
> I cannot refrain from remarking, however, that the expense of sending the Royal Engineers to British Columbia, is a charge that can scarcely with perfect justness be assigned to the Colony, seeing that after all the object in view was one purely of an Imperial character.[13]

It is indicative of Douglas's skill at delineating the young colony's position that the two Colonial Office minutes on the letter's arrival in London at the end of August 1859 understood the situation and sided with Douglas, if to no avail. As described by recently promoted junior clerk Henry Turner Irving, "it was originally intended by Sir E. Lytton that those expenses should be, at any rate for a time borne by this Country" and only "afterwards in consequence of the favorable (but as they have proved over estimated) accounts of the probable revenue of the Colony, it was decided that the cost [apart from the men's regimental pay],

---

12   Colonel Richard Moody, Royal Engineers, to Earl Carnarvon, under-secretary of state for the colonies, October 25, 1858, CO 60:3; C.E. Trevelyan, assistant secretary to the Treasurer, to Merivale, October 7, 1858, CO 60:2; Lytton to Moody, October 29, 1858, in Lytton to Douglas, No. 35, November 1, 1858, LAC RG7:G8C/6; Moody to Carnarvon, September 12, 1858, CO 60:3; Carnarvon to Douglas, No. 48, April 11, 1859, CO 398:1; Moody to Merivale, September 28 and 29, 1858, CO 60:3; Moody to Carnarvon, October 9, 1858, CO 60:3; Moody to Henry Turner Irving, junior clerk in Colonial Office, October 11, 1858, CO 60:3. On the Royal Engineers' arrival, Douglas to Lytton, No. 5, February 9, 1859, CO 305:10, and No. 142, April 25, 1859, CO 60:4. Accessible online, the Colonial Correspondence contains a host of letters in which Moody requests additional items, personnel, services, and the like.

13   Douglas to Lytton, No. 182, July 2, 1859, CO 60:4.

should be paid from the Colonial revenue."[14] The rules of the game had changed without Douglas's foreknowledge or agreement.

The second minute, from the more senior Herman Merivale, who had studied law at Oxford University and taught there prior to joining the Colonial Office, was blunt and providential respecting the Royal Engineers' consequences for British Columbia's economy and possibly also for the colony's future given American proximity:

> It is perfectly clear that the Colony cannot pay for the military force, & that any attempt to make it do so can only end in disastrous debt. The question lies between the "kind & lenient" policy advocated by the Governor, and that of withdrawing almost all the military force & leaving the Colony to take care of itself…
>
> There is no doubt this latter policy requires firmness & nerve to follow, &, above all, that it cannot be pursued unless we are determined to disregard the apprehensions arising from the American character of the population. Probably the experiment might be safely risked. But it is not to be forgotten, that this corner of the world is becoming a very important point with a view to foreign affairs. Indian hostilities & other causes have established in Oregon a large detachment (relatively speaking) of the small American army.[15]

The uncertainty occasioned by the Royal Engineers was compounded by the self-importance of its head, who was also appointed "Commander of Lands and Works," which came with an additional salary and status, or so Moody considered. As early as August 1858, almost certainly fed by Moody, rumours flew, as they would do until his departure from British Columbia five years later, that

---

14 Minute by HTI [Irving], August 30, 1859, on Douglas to Lytton, No. 182, July 2, 1859, CO 60:4. Writing on October 18, 1858, Benjamin Disraeli, then Chancellor of the Exchequer, confirmed to Lytton (as noted in Chapter 2) that "it was understood that the regimental [underlining in original] pay of the detachment of Royal Engineers, sent to British Columbia, should be paid by the War Office, and that the working, or extra pay, should be by the Colony," which "is in accordance with previous practice."

15 Minute by HM [Merivale], August 31, 1859, on Douglas to Lytton, No. 182, July 2, 1859, CO 60:4.

CHAPTER 3

"Col. Moody has been appointed Govr of the new Colony of British Columbia."[16] The claims may have originated in his also being named lieutenant governor in what, Lytton explained to Douglas, was a "dormant" position whose "functions in that capacity will commence only in the event of the death or absence of the Governor."[17] Moody's wife, a British banker's daughter with, like her husband, a strong sense of self, anticipated—as indicated by her private correspondence and by their being quartered in what was named "Government House," where Douglas also stayed when in the colony's capital of New Westminster—that her husband would soon accede to the governorship, their large family thereby becoming "luxuriously comfortable."[18] The Moodys viewed his position as a stepping stone to greater things as opposed to an end in itself.

Moody's view of himself was not shared by others. Pointed minutes began to appear in the Colonial Office's internal correspondence even before the Royal Engineers left England and would continue throughout Moody's years in British Columbia:

> I so entirely mistrust Colonel Moody—who is always in a hurry & frequently wrong. AB^d[19]
> There is no end to the wants of R. Engineers. AB^d[20]

---

16   Two of the earliest rumours respecting Moody being named governor originated with men he knew from his previous posting. See "his Graces humble Servants of several years experience of the Falklands Islands in Gov Moody's time" to Lytton, August 21, 1858, CO 6:27; and P. Cadell to Lytton, August 23, 1858, CO 602; also William Kernaghan to Carnarvon, August 23, 1858, CO 6:28. About the same time the principal London newspaper, *The Times*, declared Moody to Lytton's annoyance having been named "Lt Govr & Commander in chief." Minute by AB^d [Blackwood], August 21, 1858, on Storks to Merivale, August 20, 1858, CO 6:26.

17   Dorothy Blakey Smith, "The First Capital of British Columbia: Langley or New Westminster," *British Columbia Historical Quarterly* 21, 1–4 (January 1957–October 1958): 33.

18   Jacqueline Gresko, "'Roughing it in the Bush' in British Columbia: Mary Moody's Pioneer Life in New Westminster, 1859–1863," in Gillian Creese and Veronica Strong-Boag, eds., *British Columbia Reconsidered: Essays on Women*, 38–54 (Vancouver: Press Gang, 1992), 41–42.

19   Minute by AB^d [Blackwood], October 23, 1858, on Moody to Carnarvon, October 23, 1858, CO 60:2.

20   Minute by AB^d [Blackwood], October 26, 1858, on W. Driscoll Gosset, Royal Engineers

With regard to provisions, ... I have never yet heard it surmised that we are to feed either the functionaries or the population of British Columbia from England. TFE[21]

Captn Moody's requisition is of reckless magnitude. TFE[22]

A little over a year later from within the Emigration Office, also in London:

The Engineers appear to have done very little useful work [building roads] in B. Columbia, and to have devoted themselves mainly to military duties, & laying out capital cities. Might it not be useful to address the Gov[r] [Douglas] on this subject, if the Engineers are continued? I am much inclined however to think that they wd. be better away as a military [underlining in original] body—only a sufficient number being retained to direct the labour of others in roadmaking & surveying.[23]

And two years later from a long-time Colonial Office employee:

If anything went wrong it was entirely owing to Colonial Moody's personal share who is the worst man of business I ever encountered.[24]

The impasse between Douglas and Moody widened due to the latter's repeated demands for additional funds which the mainland colony did not have the means to provide, and so were passed on to the Colonial Office to be added

---

and colonial secretary of the colony of British Columbia, to Carnarvon, October 26, 1858, CO 60:3.

21 Minute by TFE [Elliot], October 27, 1858, on Gosset to Carnarvon, October 26, 1858, CO 60:3.

22 Minute by TFE [Elliot], October 28, 1858, on Moody to Carnarvon, October 28, 1858, CO 60:3.

23 Minute by CF [Chichester Fortescue], February 10, 1860, on Murdoch and Rogers, Colonial Land and Emigration Office, to Merivale, February 7, 1860, CO 60:9.

24 Minute by AB[d] [Blackwood], June 5, 1862, on Frederick Peel, financial secretary to the Treasury, to Frederic Rogers, permanent under-secretary of state for the colonies, June 3, 1862, CO 60:14.

to British Columbia's growing debt to be repaid at some future date.[25] Moody seems to have made at best a middling attempt to accommodate the colony's priorities, so Douglas regretfully informed the Colonial Office in March 1859: "Moody is of opinion that they will be able to do little more than to attend to the Survey of Town Lots, and that the rural Surveys, the construction of Roads and Bridges, and opening of the great communications of the country must be otherwise provided for."[26]

A thoughtful internal minute of March 1859 respecting British Columbia's finances, by the twenty-seven-year-old Earl of Carnarvon—then undersecretary for the colonies, who would eight years later in 1867, as secretary of state, secure passage of the British North America Act, bringing the Dominion of Canada into being—indicates the considerable extent to which Lytton's increasingly hard line was not shared across the Colonial Office.

> Sir Edward Lytton
>
> Though you have expressed a strong opinion upon Colonial expenses in B. Columbia... I must trouble you with a somewhat different view of the case... It is hopeless to expect that during the first year of its existence a sufficient revenue can be raised to defray the necessary expenses of establishing a government and organising a civilized community. No Colony can be created under the circumstances of B. Columbia without some sacrifice: & if it is not the sacrifice of law and order, as was the case in California, it must be a sacrifice of money. Hitherto we have been remarkably fortunate in B. Columbia, but the good fortune is owing to the remarkable ability & firmness of Gov[r] Douglas & to the presence of a certain amount of military force... To say that we will supply him with men but that he must pay for them amounts in fact to a refusal.[27]

Lytton's April 1, 1859, response to Carnarvon makes clear that Douglas's one-time ally was no more. The glow was gone, and Lytton had moved on in his

---

25 As an example, Douglas to Lytton, No. 112, March 10, 1859, CO 60:4.

26 Douglas to Lytton, No. 117, March 19, 1859, CO 60:4.

27 Minute by C [Carnarvon], March 25, 1859, on Lord Naas, chief secretary for Ireland, to Merivale, No. 117, March 21, 1859, CO 60:6.

priorities. His condescending minute signalled Douglas's easy disposal should need be:

> No doubt in all Gold Colonies, violence will ensue. So there also in public schools—if a boy gets a black eye is he to send home for his Nurse. If at a gold Digging, there is a row are the Colonists to send home to the Mother Country for police? If so the boy will never be a man nor the Colonists worthy to be free men... If this Colony is to be a Colony of Men it must protect itself & pay for that protection by a local Tax... The first duty of a Colony pretending to be English is to fund its own police... That before he undertakes to pay for them, he will pay the Colonial Charges of Col. Moody... If he cannot do it I will get a Governor who can & who will.[28]

Lytton's minute signalled the full extent to which colonies such as British Columbia and Vancouver Island were below "the Mother Country" in status, their governors dispensable.

It was not only the Engineers themselves who had to be accommodated at British Columbia's cost. Dispatched from England at the time the 150-some men came, or subsequently, were men's wives or women to whom men were betrothed, and children, half the cost of whose voyages was to be "repayed by stoppages on the men's pay," the other half added to British Columbia's debt.[29]

Men's families lived respectably in housing provided for them at Sapperton near present-day New Westminster, but that was not sufficient.[30] Moody routinely demanded additional services at British Columbia's cost, including a separate hospital and the salary of a teacher for the growing numbers of

---

28   Minute by EBL [Lytton], April 1, 1859, on Naas to Merivale, No. 117, March 21, 1859, CO 60:6.

29   For details of the repayment process, minute by VJ [Jadis], January 2, 1864, on Douglas to Newcastle, No. 64, Military, November 3, 1863; by TFE [Elliot], January 20, 1864, in Edward Lugard, War Office, to Rogers, January 27, 1864, CO 60:20; and George A. Hamilton, Treasury, to Rogers, February 23, 1864, CO 60:20, including minutes on the letter.

30   Douglas to Newcastle, No. 52, Military, May 12, 1860, CO 60:7.

children.[31] By the beginning of 1863 there were "about 120 children who increase at the yearly rate of 25."[32] A laudatory article written from within the community on the centennial of the Engineers' arrival evokes what appears to have been in effect seasonal employment in its description of how "the detachment gathered each winter, from November until March, in its camp at Sapperton, and their camp was then the centre of the social life and activity of the community," their theatre "the scene of all kinds of dances and parties and balls."[33]

Commending what the Royal Engineers did accomplish

For all of the tension ensuing, virtually from the first contact between James Douglas as governor and Richard Moody as head of the Royal Engineers, Douglas did his best to commend what they accomplished.[34] He applauded to the Colonial Office in June 1859 how "a body of Royal Engineers" along with "civilian labourers...improving the Harrison River Road into a good wagon Road... will open a safe, easy, and comparatively inexpensive route into the interior of British Columbia and give facilities at present unknown to the miner and merchant, for the development of its material resources." A road from Fort Hope to Lytton was also in process, owing, Douglas added, not to the Royal Engineers, but rather to local inhabitants having "with great spirit immediately raised the sum of Two Thousand Dollars ($2000) among themselves for the purpose of opening a horse-path," whereupon two Engineers were dispatched, but only to assess its quality.[35]

A month later Douglas again drew the Colonial Office's attention to the Royal Engineers' contributions to roadbuilding:

> The opening of roads through the mountainous districts of British Columbia into the interior, is now the object which has the strongest claim upon our attention. A party of Royal Engineers are now employed in making the road from Fort Hope to Boston

---

31 Douglas to Newcastle, No. 221, Military Expenses, October 19, 1859, CO 60:5.

32 January 1, 1863, entry in "The Journal of George Hills," 1863: 1.

33 Untitled essay in *The Sapper: Regimental Journal of the Royal Engineers* 5, 1 (June 1958): n.p. [pp. 1–2], searchable online by title.

34 For example, Douglas to Lytton, No. 104, February 19, 1859, CO 60:4.

35 Douglas to Lytton, No. 167, June 8, 1859, CO 60:4.

Roadbuilding was a leading priority of James Douglas, who knew that British Columbia's many natural resources would remain inaccessible, and thus unprofitable to Great Britain, without "a great system of roads" to connect the many remote communities of the colony. *Image D-08062 courtesy of the Royal BC Museum.*

Bar, and a detachment of Royal Engineers and Royal Marines [stationed on a ship then surveying the maritime portion of the boundary established in 1846 between Britain and the United States], exceeding one hundred (100) men are employed in widening and improving the Harrison Lillooet Road.

The transport by that road is already very great. About one hundred (100) pack mules leave Douglas [named after the governor, with a population of 150 whites] weekly with freight for Bridge River.

Based on returns made up at Douglas, 3,600 tons of provisions were carried over the road from its opening in November 1858 through the first half of 1859.[36]

---

36   Douglas to Lytton, No. 185, July 4, 1859, CO 60:4.

CHAPTER 3

Roadbuilding's complexities

Opening up the large interior topped Douglas's agenda for the mainland colony. Realizing roadbuilding's complexities, Douglas shared with the Duke of Newcastle, secretary of state for the colonies, in February 1860 his long-held reservations respecting the Royal Engineers being the means for achieving that goal:

> I was directed by the Despatches of Sir Edward Lytton, Nos 30 and 31 of the 16th of October 1858, to rely entirely upon Colonel Moody and the Royal Engineers under his Command, for the great work of opening the communications of the Country. Experience has proved that the Force in question is utterly unable to grapple with the great difficulties with which it has had to contend, or to make any perceptible impression upon the rugged mountain passes which lead into the interior. Knowing therefore that if I relied upon the Royal Engineers the day would be far distant when this much desired end could be attained, I have felt it imperative on me not to delay longer in the employment of civil labour, and failing assistance from Her Majesty's Government, I have resorted to the expedient of levying a Tax of £1 Sterling upon all pack animals leaving Douglas and Yale, in order to raise the funds necessary for the Expenditure required.[37]

Douglas's initiative was applauded within the Colonial Office. Assistant Under-Secretary Thomas Elliot and Parliamentary Under-Secretary Chichester Fortescue noted in joint minutes of April 21 and 23, 1860, "the uselessness of the Sappers and Miners in B. Columbia." A day later Newcastle noted how "if the Sappers & Miners could be replaced by an equivalent but less expensive force it would be well to do so."[38]

---

37 Douglas to Newcastle, No. 27, Financial, February 25, 1860, CO 60:7; see also *The Work of the Royal Engineers in British Columbia, 1858 to 1863* (Victoria: R. Wolfenden, 1910).

38 TFE [Elliot], April 21; CF [Fortescue], April 23; and N [Newcastle], April 24, 1860, on Douglas to Newcastle, No. 27, Financial, February 25, 1860, CO 60:7.

Managing the two colonies

So as to keep watch on roadbuilding and to oversee British Columbia generally, Douglas regularly visited the mainland colony. He described Queen Victoria's birthday in New Westminster on May 24, 1860, with a clear sense of relief at how "never I believe has any part of Her Majesty's dominions resounded to more hearty acclamations of loyalty and attachment, than were had on that occasion, … a fact which I record with pleasure as a proof of the growing attachment of the alien population of the Colony to our Sovereign, and to the institutions of our Country."[39]

Come autumn 1860 Douglas travelled "the newly-formed Waggon Road, then nearly finished as far as the lesser Lillooet Lake, 28 Miles from Douglas," which he termed "a work of magnitude, and of the utmost public utility…laid out and executed by Captain Grant and a Detachment of Royal Engineers under his command, with a degree of care and professional ability reflecting the highest credit of that active and indefatigable Officer." To Douglas's pleasure respecting his namesake community, "a number of Waggons, imported by the enterprising merchants of Douglas, have commenced running on the new Road; and the cost of transport has already been greatly reduced."[40] By the time Bishop Hills visited the next May, Douglas had acquired as temporary, possibly permanent, residents "Italians, Germans, Norwegians, French, Africans," along with "Americans, Scotch, English, & Irish—Canadians were also seen."[41]

Douglas also "fell upon the new Road from Hope, which is carried over an elevation of 4000 feet without a single gradient exceeding one foot in twelve, a fact very creditable to Sergeant McCall and the detachment of Royal Engineers employed in marking out the line." Respecting a "Horse-way from Yale to Spuzzum," Douglas explained to the Colonial Office how "the arduous part of this undertaking—excavating the mountain near Yale—was executed entirely by a Detachment of Royal Engineers under Sergeant Major George Cann, and it has been completed in a manner highly creditable to themselves, and to the officers who directed the operation."[42] The next spring Douglas enthused how "Captain Grant with a detachment of 80 Royal Engineers under his command,

---

39 Douglas to Newcastle, Separate, May 31, 1860, CO 60:7.
40 Douglas to Newcastle, Separate, October 9, 1860, CO 60:8.
41 May 31, 1861, entry in "The Journal of George Hills," 1861: 61.
42 Douglas to Newcastle, Separate, October 25, 1860, CO 60:8.

and about 80 Civilian labourers" were roadbuilding from Hope "towards Shimilkomeen [Similkameen]."[43]

In their personal lives, the engineers followed a variety of pathways. Cann and Grant had arrived with their wives, while McCall came on his own. Cann also had a daughter, and Grant fathered three daughters in the future British Columbia. McCall soon arranged for his wife and four young children to join him from England, on which condition he committed to remaining in British Columbia. While Cann and Grant purchased land out of their wages, when the time came to decide, both families returned to England.[44]

Enter the Cariboo gold rush

Even as the Fraser River gold rush continued to demand Douglas's attention, a wholly separate rush sprang to life. It became a matter of not only managing what was, but also dealing with a huge, almost wholly Indigenous, chunk of British Columbia accessible only with difficulty. Reporting to the Colonial Office in the spring of 1861, Douglas fretted over "men whose excited imaginations indulge in extravagant visions of wealth and fortune to be realized in remoter diggings."[45] He was by then daily receiving "the most extraordinary accounts" respecting the region known as the Cariboo,[46] which was "distant some 500 miles" from New Westminster.[47] There was in consequence, Douglas explained to the Colonial Office, a fundamental shift in the geography of gold mining, itself just three years old in British Columbia:

---

43 Douglas to Newcastle, Separate, June 4, 1861, CO 60:10.

44 Information drawn from The Royal Engineers Living History Group (website), www.royalengineers.ca.

45 Newcastle to Douglas, No. 20, April 24, 1861, CO 60:9.

46 Even the name of the new area was distinctive. Douglas explained to the secretary of state for the colonies that he had "adopted the popular and more convenient orthography of the word [Cariboo]—though properly it should be written 'Cariboeuf' or Rein Deer, the country having been so named from its being a favorite haunt of that species of the deer kind." Douglas to Newcastle, Separate, September 16, 1861, CO 60:11.

47 Douglas to Newcastle, Separate, June 4, 1861, CO 60:10, and No. 75, Military, November 30, 1861, CO 60:11.

Photographer Frederick Dally captured this image of the Alturas mining claim at Stouts Gulch, ca. 1868, which typifies the infrastructure and cooperation necessary to profit from the gold rush in the Cariboo. *Image A-04919 courtesy of the Royal BC Museum.*

> The Mining Districts of Thompson's River, and of the Fraser below Pavillion, have been almost abandoned by the white Miners of the Colony, who have been generally carried away by the prevailing excitement of the Cariboo and Antler Creek Mines... About 1500 men are supposed to be congregated in those Mines, and the number is continually augmented by the arrival of fresh bodies of Miners.[48]

For those making it to the Cariboo, work processes were very different than with the earlier finds. Rather than men panning for gold near the surface on their own or in small groups, the Cariboo was, in Douglas's words, "what may be styled the Company era where individual Miners must club together, and the possession of a certain amount of Capital is requisite for sinking Shafts, running drifts, rigging drafts, rigging pumps, bringing in water, before Gold can be obtained."[49] The expense and practical difficulties meant that while men dream

---

48 Douglas to Newcastle, Separate, July 16, 1861, CO 60:10.

49 Douglas to Newcastle, Separate, November 13, 1864, CO 60:16.

ing of a better future nibbled at the edges, profiting from the Cariboo rush was complex, expensive, and seasonal due to the inclement winter weather, with many of those reaping the profits returning to their distant homes as opposed to settling down to the two colonies' benefit.[50]

Travelling the mainland colony in the summer of 1861 to hold court, Judge Begbie not unexpectedly stressed the need for roadbuilding:

> It is of course impossible that any roads or trails can be pushed in such a country so as to keep even within sight of the eager swarms who scattered themselves in every direction in search of gold. But the Caribou [spelling in original] may now probably be deemed an ascertained auriferous district of considerable extent and very attractive richness; and trails will be required next year for the passage of 5000 or 6000 men at the least—and their provisions, during 5 months of the year.[51]

Uncertainty over the mainland colony

Whereas the longer-settled Vancouver Island held few surprises as a British colony, its mainland counterpart was a different matter. In addition to ongoing attention to gold miners was financial uncertainty arising from the cost of the Royal Engineers.[52] Had not a gold rush to the distant Cariboo

---

50   Douglas to Newcastle, Separate, July 2, 1863, CO 60:16, reported on four such men, being William Wallace Cunningham and Hugh Nathaniel Steele of Kentucky, Nelson Dutoux of Lower Canada, and John R. Adams of New Brunswick; Peter O'Reilly, gold commissioner, to Douglas, June 11, 1863, enclosed in Douglas to Newcastle, Separate, July 2, 1863, CO 60:15, reported in one instance J.P. Diller of Pennsylvania, James Loring of Boston, and Hard Curry of Georgia; and in a second instance David Grier of Wales, John Fairbairn of Scotland, Michael Gillain and "Captain O'Rourke" of Ireland, and John Wilson of Canada West.

51   "Report of M.B. Begbie 30/11/61," enclosed in Douglas to Newcastle, No. 7, February 5, 1862, CO 60:4.

52   Douglas's attention to, and ambivalence toward, Indigenous peoples, including their title to the land, runs through his correspondence, as examples from the many letters referencing them: Douglas to Newcastle, No. 34, July 7, 1860; No. 39, August 8, 1860, CO 305:14; No. 24, Legislative, March 25, 1861, CO 305:17; Murdoch, to Rogers, June 12, 1861,

ensued just as its predecessor was losing its lustre, it is impossible to know, but intriguing to ponder, the fate of the mainland colony, or for that matter of both colonies.

It was also the case that, even as events on the mainland played themselves out, the United States lurked just next door, both to the south and to the north, and might well have pounced to retrieve territory many Americans felt should have been theirs in the 1846 boundary settlement. Indicative of the ongoing tension was a January 1861 suggestion by the British Foreign Office to the Colonial Office consequent on British Marines being dispatched to San Juan Island, then in dispute between the two countries:

> A Battalion might be usefully stationed in Vancouver's Island, where, and in the adjoining Colony of British Columbia, we have large interests at stake, while, on the other hand, the neighbouring provinces of the United States abound in a squatter population only too ready to create disturbance, but against which, if directed towards the British provinces, such a force might exercise a very salutatory check.[53]

The roads so critical to making the mainland colony accessible had as a complement, Douglas pointed out in July 1859, the Colonial Office's goal of making land accessible. "The regular settlement of the country by a class of industrious cultivators is an object of the utmost importance to the Colony, which is at present dependent for every necessary of life, even to the food of the people on importation from abroad." Although "Colonel Moody is making great efforts to bring surveying parties rapidly into the field,... no country land has as yet been brought into market," for which "there is much popular clamour."[54]

The Colonial Office was in consequence not best pleased, as indicated by Henry Irving's minute on Douglas's letter: "The delay in bringing the country lands into the market is a serious evil... It is probable too that the R. Engineers are not very rapid surveyors."[55]

CO 305:18.

53 Edmund Hammond, Foreign Office, to Rogers, January 21, 1861, CO 305:18.
54 Douglas to Lytton, No. 185, July 4, 1859, CO 60:4.
55 Minute by HTI [Irving], August 29, 1859, on Douglas to Lytton, No. 185, July 4, 1859, CO 60:4.

CHAPTER 3

Newcastle's minute respecting landholding was both critical and providential: "I believe we must resort to the American fashion. The very neighbourhood to U.S. territory renders it next to impossible to maintain the present system."[56] The reference was to pre-emption, whereby in the United States land could be marked out, registered, and taken up prior to surveying and payment. Adopted on the mainland in 1860 as a temporary measure, except in New Westminster where land continued to be, following the earlier practice, sold at auction, pre-emption remained in place until entry into Confederation in 1871.[57]

In August 1859 Douglas forwarded a report from Moody respecting landholding which, on the way to Newcastle's desk, was minuted by the experienced Arthur Blackwood:

> I know not to what it is owing, but this is the first report from an Engineer Officer on the interior of the Country which we have rec^d. And this only refers to a Section up the Harrison River. The Engineers were sent out to explore, survey, lay out lands, make roads & Bridges. They have been for nine months in the Colony, & with the exception of laying out some Lots of land at Langley, & New Westminster, (and making a very few miles of road) this is all the produce of their Labors.[58]

While taking no action, the secretary of state for the colonies, the Duke of Newcastle, responded crisply in a follow-up minute how "I have for some time thought that the labours of the Engineers make very little show!"[59] Caught in the middle, Douglas continued to update the Colonial Office as best he could, commending the Royal Engineers for what they did accomplish, even as the colony racked up a growing debt on their behalf.

---

56   Minute by N [Newcastle], August 29, 1859, on Douglas to Lytton, No. 185, July 4, 1859, CO 60:4.

57   For a pithy overview, see Phyllis Mikkelsen, "Land Settlement Policy on the Mainland of British Columbia, 1858–1874" (master's thesis, University of British Columbia, 1950), esp. 89–117.

58   Minute by Ab^d [Blackwood], October 12, 1859, on Douglas to Lytton, No. 206, August 18, 1859, CO 60:5.

59   Minute by N [Newcastle], October 18, 1859, on Douglas to Lytton, No. 206, August 18, 1859, CO 60:5.

The Colonial Office rethinking the Royal Engineers

What Douglas may not have realized was that it was at this point the Colonial Office began to rethink the Royal Engineers' presence in British Columbia, commissioning an internal report which concluded that "the amount of work done is insignificant."[60] Responses from within the Colonial Office reinforced its conclusions. Chichester Fortescue, parliamentary under-secretary for the colonies, got to the point of the matter:

> I have no doubt that they are an extravagant failure…They have done nothing in the way of laying out country lands [intended to pay for their keep] & very little in the way of road making…I feel myself no doubt that the best thing that could be done would be to recall Col. Moody & the Sappers…& giving all the option of taking their discharge in the Colony & receiving grants of land.[61]

The Duke of Newcastle's minute validated Douglas's long-held concerns respecting the cost of the Royal Engineers, acknowledging that British Columbia was effectively funding Britain's foreign policy, to the detriment of colonial revenues:

> I have no doubt that the Engineers in B. Columbia are a "Mistake" and I was meditating their withdrawal when the S: Juan affair broke out. This affair renders a [underlining in original] Military force Necessary & I should not feel justified in withdrawing the Engineers without the substitution of another force which I admit might easily be both better and cheaper…I greatly deprecate this heavy expense for little practical result.[62]

---

60   Henry T. Irving, Colonial Office clerk, "The Royal Engineers in British Columbia, April 1860," memorandum for the Duke of Newcastle, included in Frances Woodward, "'Very Dear Soldiers' or 'Very Dear Laborers': The Royal Engineers in British Columbia, April 1860," *British Columbia Historical News* 12, 1 (November 1978): 8–14, with memorandum on 10–13 and quote on 13.

61   Minute by CF [Fortescue], July 5, 1860, on Irving, "The Royal Engineers in British Columbia, April 1860," included in Woodward, "'Very Dear Soldiers' or 'Very Dear Laborers,'" 14.

62   Response from N [Duke of Newcastle], July 7, 1860, on Irving, "The Royal Engineers in

Newcastle's reference was to the ongoing dispute over San Juan and neighbouring islands which straddled the forty-ninth parallel between British and American possessions, where an American military force had landed in July 1859. In 1872 an international arbitrator would award the San Juan Islands to the United States.

Funding roads

As Douglas discovered, the Colonial Office commending and funding roadbuilding were two very different matters. His frustration with the slow course of events caused him in a letter of August 28, 1860, to propose a more direct approach. Douglas used as the impetus for doing so the cross-border consequences of "great discoveries of Gold in the Shilmilcommen [Similkameen], and on the Southern frontier of British Columbia near Colvile [Washington]":

> Prodigious efforts have hitherto been made by the people of Oregon to throw supplies, by means of the Columbia River, into the Southern frontier of the British Possessions, and since these new discoveries are so close to their own Territory, these efforts have been redoubled, and unless we adapt instant and effective measures, the revenues of the Colony will suffer to an extent which we can hardly now foresee.

Because the funds needed to construct the necessary roads were far beyond "the means of payment in the Colony," the "only resource" for "the youngest of Her Majesty's Colonies" was, in this unexpected circumstance, Douglas explained to the Colonial Office as persuasively as he could in a letter of August 28, 1860, to "turn to the Mother Country to endeavor to effect a Loan to the extent of Fifty thousand pounds" at a rate "paid by other British Colonies of the same Continent."[63]

On the letter's arrival in London in early October, seasoned employee Arthur Blackwood, with over a third of a century of Colonial Office experience, acted on his own initiative to determine whether such a loan was feasible. As to the reason he did so:

British Columbia, April 1860," included in Woodward, "'Very Dear Soldiers' or 'Very Dear Laborers,'" 15.

63 Douglas to Newcastle, No. 84, Financial, August 28, 1860, CO 60:8.

It would be the making of B. Columbia to have a sum of money to spend in the construction of roads, or even paths capable of conveying provisions & merchandize into the inaccessible interior of the Country in return for the gold, the produce of the Miners' labour. But money cannot be obtained on the spot. The Governor hence appeals to the S. of State to help him to effect a loan here. He wants £50,000...The Colony with no other security to offer than tracts of wild land, at present almost worthless, I had misgivings as to the possibility of the Crown getting the money it wants on any terms in London; but happening to meet an eminent Banker and acquaintance of my own, I endeavored to ascertain from him whether it was at all likely that the loan c^d be effected.[64]

Having reviewed the relevant documents, the banker acquaintance informed Blackwood on October 23, 1860, that a loan was feasible at 6 per cent interest on bonds payable in twenty years with "the revenue and Crown property of British Columbia" as "an efficient security."[65]

In what was a trenchant critique of Douglas from within the Colonial Office, Blackwood added in his minute of October 24 that, if possible and agreed by the Colonial Office, "the distribution of the money should be settled by the Governor in concert with some of the principal officials in B. Columbia," not "to deprecate the honor and integrity of Governor Douglas," but to prevent "a whisper raised...in a Colony where he is perfectly despotic in power."[66] The parliamentary under-secretary, Oxford University graduate Chichester Fortescue, added on October 27 that if the proposal went ahead, "a Council of some kind sh. be associated with the Govr, the reasons for which wd. be increased by the fact of his having a Loan to expend on Road-making."[67] Douglas needed minding.

---

64 Minute by AB^d [Blackwood], October 24, 1860, on Douglas to Newcastle, No. 84, Financial, August 28, 1860, CO 60:8.

65 Statement by J.W. Bosauquet to AB^d [Blackwood], October 23, 1860, in Douglas to Newcastle, No. 84, Financial, August 28, 1860, CO 60:8.

66 Minute by AB^d [Blackwood], October 24, 1860, on Douglas to Newcastle, No. 84, Financial, August 28, 1860, CO 60:8.

67 Minute by CF [Fortescue], October 27, 1860, on Douglas to Newcastle, No. 84, Financial, August 28, 1860, CO 60:8.

CHAPTER 3

Three months later the resourceful James Douglas prepared a letter summarizing for the Colonial Office British Columbia's 1860 revenue and expenses. Its two principal sources of income were duties on imports totalling £35,519 and land sales of £10,962, with total expenditures excluding the cost of the Royal Engineers totalling £44,124.[68] Within this frame of reference, Douglas audaciously proposed nine roadbuilding projects for 1861 totalling 358 miles:

Cart Road	Pemberton to Cayoosh [Lillooet]	36 miles
Same	Hope to Similkameen	74 miles
Horse road	Boston Bar to Lillooet	30 miles
Same	Lytton to Alexandria	150 miles
Same	Cayoosh to Lytton junction	30 miles
Road in progress	New Westminster to Langley	15 miles
Same	New Westminster to Burrard Inlet	9 miles
Same	US boundary to Semiahmoo Bay	14 miles
Same	Spuzzum to Boston Bar	20 miles[69]

Douglas was well aware that by writing as he did, he was challenging the boundaries of his authority and had for that reason made explicit the proposed roads' locations, distances, and financing.

Douglas's letter generated favourable responses. A minute by Thomas Elliot on March 30, 1861, seconded by Chichester Fortescue on April 3 and by Newcastle on April 7, read: "This is on the whole, a satisfactory account of the progress of Revenue in B. Columbia. Probably it will be acknowledged, with an intimation to that effect."[70] After more back-and-forth, the Treasury approved on February 27, 1862, Douglas's "raising of any sum not exceeding £100,000 on the security of the Revenue of British Columbia."[71]

Not so fast.

---

68   Douglas to Newcastle, No. 7, Financial, January 26, 1861, CO 60:10.
69   Douglas to Newcastle, No. 7, Financial, January 26, 1861, CO 60:10.
70   Minute by TFE [Elliot], March 30, 1861, on Douglas to Newcastle, No. 7, Financial, January 26, 1861, CO 60:10.
71   Newcastle to Douglas, No. 107, March 1, 1862, NAC RG7:G8C/10. See also among other letters, Douglas to Newcastle, No. 70, Financial, November 15, 1861, CO 60:11; Separate, May 29, 1862, CO 60:13; No. 38, Financial, August 2, 1862, CO 60:13; and No. 43, September 3, 1862, CO 60:13.

Assessing British Columbia's finances

In the meantime, back charges owed by British Columbia to the Treasury were brought to the attention of the Colonial Office. In a letter to Douglas of February 22, 1862, Newcastle pointed out that British Columbia already owed £26,958.9^{s}10^d. Also owing was £6,900 for silver coins sent out from London to British Columbia in 1860 at a time when none were available in the colony, for which Douglas had promised repayment but not done so.[72]

Thomas Elliot's astute minute of February 27, 1862, on the Treasury's letter respecting British Columbia's debt pointed out how the silver coins' repayment would, "as the Treasury themselves point out with some satisfaction, reduce the Colony to bankruptcy," and, "with all respect, I cannot but think this more petulant than statesmanlike."[73] Chichester Fortescue's minute may have impacted Douglas's future as governor: "Whatever we may think of the tone & temper of the Try [Treasury], they have disclosed to us conduct on the part of the Govr most insubordinate and unfair to the Sec. of State [for the Colonies]."[74]

The complexities of British Columbia's finances originating with the Royal Engineers did not end there. The Treasury followed up with the Colonial Office respecting the £100,000 loan Douglas requested for roadbuilding "to be raised on the security of the Colonial Revenue of British Columbia." The Treasury was doubtful, given that it was already bearing half the colonial expenses of the Royal Engineers, as opposed to their being wholly absorbed by British Columbia. In consequence "they are of opinion that the Governor should be informed that any immediate proceedings for raising the Loan must be suspended."[75]

Assistant Under-Secretary Thomas Elliot's minute of March 24, 1862, on the Treasury's letter was by contrast sympathetic to Douglas on the grounds that in his letters "the Governor made out a striking case for the necessity of Roads, and of borrowing money for their construction." Elliot reminded the others how

---

72   Newcastle to Douglas, No. 104, February 22, 1862, CO 398:2. The total of unpaid back charges British Columbia owed was reduced by £16.9^{s}10^d in a detailed follow-up letter from the Treasury Department to the Colonial Office: Peel to Rogers, February 27, 1862, CO 60:14.

73   Minute by TFE [Elliot], February 27, 1862, on Peel to Rogers, February 28, 1862, CO 60:14.

74   Minute by CF [Fortescue], February 27, 1862, on Peel to Rogers, February 28, 1862, CO 60:14.

75   Peel to Rogers, February 28, 1862, CO 60:14.

"in most new Settlements, as well as in a large proportion of all the British Colonies, the entire Military expenditure is defrayed by the Mother Country, British Columbia will not be doing less in this respect, but more, than most other Colonies."[76] To push home the case, Elliot in his very long minute pointed out, along with the time that had elapsed since Douglas made his request, the reality of American proximity combined with British Columbia's physical isolation:

> So far back as in a despatch from hence of the 1st of March 1861, the Governor was told that his plan was viewed very favorably, provided that he could supply certain information. This information he has supplied, and believes it (on grounds which seem to me reasonable) to be sufficient.
>
> The value of time must be considered. More than a year and a half has elapsed since the Governor wrote his despatch of August 1860 which convinced the Secretary of State—and indeed the Treasury itself—of the necessity of a speedy provision for the construction of roads but the Treasury wanted further information, and now that it has come, they call for more.
>
> At this rate there will be no end of correspondence with a place which is one of the most inaccessible of British Possessions. Nor is real help to be expected from the Governor; in the past he has furnished his information; the future must be judged of by the light of experience and on general considerations which ought to be at least as well understood at home as by the Governor of British Columbia.
>
> Whilst we are writing, American speculators are acting; and it would be a serious responsibility if by mistrust and a craving for more certainty than is attainable in human affairs, the Home Authorities should find that the progress of the Colony was crippled, and possibly foreign channels opened for its supplies.[77]

---

76   Minute by TFE [Elliot], March 24, 1862, on Peel to Rogers, February 28, 1862, CO 60:14. Douglas described his proposal to raise "a loan of £15,000 or £20,000 in this Country" in his letter to Newcastle of October 24, 1861, Separate, CO 60:11.

77   Minute by TFE [Elliot], March 24, 1862, on Peel to Rogers, February 28, 1862, CO 60:14; also minute by same, April 8, 1862, on Peel to Rogers, April 2, 1862, CO 60:14.

Douglas's plan as supported by Elliot was not, however, the Colonial Office's plan. Writing on May 13, 1862, Newcastle summarily informed Douglas that henceforth one half of the Royal Engineers' annual pay of £22,000 "must be defrayed by Colonial Revenue." He went on to remind Douglas of previous "heavy over drafts made by you" to pay bills incurred by the Royal Engineers, which was from Newcastle's perspective "to appropriate British money to the use of the Colony without leave." Newcastle did, however, conclude his admonitions with a consolation prize of sorts:

> I am well aware that the proposed repayments relating to the cost of the Royal Engineers will seriously impair your current means for the important object of the construction of roads, which is in itself so material to the prosperity of the Colony. I have however conveyed to the Lords Commissioners of the Treasury my strong recommendation that you should be authorized to make a fresh law providing for the creation of a loan for this purpose, limited to the extent of £50,000.[78]

Douglas's request for £50,000 had, it appears, come full circle.

Tallying up the cost of the Royal Engineers

The Royal Engineers' demands, which Douglas had no authority to refuse, ate away at British Columbia's finances.[79] In August 1862 he responded at length to the Colonial Office in respect to claims of overspending:

> I earnestly hope that it may be within my power to shew that the sums which I am charged with having improperly drawn have been expended solely on account of the Royal Engineers, under the immediate control and superintendence of their Commanding Officer, Colonel Moody, and that the particular sum of £10,704, occurring under the head, Roads, Bridges, and Surveys,

---

78 Newcastle to Douglas, No. 123, May 13, 1862, NAC 124.

79 For one of Moody's schemes which Douglas did manage to circumvent, see "Confidential Report upon the characters and qualifications of Public Servants," 1863, enclosed in Douglas to Newcastle, Confidential, February 18, 1863, CO 60115.

is for the most part, if not wholly made up of items of expenditure peculiar to the Royal Engineers, and of no benefit to the Colony...

I have kept the public works going by various expedients of short loans, and that I hope to continue to do so, and with your Grace's kind co-operation to bring the Colony satisfactorily out of her present financial embarrassment.[80]

The next spring, April 1863, Douglas again reminded the Colonial Office of "the heavy expenses incurred by this Detachment—expenses that I cannot but think are not proportionate to its strength, and are certainly not proportionate to the circumstances of the colony." Excluding Moody's "£1200 Civil Salary as Chief Commissioner of Lands and Works" paid him in England, in 1862 "the expenditure of The Royal Engineers within the Colony amounts to the sum of $22,325," of which £10,500 was offset by the Imperial Treasury, leaving "a balance provided by the Colony of nearly £12,000" that somehow had to be got.[81]

The same month Douglas provided the Colonial Office with an accounting of what British Columbia got in exchange. "From a Return which I have just received from Colonel Moody, I find that the value of the works performed by the Royal Engineers during 1862 may be estimated at about £3,500." To this amount Douglas added £1,500 for miscellaneous services for a total of £5,000, which left "a sum of £7,000 actually paid out of the Revenue of the Colony, for which no appreciable return is received." Adding to that the £10,500 funded by the Imperial Treasury and Moody's "£1200 Civil Salary," £23,525 was expended in 1862 on the Royal Engineers for £5,000 worth of services.[82]

Douglas shared with the Colonial Office his lengthy search to secure an accurate accounting of Royal Engineers' expenses:

I have long intended to represent to your Grace the heavy expenses incurred by this Detachment—expenses that I cannot but think are not proportionate to its strength, and are certainly not proportionate to the circumstances of the Colony—and I desired to

---

80 Douglas to Newcastle, No. 38, Financial, August 2, 1862, CO 60:13.

81 Douglas to Newcastle, No. 23, Financial, April 22, 1863, CO 60:15.

82 Douglas to Newcastle, No. 24, Financial, April 22, 1863, CO 60:15.

accompany my representation with certain statistical information which I could only obtain from Returns to be furnished by Colonel Moody.

I have called upon Colonel Moody for these Returns but from the delay that has taken place in procuring them in the shape I wished, and from a positive refusal being made in one case, I regret that I cannot testify to Colonel Moody's cheerful co-operation in this matter. With respect to the case of refusal, as a very serious point is involved I beg herewith to enclose Colonel Moody's letter upon the subject: for I feel that it is scarcely just that the Colony should be compelled to bear so heavy a burden, without having the least control in the matter of expenditure.

Colonel Moody declines to comply with my request upon the ground that it would be an infringement of Military Rule. It is remote from my desire to trespass in any way upon Colonel Moody's province so far as his Military duties are concerned, and I have always made it a point most carefully to abstain from doing so; but as it seems to me that the request I made, which was simply to be furnished with a nominal List of all persons rationed at the public expense, has more of a financial than a Military bearing, I cannot accept as satisfactory Colonel Moody's explanation for declining to render the required Return. My reason for asking for it was this: I was anxious to place before your Grace, the numbers and qualities of the different persons rationed, more especially the women and children, the wives and families of officers and men; but as several attempts to obtain the numbers properly classified, failed, I, to avoid further correspondence and delay sought to obtain a nominal list of the persons rationed, from which, the information I required, could have readily and satisfactorily been gathered.

The expenditure of the Detachment during 1862 has exceeded the expenditure in 1861 by £2271. The increase is mainly found under the head of Rations—the Provisions in 1861 costing £6020 in 1862 £7805 a difference of £1784. At present I do not exactly know how to account for this large increase, but a proportion of it is no doubt attributable to the greater number of persons rationed—the number of children in the Detachment having been more than trebled since it left England, and the number is increasing every day. I believe the number of women and children rationed at present exceeds 150 and as this is beyond the strength of the whole detachment I believe it is out of all proportion to what is authorized by the regulations of the Army.

Under these circumstances I do not hesitate to beg that your Grace will authorize me to reduce the establishment by granting a discharge to those who may have large families and to those who may wish to settle in the Colony; I believe many so circumstanced would readily avail themselves of the offer, and in the cases of invariable good conduct the grants of land referred to in Sir Edward Lytton's Despatch No 14 of 2nd September 1858 might be made, by which means the cost of the Detachment could be considerably reduced.[83]

Moody, in the letter Douglas enclosed, written nine months earlier on August 1, 1862, had waxed indignant "that for an Officer com[mandin]g in a Colony to be called on to supply, even to a Governor, a Nominal [underlining in original] Roll of Troops is so far out of all Military Rule that I trust your Excellency will not press it."[84]

The Royal Engineers' departure

By the time Douglas's long and detailed letter reached the Colonial Office in June 1863 it had already been decided to withdraw the Royal Engineers. Arthur Blackwood noted how "this report strengthens the propriety of the measure resolved upon by the Duke of Newcastle of withdrawing the R. Engineers from B. Columbia," with their "shipping" already arranged.[85] In a joint minute, Thomas Elliot, Chichester Fortescue, and Newcastle were grateful to Douglas for supporting the decision:

---

83 Douglas to Newcastle, No. 23, Financial, April 22, 1863, CO 60:15.

84 Moody to Douglas, August 1, 1862, in Douglas to Newcastle, No. 23, Financial, April 22, 1863, CO 60:15.

85 Minute by AB^{d} [Blackwood], June 18, 1863, on Douglas to Newcastle, No. 23, Financial, April 22, 1863, CO 60:15.

This despatch contains proof of the great costliness of the Engineers and affords evidence of their having rendered a very disproportionate amount of service to the Colony. It seems to me to show that they are likely to have been so much spoilt as to render it questionable whether we should endeavour to retain any of them for a further period.[86]

Two months earlier Assistant Under-Secretary Thomas Elliot reflected in another context on what might be the Royal Engineers'—and more particularly Moody's—epitaph:

I do not think that the officers of the Royal Engineers employed in B. Columbia have done themselves credit. They have shown much too great a disposition to employ their time in agitation, and in attempts to show that they could manage matters better than the Governor, than which nothing could be more remote than the truth.[87]

The departure of the Royal Engineers from British Columbia in the summer of 1863 seemed like an afterthought.[88] One hundred of the 165 men, many of whom had already received financial assistance in bringing wives and children to British Columbia, opted to remain. Those doing so were eligible to take up "grants of agricultural land, not exceeding thirty acres...on condition of residence and Military Service in the Colony if called upon," but as of October 1865 only one had done so.[89]

Many of the Royal Engineers settled on their own resources near where they had been based in New Westminster, variously contributing to their new home as constables, surveyors, craftsmen, and merchants, with descendants

---

86   Minutes by TFE [Elliot], June 19; CF [Fortescue], June 24, and N [Newcastle], June 28, 1863, on Douglas to Newcastle, No. 23, Financial, April 22, 1863, CO 60:15.

87   Minute by TFE [Elliot], April 17, 1863, on Douglas to Newcastle, Confidential, February 18, 1863, CO 60:15.

88   Douglas to Newcastle, No. 28, Financial, July 20, 1863, CO 305:20.

89   "Out of the hundred men who elected to take their discharge, only one was found willing to undertake the obligations he would incur in accepting the free grant." See Arthur Birch, colonial secretary of British Columbia, to Cardwell, No. 113, October 2, 1865, CO 60:22.

CHAPTER 3

commendably doing so into the present day.⁹⁰ Left behind as a souvenir of sorts was "a quantity of stores," being the remains of the two tons of mainly food supplies Moody had demanded be taken with the Royal Engineers to the faraway colony. No one in the Colonial Office knew quite what to do with them and wondered if "Colonel Moody might be able to advise as to the best mode of proceeding."⁹¹ What ensued has been lost from view.

Moody and his family were among those returning to England. They did so despite his having acquired during their time in British Columbia over three thousand acres of land on which he had created what British Columbia's most eminent historian Margaret Ormsby terms "his model farm."⁹² What might have spurred Moody to do so was his perceived claim, made even before leaving England, that he was Douglas's successor in line with his secondary position as chief commissioner of lands and works and his dormant position as lieutenant governor. Newcastle minuted on a letter respecting Moody at the time the Engineers left British Columbia in April 1863, "There is no doubt he is looking to the Governorship, (for which he is not fit) and would be a discontented Subordinate to Mʳ Douglas' successor."⁹³

Indicative of Moody's legacy as viewed at the time, Colonial Office staff were alerted to "be careful not to employ any terms which will give Colˡ Moody an oppʸ of offering to stay in B.C. in the capacity of Ch. Commʳ."⁹⁴ The immediate

---

90   On numbers of dependents brought to British Columbia, see Douglas to Newcastle, No. 24, April 22, 1863, CO 60:15; on subsequent occupations, Francis M. Woodward, "The Influence of the Royal Engineers on the Development of British Columbia," *BC Studies* 24 (Winter 1974–1975): 3–48. Among other sources, Beth Hill, *Sappers: The Royal Engineers in British Columbia* (Ganges, BC: Horsdal & Schubart, 1987), 123–68 on those who stayed and their legacies; and Woodward, "The Influence of the Royal Engineers," 3–51, which profiles the 125 men who made their lives in British Columbia. I am grateful to Royal Engineers descendant Anita Bonson for her insights.

91   Untitled memo attached to Douglas to Newcastle, No. 76, Financial, December 19, 1863, CO 60:16.

92   Margaret Ormsby, "Richard Clement Moody," *Dictionary of Canadian Biography*, vol. 11, http://www.biographi.ca/en/bio/moody_richard_clement_11E.html.

93   Minute by N [Newcastle], April 22, 1863, on Edward Lugard, War Office, to Elliot, April 18, 1863, CO 60:17.

94   Minute by ABd [Blackwood] and TFE [Elliot], May 29, 1863, on Lugard, War Office, to Elliot, May 28, 1863, CO 60:17.

reason for doing so was, as spelled out in two minutes, "the recent eposé [underlining in original] by Governor Douglas of the fact that the whole of the numerous wives and families of these Engineers were drawing rations, at an immense cost to the public, whilst the Governor could not obtain so much as even a list of the recipients, and whilst the whole value of the labor performed by the Royal Engineers for the Colony in 1862 was £3,500 [underlining in original]."[95] An unsigned sidebar on the minute penned from within the Colonial Office reads "43 women 29 children." Moody had, from the perspective of the Colonial Office, finally gone too far. But he did exact a petty revenge, vetoing Douglas's proposed appointment of a successor as commissioner of lands and works from within the ranks of the Engineers who had served under Moody in British Columbia.[96]

Describing himself in the 1871 British census as a "retired Major General of the Royal Engineers with full pay," Moody, along with his wife and by then eleven children aged from two to seventeen years (of whom the three between ages eight and eleven had been born in British Columbia), were living at Caynham House in the small village of Caynham in Shropshire, England.[97]

Change in the making in British Columbia

Douglas's letter of October 27, 1862, describing his seasonal trip through the British Columbia interior gives a sense, as it was intended to do, of the state of "these most indispensable public works in British Columbia" on the eve of the Royal Engineers' departure.[98] "I cannot speak too favourably of the newly formed Roads. In smoothness and solidity they surpass expectation."[99]

Indicative of Douglas's predisposition against gold miners as such, he found

---

95 Minute by TFE [Elliot], July 4, 1863, on Lugard, War Office, to Elliot, Assistant Under-Secretary, May 28, 1863, CO 60:17.

96 Douglas to Newcastle, No. 36, September 14, 1863, CO 60:16; and Moody to Douglas, November 13, 1863, enclosed in Moody to Chichester Fortescue, under-secretary of state for the colonies, December 19, 1863, CO 60:17.

97 Household 63, Cainham House, Cainham, Shropshire, England, 1871, England census on Ancestry; Lillian Cope, "Colonel Moody and the Royal Engineers in British Columbia" (master's thesis, Department of History, University of British Columbia, 1940), 116–70, also 175–205.

98 Douglas to Newcastle, No. 58, Financial, December 15, 1862, CO 60:13.

99 Douglas to Newcastle, Separate, October 27, 1862, CO 60:13.

CHAPTER 3

"a striking improvement in all the principal towns, except Hope, which is almost deserted in consequence of the migration of the inhabitants to Carribou [spelling in original] and other places; an evil to which gold producing countries, occupied by a purely mining population, are peculiarly exposed." Changes of which Douglas approved continued to be linked to his long-lived hope for arrivals from Britain so as to realize the British Columbia of his dreams and aspirations:

> I noticed Settlers are beginning to take up Public Land along the course of the Public Roads, and are turning their attention to tillage and Stock raising. A few successful experiments showing how profitable farming may be made in British Columbia will induce other persons to follow their example; and I apprehend the majority of British emigrants will probably find agricultural pursuits better adapted than mining, to their tastes and former habit of life.[100]

What Douglas, or for that matter the Colonial Office, may not have realized was that settlers were arriving, quietly and independently, of their own accord. In May 1861 at Saanich, a few miles north of Victoria, Bishop Hills encountered at an "evening camp meeting," a Protestant social event, "a party of settlers with cattle, wagons & horses on their way to find a settlement." As described by Hills in his journal, the arrivals were James Douglas's ideal settlers: "They were Englishmen, lately arrived from Oregon preferring the old English farmer to the Stars & Stripes. They have been some years in the States, one of them was from Gloucestershire, another from Wales." Hills summed them up as "wayfarers in the wilderness," and it is intriguing to wonder where they ended up and how they fared.[101]

Douglas also reported in his October 27, 1862, letter on overland communication with Canada, describing how some of those arriving by a different route than his road in the making "suffered a good deal of privation" along the way. Douglas's commitment to linking British Columbia eastward across the Rocky Mountains is evident in his hopeful suggestion that

> Should Her Majesty's Government deem it a matter of national importance to open a regular overland communication with Canada, I submit that parties of workmen might be dispatched from

---

100 Douglas to Newcastle, Separate, October 27, 1862, CO 60:13.
101 May 21, 1861, entry in "The Journal of George Hills," 1861: 52.

this Colony at less expense than from Canada to carry their views [of an overland route] into effect.[102]

Douglas's unrelenting roadbuilding

In his follow-up letter of December 4, 1862, Douglas once again directed the Colonial Office's attention to roadbuilding "as soon as the ground thaws in Spring," in this case to "be continued to Alexandria, from whence Fraser's River is navigable to the very bases of the Rocky Mountains," for which "I shall be pressed for funds...and shall be under the necessity of again appealing to Your Grace for assistance."[103] Blackwood's minute on the letter observed a bit wearily how "Governor Douglas threatens us with further appeals for money for his road in B. Columbia," a second by Newcastle how "I suppose he means more loans," which is indeed what he meant.[104]

Douglas wrote again a week and a half later, December 15, 1862, regarding "the precise position in which I am placed with respect to these most indispensable public works in British Columbia."[105] Douglas's long description exemplifies his untethered commitment to roadbuilding even in the difficult terrain that still today characterizes parts of British Columbia. A critical section had been contracted to Joseph Trutch, a recently arrived English surveyor and engineer who would become a strong supporter of entry into Confederation and the new province's first lieutenant governor.[106]

In his very long letter of December 15, Douglas pointed out the great difference that the completion of roads made to the colony's development and to residents' well-being:

> Up to the end of last summer the lowest charge for carrying from Douglas by way of Lillooet to Alexandria was 61 cents per pound, or £1366 per Ton! Now in anticipation of the completion

---

102   Douglas to Newcastle, Separate, October 27, 1862, CO 60:13.

103   Douglas to Newcastle, Separate, December 4, 1862, CO 60:13.

104   Minutes by AB[d] [Blackwood], January 31, 1863, and N [Newcastle], February 3, 1863, on Douglas to Newcastle, Separate, December 4, 1862, CO 60:13.

105   Douglas to Newcastle, No. 58, Financial, December 15, 1862, CO 60:13.

106   See Robin Fisher, "Sir Joseph William Trutch," *Dictionary of Canadian Biography*, vol. 13, http://www.biographi.ca/en/bio/trutch_joseph_william_13E.html.

of the road, one of the most substantial Carriers in the Colony has lately tendered for the transport of all Government stores required in 1863 over the same line, at the rate of 21 Cents per pound: that is at a reduction of no less than 40 cents per pound or 896 dollars per ton, as compared with the rate charged in 1862, being in short a saving to the public to that extent upon all goods carried from Douglas to Alexandria, merely from the effect of forming Roads.

Douglas concluded with the plea which underlay his writing in such detail: "I trust I have said sufficient to convince Your Grace of the Propriety of my being permitted to extend the British Columbia Loan to £100.000."[107]

Funding roadbuilding

Douglas's plea worked. The three minutes on his December 15, 1862, letter—one by Thomas Frederick Elliot, who had been for the past decade and a half assistant under-secretary, another by parliamentary under-secretary Chichester Fortescue, and the third by the letter's recipient, the Duke of Newcastle—could not have been more complimentary of the hard work that had gone into roadbuilding and more immediately into the letter.

> Having raised £50,000, Governor Douglas asks leave to extend his loan to £100,000 for the important object of increasing the means of communication in the Colony. The question is, may this be recommended to the Treasury? TFE[108]
>
> To me the Governor's appeal seems irresistible, and the object upon wh. the money is to be spent—Road-making—one for which a young Colony may fairly borrow. There is probably no country in the world where Roadmaking is so vital, & likely to be so reproductive, as B. Columbia. CF[109]

---

107 Douglas to Newcastle, No. 58, Financial, December 15, 1862, CO 60:13.

108 Minute by TFE [Elliot], February 16, 1863, on Douglas to Newcastle, No. 58, Financial, December 15, 1862, CO 60:13.

109 Minute by CF [Fortescue], February 18, 1863, on Douglas to Newcastle, No. 58, Financial, December 15, 1862, CO 60:13.

I entirely agree. Moreover an early [underlining in original] permission to raise the loan is almost as important as the loan itself. Will Mr Fortescue endeavour to get Mr Peel to attend to this as soon as the letter goes to the Treasury. N[110]

Newcastle's March 12, 1863, response was in the spirit of the three minutes. Respecting Douglas's request "to extend the Loan for the construction of roads in British Columbia to £100,000,…the grounds alleged by you appear to Her Majesty's Government sufficient…for raising a further sum of £50,000 by loan upon the security of the general revenue of the Colony."[111]

Douglas replied a month later on May 14 that the necessary law "similar to the British Columbia Loan Act of 1862" had been passed, meaning the task Douglas had set for himself as governor to open up British Columbia was on its way to completion:

> By the completion of this road, the two great thoroughfares of the country will be established. From the Coast to Douglas, and from the Coast to Yale, the Fraser is navigable. From these two points roads are carried to Alexandria, by which a vast district which has no water communication is rendered accessible. From Alexandria to the Rocky Mountains even, the Fraser is again navigable, and private enterprise has already launched a Steamer on the Fraser at Alexandria. These great road works being accomplished, the Government has faithfully done its duty to the Country, and the development of its valuable resources may safely be left to the energy & enterprise of the people governed by wise and wholesome laws."[112]

And so Douglas got more of his road, which was at the very heart of his governance of British Columbia. In consequence, as of September 14, 1863:

---

110   Minute by N [Newcastle], February 19, 1863, on Douglas to Newcastle, No. 58, Financial, December 15, 1862, CO 60:13.

111   Newcastle to Douglas, No. 14, March 12, 1863, NAC 34; also Douglas to Newcastle, No. 43, September 3, 1862, CO 60:13, enclosing the act for the new loan, and No. 30, Financial, May 14, 1863, CO 60:15, following up.

112   Douglas to Newcastle, No. 30, Financial, May 14, 1863, CO 60:15.

The whole journey from New Westminster to Alexandria may now be readily made in eight days by a connected line of Steamboats and stages running constantly between these places. From Soda Creek below Alexandria, a river Steamer plies on Fraser River to Quesnel and a good horse road, formed this season, connects the latter place with Richfield, sixty three miles (63 miles) distant, thus completing the chain of communication between the Coast and the centre of the Carriboo District. These works have been necessarily expensive, but they are of incalculable advantage to the Colony.

The consequences were wide-ranging, among them "the charge for packing has very materially decreased, prior to that period, it averaged 25 to 30 cents per lb but now it has fallen to 12 and 15 cts."[113]

In the aftermath of success, Douglas acknowledged to the Duke of Newcastle how he considered "the work of opening roads—the very essence of the existence of the Colony—and what an anxious and uphill task I have had in endeavouring to compass a work of so much magnitude and importance."[114]

The changing positions of British Columbia and Vancouver Island

The Colonial Office's approval of roadbuilding was almost certainly due, at least in part, to changing perceptions of the Cariboo gold rush and thereby of the mainland colony more generally. The influential London newspaper *The Times* had tracked the British Columbia gold rush as it leapt from the faraway colony's southern edge into its vast interior, where James Douglas's roads headed. The arrival of Douglas's letter of request on March 14, 1863, followed a flurry of articles published over the previous couple of months highlighting the Cariboo rush, British Columbia as a whole, and the feasibility of overland travel from the Cariboo to Canada.[115]

---

113   Douglas to Newcastle, Separate, September 14, 1863, CO

114   Douglas to Newcastle, No. 53, Financial, September 2, 1863, CO 60:16.

115   As examples of early 1863 *Times* articles headlined "British Columbia," January 1, p. 11; January 22, p. 9; January 28, p. 8; January 30, p. 7; also the separately titled "British Columbia and California," January 29, 1863, p. 9, and "Overland to British Columbia," February 7, p. 5.

Vancouver Island was a different matter, Douglas explained to the Colonial Office a couple of months later:

> The total white population does not exceed eight thousand (8000) souls; about two thirds of these are engaged in trade and mechanical pursuits; the remaining third are agricultural Settlers, and day labourers working for wages. The agricultural classes are, with few exceptions, persons of small means and not possessed of much enterprise or intelligence. Their operations are of the most limited kind, and chiefly effected by their own labour.[116]

If Vancouver Island lost out, British Columbia was the beneficiary of the changing times in more ways than gold mining:

> Continual accessions are being made to the general population of the upper Country, the newly formed roads having given a prodigious impulse to settlement, by opening up valuable farming Districts which before were virtually closed to men of moderate means by difficulties of access, and the enormous cost of transport, and impenetrable at any cost for all kinds of Machinery except such as could be taken asunder, and packed through the mountains on Mules.[117]

Douglas reported to the Colonial Office that Gold Commissioner Peter O'Reilly had similarly observed, on his way from Lillooet to the Cariboo in the spring of 1863, "large tracts of land that were fenced in, and at all the way side Houses great preparations for embarking largely in farming operations; and moreover in the District between Bridge Creek and Williams Lake he states that 500 acres of land were actually under crops of various kinds."[118]

By late spring and summer 1863, Douglas took pleasure in reporting how, in the mainland colony, "the immigration of this year so far consists of about four thousand five hundred persons (4,500 persons), chiefly able bodied men, exclusive of women and children, a class of which this Colony is still lamentably

---

116   Douglas to Newcastle, No. 27, Miscellaneous, July 14, 1863, CO 305:20.

117   Douglas to Newcastle, Separate, May 18, 1863, CO 60:16.

118   Peter O'Reilly quoted in Douglas to Newcastle, Separate, May 18, 1863, CO 60:16.

deficient," with "about 2000 persons" passing through Yale "on their way to the Upper Country," and another two thousand otherwise arriving."[119] Come November Douglas anticipated that "a considerable number of people will remain here during the winter—it is generally said about 1000," while others "are now retreating in great numbers from Carribou [sic] and other remote Districts of the Colony on account of the apprehended severity of winter."[120] Douglas was optimistic that "Carribou and other Districts of British Columbia will surpass in the extent and richness of their auriferous deposits, every other Gold Country in the world," not surprising given "the annual produce of Gold in the Carriibou District is estimated at One Million sterling."[121]

Repeated requests for more equitable governance

Alongside the challenges posed by the Royal Engineers and road construction was everyday governance. Douglas had, from the time he took charge of Vancouver Island in 1851 and of British Columbia in 1858, been subject to complaints respecting a ruling style perceived by those not directly benefiting from it as authoritarian. From the perspective of British Columbia residents, Douglas's governorship advantaged Vancouver Island at the expense of the newer colony. Following a meeting held in the mainland capital of New Westminster on May 22, 1860, signatories of a memorial denounced Douglas in personal terms for "His Excellency not being an English Statesman," and called for "a Representative Government."[122] The memorial, which in Douglas's words "purports to be signed by the British Residents in the Colony of British Columbia," had 413 signatures from across British Columbia, one of them being crossed out as "not a British subject," with another 200 names added later.[123] This was at a time when the colony's White population was about three thousand people.

---

119 Douglas to Newcastle, Separate, July 2, 1863, CO 60:16; May 18, 1863, CO 60:15.
120 Douglas to Newcastle, Separate, November 13, 1863, CO 60:15.
121 Douglas to Newcastle, Separate, May 18, 1863, CO 60:16.
122 Original of the petition of May 22, 1860, from New Westminster residents to secretary of state for the colonies, including the signatures, enclosed in W. Elmsley to Under-Secretary of State, July 21, 1860, CO 60:9; also G.C. Lewis to Douglas, July 16, 1860, with attached documents, CO 410:1.
123 Douglas to Newcastle, No. 58, June 22, 1860, CO 60:7.

Douglas's defence for having diverted British Columbia's governance from the pattern of Vancouver Island, where a House of Assembly had been established in 1856 at a time when, according to the Colonial Office, "the population cannot have exceeded 500 persons of all ages and sexes," was that while he had "established Municipal Bodies at New Westminster, Hope and Yale, ... for a Representative Government the country is not yet sufficiently settled; and the British element in the population is still so small."[124] Blackwood agreed:

> It cannot be said that, with the exception of a very few Officers of the Engineers, & a sprinkling of other persons of the same standing in society, there is any settled respectable class of people in B.C. from whom you could create two creditable Houses of Parliament."[125]

Chichester Fortescue, who also sided with Douglas, took note of the paucity of women and children among the "fixed population":

> It seems to me quite too soon to introduce an elective [underlining in original] House of Assembly or Council into B.C. The number of Whites [underlining in original] in the Colony in July 1860, was estimated by Judge Begbie at 3000, of wh. probably not one half is a fixed population—with scarcely any women or children—and, doubtless, almost all of the class of labouring men, while but few are British subjects.[126]

Assumptions respecting demands for a resident governor and representative government appear to have been largely shared between Douglas and the Colonial Office.

Another memorial followed in the spring of 1861 consequent on, in Douglas's dismissive words, "a series of political meetings" by eight "delegates"

---

124   Douglas to Newcastle, No. 58, June 22, 1860, CO 60:7. The British Columbia population figures were noted within the Colonial Office on the petition.

125   Minute by AB[d] [Blackwood], August 6, 1860, on Douglas to Newcastle, No. 58, June 22, 1860, CO 60:7.

126   Minute by CF [Fortescue], December 15, 1860, on Douglas to Newcastle, No. 58, June 22, 1860, CO 60:7.

from Hope, Douglas, and New Westminster, whose "total populations of British origin, and from the Colonies in North America," Douglas reminded the Colonial Office, were just 108, 33, and 164 "male adults." He had the document put aside owing not only to the small numbers, but also on the grounds that "a majority of the reflective and working classes would, for many reasons, infinitely prefer the Government of the Queen, as now established, to the rule of a party" not representing them but rather only themselves.[127] Douglas's reasoning to the Colonial Office took for granted the superiority of British descent, hence the character of non-Indigenous British Columbia as of the spring of 1861:

> Without pretending to question the talent and experience of the petitioners, or their capacity for legislation and self-government, I am decidedly of opinion that there is not as yet a sufficient basis of population or property in the Colony to constitute a sound system of representative government. The British element is small; and there is absolutely neither a manufacturing nor farming class; there are no landed proprietors except holders of building-lots in towns; no producers except miners; and the general population is essentially migratory: the only fixed population, apart from New Westminster, being the Traders, settled in several inland towns from which the Miners obtain their supplies. It would I conceive, be unwise to commit the work of legislation to persons so situated, having nothing at stake, and no real vested interest in the Colony... a power not representing large bodies of landed proprietors, nor of responsible settlers having their homes, their property, their sympathies and their dearest interests irrevocably identified with the Country.[128]

Elliot's minute on Douglas's report on the spring 1861 meeting seconded Douglas's reasoning that "the introduction of a representative Assembly in British Columbia would be premature and that the establishment of party Government would be not only premature but pernicious." In sum:

---

127 Douglas to Newcastle, Separate, April 22, 1861, CO 60:10.

128 Douglas to Newcastle, Separate, April 22, 1861, CO 60:10.

> The Governor's despatch appears to me very able, and calculated to inspire confidence in his judgment and in his intentions. The public has always seemed to me fortunate in obtaining at this remote and inaccessible settlement, so far out of the reach of much control from home, a Governor of so much self-reliance and practical ability.[129]

Another memorial urging "representative institutions" followed from nine petitioners who came together in the fall of 1861 at Hope in what they termed "The British Columbia Convention," seeking a resident governor and officials, a public hospital, direct mail service, public schools, and other amenities. Douglas described them, or rather dismissed them, to the Colonial Office as sincere "quiet well meaning tradesmen." In sending the memorial on to the Colonial Office, Douglas agreed in principle, but in practice was once again unable to act, he considered, due to the lack of a suitable British population, so he explained at length:

> With respect to the prayer of the Memorialists, that is, the redress of grievances, and the grant of representative institutions, I will observe that I fully, and cordially admit the proposition that liberty is the Englishman's birthright, and that the desire for representative institutions is common to all Her Majesty's subjects... Parliament has, however, seen fit, for good and sufficient reasons, to establish a temporary form of Government in British Columbia not unusual in the infancy of British Colonies, the Government of the Queen in Council, and Parliament, I think, adopted a wise and judicious course.
>
> For my own part, I would not assume the responsibility of recommending any immediate change in the form of Government, as now established, until there is a permanent British population to form the basis of a representative Government, a population attached to the British throne and constitution, and capable of appreciating the civil and religious liberty derived from that constitution; blessings which I venture to assert are now enjoyed in the fullest sense of the term, by the people of British Columbia.[130]

---

129   Minute by TFE [Elliot], June 11, 1861, on Douglas to Newcastle, Separate, April 22, 1861, CO 60:10.

130   Douglas to Newcastle, Separate, October 8, 1861, CO 60:11.

CHAPTER 3

The Colonial Office appears to have once again supported Douglas's position. Elliot's December 1861 minute put the issue in perspective in the larger context of the unquestioned social and racist assumptions of the time:

> I have little doubt that the postponement of Representative Government is in fact a benefit to this or to any other young Community... A large proportion of gold-diggers in the population, including a considerable admixture of Americans, would not add to the favorable prospects of popular Government. The time of course will come when this like every other British Colony situated in a temperate climate & occupied by inhabitants of European race, ought to possess a Representative Legislature.[131]

Another petition, drawn up a little over a year later "by a Clique in New West[r] numbering 8 or 10 persons, shopkeepers &c," mainly "Canadian emigrants," sought "a resident Governor." The writer lamented how "the preference has always been from the first artificially [underlining in original] given to Victoria [underlining in original] to the material prejudice of New West[r]—in all points where the interests of the two came in collision."[132] The Colonial Office's assistant under-secretary, Thomas Elliot, had a somewhat different perspective, minuting on a letter from Douglas arriving not long after:

> The representation which I have always heard on behalf of Vancouver Island is to the following effect, that the miners when they return from the diggings weary of their wild life and eager to exchange it for the pleasures and attractions of a civilized Town, will not remain at New Westminster which holds out no attractions, but hurry on to Victoria... they will not remain at an uninviting and inferior place on the river.[133]

---

131 Minute by TFE [Elliot], December 10, 1861, on Douglas to Newcastle, Separate, October 8, 1861, CO 60:11.
132 John Lindley to Newcastle, March 18, 1863, CO 60:16.
133 Minute by TFE [Elliot], June 3, 1863, on Douglas to Newcastle, No. 19, April 10, 1863, CO 60:15.

At least for the time being, British Columbia's governance under Douglas's charge went on much as before. Writing to Douglas in June 1863 Newcastle considered that "the fixed population of British Columbia is not yet large enough to form a sufficient and sound basis of Representation, while the migratory element far exceeds the fixed, and the Indian far out numbers both together." The secretary of state for the colonies was opposed to extending "a large amount of political power to immigrant, or rather transient Foreigners, who have no permanent interest in the prosperity of the Colony," or to "foreign gold diggers" who were by definition "migratory and unsettled,"[134] much less to Indigenous people who mattered not at all.

The many functions of roadbuilding

Douglas's other emphasis, be it in the Cariboo or generally, lay in opening up to non-Indigenous settlement the sprawling British colony four times the size of Britain itself. In his September 1861 letter to the Duke of Newcastle, which lauded the Cariboo, Douglas had taken special pleasure in reporting that "the great commercial thoroughfares leading into the interior of the country from Hope, Yale and Douglas, are in rapid progress, and now exercise a most beneficial effect on the internal commerce of the Colony."[135]

Writing the next April, and very familiar with long-distance travel from his many years in the fur trade, Douglas went further by detailing a feasible land route "for travel the whole way to Red river Settlement" in present-day Manitoba "in twenty-five days from Victoria." Critical to doing so was a proposed eighteen-foot-wide wagon road from Yale to Williams Lake in the heart of the Cariboo gold rush, making it possible to travel the 500-plus miles (300-plus kilometres) from Yale in the Fraser Valley to Alexandria at the entryway to the Cariboo gold rush by stagecoach in eight days. Douglas anticipated the route having "a very important bearing on the future condition of the Colony, as part of an overland communication with Canada by a route possessing the peculiar advantage of being secure from Indian aggression, remote from the United States Frontier, and traversing a country exclusively British, and which from its position, character and large resources can hardly fail, in the ordinary course of events, to become the seat of a large population." Looking ahead, "the question of overland

---

134   Newcastle to Douglas, Separate, June 15, 1863, CO 398:2.
135   Douglas to Newcastle, Separate, September 16, 1861, CO 60:11.

communication with Canada is so closely connected with the prospective interests of the Colony that I feel assured Your Grace will not regard it out of place."[136]

Douglas was energized by the Cariboo rush, describing a month later in May 1862 how "great numbers of persons, principally able-bodied men, unaccompanied by women or children, continue to arrive in this Colony, on their way to the Gold Fields of British Columbia" with up to four thousand passing through New Westminster since March, and a thousand more on their way overland. The consequence was "eight or ten thousand people residing at a distance of five hundred miles from the Coast," hence more than ever the need for roads, made feasible by drawing on revenue from a tax on goods carried by new arrivals, which he estimated would raise £16,000 a year. Douglas explained that he was "making every possible effort to push on with the roads in progress ... with economy and dispatch, as labour is abundant, and the public have unlimited confidence in the resources of this Country."[137]

Still the Royal Engineers

Douglas's dream of linking British Columbia overland with Canada was soon muddied, if not squashed, when he received the Colonial Office's disapproving letter of February 1862 heaping additional Royal Engineers charges onto British Columbia's debt and thereupon refusing to fund roadbuilding in favour of monies being used to support the Royal Engineers.[138] Douglas in his fury responded twice on May 13. In the first letter he pointed out how "numbers of people are arriving, by every Steamer, from California, Canada and England, and the rush towards the Gold Fields is incessant." By summer's end, he foretold, five thousand miners would make their way to the Cariboo, some from elsewhere in British Columbia, most from farther away. From his perspective,

> there is little doubt of a great increase in the annual revenue, if we can only succeed in retaining the population now arriving, and in keeping them from being driven from the Country by want

---

136 Douglas to Newcastle, Separate, April 15, 1862, CO 60:13. Minutes on the letter acknowledged the lack of a response to Douglas, attributed by the ministry to the Treasury's inaction.

137 Douglas to Newcastle, Separate, May 29, 1862, CO 60:13.

138 Newcastle to Douglas, No. 104, February 22, 1862, CO 398:2.

and starvation, a calamity which will inevitably happen unless the appalling cost of inland transport to Carribou, now exceeding seven hundred dollars a ton, be greatly reduced...by a saving of at least five hundred dollars on the ton, in the charges for the transport...It is in fact impossible to retain a population in the Colony unless such improvements are made, and without population there can be neither wealth, revenue, nor progressive development.

Seemingly at wit's end as to how to make the case, Douglas, unusually for him, ended his first May 13, 1862, letter with an implied rebuke:

> Whatever expenses Your Grace may have in contemplation to bring against the Colony should not, I submit, be brought forward and enforced at the very hour of its greatest need, and when it is maintaining an arduous struggle with difficulties altogether unprecedented, in the early history of Colonies.[139]

Arthur Blackwood's minute on the letter once again supported Douglas:

> It will be very difficult to resist this Appeal from the Governor for "more time." Assuming that his representations are void of exaggeration, & that he is what he ought specially to be, in the important post he occupies, worthy of credit I think that his request ought to be complied with. It w^d be a serious reproach ag^t the Col. Office if we helped to cripple this new Colony for the sake of a few thousand pounds.[140]

Douglas's second letter written on May 13, 1862, contrasted his immediate commitment to roadbuilding with the considerable sum of £11,000 coming out of the mainland colony's coffers that was going "towards the maintenance of the Royal Engineers" as "an expenditure which having been arranged by Her Majesty's Government with the Colonel Commanding and mainly left to his

---

139 Douglas to Newcastle, No. 25, May 13, 1862, CO 60:13.

140 Minute by AB^d [Blackwood], June 30, 1862, on Douglas to Newcastle, No. 25, May 13, 1862, CO 60:13.

own discretion, is almost entirely beyond my control," as indeed it was. However, by seeming to critique the judgment of the Colonial Office respecting Moody and the Royal Engineers, and basing his plea for funding roadbuilding on, in his words, "the congregation of starving multitudes" principally from "the dissatisfied of California" imminently arriving in the Cariboo and not finding foodstuffs, Douglas set himself up for a fall.[141]

Thomas Frederick Elliot, employed in the Colonial Office for over a third of a century, and with a different perspective from Blackwood, queried on Douglas's May 1862 letter "why the starving cotton spinners in Lancashire should be taxed in order to ensure these spirited young men against the inconvenience of neglecting to provide themselves with sustenance," especially given "a large proportion of them consisting of Yankee Immigrants from California."[142] Americans were unwanted whatever the time or place.

To hone his points, Douglas enclosed in a follow-up letter of July 1862 the diverse reports of three Cariboo justices of the peace. Thomas Elwyn described how as of June 15, 1862, five hundred men, likely to reach a thousand in a few weeks, were preparing to mine at Antler where claims "will pay from $40 to $100 a day to the hand; over 200 men on Grouse Creek; 500 to 600 on Williams Creek." Given "a great many men principally Canadians... as a rule entirely ignorant of mining," it was not surprising that "one man actually thought... gold was found on the top of the Ground [underlining in original]."[143] Writing from Quesnelle, Peter O'Reilly estimated as of June 28, 1862, four to five thousand arrivals of whom four hundred had already left due to "the scarcity and enormously high prices of provisions."[144] The third justice of the peace, Henry Maynard Ball, along with a medical doctor, had been instructed by the Colonial Office "to vaccinate every Indian" in the district, a total of 1,790 persons, during which he also surveyed ongoing road work employing "immigrants who went into the Upper Country at the commencement of the spring [and who] have been obliged to return for want of means." Ball counted "sixty four trains of

---

141 Douglas to Newcastle, No. 26, May 13, 1862, CO 60:13.

142 Minute by TFE [Elliot], July 7, 1862, on Douglas to Newcastle, No. 26, May 13, 1862, CO 60:13.

143 Report by Thomas Elwyn, June 15, 1862, in Douglas to Newcastle, Separate, July 16, 1862, CO 60:18.

144 Report by Peter O'Reilly, June 28, 1862, in Douglas to Newcastle, Separate, July 16, 1862, CO 60:18.

animals employed packing between Yale and the Forks of Quesnelle, averaging each about 30 animals."[145]

In his letter accompanying these reports, Douglas described "the almost impassable state of the roads beyond Williams Lake, and the high price of food and of all other necessaries of life," due to which "upwards of four hundred able-bodied men have been driven from the mines by mere inability to procure subsistence during the time required for testing, and getting their claims into working order."[146] The Duke of Newcastle's minute, not unlike that of Elliot on an earlier letter, accused Douglas of wanting the government to "tax the starving people of Lancashire for the benefit of men of their own class who are making thousands [underlining in original] of pounds in a few months!"[147]

By the autumn, Douglas was on a different pathway, writing enthusiastically in October 1862 on his return from six weeks in British Columbia, visiting towns, inspecting "the new roads which are rapidly advancing towards Alexandria," and holding "free and daily intercourse with the inhabitants of all classes; hearing complaints, and granting redress wherever grievances were found to exist." He reported "a marked feeling of confidence exhibited by business men in the extent and richness of the Gold-fields, and a generally expressed satisfaction with the prospects and condition of the Colony."[148]

An example of this confidence came the next summer. Aware of the importance of roadbuilding, one of three partners in the Cariboo's very lucrative Hard Curry gold mine, James Loring from Boston, offered to lend the colony $40,000 toward constructing a needed piece of road.[149]

Indicative of British Columbia's few men in charge or able to be in charge, in May 1864 Joseph Trutch, described as "the sole proprietor of the magnificent suspension bridge which spans the Fraser at Spuzzum" (today known as the Alexandra Bridge), under whose auspices it had been constructed and on which he had the authority to levy tolls for the next six years, was appointed

---

145   Report by Henry M. Ball, July 6, 1862, in Douglas to Newcastle, Separate, July 16, 1862, CO 60:18.

146   Douglas to Newcastle, Separate, July 16, 1862, CO 60:18.

147   Minute by N [Newcastle], September 1, 1862 on Douglas to Newcastle, Separate, July 16, 1862, CO 60:18.

148   Douglas to Newcastle, Separate, October 27, 1862, CO 60:13.

149   Douglas to Newcastle, Separate, July 2, 1863, CO 60:13.

British Columbia's surveyor general.[150] The appointment was troublesome to the Colonial Office, which saw the potential for conflict of interest and rationalized as to how, as minuted by long-time senior clerk Arthur Blackwood, "Mr Trutch, who is coming home will report to us the result of his negotiations for getting rid of his property."[151] It seems almost certain that his "coming home" to England shielded Trutch from the censure he might otherwise have faced on the news of the appointment.

Douglas on the way out

On March 16, 1864, James Douglas proudly sent to the secretary of state for the colonies a copy of "The British Columbia Loan Act 1864" by which "the Governor of the Colony is empowered to raise a Loan upon Debentures for such sum or sums not exceeding One Hundred Thousand pounds Sterling (£100,000), as may be required for the purposes of surveying, constructing, and maintaining Roads, Bridges, and other public works within the Colony." Douglas explained optimistically how the past year's revenue of £110,000 was a 23 per cent increase over the previous year, with 1864 looking "to exhibit a corresponding increase."[152]

The future Douglas envisaged consequent on yet another loan bode fair with the one notable exception that it was not to be his future. The first of the minutes on Douglas's March 16 letter, by Arthur Blackwood, acknowledged with a touch of irony an imminent departure already known within the Colonial Office: "Sir Ja^s Douglas closes his Gov^t with another Loan for £100,000... If the Gold in the Colony lasts for 30 years I suppose the Loan is safe enough. But all mines come to an end."[153] So did careers.

As governor of Vancouver Island and of British Columbia, James Douglas had never been the Colonial Office's plaything he might have been had he been selected by the Colonial Office and thereby, almost as a given, deferred to its priorities. Douglas's commitment was to the two colonies over which he had

---

150   Frederick Seymour, governor of the colony of British Columbia, to Newcastle, No. 6, May 19, 1864, CO 60:18.

151   Minute by Ab^d [Blackwood], July 27, 1864, on Seymour to Newcastle, No. 6, May 19, 1864, CO 60:18.

152   Douglas to Newcastle, No. 10, Financial, March 16, 1864, CO 60:18.

153   Minute by AB^d [Blackwood], May 12, 1864, on Douglas to Newcastle, No. 10, Financial, March 16, 1864, CO 60:18.

charge, his ties to the people and the places there longer-lived than his ties to the Colonial Office as governor. In both of the French senses of knowing—*savoir* and *connaître*—Douglas was familiar with that of which he had charge, be it fur traders retired to Victoria, Indigenous groups knowing distinct places as their home since time immemorial, or the rivers along which gold miners set themselves down.

Douglas and the Colonial Office had, from time to time, jostled with each other, never more so than over the Royal Engineers, dispatched to the mainland colony in 1858 even as Douglas was appointed its governor with quite different senses of their relationship to British Columbia's well-being. Douglas's commitment to the road construction that would open up communication took priority, even at the cost of putting the colony in debt and of not playing by the Colonial Office's rules, so to speak.

With the passage of time, as indicated by minutes on his letters, Douglas's independent spirit sometimes grated even as it was applauded at other times. Not unexpectedly, given he was not a Colonial Office appointee from among the numerous such men rotated from post to post, Douglas was never, it seems, wholly trusted.

As early as December 1860 stalwart parliamentary secretary Chichester Fortescue had proposed "the removal of Gov' Douglas from B. Columbia, on the grounds of his being—an absentee—interested in the success of Victoria— and ignorant of 'English institutions.'"[154] In his view, Douglas, for all of his good qualities, should be replaced by a Colonial Office import:

> The Governor cannot, I think, be much [underlining in original] longer left to Govern B.C. single handed & despotically, issuing Laws in the shape of Proclamations. Two courses seem to be open—1. B.C. might be annexed to Vancouver's Id. & return a certain number of members to the Assembly at Victoria, wh. wd. become the capital of the united Colony... 2. The Governor might be surrounded by a Legislative Council... and I sh. think this would be the most convenient transition from the present state of things toward the introduction of representative institutions.

---

154   Minute by CF [Fortescue], December 15, 1860, on Douglas to Newcastle, No. 58, June 22, 1860, CO 60:7.

CHAPTER 3

> I do not think however that the change is urgent—and, before it is decided upon, I should be strongly inclined to send out an able man as Govr of British Columbia, in whose judgment upon such a subject you might have more confidence than, I think, can be placed in that of Govr Douglas, in spite of the good sense & shrewdness of the latter, and the favourable impression which, in many respects, his despatches produce... and I admit that things appear to go on fairly in B.C. under Govr Douglas.[155]

A little over three years later, the secretary of state for the colonies acquiesced. Concluding in March 1864 that the two colonies' "grievances," being in British Columbia for representative institutions and on Vancouver Island for those institutions' reform, "mostly resolve themselves into a demand for a New Governor" and "must be left to be dealt with by a new Governor." The Duke of Newcastle so alerted Douglas:

> I wrote privately to Mr Douglas by the last Mail telling him that I should soon deal with the subjects treated of in this Minute, and that I should when my plans were complete relieve him of both Gov^{ts}. I made this as little unpleasant to him as I could, and told him that when I wrote to him Officially I would take every care to prevent his enemies having a triumph over him.[156]

The Duke of Newcastle's carefully crafted letter to Douglas read in part:

> As you have now ruled over Vancouver Island for twelve years—twice the usual period of Governorship—and as I do not think it would be desirable to replace you by a new Governor there and leave you to take up your abode in New Westminster as Governor of British Columbia alone, I intend to relieve you of both Governments... It may be assumed however that I shall not carry out this decision in any way that can be disagreeable to you or shall give a

---

155   Minute by CF [Fortescue], December 15, 1860, on Douglas to Newcastle, No. 58, June 22, 1860, CO 60:7.

156   Newcastle, "British Columbia and Vancouvers Island," memorandum, March 27, 1863, enclosed in Arthur Helps, Whitehall, to Chichester Fortescue, June 12, 1863, CO 60:17.

triumph to those who have desired your recall...I have now recommended to the Queen your Successor in the two Governments, and I have accompanied the recommendation with one that you shall be raised to the second rank in the Order of the Bath.[157]

Sir James Douglas, as he now became, was replaced in the spring of 1864 by separate governors of Vancouver Island and British Columbia.

Douglas for his part continued to apprise the Colonial Office of his views, not unexpectedly recommending in early 1864 "against the fusion of the two Governments into one" and in favour of "the present system of Government, which has grown up naturally out of the existing circumstances and conditions of the Colonies, and may for that reason, be presumed to be better adapted to their wants than any untried system that could be devised."[158]

No question exists that Douglas had moved slowly, if at all, to loosen his control over a mainland population he clearly considered suspect in respect to governing themselves. But now he returned full-time to the family and community he had in part left behind on Vancouver Island as governor also of British Columbia.

Through six difficult years, 1858 to 1864, James Douglas had kept British Columbia together, much as he earlier oversaw Vancouver Island for the Hudson's Bay Company and then also the Colonial Office. Douglas steered the mainland through two gold rushes with a flourish that might well have stymied an outsider in charge. He held off American attempts to secure control, successfully so except for a small group of islands in a decision made from afar over which he had no control. Most significantly, through his commitment to roadbuilding he opened up today's British Columbia mainland. By doing this he very possibly played a role in Britain's unwillingness to trade away the future province following the American Civil War, when the United States had its hands out for reparations from Britain for having permitted the seceding South to build warships on its territory. It is intriguing to ponder but impossible to know what might have ensued respecting the British Columbia we today take for granted if not for James Douglas.

---

157 Newcastle to Douglas in Margaret A. Ormsby, "Sir James Douglas," *Dictionary of Canadian Biography*, vol. 10, http://www.biographi.ca/en/bio/douglas_james_10E.html.
158 Douglas to Newcastle, No. 3, Legislative, February 12, 1864, CO 305132.

CHAPTER 4

The Colonial Office in Action (1864–67)

Britain's governance of its two remote colonies of Vancouver Island and British Columbia had never been easy. Indicative on a practical level was, Douglas explained in 1863, the twists and turns that letters intended for the Colonial Office in faraway London took to get to their destination:

> Our Mails are carried between this and San Francisco by American Vessels; and from thence there are no less than four different ways letters may be forwarded, viz. By express across the Rocky Mountains, by the ordinary Mail across the Rocky Mountains, by Steamer to Panama and from thence by Steamer to New York, or by Steamer to Southampton.[1]

From Southampton on the English coast, letters travelled northeast a further 130 kilometres or 80 miles to get to the Colonial Office in London. Neither was travel between the two colonies and the mother country straightforward, being at the time seven weeks each way in duration.[2]

From one to two governors

James Douglas's dismissal as governor in 1864 made these limitations more visible. Whereas Douglas had through his self-confidence, ease with the terrain, and a bit of bullying kept any of the players, with the pithy exception of Major Moody, from overacting their parts, his successors—Arthur Kennedy as governor of the Colony of Vancouver Island, and Frederick Seymour as governor of

---

1   Douglas to Newcastle, No. 28, Financial, July 20, 1863, CO 305: 20.
2   See W. Driscoll Gosset, returning Royal Engineer, to Fortescue, July 27, 1863, CO 60:17.

the Colony of British Columbia—were outsiders, unfamiliar with the country, its inhabitants, and its politics. They were, almost as a matter of course, intended to do the Colonial Office's bidding and viewed their posts as stepping stones in their careers rather than as ends in themselves, as the governorship had been for Douglas. Thomas Elliot, the Harrow-educated head of the Colonial Office's North American Department, believed their appointments bode well and remarked in November 1864: "Now that we have two trained Governors in these Colonies accustomed to a sense of responsibility, we receive accounts which make one imagine that Sir J. Douglas has earned his honors rather cheaply."[3] The reality turned out to be quite different, with neither governor fully able to manage what were in essence unmanageable situations.

The Colonial Office's seeming comfort with its two Pacific Northwest possessions was to some extent illusory. They were not bounding ahead, nor were they falling behind; they just were. It is impossible to know whether the two colonies would have survived to be joined in a single colony in 1866 and as the Canadian province of British Columbia in 1871, as opposed to becoming one or more American states, had it not been for Douglas's familiarity with their land bases and Indigenous populations consequent on his earlier fur trade postings, his commitment to all things British, and his and the Colonial Office's tenacity and perseverance. With his departure, the two colonies were cast on their own resources.

Governing Vancouver Island

Just as gold miners preferred Victoria over New Westminster, so did the course of events, making Vancouver Island's governance, it might seem, relatively straightforward. As Douglas explained in the spring of 1863, Victoria "being more built up and settled offers greater inducement to Miners as a resort than New Westminster."[4] A minute by Thomas Elliot characterized the mainland capital as "an uninviting and inferior place on the river," whereas "nature has formed Victoria to be the Commercial Capital of the whole of the British Territory in that part of the World."[5]

---

3   Minute by TFE [Elliot], November 21, 1864, on Kennedy to Edward Cardwell, secretary of state for the colonies, No. 80, Miscellaneous, October 1, 1864, CO 305.23.

4   Douglas to Newcastle, No. 19, April 10, 1863, CO 60:15.

5   Minute by TFE [Elliot], June 3, 1863, on Douglas to Newcastle, No. 19, April 10, 1863, CO 60:15.

CHAPTER 4

Arthur Kennedy, the Colonial Office's appointee to govern Vancouver Island, brought with him, on his arrival in March 1864, a wealth of experience. Joining the Colonial Office at the beginning of the 1850s, after almost a quarter of a century in the military, his Vancouver Island appointment followed his governorships of Sierra Leone and Western Australia.[6] Indicative of Kennedy's high reputation, Parliamentary Under-Secretary Chichester Fortescue considered the new posting a waste of his talents, observing how "in view of the insignificance of the population and revenue (7500, and £35,000) of Vancouver I^d, I have some misgiving as to the necessity of sending them one of our best Governors."[7]

However much Vancouver Island might have been privileged from the Colonial Office's perspective to have Kennedy as governor, he and it did not, for all of his interest in Indigenous peoples' welfare as he perceived it, get on well during his two and a half years in charge. Unlike James Douglas, who took Vancouver Island as it was, his successor was not best pleased on reading shortly after his arrival the annual *Blue Book of Vancouver Island* compiled by his predecessor. Kennedy was dismayed by virtually everything in it from "expensive and defective postal and other communication" to "loose assertion and surmise" respecting the colony's resources.[8]

Kennedy's disquiet over the 1863 Blue Book makes a subsequent volume elaborating his governorship a potentially perceptive guide to the state of Vancouver Island. To Kennedy's dismay it was still the case by the mid-1860s that just "one town in the Colony (Victoria), has yet been incorporated... and there is but one other place in the Colony, (Nanaimo), deserving the name of a town and that containing more than 800 inhabitants who are almost exclusively coal miners and labouring people."[9] Not only that, but "the agricultural resources of the Colony may be said to be almost wholly undeveloped...The agricultural land though limited in extent is amazingly fertile and sufficient in extent for ten

---

6   For more information see Robert L. Smith, "Sir Arthur Edward Kennedy," *Dictionary of Canadian Biography*, vol. 11, http://www.biographi.ca/en/bio/kennedy_arthur_edward_11E.html, and Smith's "The Kennedy Interlude," BC *Studies* 47 (August 1980): 66–78.

7   Minute by CF [Fortescue], April 1, 1864, on Douglas to Newcastle, No. 3, Legislative, February 12, 1864, CO 305:32.

8   Kennedy to Cardwell, No. 40, Separate, July 7, 1864, CO 305:22.

9   Kennedy to Cardwell, No. 14, Financial, March 1, 1866, CO 305:28.

times the present population."[10]

Kennedy considered that "the British population of the island, women and children included, cannot much, if at all, exceed 3000," as compared to "the European, Negro, and Chinese together numbering about 8000 and the Aboriginal Indians about 10,000." From his perspective, much as it had been for Douglas, "the great want in this as in all other new countries is a fixed population, and this can scarcely be expected till the excitement attendant upon the first discovery of gold has subsided, and communication with the Mother Country is facilitated and cheapened."[11]

Kennedy counted, as of 1865, "85 retail Licences for public houses granted in the City of Victoria alone in addition to 23 wholesale licences," along with there being outside of Victoria "41 licensed retail public houses making a total of 149 licences to sell drink," which "cannot fail to produce disastrous social results."[12] The explanation lay at least in part in Victoria seeking to appeal to gold miners, especially during the winter months when mining operations for the most part shut down.

Kennedy gave sparse attention to Vancouver Island's governance apart from its being "composed of five ex officio [underlining in original] and three non-official Members nominated by the Crown," along with fifteen members elected by constituencies. Kennedy noted that, out of 890 voters—eligible to vote by virtue of being British and having taken up land on Vancouver Island—"nearly all those are resident in Victoria." Voters elsewhere were sparse, numbering fifty-eight between Esquimalt and Metchosin, twenty-four between Saltspring and Chemainus, eighteen in Nanaimo, and forty-one elsewhere for a total of 141.[13] Not included in the Blue Book was Kennedy's inability to effect the control he would have liked to have over Vancouver Island's governance. He acknowledged to the Colonial Office in May 1865, when he put the total "number of registered voters at the last general election" at 1,051, how the non-voting "American element possesses and exercises great influence over the press and voters who are connected with them in trade."[14]

A year later Kennedy considered that "the circumstances of the Colony...do not call for much comment" apart from the non-Indigenous population falling

---

10 Kennedy to Cardwell, No. 73, Separate, August 24, 1865, CO 305:26.

11 Kennedy to Cardwell, No. 73, Separate, August 24, 1865, CO 305:26.

12 Kennedy to Cardwell, No. 73, Separate, August 24, 1865, CO 305:26.

13 Kennedy to Cardwell, No. 73, Separate, August 24, 1865, CO 305:26.

14 Kennedy to Cardwell, No. 27, Miscellaneous, May 4, 1865, CO 305:25.

CHAPTER 4

from eight thousand to six thousand.[15] As explained by British Columbia historian Margaret Ormsby, it had been a year earlier, in the spring of 1865, "when the usual rush of miners from San Francisco failed to materialize that there were doubts about the colony's prospects."[16]

Vancouver Island in disarray

Governor Kennedy's letters to the Colonial Office attracted cryptic minutes. In the view of the experienced Arthur Blackwood on reading them: "The Assembly is composed of half Yankees; Canadians, & Hudson's Bay C° servants. The pure British element is very small."[17] To Thomas Elliot, "'Responsible Gov^t' in a little Community like Vancouver [Island] would be a mockery and a scramble, it seems to me."[18]

Not everyone agreed. Kennedy's December 30, 1865, letter in the Colonial Office files marked "Confidential" reported on a proposal by the respected Speaker of the Vancouver Island Legislative Assembly, John Sebastian Helmcken, to allow aliens, being non-citizens, to vote, about which Kennedy had taken a firm stand in opposition:

> At another time, and in other localities any disparagement of sound and proper nationality might be left unnoticed, but in a community such as that of Vancouver Island, where there is at present a large American element, the language attributed to Dr. Helmcken is not only to be lamented but mischievous."[19]

Nor was the proposal well received by William Edward Forster, parliamentary under-secretary of state for the colonies, who minuted, seconded by the secretary of state for the colonies, Edward Cardwell: "Dr Helmcken's propⁿ

---

15   Kennedy to Cardwell, No. 55, Separate, August 3, 1866, CO 305:29.

16   Margaret Ormsby, "Frederick Seymour," *Dictionary of Canadian Biography*, vol. 9, http://www.biographi.ca/en/bio/seymour_frederick_9E.html.

17   Minute by AB^d [Blackwood], February 14, 1866, on Kennedy to Cardwell, Confidential, December 16, 1865, CO 305:26.

18   Minute by TFE [Elliot], February 14, 1866, on Kennedy to Cardwell, Confidential, December 16, 1865, CO 305:26.

19   Kennedy to Cardwell, Confidential, December 30, 1865, CO 305:26.

is that aliens should vote without nationalizing themselves as British Subjects. I do not think this ought to be allowed."[20]

Kennedy's correspondence testifies to his being alternately exasperated and incensed by the Legislative Assembly's attitude and actions, which were alien to his way of being, as he described at length in a confidential dispatch of January 24, 1866, to the Colonial Office:

> I think the time has arrived when the existing form of Government should be reconsidered and amended if Vancouver Island is to be permanently retained as a British Colony.
>
> Two years of experience has convinced me that the House of Assembly as at present constituted is not capable of using constitutional power in a respectable manner...Their avowed object is to drive matters to extremity...[which if carried out] the large American element and influence here would render Government on constitutional or British principles no longer possible...The majority in the present Assembly is mainly composed of reckless adventurers with small stake in the Colony and in too many instances wanting in personal respectability...
>
> I regard this as a most hazardous experiment. The working classes here are attracted from distant places—strangers are continually pouring in—moral and social restraints are few and feeble, and the temptations held out by 85 licensed public houses in Victoria alone, saloons, brothels and gambling houses (some of them combining all three characteristics) far exceed those usually found elsewhere...
>
> The whole foundation of a sound and prosperous Colony has yet to be laid and I see no prospect of its being done by an irresponsible Assembly strongly imbued with republican and American sympathies...
>
> The latest effort in the way of raising Revenue consisted in the imposition of import duties upon cabbage, carrots, potatoes, beef, mutton and pork while spirits, wine, beer, tobacco, and all other luxuries are left free.[21]

---

20   Minute by WEF [William Edward Forster], March 12, 1866, and EC [Cardwell], March 13, 1866, on Kennedy to Cardwell, Confidential, December 30, 1865, CO 305:26.

21   Kennedy to Cardwell, Confidential, January 24, 1866, CO 305:28.

CHAPTER 4

From Kennedy's perspective, Vancouver Island was not only running wild, but close to falling into American hands, not unexpectedly, given, he added in a follow-up letter, "the majority of the inhabitants being foreigners."[22]

Governing British Columbia

British Columbia's governor, Frederick Seymour, had a similar background to his Vancouver Island counterpart, having been assistant colonial secretary of Tasmania followed by five Caribbean postings.[23] Responding from Belize on the northeast coast of Central America to the invitation to take charge of British Columbia, he enthused how "the prospects of a change from the swamps of Honduras to a fine country is inexpressibly attractive to me, and I trust, in the bracing air of North America to prove myself worthy of Your Grace's confidence and kindness."[24] Along with governing experience, Seymour brought with him a knowledge of current events, subscribing to newspapers in "England, California, and the Colonies," including *The Times* and *The Saturday Review of Politics, Literature, Science, and Art*, both published in London.[25]

Not unexpectedly then, among the tasks Seymour took seriously was non-Indigenous children's literacy. In November 1864 he described how the "schools supported mainly at the Public expense in this Colony, are supplied at present with American School Books of rather an objectionable kind," given "the United States are lauded at the expense of England." Seymour requested as "a favour on the Colony if you would direct the Agents General to send out a well assorted collection of school books for about one hundred children" that "should, to secure universal confidence, not be in any way of a sectarian character."[26]

Attention to Indigenous peoples

Welcomed on his arrival in New Westminster in the spring of 1864 by "arches and other decorations," Frederick Seymour was within the month caught up in the fallout from, so he described in the first of many letters on the subject, "the

22 Kennedy to Cardwell, No. 24, Financial, March 26, 1866, CO 305:28.
23 For more information, see Ormsby, "Frederick Seymour."
24 Seymour to Newcastle, September 14, 1863, CO 60:17.
25 Seymour to Cardwell, No. 33, March 24, 1865, CO 60:21.
26 Seymour to Cardwell, No. 73, November 28, 1864, CO 60:19.

massacre of 14 out of a party of 17 Europeans by the Indians at Bute Inlet in this Colony."[27] As detailed in his correspondence accessible online, the event known variously as the Tsilhqot'in uprising, Chilcotin war, and Bute Inlet massacre matters in its own right and is not followed here.[28]

High among Seymour's concerns was to keep faith with Douglas's reputation as "a great Chief...for upwards to forty years." Seymour thereupon invited "Catholic priests and others to bring in all the Indians who are willing to come to New Westminster and meet me on the Queen's birthday" on May 24, 1864. A remarkable 3,500 arrived by canoe, being formed by the priests into a welcoming procession for Seymour.[29]

At the event fifty-five "Indian Friends," Seymour's term, strategically presented the governor with a petition identifying each of them by name and location. The petition explained how "we know the good heart of the Queen for the Indians" and asked the governor "please to protect our land, that it will not be too small for us."[30] Seymour assured them how "you shall not be disturbed on your reserves" for "as you say there is plenty of Land here for both White men and Indians...I am a stranger here and don't yet know your language, but I am as good a friend to you in my heart as my predecessor."[31] The size of the reserves would begin to be reduced within the year.

More immediately, Seymour requested from the Colonial Office "one hundred canes with silver gilt tops of an inexpensive kind, also one hundred small and cheap English flags suitable to Canoes about 20 or 30 feet long" for the next May's gathering so as "to introduce into this Colony the practice which had worked very successfully in Honduras, of presenting a Staff of Office to the Chief

---

27 Seymour to Newcastle, No. 1, April 26, 1864, and No. 7, May 20, 1864, CO 60:18.

28 For Colonial Office correspondence, see https://bcgenesis.uvic.ca/; for a couple of accessible printed sources, Edward Sleigh Hewlett, "The Chilcotin Uprising of 1864," *BC Studies* 19 (Autumn 1974): 50–72; and Judith Williams, *High Slack: Waddington's Gold Road and the Bute Inlet Massacre of 1864* (Vancouver: New Star, 1996).

29 Seymour to Cardwell, No. 30, August 31, 1864, CO 60:19.

30 "Assembled Indian Chiefs" to Seymour, in Seymour to Cardwell, No. 30, August 31, 1864, CO 60:19.

31 Seymour's response to "Indian Friends" in Seymour to Cardwell, No. 30, August 31, 1864, CO 60:19. For the larger context see Megan Harvey, "Story Peoples: Stó:lō-State Relations and Indigenous Literacies in British Columbia, 1864–1874," *Journal of the Canadian Historical Association/Revue de la Société historique du Canada* 24, 1 (2013): 51–88.

of each friendly tribe."[32] He would continue to do so, reporting three years later:

> Our Indian population is prosperous & contented. I have had gatherings of the natives for several consecutive years on the Queen's birthday. This year I did not issue any invitations yet upwards of 4,000 attended to congratulate me on my return to the Colony [from time in Europe]. Some of the Chiefs from the Upper Fraser travelled nearly a thousand miles, to New Westminster & back for the occasion.[33]

Effecting British Columbia's governance

Frederick Seymour had, in addition to the usual responsibilities as governor of British Columbia, to oversee the completion of James Douglas's prized wagon road from New Westminster to the Cariboo, which was "kept up by tolls."[34] An ordinance had been passed at the first meeting of the British Columbia Legislative Council in 1864 authorizing a loan of £100,000, including "the immediate expenditure of £48,000 in the completion of the Cariboo Road," so as to make accessible what was later described as "the only known mining Region and the main support of the Colony."[35]

Seymour also authorized additional road construction and visited the Cariboo later in the year, to be overwhelmed by warm greetings from both miners and Indigenous peoples "as the representative of the Imperial Government." Seymour was so impressed he began his letter to the Colonial Office describing the trip with an apology for its being an "unavoidably egotistical despatch."[36]

Much like its Vancouver Island counterpart, British Columbia's 1865 Blue Book gives us a sense, as was intended, of what mattered from the perspective

---

32 Seymour to Cardwell, No. 46, September 23, 1864, CO 60:19.

33 Seymour to Richard Grenville, 3rd Duke of Buckingham and Chandos, secretary of state for the colonies, Private, June 26, 1867, CO 60:28.

34 Seymour to Newcastle, No. 1, April 26, 1864, and No. 6, May 19, 1864, both CO 60:18.

35 Arthur Birch, acting governor of British Columbia, to Cardwell, No. 50, July 9, 1866, CO 60:25. Also Newcastle to Douglas, No. 14, March 12, 1863, NAC 34; Douglas to Newcastle, No. 43, September 3, 1862, CO 60:13, enclosing the act for the new loan, and No. 30, Financial, May 14, 1863, CO 60:15, following up.

36 Seymour to Cardwell, No. 38, September 9, 1864, CO 60:19.

THE COLONIAL OFFICE IN ACTION (1864-67)

of whoever was in charge. Because Seymour was then on leave in Europe to get married, the Blue Book was prepared by Arthur Birch, who had been a clerk in the Colonial Office before accompanying Seymour to British Columbia as the colony's incoming colonial secretary. Almost certainly for that reason the annual report reflects a professionalism not always found in Blue Books, with its incisive portrait of the mainland colony and, by inference, of Vancouver Island.

The Blue Book acknowledged American influence, describing how, consequent on British Columbia's isolation from the mother country and proximity to the United States, "American Coinage is in universal circulation and Commercial transactions are conducted in Dollars and Cents," with an ordinance "passed to enable the Public Account to be kept in the Decimal system." In like manner, "an American company had been contracted to construct a telegraph line."[37]

Birch was aware of Vancouver Island living off British Columbia, as it had been doing, and diplomatic in explaining how "the free Port system of Vancouver Island has enabled the Merchants to live more cheaply in Victoria than on the Mainland and Victoria has thus become the depot where goods destined for the British Columbia Market have been detained, only to be reshipped in small quantities as occasion required." In respect to imports and exports, "Vancouver Island...has acted as a Toll gate to British Columbia."[38]

British Columbia's exports were assessed. The Blue Book enthused about how "the extensive Pine Forests bordering the Coast are capable of producing an almost inexhaustible supply of the finest lumber and Spars." It described how "three Steam Sawmills have been erected at New Westminster and Burrard Inlet and are capable of turning out 180,000 feet of lumber per diem" dispatched to "the Markets of Mexico, South America, the Sandwich [Hawaiian] Islands and Australia." As for coastal fisheries basic to Indigenous peoples' ways of life, "salmon abound in every river in the Colony; some 1500 barrels were exported to the Sandwich Islands in 1865."[39]

Social services were limited. Public schools had been established by inhabitants at New Westminster, Yale, and Douglas, to which the government contributed support, with $1.00 a month required per child from the parent or guardian. The Blue Book took pride in "the small amount of crime among the

---

37   Birch to Earl Carnarvon, secretary of state for the colonies, No. 72, October 31, 1866, CO 60:25.

38   Birch to Carnarvon, No. 72, October 31, 1866, CO 60:25.

39   Birch to Carnarvon, No. 72, October 31, 1866, CO 60:25.

heterogeneous community by which this Colony is peopled." Only two criminal cases had been brought before the Supreme Court in 1865.[40]

In respect to monitoring Indigenous peoples, the Blue Book explained how the fine for the sale or gifting of intoxicating liquor to them was increased in 1866 to £100 on first offence, and to twelve months' prison with hard labour without the option of a fine for a second offence. A heavy penalty had been levied for violating Indigenous graves by removing articles deposited there, which were usually items "most cherished by the deceased," including guns, canoes, blankets, and carved images. There was "a penalty of £100 with or without imprisonment for six months for rifling Indians Graves, and…a second offence liable to 12 Months imprisonment." Deer, elk, and species of grouse were prohibited from sale during the breeding season. In sum, "the large Indian population are peaceable orderly and contented and among all classes poverty can scarcely be said to exist."[41]

As for British Columbia's non-Indigenous population, land laws had been consolidated to promote permanent settlement, provide for pastoral leases and timber cutting, and make free or partially free grants to promote immigration.[42] Agriculture commanded special attention not just in the Fraser Valley, where non-Indigenous farming dated back to the fur trade, but generally. "The large and fertile tracts bordering the lower Fraser are gradually being brought under cultivation," and the rest of the mainland colony was awash with potential:

> It is however beyond the Cascade range of Mountains commencing at Lytton…that the Settlements are more extensive; there the Country opens out and the vast and almost impenetrable Forest of Pine disappears. Large benches of table-land covered with a luxurious growth of bunch-Grass border the Banks of Fraser and Thompson River and extend back to the dividing ranges. It has been proved by the experience of 1865 that by a system of irrigation (rendered necessary by the Small amount of rain that falls) this land will produce extraordinary crops of all descriptions. The root crops are not to be surpassed in any part of the world, and the

---

40   Birch to Carnarvon, No. 72, October 31, 1866, CO 60:25.

41   Birch to Carnarvon, No. 72, October 31, 1866, CO 60:25.

42   Birch to Carnarvon, No. 72, October 31, 1866, CO 60:25.

THE COLONIAL OFFICE IN ACTION (1864-67)

Cereals, both as regards the quantity and quality of the Crops, can compete with any that are grown in the Mother Country.[43]

Not only that, but agricultural options were expanding.

> Prior to 1865 little attention had been paid to the raising of Wheat in consequence of the want of Grist Mills throughout the upper portions of the Country but during the past year four were erected inducing the Settler to enter more extensively into this branch of Agriculture, and the Upper Country now produces most of the Flour consumed by the Inhabitants...
>
> The portions of the Country adapted for pasture are extensive and the grass known as Bunch-Grass most luxuriant and nutritive. In the early days of the Colony bands of Cattle driven in from the neighbouring American territories supplied the Market, but the settler has found by experience that British Columbia as a Stock raising Country is unrivalled and a large importation of Cattle during 1864 and 1865, has consequently ensued.[44]

For all of the information that had been gathered together, the Blue Book's description of the British Columbia population in 1865 was able to go only so far:

> It has been found impossible to take any correct census of the Population... Miners as a class have no fixed abode. During the Mining season they are to be found scattered over an area of 400 Miles throughout the Gold bearing range of Mountains. As Winter sets in many of those who have made sufficient money to leave the Colony do so by the many routes open to them and spend their money in Portland or San Francisco. The settled White population during 1865 did not in my opinion exceed 6,000. The Chinese may be estimated at 3,000, the Indians at 35,000. To this may be added a migratory population during summer months of an additional 3,000 Miners.[45]

---

43   Birch to Carnarvon, No. 72, October 31, 1866, CO 60:25.
44   Birch to Carnarvon, No. 72, October 31, 1866, CO 60:25.
45   Birch to Carnarvon, No. 72, October 31, 1866, CO 60:25.

CHAPTER 4

British Columbia's 1865 Blue Book impressed the Colonial Office. As minuted by Thomas Elliot, whose service went back to 1825 as a junior clerk:

> This is one of the most satisfactory reports we have rec^d from B.C., & is devoid of the inflated coloring the Reports were tinged with in the time of Sir J. Douglas. The discovery of the agricultural capabilities of the valleys of the Frazer & the Thomson Rivers is of inestimable value...The printed report...seems to me a very excellent performance for a Colony 8 years old.[46]

Colonial Office dissatisfaction

However well, or not so well, the two distant colonies were doing, dissatisfaction was in the air. Having contemplated as far back as 1863, with James Douglas's departure in view, joining the two colonies for ease of governance, the Duke of Newcastle, who had held the post of secretary of state for the colonies from 1853 to 1854 and again since 1859, had initially been cautious. He described why in an internal memo:

> The jealousies—I might almost say, hatreds—between the two have become so great and such opposition of interests have been allowed to grow up that I believe it would be almost as hopeless to attempt to amalgamate the two as it would be to rejoin the Confederate [southern slave-holding] with the Federal States [of the United States] and the act of forcing them into a union would probably retard the time for a willing and hearty junction on grounds of mutual interests, [meaning] the complete fusion is at present impossible.[47]

And writing to Douglas in June 1863 respecting the mainland colony in particular:

---

46 Minute initialed by AB^d [Blackwood], February 26, 1867; TFE [Elliot], February 25, 1867; CBA [Charles Bowyer Adderley], February 27, 1867; and C [Carnarvon], February 18, 1867, on Birch to Carnarvon, No. 72, October 31, 1866, CO 60:25.

47 Newcastle, "British Columbia and Vancouvers Island," memorandum, March 27, 1863, enclosed in Arthur Helps, Whitehall, to Fortescue, June 12, 1863, CO 60:17; also Newcastle to Douglas, Separate, June 15, 1863, CO 398:2.

> I should have wished to establish there the same representative Institutions which already exist in Vancouver Island; and it is not without reluctance that I have come to the conclusion that this is at present impossible...The fixed population of British Columbia is not yet large enough to form a sufficient and sound basis of Representation, while the migratory element far exceeds the fixed, and the Indian far out numbers both together.
>
> Gold is the only produce of the Colony, extracted in a great measure by an annual influx of Foreigners—Of Landed proprietors there are next to none—Of tradesmen not very many, and these are occupied in their own pursuits at a distance from the centre of Government and from each other. Under these circumstances I see no mode of establishing a purely representative Legislature which would not be open to one of two objections. Either it must place the Government of the Colony under the exclusive control of a small circle of persons naturally occupied with their own local, personal or class interests, or it must confide a large amount of political power to immigrant, or rather transient Foreigners, who have no permanent interest in the prosperity of the Colony.[48]

The state of affairs as set forth by Newcastle testified to Douglas's capacity to hold together, or rather keep from disentangling, the bits and pieces of non-Indigenous settlement spread out across British Columbia. The good news, as we know now, is that the future province did not collapse on his departure from governance; the bad news that apart from squabbling, nothing much happened for some time, at least from the top down, despite the usual hopeful minutes being added within the Colonial Office to spur things on in its desired direction.

Evening out the relationship between the two colonies

The Colonial Office's desire to unite the two colonies on Douglas's departure as governor had become the fodder of gossip by the time his two successors took office in 1864—so much so, both governors rallied against the possibility, which had the potential to stultify their careers.

---

48   Newcastle to Douglas, Separate, June 15, 1863, CO 398-2

CHAPTER 4

Within two months of arriving in April 1864, British Columbia governor Frederick Seymour summarily informed the Colonial Office that his colony's newly established Legislative Council was "against union upon any terms" due to its being "simply impossible, in my opinion, to govern satisfactorily the district of Cariboo from Vancouver Island."[49] To make his case Seymour compiled a capsule history of British Columbia's financial support for the governance of Vancouver Island:

> Unquestionably under the rule of my Predecessor Victoria became the principal English Port on this Coast and New Westminster commenced a retrograde course early in its history. It could hardly have been otherwise. The Governor and other Public Officers drew their full salaries from British Columbia and resided in Vancouver Island. Victoria escaped all indirect taxation while heavy duties were collected on all articles consumed on the Main land...
>
> While waiting for the Steamers [to and from San Francisco], the Miners spent their money in Victoria and thus billiard rooms and drinking Saloons arose, and the place acquired sufficient importance to depopulate New Westminster without attaining any solid foundation or considerable prosperity for itself...I had not seen even in the West Indies so melancholy a picture of disappointed hopes as New Westminster presented on my arrival...Westminster appeared, to use the Miner's expression, "played out."[50]

The situation was similarly fraught on Vancouver Island. Its governor, Arthur Kennedy, was at wit's end, writing on May 4, 1865, respecting the refusal of its fifteen-member Legislative Assembly to approve the Civil List—government officials' salaries—on the grounds that they "are too high." As explained by Arthur Kennedy's biographer, Robert L. Smith:

> The Vancouver Island Assembly, which had grown accustomed to

---

49 Seymour to Newcastle, No. 9, June 1, 1864, CO 60:18.
50 Seymour to Cardwell, No. 30, March 21, 1865, CO 60:21; also No. 14, Separate, March 21, 1865, CO 305:25.

Douglas' practice of paying the bulk of his salary and the salaries of other officials who served both colonies from British Columbia revenues, was now prepared to withhold even the temporary payment of Kennedy's salary as a means of protesting the Colonial Office's expensive and politically ominous appointment of separate governors.[51]

The appointment of two governors meant Vancouver Island's largely free ride at the mainland's expense was over.

Kennedy put the non-Indigenous population of Vancouver Island at "about 6000 souls of whom about 2000 are British male subjects—the remainder made up of Americans, Germans, French, Italians and Chinese," among whom, he added as an aside, "I am paying a Chinaman [underlining in original] for cooking my dinners, alone ₤120 per annum." From this diverse group, Americans were in Kennedy's view the most admirable: "The American element in the population possesses and exercises great influence over the press and voters who are connected with them in trade." To which Arthur Blackwood noted, "I am not sure that the American element may not be the best at first. They bring great energy & go a headism—they are excellent pioneers, & it has never been shown that they are not as good & orderly inhabitants as any of the broken down subjects of the Queen who take refuge in our Colonies."[52]

Thomas Elliot in the Colonial Office pulled no punches in responding to Kennedy's letter: "This petty body at Vancouver [Island] is exceptionally obstinate and unmanageable, and is among the worst specimens of a Colonial Assembly. The idea of Responsible Government of such a place would be preposterous. It is a little community of 6000 Souls."[53]

The genie was out of the bottle, so to speak. There had been a winner and a loser, in which process Douglas was complicit, and Seymour, on finding out, was determined that the uneven relationship in Vancouver Island's favour should not be allowed to continue. In March 1865, after Kennedy reported to the Colonial

---

51   Smith, "The Kennedy Interlude, 1864–66," BC *Studies* 47 (Autumn 1980): 70; also Smith, "Sir Arthur Edward Kennedy."

52   Kennedy to Cardwell, No. 27, Miscellaneous, May 4, 1865, CO 305:25; marginal note by Arthur Blackwood, no date.

53   Minute by TFE [Elliot], July 7, 1865, on Kennedy to Cardwell, No. 27, Miscellaneous, May 4, 1865, CO 305:25.

Office on resolutions adopted by the Vancouver Island Legislative Assembly and by the Victoria Chamber of Commerce to "unit[e] British Columbia and Vancouver Island under one Governor, one Legislature, and equal Laws,"[54] it took Seymour a matter of days to protest as to how Kennedy was thereby seeking to "procure annexation" of British Columbia, with Vancouver Island once again looking out for itself at British Columbia's expense.[55]

Seymour's reflections while on leave

Seymour slowly came around to the view that a union of the two colonies was necessary, but only if he were named governor of the new single colony. This change dovetailed neatly with Seymour going on leave in July 1865 in order to get married in Britain. His doing so would transform the almost frantic rhetoric as to which governor outshone the other into a one-man show. Seymour would win hands down by ingratiating himself with the Colonial Office while he was in London.[56] His doing so would position him as the desired governor of the two colonies on their being joined together.[57]

Having time to reflect in England, Seymour related to the Colonial Office the next February how, from his perspective, Vancouver Island had benefited from Douglas's arrangement at British Columbia's expense:

> The Government of British Columbia was carried on from the capital of another colony. The Governor and principal public officers drew full pay from the main land, and lived on the island. The people of Victoria profited by the expenditure of the proceeds of taxation levied on another community, & were at the same time, by the freedom of the port, relieved from the payment of the heavy import duties which fell on those who made of British Columbia their home.[58]

---

54   Kennedy to Cardwell, No. 16, Separate, March 21, 1865, CO 305:25.
55   Seymour to Cardwell, Separate, March 29, 1865, CO 60:21.
56   Cardwell to Seymour, No. 36, July 1, 1865, NAC RG7:G8C/12, 155; and Private, July 1, 1865, CO 398:2.
57   See the list in Ormsby, "Frederick Seymour."
58   Seymour to Cardwell, February 17, 1866, CO 60:26.

It was to Vancouver Island's benefit that things continued as they had been. More recently, however, the situation had reversed itself. "Victoria is not flourishing," wrote Seymour, but now "British Columbia is so." As for the reason:

> The discoveries of gold on the Lower Fraser first attracted to British Territory a large portion of the unattached population of Western America. The immigrants came from Oregon or California by sea. Their detention at the first place of landing created Victoria. The bars on the Fraser were gradually worked out. Now they are abandoned to the labours of Chinamen. But year by year the summer immigrants pushed further into the interior, still by the valley of the great river. Finally Cariboo was discovered and its prodigious wealth attracted large numbers of miners who were fed and supplied from Victoria. Driven from their work by the severe climate of the winter, the "Caribooites" spent some time & much money in that town & added to the profits of the merchants who had monopolized their markets during the working season. There were no large settlements in British Columbia. It was only a colony in name...
>
> Here was the real cause of the ill feeling between the two colonies. The settlers on the Fraser [River] paid gold miners duties on all they consumed while the people of the island profited by the success of the diggings & paid no import duties. Everything was done to foster Victoria... Imperial interests were assumed to be involved in the welfare of Victoria, & people affected to believe that great destinies were in store for the town... Meanwhile every man on the main land knew that the town was kept alive by the British Columbian mines. They petitioned for separation and they got it. Now,... the proceeds of their taxation are spent among them. Trade is beginning to establish itself on the Fraser...
>
> Cariboo was the great customer for Victoria, but Cariboo with its prodigious wealth has been found out to be "poor man's diggings." Not competent therefore to support a very large population. The mines are of limited extent. The gold is deep and is expensive to extract. The number of spring immigrants began early to fall off and in 1865 was smaller than usual... Victoria continued

CHAPTER 4

to do the principal business of these mines, but the population to feed was comparatively small and Victoria suffered.

So did British Columbia to a certain extent. Road side houses on the Cariboo line became bankrupt as traffic decreased by diminished immigration and accelerated travelling. The general condition of the colony was however prosperous. The customs receipts at New Westminster were, by the last account which has reached me, £15,000 in excess of the corresponding period of 1864. I learn that the British Columbia capital "is making great progress. Houses and wharves, clearing and fencing going on everywhere this autumn," and the most hopeful sign of all is beginning to shew itself; a disposition on the part of the miners to purchase land in New Westminster or its neighbourhood, and commence the systematic colonization of the Lower Fraser. These benefits in no way assist Victoria nor can it appreciate the improvement in the general condition of Cariboo which now induces many miners to winter there instead of squandering their money in Vancouver Island or San Francisco.

To the merchants of Victoria the depression they felt in 1865 appeared to extend over British Columbia, but he could only see the valley of the Fraser while a vaster view lay open before the eyes of the Government of New Westminster...From the sea to the Rocky Mountains, on both sides of the boundary line the country swarmed with eager prospectors...The revolver and bowie knife are laid aside and perfect tranquillity prevails.[59]

Seymour's perceptive narrative of a course of events differentially benefiting the two colonies continued apace. Whereas Vancouver Island was stagnant, British Columbia was bounding ahead:

> Every Surveyor and every Engineer in the Colony was in Government employ last year. Every discharged Sapper possessing anything like adequate knowledge was likewise induced to enter our service. A good trail for pack animals has been opened from the Fraser to the Kootenay...A sleigh road had been opened from the seat of Government to Yale running for upwards of a hundred

---

59   Seymour to Cardwell, February 17, 1866, CO 60:26.

Appointed governor of the mainland colony of British Columbia in 1864, Frederick Seymour was named governor of the merged colonies of British Columbia and Vancouver Island in 1866. He was photographed visiting the Heron mining claim in the Cariboo near Barkerville the following year. Seymour is at far right. *Image F-08565 courtesy of the Royal BC Museum.*

miles through the dense forest of the lower Fraser...Upwards of twenty thousand pounds have been expended in the completion on the high road into Cariboo allowing machinery, at last, to be introduced into Williams Creek...A good road now connects New Westminster with the sea at Burrard Inlet...A light ship, public libraries, new school buildings testify to the energy of the Government...For the telegraphic communication & the new line of steamers the Government can only claim the credit of the earnest efforts it has made to second the enterprise of our republican neighbours.[60]

The British Columbia mainland was, in effect, fast becoming the entity it remains into the present day.

---

60   Seymour to Cardwell, February 17, 1866, CO 60:26

Seymour concluded his lengthy letter to Edward Cardwell with his support for the union of the two colonies, but with a warning that the residents of the mainland colony did not agree.

> Your predecessor [the Duke of Newcastle], listening to the voice of the protesting colonists, effected the separation [signified by there being two separate governors] so joyously received in British Columbia. I say confidently that that colony has not altered its views. It has had the one great wish gratified and dreads all change...I am for many reasons anxious that the desire for union should exist in British Columbia. It does not.

In contrast, Seymour told the secretary of state for the colonies, "so great is the anxiety for union existing in Victoria...that the conditions are left entirely for you to determine," while "Nanaimo, the second town, I believe, faintly wishes for amalgamation of the two colonies, but the people are prosperous, contented, and the best feeling exists between them and the colonists of the mainland."[61]

"A lunatic House of Assembly, and a bankrupt Government"

Less than two weeks later, on March 1, 1866, Arthur Kennedy wrote a letter respecting the Vancouver Island Legislative Assembly's abolition of numerous taxes and import duties, complemented by "the contraction of two loans of $100,000 (£20,681) and £50,000 ($242,00)" to be added to a recent loan of £4000 ($19,400).[62] The letter, on its arrival in the Colonial Office in early April, pushed Elliot and Blackwood to new levels of exasperation:

> These despatches disclose a sad state of things at Vancouver Island—A lunatic House of Assembly, and a bankrupt Government...Unfortunately in Vancouver Island the power of initiating

---

61 Seymour to Cardwell, February 17, 1866, CO 60:26.

62 Kennedy to Cardwell, No. 14, Financial, March 1, 1866, CO 305:28; on the follow-up, same to same, No. 45, Financial, June 26, 1866, CO 305:28; No. 50, Financial, July 12, 1866, CO 305:29; No. 61, August 8, 1866, CO 305:29.

money votes is not reserved to the Governor—so the Assembly run wild. AB[d] and TFE[63]

There is but one remark which I have to make, & that is that the members of the V.C.I. Assembly are eminently unfit for their places. AB[d64]

James Douglas's watching brief

Even as those currently in charge were looking for solutions, so was their predecessor. In September 1866 James Douglas, who had kept a watching brief from Victoria, detailed to the Earl of Carnarvon, who was now the secretary of state for the colonies, his long-held view of the two colonies in relation to each other:

> No art can ever make New Westminster, what Victoria now is—a resort for Ocean going ships. Were Victoria destroyed New Westminster would not profit by the loss, on the contrary, it would be to her, the greatest possible calamity. Its effect would be to throw the trade of the coast into the American Ports in the Straits of De Fuca, and British Columbia would become, commercially, a dependency of the United States.[65]

The Colonial Office was not convinced. Minutes on Douglas's letter pinpointed its view of his legacy, Blackwood doing so in respect to Vancouver Island:

> V.C.I. was an insignificant place before the discovery of Gold in B.C. Victoria then naturally became the rendezvous for the Miners. Store shops & so called Merchants established themselves there. They got rich, speculated largely, & relied upon the free trade & the everlasting continuance of the gold fields in B.C. But miners were migratory, & these have been for a time seduced by Oregon & California by the reports of other gold miners. They

---

63 Minute by AB[d] [Blackwood], April 12, 1866, and TFE [Elliot], April 12, 1866, on Kennedy to Cardwell, No. 14, Financial, March 1, 1866, CO 305:20.

64 Minute by AB[d] [Blackwood], April 16, 1866, on Kennedy to Cardwell, No. 14, Financial, March 1, 1866, CO 305:28.

65 Douglas to Carnarvon, September 14, 1866, CO 305:30.

CHAPTER 4

returned, however, to B.C. which must, like all gold producing Countries be fluctuating in its prosperity. Except for the Royal Engineers who were sent there it has cost this Country nothing...

I do not dispute the fact stated by Sir J.D. [Douglas] that Victoria is in a bad way...due solely to over trading, smuggling, dependence on the success of B.C. as a gold Colony and to the incubus of an Assembly which by its legislation or perhaps want of proper Legislation has frustrated every attempt on the part of an able, an honest & a patient Governor to direct its course into channels wh^h w^d be beneficial to the Community.[66]

Blackwood noted Kennedy's confidential dispatch of January 24, 1866, respecting Vancouver Island in which he had described how the majority of the Assembly was composed of "reckless adventurers with a small stake in the Colony," some "notoriously insolvent."[67]

A very knowledgeable Frederic Rogers, Baron Blachford, the permanent under-secretary for the colonies, pointed to Douglas's history of entitlement:

Sir J.D. unfortunately is the man in the whole world whose personal authority is least valuable on this question. He (Governor) acquired a large property in V.C.I. and is accused I do not say whether justly or not of having so carried on the Gov^t of the two Colonies, as to give value to property in V.C.I. Certain it is—as he complains himself—that since B.C. has had an independent Governor the value of property in V.C.I. has been destroyed. Very likely from the causes enumerated by Mr Blackwood—but very likely in part also from successful attempts made by the B. Columbian merchants to retain the custom of B.C. miners who used to spend their money in Victoria—or by buying imports from Victoria.[68]

---

66 Minute by AB^d [Blackwood], October 31, 1866, on Douglas to Carnarvon, September 14, 1866, CO 305:30.

67 Kennedy to Cardwell, Confidential, January 24, 1866, CO 305:28.

68 Minute by FR [Rogers], November 1, 1866, on Douglas to Carnarvon, September 14, 1866, CO 305:30.

Vancouver Island's assumption of superiority over British Columbia, as effected under Douglas's governorship, had finally run its course.

Uniting the two colonies

Unbeknownst to Douglas, the fate of the two colonies had already been decided. In the time it took Arthur Kennedy's March 1, 1866, letter respecting the sad state of affairs on Vancouver Island to make the rounds of the Colonial Office, the parliamentary under-secretary, William Forster, was able to formulate an action plan to unite the two colonies, as he minuted May 3 on Kennedy's letter:

> Mr Blackwood tells me that without special instructions the Governor would not summon a new assembly before Oct this year at the soonest.
> This gives time for us to pass our Union Bill. I think, considering the past conduct of the Assembly & the probability that next year will start both colonies on a new course, it would be well to suggest by a Confidential Despatch to the Governor to take no more steps toward summoning a new Parl^t until the fate of our Union Bill be decided.[69]

The Colonial Office had in effect been working to implement a union of the two colonies, even as current and former governors were propounding their views on the matter.

Victoria residents also made their voices heard. At the beginning of December 1865, Kennedy had forwarded to the Colonial Office a petition against the union "from certain Merchants, Traders and others resident in Victoria" numbering eighty-eight British subjects, thirty-three Americans, twenty-one Germans, eight French, and seven unknown for a total of 157 persons. Kennedy's covering letter threw some of their claims back onto the petitioners, blaming the "great commercial depression" described in the petition on "a system of reckless credit, competition, and overtrading" on "the Cariboo market," on the merchant petitioners not taking into account "the cost of carriage" to the Cariboo, and

---

69 Minute by WEF [Forster], May 3, 1866, on Kennedy to Cardwell, No. 14, Financial, March 1, 1866, CO 305:28.

on the supply having "far exceeded the demand," leaving "Victorian merchants without payment for the goods they supplied."[70]

On December 12, 1865, Kennedy sent to the Colonial Office resolutions passed by the Vancouver Island Legislative Assembly concerning which the exhausted Blackwood's minute not unexpectedly began: "This half Yankee Assembly now expresses…"[71] The petitions and memorials kept coming, leading Kennedy to editorialize the next June how "the Members of the Assembly so far as my experience of that Body has extended, have not evinced any sense of responsibility to their constituents, to each other, or to their Sovereign."[72]

Blackwood minuted in response how "this despatch is an abundant proof, had any more proof been necessary, of the urgent need of suppressing this mockery of representative Institutions."[73] In a minute of the same day, Rogers, the permanent under-secretary, expressed confusion that after Vancouver Island had, in the course of negotiations respecting a union, reluctantly given up its representative assembly and Victoria's status as a free port "in consideration of being united with B.C.," it now seemed to have changed its mind.

> Now the Assembly has passed Resolutions virtually negating this understanding—& have asked the Gov. to telegraph them in time to stop the Parliamentary action based on the previous understanding. This the Gov[r] has refused to do (rightly enough I dare say) & the Resolutions reach us too late to stop the Act of Parl[t]—but not too late to stop the Proclamation of the Union issuable under it.[74]

The British Parliament had, for its part, rushed the Union Bill through to receive royal assent on August 6, 1866. What had been mooted prior to Douglas

---

70   Kennedy to Cardwell, No. 92, Separate, December 1, 1865, CO 305:26.

71   Minute by AB[d] [Blackwood], February 12, 1866, on Kennedy to Cardwell, No. 97, Separate, December 16, 1865, CO 305:26; also Kennedy to Cardwell, No. 10, Financial, February 13, 1866, CO 305:28.

72   Kennedy to Cardwell, No. 48, Separate, June 26, 1866, CO 305:28.

73   Minute by AB[d] [Blackwood], August 8, 1866, on Kennedy to Cardwell, No. 48, Separate, June 26, 1866, CO 305:28.

74   Minute by FR [Rogers], August 10, 1866, on Kennedy to Cardwell, No. 48, Separate, June 26, 1866, CO 305:28.

leaving office in 1864 now came to fruition with the two colonies joined as the United Colony of British Columbia, whereupon, as spelled out in the legislation, "the Form of Government existing in Vancouver Island as a separate Colony shall cease" in favour of that of British Columbia extending "to and over Vancouver Island."[75] And in spite of the Vancouver Island petition, the bill was proclaimed on November 19, 1866, by Governor Frederick Seymour.[76]

As for Arthur Kennedy, his two and a half years in charge of what Blackwood and Elliot termed "a lunatic House of Assembly" had not been a happy time.[77] All was not lost, however, for he was rewarded on his return to London with a knighthood and would subsequently govern Hong Kong, and Queensland in Australia.[78]

Deciding on a capital

The now united colony had to have a capital, and locating it was no easy matter. James Douglas had, in expanding his turf from the governorship of Vancouver Island to that of the mainland, and on its coming into being as the colony of British Columbia consequent on the 1858 gold rush, continued to make his home in Victoria. The principal mainland settlement of New Westminster remained in the shadows, although it gained some prominence due to the nearby headquarters of the Royal Engineers prior to their departure in 1863.

Seymour's earlier governorship of British Columbia made him sympathetic to New Westminster, being "the most respectable, manly and enterprising little community with which I have ever been acquainted," getting its due as the

---

75   "Act for the Union of Vancouver Island with the Colony of British Columbia," August 6, 1866, 101–2, online at archives.leg.bc.ca, item 741793246 (Appendix 3 in "Journals, Colonial Legislatures VI and BC 1851 to 1871, Volume I, Councils, 1851 to 1866").

76   Ormsby, "Frederick Seymour."

77   Minute by AB^d [Blackwood], April 12, 1866, and by TFE [Elliot], April 12, 1866, on Kennedy to Cardwell, No. 14, Financial, March 1, 1866, CO 305:28. For a detailed account of the Legislative Assembly's proceedings from Kennedy's perspective, see Kennedy to Cardwell, No. 60, Financial, August 8, 1866, CO 305:29; No. 61, CO 305:29; No. 69, Financial, September 3, 1866, CO 305:29; No. 71, Separate, September 4, 1866, CO 305:29; No. 73, Financial, September 8, 1866, CO 305:29.

78   Smith, "Sir Arthur Edward Kennedy."

CHAPTER 4

capital of the united colony.[79] Not so fast. As explained by Seymour in the summer of 1867:

> I have met with the unscrupulous hostility of the Victoria politicians. It was not to be allowed that British Columbia would stand alone and be independent...The inhabitants of the Island commercially levied a toll on everything consumed on the mainland and evaded all indirect taxation. British Columbia was practically a dependency of Victoria, its gold fields, fishing and hunting ground. If the mines proved rich, Victoria prospered...[and] by the assistance of the Government, Church, Navy, Banks and a great commercial Company was raised to a place of considerable importance. But its prosperity was artificial, to a certain extent, and had no solid foundation.[80]

From a non-Indigenous perspective Victoria had had charge of Vancouver Island from the time it came into being as a Hudson's Bay Company entity and then as a British colony under the aegis of the Colonial Office based in London. Its non-Indigenous residents took for granted Victoria would be the capital of the united colony. Thanks in good part to James Douglas's manoeuvrings, governance, commerce, and organized religion were all based there and Victoria residents assumed they would continue to be so. When the energetic George Hills arrived as bishop, to establish the Church of England in the future British Columbia, he was based in Victoria, testifying to that community's pre-eminence in things spiritual as well as worldly.[81]

Victoria now harnessed all its efforts, including petitions to the Colonial Office and deft manoeuvring by the experienced Dr. Helmcken, to get its way so that in the end, as Frederic Rogers put it realistically in a Colonial Office minute, "it will be soon necessary to make Victoria the Capital of the Colony,"

---

79   Seymour to Buckingham, No. 87, July 13, 1867, CO 60:28.
80   Seymour to Buckingham, No. 87, July 13, 1867, CO 60:28.
81   See Jean Friesen, "George Hills," *Dictionary of Canadian Biography*, vol. 12, http://www.biographi.ca/en/bio/hills_george_12E.html; Roberta L. Bagshaw, *No Better Land: The 1860 Diaries of Anglican Colonial Bishop George Hills* (Victoria, BC: Sono Nis Press, 1996); and "The Journal of George Hills," 1861–92, typescript in Ecclesiastical Province of British Columbia Archives.

Governor Seymour thought that New Westminster would make an excellent capital for the merged colonies. However, by 1867, when this photo was taken, it had lost out to Victoria. Image A-03084 courtesy of the Royal BC Museum.

with Seymour "preparing the way to yield with decorum."[82] So Seymour did, having been given leave by parliamentary under-secretary Charles Adderley that, "if he wishes, he may quote authority from home in favour of Victoria."[83] Seymour was still agonizing over the choice three months later, concluding reluctantly in December 1867 that if "we consider the question merely as how to please immediately the greater number of persons the selection of Victoria as a capital would be the most advisable."[84] And so Victoria has continued to be into the present day.

---

82   Minute by FR [Rogers], September 16, 1867, on Seymour to Buckingham, No. 87, July 13, 1867, CO 60:28.

83   Minute by CBA [Adderley], September 17, 1867, on Seymour to Buckingham, No. 87, July 13, 1867, CO 60:28.

84   Seymour to Buckingham, No. 161, December 10, 1867, CO 60:29.

CHAPTER 5

The Moderating Influence of Bishop Hills (1860–63)

For all of the amazing tales of the origins and survival of the two remote British colonies of Vancouver Island and British Columbia, huddled together as they were on the far west coast of North America, when this history is viewed from the top down the outcome seems almost predictable. Yet the reality was very different. Even as James Douglas, sustained by the Colonial Office, made the two colonies his own, others, notably Anglican bishop George Hills, provided a moderating influence. By tagging along with Bishop Hills following his arrival in Victoria at the beginning of 1860, four years before Seymour and Kennedy replaced Douglas as the single governor of two colonies, and six years before the two colonies were merged, we get a more nuanced perspective on these two remote colonies' early years, when their futures were very much in play.

Introducing Bishop Hills

The same day the newly appointed Anglican bishop arrived from England on January 6, 1860, he began a private journal whose opening sentence reads: "We are within a few hours of Victoria."[1] Continuing to write with a similar matter-of-factness, Hills chronicled his attitudes and actions, his feelings and outlook, and by virtue of doing so provides a useful second opinion to the letters that those in charge exchanged with the Colonial Office in London. Whereas James Douglas wrote strategically to persuade others, Hills's journal was for his eyes only. In

---

1   "The Journal of George Hills," 1860 to 1895, the year of his death, typescript in Ecclesiastical Province of British Columbia, Archives, which generously made a copy of the typescript available to me. See also Roberta L. Bagshaw, *No Better Land: The 1860 Diaries of the Anglican Colonial Bishop George Hills* (Victoria, BC: Sono Nis Press, 1996), 11–12, 19–20. For the 1860 diary in its entirety, 47–382, I have preferred the typescript.

consequence, it opens a window on a British Columbia in the making otherwise hidden from view or obscured.

It is also the case that, as with all our accounts, Bishop Hills's journal tells us only part of the story. "Born into a stern, disciplined naval family," according to Jean Friesen in *The Dictionary of Canadian Biography*, Hills earned undergraduate and graduate degrees from the University of Durham, followed by two decades of parish work in England before his appointment on January 12, 1859, as the founding Anglican bishop of British Columbia. He was consecrated at Westminster Abbey in London a little over a month later on February 24.[2]

George Hills was no ordinary appointee. His position was initiated and funded by the very wealthy English heiress and philanthropist Angela Burdett-Coutts, who oversaw his selection, provided generous financial support, and threw into the arrangement a corrugated iron building to be shipped in pieces around South America to Victoria to become, in 1860, the first consecrated Anglican church in today's British Columbia, along with a smaller structure to house its bishop.[3] In October 1858, with events already in play, the secretary of state for the colonies, Sir Edward Bulwer Lytton, forwarded to Governor James Douglas "a letter from the Archbishop of Canterbury announcing to me the munificent endowment offered by Miss Burdett-Coutts for the foundation of a See in British Columbia." In his letter to Lytton, the Archbishop explained the endowment's impetus in the gold rush:

> In consequence of the importance which is likely to belong to the colony of New Columbia [sic], & the expediency of providing for the spiritual instruction of the population assembling there, Miss Burdett Coutts has empowered me to propose the appointment of a bishop there, who may take the oversight of the Clergy & superintend the religious interest of the country & people; and for that purpose she is prepared to furnish an Endowment of the See, to the amount of £15,000.[4]

---

2 Jean Friesen, "George Hills," *Dictionary of Canadian Biography*, vol. 12, http://www.biographi.ca/en/bio/hills_george_12E.html.

3 For a contemporary perspective, Anonymous, *Baroness Burdett-Coutts: A Sketch of Her Public Life and Work* (London: Unwin Brothers, 1893; reprinted New York: Cambridge University Press, 2013).

4 J.B. Cantuar, Archbishop of Canterbury, to Lytton, September 27, 1858, in Lytton to Douglas, No. 32, October 19, 1858, LAC RG7:G8C/6, 292.

CHAPTER 5

Bishop George Hills, shown here ca. 1860, came to Victoria in January 1860 as the first Anglican bishop of British Columbia. He remained in that position until 1892. *Image G-05683 courtesy of the Royal BC Museum.*

To supplement the endowment, Hills during the first ten months of his appointment had raised funds in England, Ireland, and Scotland in the form of five-year pledges to the Columbia Mission, founded to sustain his work in the distant British colony.[5]

---

5   For the particulars of Hills's appointment, see Bagshaw, *No Better Land*, 17–18.

Nor was George Hills without his own needs. In a private letter to British government officials of October 1859, he requested passage "to B. Columbia by the W. India Mail Steamer on the 17th of November" not only for himself but also for "two servants," being "a man & wife," Samuel and Jane Bridgman.[6] While unmentioned in his journal, they were fundamental to his everyday well-being.

Four fractures

However prepared Hills might have considered himself to be for his big adventure, on his arrival in January 1860, the way of life he had up to then taken for granted would fracture in four important ways, wresting Hills from his assumptions about the way things were and therefore ought to be. These four fractures would cause Hills to bring new eyes, ears, and feelings into play respecting the two British colonies under his watch on behalf of the Church of England.

Hills's first task on arriving was "to pay my respects to the Governor," who lived not far from the temporary accommodation that had been found for Hills. For a brief moment he may have hesitated. As to his almost certain reason for doing so, he was already aware that "Mr. Douglas' wife is a half caste."[7] Meeting her on being invited for dinner, Hills wrote in his journal without further comment: "Dined with the Governor. Met Mrs. Douglas for the first time."[8]

Indicative of the biases we all share from time to time, a few days later Hills would similarly differentiate the wife of the couple living next door to him:

> In a neighbouring house is an Indian woman the wife of a respectable white man named Cotsford. She is a nice clean & well ordered person—will not speak but understands English. I saw her little girl a pretty child you would not tell her from an English girl—speaking English well. The other day the mother of Mrs. Cotsford went out at 8 o'clock, got drunk & died at 10. She was placed in a coffin with 15 Blankets. Her head did not lie easy & two new blankets were brought—they put inside a work bag—a looking glass, a box of matches & many such articles.[9]

---

6   George Hills to Newcastle, October 4, 1859, CO 60:6, No. 9938, 419.
7   January 6, 1860, entry in "The Journal of George Hills," 1860: 4–5.
8   January 31, 1860, entry in "The Journal of George Hills," 1860: 20.
9   February 3, 1860, entry in "The Journal of George Hills," 1860: 22.

CHAPTER 5

Thomas Cotsford was an English-born Hudson's Bay Company employee based at Fort Victoria who had purchased a town lot there in 1854.[10] He had a family with Betsy, whose English-born father John Thompson Dunn had arrived at Fort Vancouver with the HBC in 1821. Dunn was well-known as the author of *History of the Oregon Territory*, published in London in 1844 and for sale into the present day.[11] Betsy's mother was, according to a grandson, "a Russian girl" from today's Alaska, then a Russian possession.[12] The Cotsford daughter who caught Bishop Hills's eye was six-year-old Harriet, who would in due course marry Scottish-born Donald McKay. Their daughter wed Irishman John Hart, who would become British Columbia's minister of finance (1917–24 and 1933–47) and premier (1941–47).

The mixed Indigenous and white descent of Amelia Douglas, Betsy Cotsford, and other "half breeds," as Hills would sometimes term persons of mixed Indigenous and non-Indigenous descent, was the first of four fractures of everyday life, whose racial parameters Hills had up to then either been unaware of or taken for granted.[13]

A second fracture may have earlier come to Hills's attention on his being informed that the house prepared for his arrival belonged "to a Coloured man."[14] Possibly not digesting the information at the time, it became visible, along with a third fracture, at Hills's inaugural church service on January 8 when, he wrote in his journal, "about 42 Communicants were present—among them several coloured people—and a few Indians stood near the door."[15]

---

10   "Thomas Jonathan Cotsford" in Bruce McIntyre Watson, *Lives Lived West of the Divide: A Biographical Dictionary of Fur Traders Working West of the Rockies, 1793–1858* (Kelowna, BC: University of British Columbia Okanagan, 2010), 290.

11   "Thomas Jonathan Cotsford" in Watson, *Lives Lived West of the Divide*, 290; John Dunn, *History of the Oregon Territory and British North America Fur Trade, with an Account of the Habits and Customs of the Principal Native Tribes on the Northern Continent* (London: Edwards and Hughes, 1844).

12   Frederick William Pamphlet, conversation with Major Matthews, Vancouver, May 6, 1938, Vancouver Archives, Add. Ms. 54.

13   The earliest use of "half breed" noted in Hills's journal was in reference to the mother of John Tod, who "had been brought up at the Red River settlement" and "mother who is a half-breed." January 18, 1860, entry in "The Journal of George Hills," 1860: 70.

14   January 6, 1860, entry in "The Journal of George Hills," 1860: 4. On Hills's house, January 6, 1860: 4.

15   January 8, 1860, entry in "The Journal of George Hills," 1860: 5–7.

The fourth fracture upending a familiar status quo alongside racial mixing; "coloured people," who we now know as Black people; and an everyday Indigenous presence were Chinese men come to mine gold. Hills noted in his journal the presence of "Indians & Chinese as well as miners & labourers & artisans of other nations" at an "open air Mission" run by fellow Anglican priest Alexander Garrett that Hills passed by on his way home from holding services.[16]

Six days later Hills crossed the Strait of Georgia, which separates Vancouver Island from the mainland by a three-and-three-quarter–hour water voyage, in order to preach there. His journal recorded without further comment "two young Chinese—three Coloured men & others" turning up at his Sunday afternoon service.[17] Three days later Hills helped to inaugurate Trinity Anglican Church in New Westminster where Douglas, who had earlier laid the cornerstone, was received by a guard of Royal Engineers, and by their head Richard Clement Moody, at a service that was widely attended, including by "about 300 Chinese, Indians & other nations."[18]

Individuals who those in charge may have perceived as fractures sought in their everyday lives to get on equitably with those around them, and it was up to Hills and others identifying themselves as white to decide whether they were permitted to belong.

Initially Hills likely viewed the four fractures mostly in passing, not unexpectedly so given how much he had to absorb in the everyday. It took him a very short time to be made aware of "much rivalry between the two British colonies," this on learning from a British Columbia resident "how anxious the people are in that Colony that I should come and live there" rather than remain in Victoria and only visit the mainland.[19] As for how Hills fared: following a few days of milk being delivered to the accommodation provided for him, "no one came & no milk was there to be had," whereupon he discovered respecting the milkman that, "as he was a Roman Catholic he could not think of supplying milk to a Bishop of the Church of England!"[20]

---

16   May 13, 1860, entry in "The Journal of George Hills," 1860: 80.
17   May 19, 1860, entry in "The Journal of George Hills," 1860: 83.
18   May 12, 1860, entry in "The Journal of George Hills," 1860: 84.
19   January 13, 1860, entry in "The Journal of George Hills," 1860: 8.
20   January 13, 1860, entry in "The Journal of George Hills," 1860: 9.

CHAPTER 5

Visiting Freezy

In mid-January 1860 Hills was put in closer contact with Indigenous life on being introduced to the indomitable Freezy.[21] "Mr. Pemberton, the Magistrate, & Mr. Cridge accompanied me to the Indian reserve on the Esquimalt side of the Harbour," Hills wrote in his journal. "We happened on our road to meet the chief of one tribe—the Songish [Songhees]—his name is 'Freesy.'"[22] Joseph Despard Pemberton, grandson of a Lord Mayer of Dublin, was a surveyor, and Cambridge University-educated Edward Cridge was rector at Anglican Christ Church in Victoria.[23] The meeting was followed by a formal visit to Freezy's abode:

> I was placed in the middle as the Tyhee or chief. Presently more came in... These were Freesy's Councillers... Mr. Pemberton was interpreter—the language was Chinook—or rather Jargon, for it is no language—only a trading medium composed of words of different language & cant terms.
>
> Mr. Pemberton explained to them that I was a King George or English Tyhee & that I was come to endeavor to do them good...
>
> They spoke several times in reply & said they were glad anyone would be their friend and do them good & they would like to be better educated & have better houses. They had heard it said they were going to be removed—this grieved them much. What could they do if sent away—now they could get work & dollars & food but if sent away they must starve... Freesy was dressed in coat & trousers & if seen in England would be taken for rather a shabby Irishman. The others had blankets wrapped round them.[24]

---

21   Freezy and some of his family are introduced in Jean Barman, "Race, Greed, and Something More," in *On the Cusp of Contact: Gender, Space and Race in the Colonization of British Columbia*, ed. Margery Fee (Madeira Park, BC: Harbour Publishing, 2020), 15–16.

22   January 17, 1860, entry in "The Journal of George Hills," 1860: 10.

23   Richard Mackie, "Joseph Despard Pemberton," *Dictionary of Canadian Biography*, vol. 12, http://www.biographi.ca/en/bio/pemberton_joseph_despard_12E.html; Gail Edwards, "Creating Textual Communities: Anglican and Methodist Missionaries and Print Culture in British Columbia, 1858–1914" (doctoral dissertation, University of British Columbia, 2001), 446–47, 456, 452; on Cridge, 442.

24   Indigenous peoples' removal from Victoria is considered in Barman, "Race, Greed, and

THE MODERATING INFLUENCE OF BISHOP HILLS (1860-63)

From the Songish [Songhees] Indians I went to the Northern Indian Encampment. They are the Chymsyan [Tsimshian] from Fort Simpson & the Hydas [Haidas] from Queen Charlottes Island. They are a finer & fairer race then the Songish. Some of the faces were no darker than my own & had a healthy tint on the cheeks.[25]

As Hills's early journal entries indicate, physical features and skin tones mattered to him, but were at the same time not determinants of his actions and outlook. Hills would become fluent in the Pacific Northwest trading jargon of Chinook, comprised of words from English and French along with Indigenous languages.[26] It was expected that anyone in ongoing contact with Indigenous people would be familiar with the jargon, be it the governor of the colony, the Anglican bishop, or an everyday Indigenous person.

Getting to know his new home

There was much to learn, and Hills was keen to do so, often from different perspectives than Douglas or the others who had by now come to accept the way things were. Visiting New Westminster in mid-February 1860, Hills was impressed by its location "on the slope of a hill," with "about 400 people...in addition to the 300 at the Camp" of the Royal Engineers, dispatched from England to assist the mainland colony's beginning.

From there Hills and a fellow Anglican minister walked about five miles along a track "just cut out of the mighty Forest...through profuse vegetation, on either side of lofty Pines of 150 to 250 feet high towards Burrards Inlet," which "is to be the naval Harbour" and would become the city centre of today's Vancouver. Indicative of the changing times already in view, on one side of where

---

Something More," 3-25. Bishop Hills would continue to be in contact with Freezy, as, for example, the August 26, 1860, entry in "The Journal of George Hills," 1860: 206.

25 January 17, 1860, entry in "The Journal of George Hills," 1860: 10-12.

26 The February 16, 1860, entry in "The Journal of George Hills," 1860: 32, lists commonplace phrases in Chinook and English including *muck muck* for "sweet things," being more generally a generic term for food, and *mercie* for "thanks," indicating the influence of the French language. Among numerous introductions to Chinook is Itswoot Wawa Hyiu, ed., *Chinook Wawa*, 2nd ed. (self-published, 2011).

the two clerics walked, "a farmer from Canada was clearing his lot & I doubt not another year will show a plentiful harvest." On the other side was an Indigenous village where the chief's house had been built "with a gable roof in imitation of the house of Col. Moody," the head of the Royal Engineers.[27]

Crossing over the river by canoe, Hills described in his journal how, outside of the house of "Chief Tschymānā," who was not at home, one of his "three wives" was caring for her baby, "about six months old—a fine boy bound head & foot like a mummy & upon his head the heavy bandage for the flattening process... suspended in a horizontal position to the end of a bent stick placed in the ground & was rocked with a string."[28] The past, present, and future could not have been more intimately intertwined.

Hills would interact as need be with other religious denominations and was also keen on Indigenous conversion. He was respectful, if to some extent disconcerted, as to how "French priests have been instructing the Indians."[29] Not viewing other denominations as competitors, Hills did not give them much space in his journal.

"The colour question"

The next while passed in a similar fashion to what had gone on before, except that Hills repeatedly found himself faced with what he termed in his journal "the colour question," which centred on whether "no distinction is to be made in the seating of White & Coloured people" in church or whether to acknowledge Americans' "abhorrence of sitting next to a [derogatory term for a Black person] anywhere!"[30] An English friend who Hills invited to dine in early May told of how he had "mentioned to some Americans yesterday he was going to Church, they said, 'oh do you wish to go to a place where they will put a [derogatory term for a Black person] along side of you?'"[31]

Given Governor James Douglas sometimes dropped in for a chat, Hills was almost certainly aware of how he had three years earlier facilitated, at their request, a group of Black immigrants in their move north from California to

---

27 February 23, 1860, entry in "The Journal of George Hills," 1860: 36–37.

28 February 24, 1860, entry in "The Journal of George Hills," 1860: 38–39.

29 April 18, 1860, entry in "The Journal of George Hills," 1860: 71.

30 March 3 and 5, 1860, entry in "The Journal of George Hills," 1860: 44.

31 March 5, 1861, entry in "The Journal of George Hills," 1861–62: 44.

Vancouver Island. Now Hills found himself similarly acting as an intermediary of sorts.[32] Discussing "the colour question" with the fairly recently arrived Trutches—he an Englishman involved in road construction, his wife, in Hills's words, "an American though I should not have known it"—Hills was perturbed. Trutch "confessed he had objection to sit near some black people, not that he felt any unkind sentiment, but because of the peculiar odour," while his wife was, in Hills's words, "patronizing with pity rather than honour & respect as fellow mortals & equal in the sight of God."[33]

Three days later, "Mr. Papeus came to tell me the troubles of the Coloured people." Many had come expecting to find peace from the bitter prejudice in the United States, and Hills was himself caught up in this saga of "injustice which exists against them in America. They are fearful they shall not be free even on British soil. They are all very sad about things which have recently happened." Papeus described events of the past week:

> A merchant (Mr. Little) sent his daughter to the Female school of the Roman Cath. Sisters. There were at it also some seven or eight Coloured children, among which the niece of Mr. Papeus a girl of 14. Mr. Little informed the Sisters that all the white children would be taken away unless a separation was made. The Sisters had thereupon set up a separate Room for the Coloured children. Upon this the Coloured children have been withdrawn & the parents are in perplexity where to send them...I told Mr. Papeus he might rely upon it the Anglican Church would never make any distinction...
>
> He thanked me with tears for the Consolation he said I had given him—for all these things had made him nervous & very sad. For if on British soil rest & peace & justice to the Coloured people were not to be had where else in the world could they look?[34]

---

32   On the early presence of Black people, see Crawford Killian, *Go Do Some Great Thing: The Black Pioneers of British Columbia*, 3rd ed. (Madeira Park, BC: Harbour Publishing, 2020).

33   March 15, 1860, entry in "The Journal of George Hills," 1860: 47; also Robin Fisher, "On Joseph William Trutch," *Dictionary of Canadian Biography*, vol. 13, http://www.biographi.ca/en/bio/trutch_joseph_william_13E.html.

34   March 18, 1861, entry in "The Journal of George Hills," 1861–62: 49–50.

CHAPTER 5

The colour question would follow Hills. Five days later "a respectable Coloured person Mrs. Washington called on me," concerned as to how "she is a Communicant, but had felt an intruder, not having been...recognized by the Clergyman." Asked by Hills what she considered to be "the ground of the American prejudice against the Coloured race," she impressed him with her response. She had heard that some consider the African race an inferior one, but "some of her race were quite white & yet the same prejudice existed against them," and "she believed they were afraid the race would become more powerful & therefore had to keep them down."[35]

By now viewed as an intermediary, three days later Hills was visited by "two Coloured gentlemen," businessmen Mifflin Gibbs and Jacob Francis, who explained to him how, "as soon as this Colony was formed & before any idea the gold existed they had come here to be in quiet & to find rest." Now they were caught up in "the prejudice against their race" that "is ever more bitter than in some of the States of America." Among other actions, "the Coloured people had been excluded from the Philharmonic and the young men's Xtian [Christian] association," as well as churches, each of which, they were told, "made its own regulations."[36]

Soon Hills was himself caught up. He invited to dinner a New Yorker briefly in Victoria who he knew from his travels. Hills's guest had earlier attended an Anglican service and "was much surprised to see the Coloured people sitting in all parts of the Church & spoke of it as something quite wrong." When Hills asked why this surprised him, "he said 'their colour' showed it was not right & they had not been made equal to the white nor had they advanced even to equality & therefore it was not intended they should be equal." Not convinced by Hills's "obvious answers," his guest continued, "If you allow them this equality how can you prevent amalgamation—there would be intermarriages." From Hills's perspective, so he wrote in his journal: "This caste prejudice [underlining in original] the Gospel entirely opposes & a pure Xtianity must have more effect upon the Americans than at present if this unhappy prejudice is to be rooted out."[37]

---

35   March 23, 1861, entry in "The Journal of George Hills," 1861–62: 54.

36   March 26, 1860, entry in "The Journal of George Hills," 1860: 56. On Mifflin Gibbs, see Sherry Edmunds-Flett, "Mifflin Wistar Gibbs" in *Dictionary of Canadian Biography*, vol. 14, http://www.biographi.ca/en/bio/gibbs_mifflin_wistar_14E.html; on both men and generally, Killian, *Go Do Some Great Thing*.

37   April 7, 1860, entry in "The Journal of George Hills," 1860: 67.

THE MODERATING INFLUENCE OF BISHOP HILLS (1860–63)

Mifflin Wistar Gibbs was one of several Black residents of Victoria who sought Bishop Hills's assistance in confronting anti-Black prejudice. A veteran of the California gold fields, he came to Victoria in 1858 and set up what was reportedly the first mercantile business in the colony outside the Hudson's Bay Company. *Image B-01601 courtesy of the Royal BC Museum.*

CHAPTER 5

What to do? How to act? There were no easy answers, or perhaps no answers at all, so Hills pondered over the next weeks and months.

Even as Hills did so, on April 9, 1860, his future was set in stone, or rather in iron, with the news of "the Iron House taken this day out of the warehouse & deposited on the 5 lot on Vancouver S^t ready for erection."[38] The physical manifestation of Hills having committed short months earlier to this far distant place was about to appear in the form of the first consecrated Anglican Church in what is now British Columbia, soon to be designated a cathedral, alongside an adjacent iron structure, "the Bishops residence," into which he moved.[39] There was no turning back.

In the business of saving souls

As Hills was soon made aware, his business of saving souls across the two British colonies of Vancouver Island and British Columbia had its complexities. In early June 1860 at Hope in the Fraser Valley, Hills recorded in his journal:

> Had a conversation with a man named Yates—a servant of the Hudsons Bay C. 11 years in their employment. Speaks the native language. Lives with an Indian woman & has a child. Is not married. Defends the unmarried state as happier. Has known instances where men have been married & of unhappiness resulting. A French Canadian at the instigation of the Priest was married. His wife took advantage of his being bound to her & resorted to many of her own ways which from fear of dismissal, before she had abstained from.[40]

Yates's perspective disputed Hills's easy assumption that sexual relations were to occur only within Christian marriage, preferably with someone of the same skin colour. Yates was not a heathen and so could not be excused for lack of understanding. "He came from Orkney—was a Methodist. Attends the Methodist Chapel here." Hills persevered:

---

38   April 9, 1860, entry in "The Journal of George Hills," 1860: 68.
39   George Hills to Newcastle, January 21, 1864, CO 305:24.
40   June 4, 1860, entry in "The Journal of George Hills," 1860: 98.

I asked if he would be comfortable to live in an unmarried state in his own country. He said there was a great difference. There were Churches in Orkney & white women. I shewed him that the sin was the same here as in Britain. He allowed it was not right—but said he had been very comfortable.[41]

The end result of Hills's conversation with Yates was likely a standoff. A similar encounter a month later on the same trip may have had more direct consequences:

About 10 or 12 miles from Lytton is Spitlums flat, a place where mining goes on. I called in at a store, the only one, it was kept by a Dane who lives there with an Indian wife. He has been many years in the country. At this place the prices were:
Flour 23$ per 100 lb   11d/ ½ p lb. 13$/5 per stone
Bacon 45c per lb[42]

Less than a year later, on May 18, 1861, Frank Gottfried, who had been born in Copenhagen in about 1824, would be married at Spitlums flat to Susanna, described as a Lillooet woman whose Indigenous name was Kekachunchalee according to her son Frank Gottfriedson—the addition of "son" to a male offspring's surname being commonplace in Denmark.[43] The officiant at the wedding was the Anglican priest at nearby Lillooet, University of Edinburgh–educated Robert Lundin Brown, who had arrived in British Columbia in 1860 and was immediately posted there.[44]

An array of learning experiences

Bishop Hills's array of learning experiences mattered to him, just as they do to our understanding of British Columbia as it was so long ago. Over the course

---

41   June 4, 1860, entry in "The Journal of George Hills," 1860: 98.

42   July 3, 1860, entry in "The Journal of George Hills," 1860: 147, 148.

43   Rev. Wilfred Scott, O.M.I., Indian Missionary, "Last Chapter Written in Indian's Colorful Career," *Vernon News*, January 18, 1951.

44   Records of St. Mary's Anglican Church, Lillooet, 1861–1917, in British Columbia Archives, Reel 22A; Edwards, "Creating Textual Communities," 440.

of his inaugural May to August 1860 road trip, Hills, as he related in his journal, introduced himself and preached to both newcomers and Indigenous peoples, sometimes using an interpreter with the latter group, and at other times trying out his growing familiarity with Indigenous languages.[45]

Encountering at the end of June near Boston Bar "a miner from California with a Revolver on one side and a Bowie knife on the other," Hills began a conversation, to be informed by the miner "how they [the weapons] were needed in California but not here." Hills reflected that the difference between California and the British Columbia colony was "all classes are well treated. Chinamen, Indians & Blacks have justice as equal as to others. Indeed it is evident that what the Californian looked for as a sign of high spirit & courage he is now ashamed of."[46]

A day later, approaching a bridge over a creek "for which according to a notice 25.c or 1 1/0 was charged for foot passengers, a dollar for a mule or horse," Hills was pleasantly surprised by how, "on the arrival of my party 6 on foot & two horses—the Chinaman in charge refused to take anything." Through "much talk" with Ah Fah, Hills learned how "an American had placed over the river...a sort of bridge," for which to cross "he charged everybody high & when the poor Chinamen came with no money he would take their mining implements." The magistrate at Lytton had thereupon advised the Chinese men to make their own bridge, whereupon the American sold his right to charge a fee to Ah Fah.[47]

Coming the next day, June 29, to a larger bridge, "a Chinaman, named Ah Soo," similarly did not charge them. "No Englishman he said pays to go over the bridge & no poor Chinaman... He charges Boston man (American). 'Boston man charges Chinaman very high in Californy—Chinaman now charges Boston man ha ha.'"[48]

In a section of his daily journal Hills headed "British soil a welcome home for all races," he made three general points in quick succession respecting what he had learned so far on the trip. He first noted how, based on an estimate he was given, three thousand or so Chinese men "are selling out their mining claims in California to come up here & are purchasing claims of the white miners." Second and third:

---

45   The July 10, 1860, entry in "The Journal of George Hills," 1860: 159–60, details the content of a two-hour sermon, as also does the August 5, 1860, entry on 187.

46   June 28, 1860, entry in "The Journal of George Hills," 1860: 136.

47   June 29, 1860, entry in "The Journal of George Hills," 1860: 139.

48   June 29, 1860, entry in "The Journal of George Hills," 1860: 139–40.

The Indian race is comparatively happy here. Every where King George men (English) are looked upon as their friends. They come & shake hands & hang about us. What a contrast to the constant massacre in the American Territory. A third race badly treated by the Americans is the African. Here everywhere they are treated fairly. Thus in these three instances is British soil a welcome Home.[49]

Hills's understandings continued to grow. In August 1860, by which time Hills was on his way back to Vancouver Island and staying with Major Moody at the Royal Engineers' enclave at Sapperton near New Westminster, "Taschclak an Indian came to see me, shewed me a paper in which he promises to be sober."[50] The next day he returned:

> Taschclak came to day again & brought his two wives—Tsahtsalote and Khalowit & his two boys Malasleton & Karkaywile. One wife looked a dozen years older than the other. The elder had 11 rings, the younger 10 rings on the hands. He had had 8 children by his two wives. Had lost six... He told me he endeavoured to bring up his children peaceably & would not let them steal. He said he never got angry & gave himself otherwise an excellent character, with which his wives agreed. He concluded by asking for a bit of paper with some writing on it. The two women were extremely well behaved. Their heads were nicely covered & their hair braided they had one each a comfortable English Shawl & were dressed in coloured cotton gowns as country people in England.
> Tashclak said he should be very glad if his children could be instructed. I spoke to them about God & the work of X^t [Christ].[51]

That day being a Sunday, it had another critical component, which was "preaching to Indians at Hope." Doing so gave Hills an opportunity to try out in his sermon the new language skills he had been acquiring since he began missionizing in the two British colonies:

---

49 June 29, 1860, entry in "The Journal of George Hills," 1860: 139.
50 August 3, 1860, entry in "The Journal of George Hills," 1860: 185.
51 August 5, 1860, entry in "The Journal of George Hills," 1860: 186.

At about ½ past 3 Indians began to assemble and soon filled the place, a large store. Several White men also came in. Old Pa-hallak was in his place. I explained to the white persons my desire to instruct the Indians & leave an impression of one or two chief points...

I then addressed the Indians. Many of them knew the Thompson Dialect. So with Chinook, with Kookptchin, with Lillooet, & some Cowichan. I managed to speak to them for nearly an hour. There was much attention. Occasionally some would repeat to others in their own words what I said.[52]

Hills reflecting on what he had learned

As indicated by his journal entries, Bishop Hills had during the summer of 1860 no ordinary adventure: "I have travelled during the 12 weeks upwards of 800 miles—in Steamboat, Canoe, horseback & on foot... I have found myself able to walk nearly 20 miles a day." Not only that, "I have learnt to sleep as soundly upon the floor of a log hut, or on the ground, as in a bed, to wake refreshed & thankful. I clean my own shoes, wash my clothes, make my bed, attend to horses, pitch tents & all such matters have become easy duties."[53]

Consequent on "the last three months of journeyings & perils by land & by water amidst a strangely mixed & peculiar population, my belief in the progress of the Colony has been confirmed." From Hills's perspective, "nothing would have opened this tract except its mineral produce," with "the formation of roads" being the means for realizing the colony's potential. Hills was intrigued by, and respectful of, the diverse nature of the population that had arrived during the gold rush:

> Variety of race is a remarkable feature & a difficulty in dealing with the population in this country. The Christianity of England is the last known even amongst those who would not pay disrespect to religion. French, Spaniards, Italians, Mexicans & some Germans & Irish are mostly Roman Catholics... Germans, most Americans, & Scotch are Presbyterian or Congregational, or Unitarian... Yet they are the truth of the people.[54]

---

52   August 5, 1860, entry in "The Journal of George Hills," 1860: 187.
53   August 8, 1860, entry in "The Journal of George Hills," 1860: 194.
54   August 8, 1860, entry in "The Journal of George Hills," 1860: 193.

Despite Hills's growing understandings, all was not well. From a solely religious perspective he was beside himself:

> The state of religion is as low as it can possibly be amongst civilized people. There is no recognition of it. Sunday is a day of business & pleasure & reveling. Most of the mining class are open profaners of the name of God & many are what are called "free thinkers." Morals I fear are as far from what is right as the case of religion…
>
> We complain in England of the little hold religion has upon many of the Artisan Class,… but I never met with anything at all approaching the calculating & matter of fact infidelity which prevails amongst many who have been trained in America. They seemed to have had full license to pursue every unfaithful thought & seem to have been unreached by any witness or influence of truth.[55]

Hills was all the same accepting of what was. As to the reason:

> Yet with all this, there is a kindness…in the American miner which is a great contrast to any thing amongst Englishmen. I was everywhere kindly received & in some cases I believe welcomed for religious sake. Allowance must be given no doubt for the frontier life which many of these have led & the absence of all opportunities of grace. But the state of religion is nevertheless a phase of work before us which is not to be seen elsewhere in a British territory & which calls for special exertion, patience & Prayer.[56]

Expanding obligations and new complexities

"Glad to find myself in my own cottage," Bishop Hills wrote on his return to Victoria in August 1860.[57] The two British colonies over which he had oversight on behalf of the Church of England were large in size and also in opportunities. Interracial unions, Black, Chinese and Indigenous peoples no longer challenged Hills's familiar way of life, but were accepted as part of the way things were.

---

55   August 8, 1860, entry in "The Journal of George Hills," 1860: 192.
56   August 8, 1860, entry in "The Journal of George Hills," 1860: 193.
57   August 9, 1860, entry in "The Journal of George Hills," 1860: 197.

CHAPTER 5

In mid-August Hills spoke to a group of "Chymsean" (Tsimshian) "in Chinook which many understood," but which was "more fully interpreted in Chymsean." Hills then visited the Haida camp, where he despaired at "some of the women decked out in every sort of vulgar finery—even to the wearing of crinoline & hoops," deemed by him "the unmarried wives of white men—& worse instances were there than even this."[58]

Hills's patience had its limits, especially when it came to religious denominations he had come to perceive as competition. While on Saltspring Island in the beginning of September 1860, "an old chief came on board" the vessel Hills was on with "a chain round his neck on which was appended a crucifix." Hills lamented in his daily journal how "I wish I had something to give these poor creatures...instead of Romish toys—and yet how much better to give them the treasure which rust & moth do not corrupt, but they are like children & Rome deals with them as such."[59]

As Hills was soon made aware, it was not so much a matter of Indigenous people being taken in by others' religious beliefs as it was their using what was offered them as strategically as possible. Later the same day, Hills was invited into a lodge in which was hanging "the Catholic Ladder," being "a representation of events of the Bible & the Church," which, he was informed, depicted how "Americans all went to the flames, but King George men went the right way."[60] "King George men," being Englishmen, had a pass into heaven.

A few days later, "Mr. Richardson, a Coloured person" Hills had met earlier, invited him to visit the "Ganges Harbour Settlement" on Saltspring, where there were "a good many Coloured people" whose "clearings compare with those of others."[61] As explained by historian Crawford Killian, early on "a considerable number of Black pioneers seized the opportunity to pre-empt land on Saltspring Island" to become an enduring community there.[62]

At the consecration a week later of a new Anglican church in Victoria, "two coloured gentlemen" were among the fifty invited.[63] Indicative of the range of

---

58   August 12, 1860, entry in "The Journal of George Hills," 1860: 197–98.
59   September 7, 1860, entry in "The Journal of George Hills," 1860: 214–15.
60   September 9, 1860, entry in "The Journal of George Hills," 1860: 214–18.
61   September 6, 1860, entry in "The Journal of George Hills," 1860: 211.
62   Killian, *Go Do Some Great Thing*, 129, also 127–51, 189, 209–10.
63   September 13, 1860, entry in "The Journal of George Hills," 1860: 220. The church was St. John's.

contacts Hills nurtured, he had only just returned when "Freesy, chief of the Songhees asked me to preach" at the "Indian school on the Reserve" on Sunday, September 16.[64] A week later Hills gave an invited talk respecting "the profligate condition of the population," by whom he meant Indigenous women. "The road to Esquimalt on Sunday is lined with the poor Indian women offering to sell themselves to the white men passersby—& instances are to be seen of open bargaining." A fellow Anglican cleric had earlier described to Hills "houses where girls of not more than 12 are taken in at night & turned out in the morning—like cattle."[65]

For all that Hills by his actions sometimes treaded close to the sensibilities line for appropriate behaviour, it was only at the beginning of October 1860 that, it appears, the consequences became public. On October 4 "a respectable trader" chose not to subscribe to his local Anglican church, due to his having "heard that the Bishop had invited Mr. Lester (a Coloured gentleman) to luncheon on the day of Consecration" of the new church.[66] Peter Lester was a Victoria businessman.

Back to the everyday

Bishop Hills proudly reported in his journal on November 1, 1860: "A Turnip taken up in my garden (white) weighs 25 lbs & is 42 ½ inches in circumference."[67] Whoever we are, however important we might be or think we are, some of our greatest accomplishments and pleasures are particular to ourselves in our place of being, which Victoria had become for him.

Countering the everydayness of that pleasure was another encounter in his principal business of saving souls. Hills was again educated by Indigenous women respecting that side of the gender equation: "Two women complained in December 1860 of the treatment they receive from Americans. They say evil men come & steal away even the wives in the face of their husbands for evil purpose. They struggle & they cry but frequently it is of no avail." Likely for lack of options, Hills "told them to appeal to the English Magistrate he could be their

---

64 September 16, 1860, entry in "The Journal of George Hills," 1860: 220.
65 September 24, 1860, entry in "The Journal of George Hills," 1860: 227–28.
66 October 4, 1860, entry in "The Journal of George Hills," 1860: 230.
67 November 1, 1860, entry in "The Journal of George Hills," 1860: 245.

friend & not allow such conduct."[68] This minimal advice did not indicate a lack of empathy, Hills having written reflectively and admiringly during his canoe trip earlier in the year:

> The Indian women take a full share of labour. Even more is carried by them than by men. They were paddling with as much strength. One woman was steering a canoe and came close to us. Indeed we passed it. She had 3 silver rings on two fingers of her left hand—& six bracelets. They have earrings also & sometimes anclets. These ornaments are made out of silver dollars.[69]

As Hills had by now come to realize, while he could not as a preacher be everything to everyone all the time, it did not mean he should not try to be so. And by virtue of Hills acting as he did toward persons of mixed descent, Black and Chinese people, Indigenous peoples, and others, they belonged or almost so, at least in the moment. Bishop Hills's moderating presence accommodated diversity.

Entertaining Lady Franklin

Soon taking centre stage for Bishop Hills was a wholly other experience initiated by the arrival in Victoria on February 22, 1861, of "the widow of the celebrated Arctic navigator" Sir John Franklin, who had disappeared in 1847 on an expedition in search of a Northwest Passage across northern North America. Sixty-eight-year-old Jane, Lady Franklin, had devoted herself to finding out as much as she could about his fate, and she came to Vancouver Island to meet with an old friend who had helped search for Franklin and was now involved with marking out the boundary line between Britain and the United States. Lady Franklin's purpose neatly coincided with a request by Angela Burdett-Coutts for her to check up on Hills so as to determine how the mission she had funded was getting on.

Lady Franklin was accompanied by her personal maid, in the person of her husband's forty-four-year-old niece, Sophia Cracroft, whose detailed account of the trip in letters home to England have fortunately survived.[70] Her candid

---

68   December 4, 1860, entry in "The Journal of George Hills," 1860: 271.
69   June 23, 1860, entry in "The Journal of George Hills," 1860: 122.
70   Dorothy Blakey Smith, ed., *Lady Franklin Visits the Pacific Northwest: Being Extracts from*

descriptions of a Victoria and British Columbia in the making complement Bishop Hills's journal entries with the perspectives of two very intelligent and perceptive women. The following excerpts, evocative of time and place, are taken from the letters:

> **Sunday, Feb 24, 1861.** We ... entered Victoria about 3–30—glad to get to our lodging, the very best in the place & really *very* [italics in original] tolerable—a tidy little sitting room & bedroom behind for my Aunt—the landlady giving up her own room to me.
>
> It is kept by a coloured man & his wife ... They are very respectable people. He is a hair cutter & has a shop ... & his wife has the reputation of being a first rate cook. They are probably one generation if not farther from being the pure Negro, & Mr Moses [born in Britain[71]] calls himself an Englishman, which of course he is politically & therefore justly. She is a queer being, wears long sweeping gown without crinoline—moves slowly & has a sort of stately way (in intention at least) which is very amusing. Sometimes she ties a coloured handkerchief round her head like the American negroes (she is from Baltimore) but on Sunday she wore a sort of half cap with lace falling behind, her hair being long enough to be parted. The language of both is very good ...
>
> As we were emerging from the back of our 'express waggon' at Mr Moses' door, the Bishop passed down the other side of the street, & came to us to welcome us to Victoria ... After a short walk over plank side walks, we found ourselves within *the* [italics in original] iron church brought out by the Bishop, forming (I *think* [italics in original], but am not quite sure) part of Miss Coutts' provision for the Diocese. The *skin* [italics in original] only is iron; it is lined with wood, the pieces being placed diagonally on the walls with excellent effect ... The cold was very painful in spite of a blazing stove, and the easterly gale roared and clattered so loud that sometimes we could hardly hear the preacher, tho' a clearer voice there could not be ...

---

the *Letters of Miss Sophia Cracroft, Sir John Franklin's Niece, February to April 1861 and April to July 1870* (Victoria, BC: Provincial Archives of British Columbia, 1974), 1–93.

71   Information in brackets is taken from Killian, *Go Do Some Great Thing*.

CHAPTER 5

Monday, February 25. The Bishop called early & paid us a long visit which was full of interest. He is a most fortunate man in being thus early in the field, while the colony is in absolute infancy—& in the clergy by whom he works... It is said that he has shewn singular tact & wisdom, and that thus he has gained over most influential persons who were disposed to oppose him... This was the case with the Governor, a Hudson Bay Co^s officer of long-standing—but he is now openly desirous of assisting the Bishop to the utmost...

As might be expected, one element in the motley population of Vancouver's Island, is the negro, or coloured class—the term "coloured" is not applied to the Indian, but only the negro race. You know that everywhere in America, they were treated as unworthy to be in contact with whites except as utterly inferior beings. They have separate churches & separate schools & the mixture of races which is often pointed out to you in the American common schools never includes the negro. The same exclusive system was attempted to be introduced here in consequence of the American prejudice—the Americans threated to withhold their children from the schools if the coloured children remained. The Romanists yielded—so also the Independents... The same feud was excited in Church schools, but the Bishop was not likely to give way upon such a point, and his firmness met with its reward—the threatened withdrawal of the other scholars never took place, and saw the unmistakable descendants of negroes... side by side with the English and American girls...

Another difficulty the Bishop encountered was with the Jews attending the schools. The basis of the teaching is essentially Christian, and no pupil is exempt... This however did not satisfy the Jews who are pretty numerous here... the parents threatened to remove them. The Bishop would not consent... & again he gained all by firmness, for they were not removed... Remember that all this has been accomplished within one year...

Mr. Douglas is the Governor... His wife is a half caste Indian, and he has 6 children of whom Mrs Dallas is the 2nd... Mrs Dallas is a very natural, lively & nice looking person, just 22... but the Indian type is remarkably plain, considering she is two generations removed from it... Even her intonation & voice are characteristic (as we now perceive) of her descent...

Tuesday, February 26. At two o'clock, the Bishop came to take us to the Collegiate Schools. We went first to that for girls—and found them assembled 25 in number—others being absent on account of the recent bad weather which prevented them from getting over from Esquimalt. These were the young ladies of the colony—those requiring the best education, including music, singing, drawing, French, Italian, German & Spanish. They were apparently of all ages between 8 and 18, and several were coloured...

The Bishop had conveyed to my Aunt an invitation to take luncheon the next day with M^r & Mrs Harris, a very rich butcher, who is also contractor to supply the Navy here with meat. They are excellent people... but are not blessed with over much education, more's the pity!...

This afternoon my Aunt received from our landlord, a paper on which were the names of some 20 of his coloured brethren, all in most respectable positions here, who wished to be allowed to pay their respects to her. The Bishop is particularly pleased at this, and has asked if he may be present when they come.

Wednesday, Feb. 27. The Bishop came to take us to our luncheon at Mr Harris's. He has one of the best houses here, a substantial building of brick, some distance from the shop. They are plain, worthy people, without any pretension. He is making a great deal of money, is living in as much comfort as can be obtained in the colony, educating his children as well as he can, buying property and improving it extensively—and is therefore a public benefactor... Mr. Harris is just the sort of man to meet half way in his upward career... We liked our visit very much—everything was in good taste without affectation of any kind.

After luncheon, Mr Hankin [British Naval officer serving as an escort to the two women] managed to find a sort of American gig in which my Aunt could go to the native school, I walking with the Bishop. The building is circular (or octagonal) of wood lighted form the roof—standing upon a hill overlooking the harbour, and close to the Indian reserve on which all the Indians live...

CHAPTER 5

we found the school at work. They were in 2 divisions seated on benches... in separate tribes, the 2 larger divisions being occupied by the Hydah [Haida] & the Sang soo [Songhees] tribes, who are hostile to each other. Stray children of other tribes were on the small benches, the upper ones of which have a desk before them for writing.

They were all decently dressed, & many of the girls were wrapped in gay plaid shawls given them for good conduct; some, both boys and girls, were huddled up in the usual fashion in a dirty blanket, others wore a gay kind of wrapper made by themselves in red & blue cloth ornamented with rows of mother of pearl buttons, with pretty effect. We often see them on the streets here. Some wore rings of silver in their lips, ears & noses; and most of the bigger girls had bracelets of silver. One had 6 or 8 on one arm. They were much cleaner than we had any idea of expecting—even their lanky hair had evidently been combed, thought it was somewhat of a fuzzy crop and hung over their foreheads...

The school has been but a very few months at work yet already the children have learned to read small words in English & some of them write with wonderful neatness.

Bishop Hills wrote his own account of the school visit.

Went with her to the Indian School, which... was assembled. The children sang Xtian Hymns. Classes were examined on reading. The copy books were inspected. Edenshaw the great Hyda Chief was present & sold a couple of silver bracelets beautifully graven. The Indians are proud of their work. Some presents were distributed—scissors & balls...We visited also several Lodges & saw 2 Indian babies with the pressure bandage on their foreheads. I remonstrated & the Indian woman declared she considered the straightness..."not good"—in answer to my declaration that the flattened forehead was "not good." So she adheres resolutely to the fashion of the Flatheads.[72]

---

72 February 27, 1861, entry in "The Journal of George Hills," 1861: 25.

Sophia Cracroft continues with her description of her aunt's visits with citizens of Victoria.

Thursday Feb 28. We were engaged today to take luncheon with the Governor's wife Mrs Douglas... Have I explained that her mother was an Indian woman, & that she keeps very much (far too much) in the background; indeed it is only lately that she has been persuaded to see visitors, partly because she speaks English with some difficulty; the usual language being either Indian, or Canadian French w^h is a corrupt dialect. At the appointed time [the Douglases' daughter] Mrs Dallas came to introduce a younger sister Agnes, who was to take us to their house. She is a very fine girl, with far less of the Indian complexion & features than Mrs Dallas...

The Governor's house is one of the oldest in the place... it is 12 years old—standing in a large old fashioned garden with borders of flower enclosing squares of fruit trees & vegetable too I think. The house is a substantial plain building, with very fair sized comfortable rooms. Mrs Douglas is not at all bad looking, with hardly as much of the Indian type in her face, as Mrs Dallas, & she looks young to have a daughter so old as Mrs Helmkin [Helmcken] the oldest, who is 26. Her figure is wholly without shape, as is already Mrs Helmkin we hear, & even Mrs Dallas...

At 5 o'clock the Bishop came to be present at the visits of the coloured people who had asked my Aunt to see them, that being the appointed hour. The first was M^r [Mifflin] Gibbs, a most respectable merchant who is rising fast. His manner is exceedingly good, & his way of speaking quite refined. He is not quite black, but his hair is I believe short & crisp. Three other men arrived after him & he took his leave soon after, having acted rather as spokesman for the others, who then explained that they were the Captain & other officers of a Coloured Rifle Corps, & the Captain proceeded to speak very feelingly of the prejudices existing here even, against their colour. He said they knew it was because of the strong American element which entered into the community which however they hoped one day to see outpowered by the English one;—that they had come here hoping to find the true

CHAPTER 5

freedom which could be enjoyed only under English privileges, & great had been their disappointment to find that their origin was against them. My Aunt sympathized with them of course & said she knew that their claims had been always maintained by the Bishop as representing the Church. This observation was eagerly taken up by the Lieu^t who said but for the stand made on their behalf by the Bishop & his clergy, the coloured population would have left the colony in a body. We sh^d thus have lost a most orderly and useful and loyal section of the community. They naturally detest America & this Rifle corps has the San Juan claim, still pending. As he went out, the Captain said "Depend on it Madam, if Uncle Sam goes too far, we shall be able to give a good account of ourselves." You can imagine how gratified the Bishop was by this emphatic declaration of their obligations to himself & his clergy.

This party was followed by a M^r and Miss Lester (his daughter). He is the partner of Mr Gibbs—certainly one or 2 degrees from the pure negro & his daughter is as fair as I am, with nice ladylike manners & appearance. With these, the conversation was more general, and after they were gone the Bishop told us that Miss Lester was actually expelled from a school in San Francisco where she was carrying off prizes, because her nails exhibited a dark shadow which is said to be the very last discernible trace of negro blood! She is very well educated, and her younger sister is in Mrs Woods school, probably as fair as any of her companions.

I need not tell you that all these people expressed their feeling of pleasure at seeing my Aunt, and they certainly do speak with a propriety & a degree of refinement which is peculiar to their race & certainly superior to the same rank among Englishmen... All of them who called are church people, attending constantly, and he [Hills] knew them all.

Bishops Hills also described this visit.

> I was present with Lady Franklin when she received a deputation of Coloured people. They surprised her by their intelligence & good manners—equal if not superior to any of their positions

in society—the sons of tradesmen. They told her they had much to suffer from the prejudice & that had it not been for the stand made by the Ch of England they would all have gone away from the Colony.[73]

Lady Franklin and Sophia Cracroft commented on the shops in Victoria and took part in quite a social whirl.

> **Friday March 1.** We managed to get in some shopping today & were surprised to find things so good & plentiful...We were surprised at the excellence of the restaurants, conducted after the French fashion & refuge of the numerous bachelors...
> This evening we were to dine at the Colonial Secretary's... You would be amused to see us trudge on foot to dinner parties...As we walked, we heard shouting & singing at a distance, & learned that it came from a party of Indians from the north, who had arrived in canoes during the day...We got home all the safer for the Bishop's lantern he coming round by our house to give us the benefit of it...The perfect quiet and order of Victoria at night is surprising—there is not the smallest approach of any annoyance...
> **Saturday March 2.** We also visited the Hudson Bay Company Store. They import direct from England everything you can think of in the way of dress, as well as groceries and other stores, of course at a very great advance on their original cost.
> At another place we saw some of the Fraser river gold, in dust, in scales, in nuggets, 7 in lumps made of dust amalgamated by quicksilver...
> **Sunday March 3.** Mr and Mrs Dallas & Mr Mayne [Royal Navy officer] came to take us to Christchurch. We sat in the Governor's pew—a large square one under the organ gallery...The congregation was a very good one, and we were struck by the large proportion of coloured people. You must remember that they are *never* [italics in original] seen in America, but have churches all to themselves...Mr [Edward] Cridge [the cleric] read the prayers...

---

73   February 28, 1861, entry in "The Journal of George Hills," 1861: 26.

CHAPTER 5

Monday, March 4. At 2 o'clock the Bishop came to take us to the Boys' Collegiate School...We found between 40 and 50... they a very nice looking set of boys—in rank, from the Governor's son, downwards. They were not more than 2 or 3 coloured boys & even those are not very dark. One however is a fugitive slave...On leaving, they cheered my aunt uproariously... & told her they had just unanimously declared that they would name their Cricket Club after her!...

Tuesday, March 5. We started at 7 to go on board the "Otter" belonging to the Hudson's Bay Company, which goes weekly to New Westminster. Mr. Dallas came to take us on board & introduce us to the Captain (Mowatt) who kindly gave us the use of his cabin, on deck, where we passed the greater part of the day...We passed close under the disputed Island of San Juan & it was rather tantalizing not to be able to land...

We had a beautiful view of the mountains as we crossed the Georgian Gulf & entered the Fraser river between low banks covered with tawny reeds, which looked like tracts of cornland ready for the harvest. Our fellow passengers were pretty numerous, chiefly miners & of many races. French, German & Spanish were spoken, to say nothing of unmitigated "Yankee."...There was also a party of theatrical ladies & gentlemen—one of the former, very pretty.

The two women spent the night with Colonel Moody and his family at the Royal Engineers camp near New Westminster. The next morning before they embarked on a trip up the Fraser River, they "walked about the Camp, admiring the taste & order which reigns throughout it."

Wednesday, March 6. The Engineers are 120 in number, all volunteers, come out for 6 years, at the end of which period they may either remain in the service & return home, or be discharged & receive a grant of 30 acres. Meanwhile they receive additional pay & are already buying bits of land. Thus a most useful class of colonists is being created, for in the Engineer corps every man is taught a trade...

We embarked on the "Maria"...Gold is found almost everywhere along the banks of the Fraser above New Westminster...

miners have been continually penetrating farther & farther into the heart of the country...Yale is the farthest point of steamboat navigation...The intervening settlements are at Langley, Old and New, about a mile apart, and Hope...

Miners have been constantly penetrating farther & farther into the heart of the country. These are the most adventurous & hardy, & the ground they have abandoned is now being worked chiefly by the Chinese who have come over in thousands, live mostly upon rice, and are content with a small return for hard work...

We had a good many passengers, including 2 Chinamen miners—the better class slept in *the* [italics in original] cabin, the dining tables being shoved aside, & mattresses put all over the floor. The upper end of the cabin had 3 sleeping cabins on each side with 2 berths in each, but the manager kindly ordered that I should have a cabin all to myself Buckland [Lady Franklin's maid] being in another...The narrowed part of the main cabin between these for sleeping formed a kind of after cabin in which was a small table which was treated as *our* [italics in original] property—here my Aunt & I breakfasted whenever we pleased, & had our tea also...

Thursday, March 7. We untied ourselves & started again by daylight... A little beyond one of the villages was a burying place, consisting of rows of large boxes or chests raised from the ground, and ornamented with figures carved in relief...

We passed a few miners only—all Chinamen, on the edge of the river, rocking their cradle so constantly & intently, that they seldom even raised their heads as we passed. They keep to their own costume & look as quaint as they do in pictures, with their round, pointed hats. Behind them was either a cotton tent, or a little wooden hut sufficient for the 2 of them. They were rarely more.

Friday, March 8. We were fortunate in finding here [at Yale] one of their winter habitations, which again reminded me of the pictures in my child's book of this part of the world. It consists of a great hole, or excavation, or rather burrowing sufficiently large to hold many people. I believe several families occupy one, as they do a single lodge. Over the top a great mound of earth is raised,

CHAPTER 5

and trodden into a compact roof in the centre of which is a hole which alone affords light & air, and the means of getting in and out by a ladder made of a notched trunk of a tree. We looked down this hole into the "sweating house" as it is called—now empty— but Mr Crickmer [Anglican cleric at Yale] came down into it some little time ago when it was fully occupied by its usual winter population. He says the heat was something awful!

Monday, March 11. [Returned to the Moodys' house.] The main point at issue here is the union of the vast territory of British Columbia, with the vastly smaller one contained within Vancouver Island. The fact that B. Columbia is governed by a Chief residing in Vancouver Is^d is a pill too bitter for the pride of a British Columbian! It irritates them even to reason upon the point; and they argue that the Governor ought to pass half his time with *them* [italics in original] & spend half his salary for their benefit...

All people speak with great admiration of the Governor's intellect—and a remarkable man he must be to be thus fit to govern a colony... He has read enormously we are told & is in fact a self educated man, to a point very seldom attained. His manner is singular, and you see in it the traces of long residence in an unsettled country, where the white men are rare & the Indians many. There is gravity, & a something besides which some might & do mistake for pomposity, but which is the result of long service in the H.B.Co^s service under the above circumstances...

Back in Victoria the women "went over the bridge, to an iron foundry & near the Indian village."

Thursday, March 22. We walked home through a street hitherto unknown to us, chiefly the resort of the Indians (who however are seen everywhere throughout the towns—in the morning carrying cut wood for sale; the women, baskets of oysters, & clams)—with shops kept mostly by foreigners, fish being generally sold by Italians. We stopped at one & my Aunt said a few words to him in Italian which enchanted him I could see. There were many Germans & plenty of Chinese—"Wo Sang—washing & Ironing done here"—"Gee Wo—washing"—I only remember these two names at this moment—the Chinese wash & iron particularly well. They are very industrious & well behaved.

There are also many Jews in the Community—most of them from Central Europe.

Sunday, March 24. [Left for San Francisco.] Altogether this visit to Vancouver Is^d & British Columbia has been a very pleasant, as well as a deeply interesting one, and we trust to see the colonies encrease in prosperity—the foundation of which must be laid in emigration from England, or at least from English colonies, so as to absorb (or at least outweigh) the American element...

It is the ladies who are most to be pitied as they must absolutely & unreservedly devote themselves to the smallest cares of every day life—at any rate they must *expect* [italics in original] to have their hands so filled day by day & be prepared for the worst. But there is a set off to this in the fact that all are in the same predicament & there is not the least pretense to anything better. There is not a single lady in the colony who has a nurse, a cook, & a housemaid, so she has to be one of these, if not all three—this state of things saps mere conventionality at the very root—strong friendships are formed, and people are ready to help one another. There is something very interesting too, in watching the growth of a young colony which is making rapid strides as this does, especially when a good standard of civilization & morals have existed from the very first. Nothing could have produced this but the constituting it into a distinct See with a resident Bishop, whose vocation is a standing witness against the sordid tendencies of a gold producing colony.

As a community, the people of Vancouver's Island seem a very contented one—enterprising, yet without the grasping of Americans who are never satisfied unless they find themselves preeminent, if not alone in the field; and the wonderful growth of the colony during its 2 years only of existence, is highly to the credit of its people.[74]

---

74   Blakey Smith, ed., *Lady Franklin Visits the Pacific Northwest.*

CHAPTER 5

Back to the everyday life of Bishop Hills

The departure of Lady Franklin and her niece Sophia Cracroft in late March 1861 returned Bishop Hills to the everyday, whose successes and failures he interspersed, as was his wont, with new adventures and understandings.

A week later Hills garnered a small victory respecting the admission into the girls' school of a student whose mother had "a strong prejudice against Colour," but who then "gave way & confessed she had managed her scruples & would now place her child & keep her there until she was full educated."[75]

In early April Hills visited "an earnest & intelligent...coloured family" in New Westminster he had known almost since his arrival, who lived opposite the school of the Catholic Sisters of St. Ann, which their daughter attended, informed how when "the Americans & others (English) objected to the mixture of Coloured & others (English)," the Catholic bishop had obligingly ordered their separation, whereupon "the Coloured children were then all withdrawn."[76] It was, and continued to be, one step forward, one step back.

Another yearly round in British Columbia

In May 1861 Bishop Hills began his third yearly round in British Columbia. Leaving Victoria on the evening of Tuesday, May 28, he along with three other Anglican clerics arrived in New Westminster the next morning and visited locally before boarding a vessel that "reached Douglas about 6 o'clock & encamped in an unoccupied corner of the Garden of the" local Anglican cleric.[77]

The local Lillooet people were first off the mark to host the arrivals. "After breakfast an old chief & his friends came to see me" and made arrangements for a visit:

> At the Quay a handsome Canoe was waiting to take us to the Village. The crew consisted of two bright eyed & smartly dressed young ladies & two others of the same sex. We were escorted upon landing at the Village by a numerous party & soon entered

---

[75] March 5, 1861, entry in "The Journal of George Hills," 1861: 32.

[76] April 3, 1861, entry in "The Journal of George Hills," 1861: 36; Killian, *Go Do Some Great Thing*, 60.

[77] May 28–31, 1861, entry in "The Journal of George Hills," 1861: 59.

a large house capable of containing 800 people. This was the mansion of Jim Douglas, the principal Chief. About a hundred Indians were present. They laid mats. We took our places & all the rest sat down. I commenced by telling them who I was and what I had to deliver to them.

Over the course of the day spent in Douglas, Hills "went round & called upon most of the people" including "Italians, Germans, Norwegians, French, Africans," and "Americans, Scotch, English & Irish—Canadians were also seen." Later, when donations were entertained, "among contributors to Douglas Church were Americans, Germans, Norwegians, Africans." In the evening a "White Man's Service" was held, to use Hills's term, which "the Indians" requested and received permission also to attend. "They filled up the many parts of the room & stood around the door outside & listened at the windows."[78]

Come Sunday, June 2, at Douglas, Hills held three separate religious services. At 11 a.m. "people of various nations were present."

> At 3 pm we went to the House of the Indian Chief "Jim Douglas." Above 160 were present. Mats were placed for us to stand & sit on. The chief stood up in the midst of his people & directed their movements. We instructed them in simple truths. They were dressed in their best. After we had finished a party belonging to another chief desired instruction at his house & thither Mr Garrett went. [That evening] we again had service in the Town... We had fewer than in the morning... Indians were present in the morning & Evening who hung about the doors & crowded at the windows.[79]

Monday, June 3, Hills and the others were on the road again, rising "at ½ past 3" and setting off after breakfast to the 4 Mile House, 10 Mile House, where "a Swiss named Perry entertained," and "reached the 20 mile House—the Host at ½ past 2 having walked the distance including stoppages in 8 hours... In the Evening until dark Indians surrounded our tent & eagerly received our Instruction. I

---

78   May 31, 1861, entry in "The Journal of George Hills," 1861: 61.
79   June 2, 1861, entry in "The Journal of George Hills," 1861: 63.

CHAPTER 5

explained elementary Xtian Truths."[80] The next day they travelled by pack train and boat to Pemberton, but the following day was a disappointment: "Rose at 4, it rained. We waited till 11 before we started & then off in the rain. The road is bad, a mere mountain track."[81]

The days as narrated in Hills's journal had a certain similarity, the Anglican clerics trudging from place to place—Anderson Lake, Seton Lake, Cayuse, Lillooet, Lytton, Boston Bar, Spuzzum, Yale, Hope—with evening services sometimes poorly attended. "I preached...there were 10 persons besides ourselves. One of them was a Mexican"—with hopeful references in Hills's account to numbers of attendees or distinctiveness, as with the lone Mexican on June 6.[82]

Wherever Hills went he sought to preach both to whites and to Indigenous people, sometimes together, more often separately. For Indigenous people, having the bishop preach to them in their own building was a special event, as happened at Yale on the last Sunday of June 1861, during which Indigenous people seemed to believe they were genuinely interacting with whites on their own terms. And perhaps they were, at least in the moment, so Hills recounted in his journal:

> At three o'clock the Indians were assembled in the Chief's House to the number of about a hundred. They were called together by themselves by the ringing of a bell. The sight was highly picturesque. All were dressed in their best, some in good suits of black cloth, with silk neckcloths, white shirts & rings. Others had got cloth trousers with a scarlet or other bright coloured shirt a la Garibaldi with a crimson scarf. The ladies were in all stages of attire from the more humble & simple dress to the latest fashion. The hair went from the most dismal dishevelment to the neatest plait. All wore clothes in articles of foreign manufacture shewing they had completely left their native modes & that they were good customers to the shops.
>
> Mats were laid before us—and new ones on a raised seat for us... At the close of each of our addresses all uttered a loud cry of approval and we were occasionally interrupted by some one

---

80   June 3, 1861, entry in "The Journal of George Hills," 1861: 64–65.

81   June 5, 1861, entry in "The Journal of George Hills," 1861: 66.

82   June 6, 1861, entry in "The Journal of George Hills," 1861: 67.

calling out—good talk—good talk & pointing reverently upwards towards Heaven.[83]

Hills's perceptions of the state of affairs

Four days later, on July 4, 1861, as "American Guns were fired" at twelve noon to honour the United States' Declaration of Independence, signed on that day in 1776, Hills took note in his journal how "now the Flag did not wave so haughtily, since no longer are the States United." The American Civil War was in play; slave-owning southern states had broken away from the eighty-five-year-old union, putting its future into question. "In firing the guns at 12 the attempt was made to raise a cheer but no hearts or voices were in turn."[84]

A week later, amidst his daily entries, Hills ruminated on race, this time less hopefully than earlier. Drawing on what a local Hills considered credible had shared with him, the information found its way into his journal without editorial comment:

> The half breeds he said do not turn out well. When brought up in good company they do. Otherwise they drink & are dissolute. The cause of their failure thus far is that men from Canada, not the best but worst, came amongst the Indians. Only the scum of the women w^d consent to receive them. So the alliance on both sides was low.
>
> The better Indian woman would not allow a white man to catch them. In some tribes rather than such should happen a woman would destroy her own life.[85]

It was almost inevitable that race won out in his journal entries, especially when it was joined in Hills's mind with an uneasy attitude toward what he perceived, perhaps despite himself, as unacceptable female behaviour.

Following stops in the Fraser Valley, Hills returned to Victoria on August 3, 1861, a little over two months after starting out on his summer road trip.

---

83   June 30, 1861, entry in "The Journal of George Hills," 1861: 90–91.
84   July 4, 1861, entry in "The Journal of George Hills," 1861: 96.
85   July 11, 1861, entry in "The Journal of George Hills," 1861: 104.

CHAPTER 5

Another mighty adventure

Bishop Hills's pursuit of souls across much of today's British Columbia almost inevitably lured him to the Cariboo gold rush. Heading there from Victoria on June 16, 1862, Hills and two others took the sternwheeler *Enterprise* to New Westminster along with "10 horses six of whom were heavily laden," and in the company of "a good number just arrived from N. Zealand & Australia" to try their luck in the Cariboo rush. The contingent boarded a "River boat with 84 Passengers & 40 Horses" with an overnight stop at Hope to stay with the local Anglican cleric, doing much the same at Yale. There Hills preached on Sunday morning "at the House of Tom the Indian Chief, where about 98 Indians were assembled," and later in the day for whites "hardly supplying a dozen," which he attributed to the population consisting "almost entirely of Jews & Americans."[86]

Aware that smallpox had "made its appearance," Hills and the others came prepared and while at Yale vaccinated "about 30 or 40 of the Spuzzum tribe" and later others as requested. Hills described the process:

> The scene was very striking as Indians of all ages were grouped around with one arm bare waiting for their turn. I showed them the mark on my arm & told them it was done when I was an infant…The readiness with which these tribes trust us & yield to our advice is a great proof of their confidence in us of the opening for higher and better objects than care of the body.[87]

Next came a stop at Lytton, where to Hills's and the others' disappointment they only "met 3 or 4 British subjects, the rest of the people are French, American & Mexican." Hills had brought with him "a plan for a Church at Lytton but… found no encouragement to propose it." Stopping at a nearby farm, he was all the same impressed by barley being cut for hay, and potatoes "looking well" as did turnips and beets. They once again camped before Hills and one other headed to Lillooet, where they had the advantage of new road construction.[88] "The change is like magic," Hills observed in his journal on July 3.[89]

---

86   June 23, 1862, entry in "The Journal of George Hills," 1861–62: 62–68.

87   June 23, 1862, entry in "The Journal of George Hills," 1861–62: 69–70.

88   June 29–30, 1862, entry in "The Journal of George Hills," 1861–62: 74.

89   July 3, 1862, entry in "The Journal of George Hills," 1861–62: 77.

Hills and the others pushed on, holding religious services at road camps on Sundays, admiring working farms from time to time, and reaching Williams Lake on July 14, 1862, Alexandria a few days later. Hills now considered himself "in the Cariboo country," so he penned in his journal. His entries would be awash over the next two months, to mid-September, with the requisite gold miner stories, interspersed with weekly religious services so far as feasible. Among the bits of information Hills jotted down in his journal was, after a discussion with a "Frenchman... long away from France," how a "miner can live for 3 or 4$ a day, giving himself three meals a day, with flour, beans, bacon, sugar, tea, coffee, dry apples xc."[90]

Sunday, September 7, Hills held two services at Williams Lake with "not a dozen present at either."[91] Leaving Dog Creek on September 10, Hills and the others were joined by various persons along the way. Reaching Yale on September 22, Hills learned from the recently appointed Anglican cleric, Henry Reeve, how "a subscription has been commenced for a Church," with contributors including twenty names, likely local merchants, in a community where, Reeve told Hills, "there were about 200 residents," of whom "but 5 are Englishmen." As for the evening's congregation, "there were present 2 Jews, 1 Romanist [Catholic], 2 Methodists, 1 Cantonese," and "one a professing member of the Ch of England." Not unexpectedly, Henry Reeve looked "to the Chinese & Indians with more encouragement than that of the white population... Such is our work," Hills editorialized at the end of his journal entry.[92] The Anglican Church was in effect doing double duty, not only attending to parishioners, but also looking after the community.

Yet another adventure

Less than a month after returning to Victoria at the end of September 1862, Hills was off again. Almost as soon as the *Grappler* left Victoria on October 27, fog caused it to anchor. Given "there was a goodly gathering of the ships' company & settlers on board & the awning was lighted by lanterns," Hills, never one to pass over an opportunity to do so, preached.

Two days later at Comox, which Hills described as a "very active & bona fide settlement" with substantial log and lumber houses, and rich soil, he "went

---

90 August 13, 1862, entry in "The Journal of George Hills," 1861: 122.
91 September 7, 1862, entry in "The Journal of George Hills," 1861–62: 143.
92 September 22, 1862, entry in "The Journal of George Hills," 1861–62: 152.

CHAPTER 5

on shore to visit settlers." There he "found Mr. Pidcock son of a Clergyman in England," who had brought letters of introduction when he arrived in British Columbia and was now keeping a store. Hills noted how "there were about 37 or 40 settlers, amongst them but two women."[93]

When Hills returned to preach in Comox three years later in November 1865, he would count "about 70 white inhabitants" with "six white families." Hills was not best pleased by some of their behaviour:

> I visited a Settlers House close by—(Mitchell) who lives with an Indian wife... Many settlers live with Indian women. Such is the fall of a young man (named Pidcock) son of a Clergyman in England & himself once a Communicant. As the Indians passed his hut they shouted in a way showing they had but little respect for him.
>
> Another case is that of (Muster) the son of an English Clergyman who lives unmarried with a person who was a servant in the family & has two children. He has an allowance & refuses to marry her because he says his allowance [almost certainly from his family in England] would be withdrawn if he did. He drinks and ill uses her. She has once or twice gone to live with another & even now while living with Muster contemplated being married to a man expected shortly from Cariboo. Can anything be more melancholy than such a state of things! Then the poor Indians are close lookers on upon all this depravity in the white race...
>
> I visited the house of a man (named Wilson) who once lived with Indians in the way above stated he has under better influence given up his sin heartily ashamed.[94]

The gender disparity, according to Cowichan historian Eric Duncan, may have arisen because sixty some single Englishmen, including Reginald Pidcock, who had previously been a clerk in London, arrived there in 1862. They accomplished much, including building the first sawmill.[95] But Hills had by now

---

93   October 28–29, 1862, entries in "The Journal of George Hills," 1861–62: 164–65.
94   November 21, 1865, entry in "The Journal of George Hills," 1865–66: 97–98.
95   Eric Duncan, *Fifty-Seven Years in the Comox Valley* (Courtenay: Comox Books, 1979; orig. 1934), 31.

almost certainly garnered another insight, becoming aware that, given almost all newcomers were men on their own, and white women were in short supply if accessible at all, even some men respectable by his lights had partnered, or would partner, with Indigenous women.

The 1862 trip continued with stops at Nanaimo and then the Cowichan where "several young English Gentlemen offered to do all they could to help" so as "to have everything English & reproduce English religion & civilization." Hills "observed that Settlers when they first come out are more anxious about such higher advances than they are afterwards," hence "we sh^d take hold of this good feeling while it is warm."[96] Hills returned to Victoria on November 6 from his eleven-week mighty adventure.

Victoria's conflicted sense of self

Four days later, on November 10, Hills attended what he termed "a fitting observation of the coming of age of the Prince of Wales." Born in 1841, Queen Victoria's eldest son, Edward, known as Bertie, would remain her heir for almost four decades until his mother's death in 1901. The celebratory dinner to which Hills was invited was chaired, he described in his journal, by "Major Thomas Harris a patriotic Englishman who by industry as a Butcher & Contractor has attained the honorable position of first Mayor of the City of Victoria." This was the man Lady Franklin had visited in 1861, who Sophia Cracroft had described as "plain, worthy people, without any pretension." At the table, Hills noted proudly, "the Governor [was] on his right hand & myself on the left." Other dignitaries including Captain G.H. Richards, head of the British survey of Vancouver Island then underway, and the "R. Cath. Bishop" were accorded lesser positions at the dinner table.[97]

All well and good, but not quite.

Continuing with his description of the celebratory event, Hills wrote in his journal, "The most intense Patriotism seemed to prevail, I was struck also by the strong southern sentiment."

> There were French & American residents present the latter from the South. The Band amongst other tunes played "Dixie land" which carried the people beyond all bounds, they stamped—shouted &

---

96 November 4, 1862, entry in "The Journal of George Hills," 1861–62: 170–71.
97 November 10, 1862, entry in "The Journal of George Hills," 1861–62: 175–76.

encored. The Mayor & Capt. Richards the senior naval officer were anxious to stop it, lest it should seem a demonstration of British authorities upon the question. They would not be stopped, nor would the band obey orders, but Dinner went on. The Governor made an admirable speech.[98]

It turned out, Hills described in his journal, that an event earlier in the day backgrounded the evening's proceedings:

> In the morning a Secession Flag had been hoisted in the Town, upon which the American Consul hauled his down & was followed by all the N. American Inhabitants who took no part in the proceedings of the day. Towards the afternoon the Consul thought better of it & raised his Flag again, but not before he had written to the Governor a letter to say why he & others of his nation took no part in the proceedings. This circumstance, a sad mistake on the part of the American, may have added intensity to the feeling of the Evening.
>
> The tone of the company was rough & unruly, at the end one individual insisted upon returning thanks to the Municipal Council. The Mayor had already done so. Being also somewhat inebriated & threatening to say something, a body of either his friends or his foes or both forcibly carried him out of the room. His Excellency [Douglas] previous to this had retired from the disorder.[99]

Hills was not sure what to make of the evening's events, recording in his journal how "on the whole I think good will have come from this demonstration of loyalty."[100]

The middle way

Hills continued his daily and seasonal rounds in much the same fashion until his return to England in the spring of 1863 to raise funds to sustain his work in British

---

98   November 10, 1862, entry in "The Journal of George Hills," 1861–62: 176.

99   November 10, 1862, entry in "The Journal of George Hills," 1861–62: 176–77.

100 November 10, 1862, entry in "The Journal of George Hills," 1861–62: 177.

Columbia. While there, Hills married a vice-admiral's daughter, with whom he returned to British Columbia at the beginning of 1865. Four years after her death in 1888, Hills resigned as bishop of British Columbia and again returned to England, where he died three years later in 1895.[101]

In those critical years of the early 1860s in present day British Columbia, Bishop Hills provided a middle way between the top-down approach of the governor and the Colonial Office concerned with income and expenses, roads and settlements—and the occasionally racist and sexist views of white settlers and gold miners who did not see Black, Chinese, and Indigenous peoples, including Indigenous women, as human beings like themselves. Although Hills came with his own assumptions and biases, he for the most part tolerated and accepted everyone—though maybe not Roman Catholics—welcoming them to his church and enjoying their company, setting an example for others.

---

[101] The information comes from Bagshaw, *No Better Land*, 17–18 and 38, fn 16; and Friesen, "George Hills."

CHAPTER 6

Taking Gold Miners Seriously (1858–71)

Beneath the surface of events, as penned from the top down—be it by James Douglas, Bishop Hills, or from within the Colonial Office—everyday life from 1858 onward was, in the future British Columbia, all about gold miners. Given most prospective miners arrived via Victoria on Vancouver Island, and often retreated there over the winter months, which were generally unsuitable for gold mining, Vancouver Island's residents might be said to have lived off miners, whereas Indigenous women sometimes lived with them. These circumstances are obvious in retrospect, just as they were obvious at the time to those willing to acknowledge what was happening. Victoria as the major area of non-Indigenous settlement in the future British Columbia depended on gold miners' lucre, even as its residents sought to carry on their everyday lives as genteelly as possible.

It is also clear in retrospect that except for gold miners there would have been no gold rush, and except for the gold rush there would have been no mainland colony of British Columbia created in 1858. Whether Vancouver Island would have survived as a British colony cast on its own resources is impossible to know in retrospect. What is certain is that without the gold rush, today's province would have had no immediate impetus to come into being in the form it did in 1871.

Given American aspirations to have the entirety of the North American west coast, more so after the United States acquired Alaska in 1867, today's British Columbia mainland might well have gone to its southern neighbour then, if not earlier as compensation for Britain having permitted the breakaway southern states to construct ships on British territory during the American Civil War. Instead, the British colony of British Columbia, by then including Vancouver Island, became a province in 1871, thereby extending the reach of Canada across the North American continent from the Atlantic to the Pacific Ocean. This development is to a considerable extent, if not wholly so, the gold miners' legacy.

Gold miners mattered. They mattered a lot despite their almost total absence from the everyday written records originating in the Colonial Office except as objects to be critiqued and found wanting, as opposed to being actors in the course of events. If not for gold miners there would almost certainly have been no British Columbia.

Taking gold miners seriously

Taking British Columbia seriously is to take gold miners seriously. In doing so, it is necessary to keep in mind that they were real live persons in past time, not unlike ourselves in the present day.

Taking gold miners seriously is to rethink the long-held perspective, still visible in the historiography, that sees them as rowdy and contentious, as "fighty boys" to borrow my daughter's childhood characterization of some of her schoolmates. Accounts from this perspective, including some recent monographs, run the danger of marginalizing gold miners to no real gain.[1]

Accounts that sideline gold miners from the time of their arrival in the future British Columbia, from 1858 onward, echo Vancouver Island governor James Douglas's uncertain attitude toward them. Rather than accepting his observations, introduced in Chapter 3, as the way things were, we need to scrutinize them, reflecting on how his long career in the fur trade in charge of men over whom he had direct control on behalf of the London-based Hudson's Bay Company caused him to find gold miners' varied origins alien, even more so their independence of mind and action. Douglas perceived them as intruders, if not

---

[1] Among earlier monographs that come to mind are D.W. Higgins's *The Mystic Spring and Other Tales of Western Life* (Toronto: William Briggs, 1904) and his *The Passing of a Race and More Tales of Western Life* (Toronto: William Briggs, 1905), partially reprinted in David William Higgins, *Tales of a Pioneer Journalist: From Gold Rush to Government Street in 19th Century Victoria* (Surrey, BC: Heritage House, 1996). Recent accounts include in alphabetical order Marie Elliott, *Gold in British Columbia: Discovery to Confederation* (Vancouver: Ronsdale Press, 2019); Donald J. Hauka, *McGowan's War* (Vancouver: New Star Books, 2003); Christopher Herbert, *Gold Rush Manliness: Race and Gender on the Pacific Slope* (Seattle: University of Washington Press, 2018); Robert Hogg, *Men and Manliness on the Frontier: Queensland and British Columbia in the Mid-Nineteenth Century* (London, UK: Palgrave Macmillan, 2012); and Daniel Marshall, *Claiming the Land: British Columbia and the Making of a New Eldorado* (Vancouver: Ronsdale Press, 2018).

CHAPTER 6

on his turf of Vancouver Island, then on the adjacent mainland which was, from his perspective, HBC turf. Writing near the end of 1858 following a trip to the goldfields, Douglas described how, despite "some of them no doubt respectable," he had never seen "more ruffianly looking men" who "will require constant watching, until the English element preponderates."[2]

It was not only Douglas, and thereby the Colonial Office, who marginalized gold miners as "so wild, so miscellaneous," as they were described in the British House of Commons debate of July 1858 respecting the faraway mainland becoming a separate British colony.[3] Gold rushes from 1848 in California and 1851 in Australia had already informed attitudes. Prospective miners' willingness to cross long distances and unknown terrain in the hope of better lives for themselves and their families was far less newsworthy than the drama of the unexpected and its ensuing dangers.

The principal London newspaper, *The Times*, had not known initially what to make of the Fraser River gold rush. Its special correspondent Donald Fraser began reporting from San Francisco on June 4, 1858, his initial account reaching London in time to appear on Wednesday, August 4. The arrival of "a steamer from Vancouver's Island with ... news of the most glowing and extravagant tenor as to the richness of the new gold country in the British possessions" was irresistible as a news story, and its successors over the next number of years continued to be so.[4]

Fraser's accounts were initially from San Francisco, where he was based, then from the future British Columbia, to which he speedily made his way. His articles sold newspapers, encouraging some readers to head to the gold rush, others to dream of doing so or at least to follow the remarkable course of events. The dates in the following excerpts indicate when stories were written as opposed to when they appeared in London newspapers.

> San Francisco, Monday, June 16, 1858. The fever all over the State is intense and few has escaped its contagion ... the "rush" from San Francisco knows no cessation ... From the 1st of this month till

---

[2] Douglas to Merivale, Private, October 29, 1858, 586, CO 60:1.

[3] Speech by Sir Edward Bulwer Lytton, July 8, 1858, House of Commons, *Hansard's Parliamentary Debates*, vol. 151, 1090–1121.

[4] Donald Fraser, "Articles on British Columbia Printed in the London Times, Aug. 4, 1858– Aug. 15, 1862," BC Archives, E/B/F86 (hereafter "Donald Fraser Articles").

to-day (June 17th), seven sailing vessels and four steamers have left San Francisco, all for the new mines...One of the steamers carried away 1,000 persons, and another upwards to 1,200, and multitudes were left behind waiting for the next departure. There are still 13 vessels on the berth for the same destination, all filling with passengers and goods...The eagerness to get away is a mania... People seem to have suddenly come to the conclusion that it is their fate to go. "Going to Fraser's River?" "Yes, oh, of course, I must go."[5]

Victoria, Vancouver's Island, Wednesday, September 9, 1858. Visited Murderer's Bar, three to four miles below Fort Hope. Most of the miners are Cornish men, from California...Twenty log cabins erected...125 miners...The space allotted to each miner is 25 feet in width, running from the high water mark down into the river as far as he chooses to go. The miners are all satisfied with this arrangement, and all are quite ready to pay a license to Her Gracious Majesty of 1£ a-month...The miners all intend to winter on this bar in their log cabins. Provisions are cheap and abundant. They can buy plenty of salmon and potatoes from the Indians. The cost of living is $1 a-day to each man.[6]

Accounts tended to be at one and the same time dramatic and encouraging, if likely too honest for some readers:

Up the river from Fort Hope, September 12, 1858. Indians complain that the whites abuse them sadly, take their [derogatory term for Indigenous women] away, shoot their children, and take their salmon by force. Some of the "whites" are sad dogs...

The work is not heavy; any ordinary man can do it. The time of work is generally 10 hours. Every man works much or little, according to the dictates of his own sweet will. Independence and hope make up the sum of his happiness.[7]

---

[5] Donald Fraser, *London Times*, June 16, 1858, in Donald Fraser Articles.
[6] Donald Fraser, *London Times*, November 30, 1858, in Donald Fraser Articles.
[7] Donald Fraser, *London Times*, September 12, 1858, in Donald Fraser Articles.

CHAPTER 6

In his daily journal Anglican bishop George Hills, preaching in the gold fields, similarly pointed to miners' figurative, if not also literal, authority over their everyday life:

> August 27, 1862. Everything must be in accordance with the will of the miners. The habits, the mode of speaking, the dress & such like... There nobody alters his dress from one day to another & so nobody stays away on that account for want of clothes. All come in their red shirts or such like also come to Worship.[8]

The gold rush's appeal

Part of the gold rush's appeal lay in its being an ever-moving feast of possibilities for men daring to be caught up in its ethos, which was externalized in miners' dress. Robert Burnaby, a thirty-year-old Englishman with pretensions to gentility, who arrived in Victoria in late 1858 to sample the gold rush, evoked in an early letter home the "diggers from Frazer River, frozen out now, but going back again in the spring, such picturesque looking fellows with fine manly faces bearded, with red and blue shirts, etc. just as you see in drawings of them," by then circulating in the English press.[9] The vivid impression captured by Sophia Cracroft, Lady Franklin's niece (introduced in Chapter 5), after the two women travelled by steamer from Victoria to New Westminster, was more detailed but not dissimilar:

> Our fellow passengers were pretty numerous, chiefly miners & of many races. French, German & Spanish were spoken, to say nothing of unmitigated "Yankee." Most of them had their pack of baggage, consisting of a roll of blankets to the cord of which was slung a frying pan, kettle & oilcan. Some possessed the luxury of a covering of waterproof cloth to the package. Every man had his revolver & many a large knife also, hanging from a leather belt. I

---

8   April 27, 1862, entry in "The Journal of George Hills," 1861–62: 41, in typescript in Ecclesiastical Province of British Columbia, Archives.

9   Robert Burnaby to his mother, December 26, 1858, in Anne Burnaby McLeod and Pixie McGeachie, *Land of Promise: Robert Burnaby's Letters from Colonial British Columbia* (Burnaby, BC: City of Burnaby, 2002), 59.

should say that this mining costume in "highest style" consists of a red shirt (flannel), blue trowsers [sic], boots to the knees, and a broad brimmed felt hat, black, grey, or brown, with mustaches ad libitum.[10]

For a moment in time, gold miners could be who they would be, unfettered by the pretensions and assumptions of right behaviour whence they came.

The superiority of Englishness

Even as miners dressed similarly and were repeatedly so depicted, they brought with them a diversity of backgrounds, causing Governor James Douglas to lament "that so few of Her Majesty's British subjects have yet participated in the rich harvests reaped in British Columbia."[11] On the other hand, a contemporary told Hills, which almost certainly gladdened his heart, that there were "amongst the Miners such books as Gibbon, Macaulay, Shakespeare & Plutarchs' Lives."[12] Still read in the present day are Edward Gibbon's *History of the Decline and Fall of the Roman Empire*, originally published in six volumes between 1776 and 1788; Thomas Babington Macaulay's *History of England from the Accession of James the Second* in five volumes between 1849 and 1861; William Shakespeare's plays; and Plutarch's *Lives of Noble Greeks and Romans*.

That some gold miners were English was comforting to Hills and Douglas, and to lonely others. Writing in July 1860, half a year away from England, Hills enthused in his daily journal over an encounter at Canada Flat, which would become Lillooet, with "a company of 7 Englishmen" who "live in two log huts," several from Cornwall, all arrived in British Columbia via California, out of touch with their family in "the old country" and "glad to talk about old England."[13]

Douglas's predisposition for all things English not unexpectedly contained a class component. Responding in 1861 to the suggestion "that a Magistrate should

---

10   Sophia Cracroft, March 5, 1861, in letter reproduced in Dorothy Blakey Smith, ed., *Lady Franklin Visits the Pacific Northwest: Being Extracts from the Letters of Miss Sophia Cracroft, Sir John Franklin's Niece, February to April 1861 and April to July 1870* (Victoria, BC: Provincial Archives of British Columbia, 1974), 38.

11   Douglas to Newcastle, Separate, September 16, 1861, CO 60:11.

12   April 30, 1862, entry in "The Journal of George Hills," 1861–62: 42.

13   July 7, 1860, entry in "The Journal of George Hills," 1860: 154.

be appointed to reside on Admiral (or Salt Spring) Island" consequent on "an Indian disturbance," Douglas prevaricated as to how "I have made it a rule to select those local Magistrates from the respectable class of Settlers," but "none of the resident settlers on Salt Spring Island having either the status or intelligence requisite to enable them to serve the public with advantage in the capacity of local Justices, no appointment was, simply for that reason, made."[14] That such persons would be English was taken for granted.

A disdain of everyday miners extended to Douglas's other actions, as with this assertion to the Colonial Office at the beginning of 1861:

> There is no prospect of material increase in Land Sales for 1861, except through the effect of emigration from Canada and Great Britain, as there is a very small farming population in the Colony; the working classes being chiefly miners, accustomed to excitement, fond of adventure, and entertaining generally a thorough contempt for the quiet pursuits of life.[15]

If miners could not be British, being Canadian was second best. To this preference might be added Douglas's description three years later respecting the Members of Council he had just appointed for Vancouver Island that they were "gentlemen of education, approved loyalty, good estate, and high moral worth."[16]

Attitudes from the top down assuming the superiority of Englishness almost inevitably loosened, at least somewhat, over time. Writing in 1865, British Columbia governor Frederick Seymour asserted how "the Majority of the population in Lytton, Quesnel Mouth, and I believe some other towns, is alien." He was nonetheless willing, given "the central Government is sufficiently strong to enable me to do so with perfect safety to the Public," to "propose allowing those not under allegiance to the British Crown a share in the management of these small municipalities."[17]

---

14   Douglas to Newcastle, No. 5, Civil, January 8, 1861, CO 305:17.

15   Douglas to Newcastle, No. 7, Financial, January 26, 1861, CO 60:10.

16   Douglas to Newcastle, No. 15, Legislative, February 14, 1862, CO 305:17.

17   Seymour to Cardwell, No. 135, May 17, 1865, CO 60:71.

Gold miners from their own perspectives

Douglas's attitude says as much about Douglas as it does about gold miners, whether or not they came with reading material in tow. Once we take gold miners seriously, on their own terms, a more nuanced perspective comes into view. The gold rush gave a long generation of young and not-so-young men from around the world the opportunity to seek to become who they wanted to be, with greater freedom to do so than they would almost certainly have had whence they came. They could for at least a brief moment in time, perhaps for a lifetime, reimagine themselves. Everything seemed possible and eminently doable given, by one early description, "the Gold searching is principally carried on by Sluicing, which is effected by means of ditches constructed with great skill and sometimes at great length."[18]

Very importantly, it was not only Douglas but also gold miners who perforce lived at least for a time between two worlds: that of their upbringing and that of an occupation which in the moment captured their attention. For those who were British in background, the transition from whence they came to where they were headed might have been the most difficult to navigate. Long-time Colonial Office employee Arthur Blackwood, not without reason, characterized a British Columbia resident about to visit England in 1864 as "coming home."[19]

Families back home lost out, at least in the moment. Gold miners in British Columbia were beyond easy communication, and possibly had no communication at all, with the outside world until the completion of a telegraph line in the mid-1860s. During an evening stroll while preaching across the mainland in the summer of 1861, Bishop Hills came upon a miner in a solitary cabin at Lillooet who said he had a family in Cornwall with whom he had long since lost contact. "He talked of the roving and unsatisfactory life of the miner. He said many men got on hard but that they preferred it to some civilized existence. Some however went & became reckless."[20]

Not all non-Indigenous men who set down in British Columbia originated as gold miners. Two days after his encounter in Lillooet, Bishop Hills, who travelled

---

18   Murdoch and Rogers, Colonial Land and Emigration Office, to Merivale, February 7, 1860, CO 60:9.

19   Minute by AB^d [Blackwood], July 27, 1864, on Seymour to Newcastle, No. 6, May 19, 1864, CO 60:18.

20   June 17, 1861, entry in "The Journal of George Hills," 1861: 80.

CHAPTER 6

by horseback with a few others, passed by the holdings of Donald McLean, a well-educated Scot who, during his four decades as a Hudson's Bay Company employee, had children with three different Indigenous women and who, rather than abandoning them when the HBC wanted to transfer him elsewhere, abandoned the fur trade to become a rancher around the Company's post of Fort Kamloops. Another visitor at about this time considered "McLean's Station, the best farm in the colony," describing how "the enterprising and industrious proprietor has valuable stock of cattle" along with "fine turnips, cabbages, and scarlet-runners."[21] Hills found as much to praise as to query. Granted, "all of the children of Mr Mclean are from Indian mothers" and "the younger boys are fine children but wild as colts." On the other hand, McLean "has some fine cattle" and assured Hills he "should be glad of visits if a clergyman could be provided & he w^d see all things made comfortable for them."[22] It is fair to say Hills was, at least in the moment, charmed by a family setting he might otherwise have found wanting.

Hills's conversation a few days later with a group of "English miners" gave him a dose of reality, so he penned in his daily journal:

> Miners seldom get rich all allowed. Many had fine opportunities & realized large returns for a time but seldom retained the results of their labour & good fortune... They were away from home ties & restraints of society so they gave themselves up to do whatever they were tempted to do—so gambling, drinking, several pleasures soon wasted the substance. They allowed that every man kept an Indian [woman].

As if to validate the miners' perspectives, Hills noted, when he was talking soon after with the local storekeeper, "the impudent [derogatory term for Indigenous women] of whom he was ashamed & whom in vain he tried to get out of our sight," but "she would not go."[23] Indigenous women, whatever the circumstances, had minds of their own.

A talk a week later with "a shoemaker" in Hope resulted in Hills being asked to have £20 sent to the man's wife "through Archdeacon Hill at Chesterfield"

---

21 W. Champness, *To Cariboo and Back in 1862* (Fairfield, WA: Ye Galleon Press, 1972; orig. 1865), 86.

22 June 20, 1861, entry in "The Journal of George Hills," 1861: 81.

23 June 26, 1861, entry in "The Journal of George Hills," 1861: 88–89.

in England, to which Hills agreed given "he seems a worthy man."[24] The Colonial Office files in London are awash with letters from families desperate not so much for money as for word, any word at all, from sons and husbands long since out of touch.[25] How many gold miners disappeared from view by choice or circumstance is impossible to know.

The nature of gold mining

Whatever the time period, gold mining meant going where gold was to be had. Rushes were just that: mad dashes to the latest finds, the next one hopefully richer than its predecessors. Travelling up the Fraser River in November 1860, well-educated Englishman Robert Burnaby, who had arrived two years earlier with the customary gentleman's letter of introduction from the secretary of state for the colonies, Sir Edward Bulwer Lytton, to James Douglas, and had subsequently pursued this and that, observed in a letter home how "the 'Bars' [gravel ridges or bars extending across river mouths, hopefully containing gold flecks] which in '58 were crowded with diggers are now quite deserted, seamed up with trenches and heaps of 'dirt' here and there, an occasional Chinaman may be seen rewashing the leavings."[26] A bit farther up the river Burnaby mused to his faraway mother:

> The last Bar before reaching Yale is called Hills Bar and this has been as productive of Gold as any place, not only in B. Columbia, but even in California. This used to be the headquarters of the Yankee rowdies [underlining in original] —and early in 1859 there was a serious disturbance there, it used to be quite a town, with half a dozen bars, two or three Billiard tables etc., but now it is no more than a heap of gravel, and all its wealth is taken away.[27]

---

24 July 1, 1861, entry in "The Journal of George Hills," 1861: 92–93.

25 Though sometimes they *were* seeking money. For example, Elizabeth Ross, Inverness, to Cardwell, May 5, 1864, CO 60:20, was inquiring about money owed her deceased son by his employer, with minutes on the letter suggesting some ways for her to apply for help through governmental or private means.

26 Robert Burnaby to his mother, November 9, 1860, in McLeod and McGeachie, *Land of Promise*, 150; also Madge Wolfenden, "Robert Burnaby," *Dictionary of Canadian Biography*, vol. 10, http://www.biographi.ca/en/bio/burnaby_robert_10E.html.

27 Burnaby to his mother, November 9, 1860, in McLeod and McGeachie, *Land of Promise*, 152.

CHAPTER 6

The nature of gold mining was such that men reinvented themselves by chance or choice. For some it meant moving on to the next known find, then to the next, and so on. For others it meant returning home; for yet others, making new lives on the mainland or on Vancouver Island.

For Burnaby a shiny new mining option was coming into view. He described it optimistically to his sister in April 1861 from Victoria:

> We are now at the turning point of spring—when the island is most lovely—all the rocks, plains and woods turning with the prettiest wild flowers and flowering shrubs...With these flowers and sunshine our usual hopeful season arrives. In a "gold country" everything is at a standstill during the winter; the Miners cease working, come into town to "loaf" and spend their earnings—there is much talk of the past and hope for the future which bursts forth in a sort of excitement, when the start for the upper country begins. We have already been favoured with tremendous reports from the "Cariboo" country—a tract far up in B. Columbia.[28]

The news got better and better. Come October Burnaby enthused to his mother how "the news from the goldfields is as wonderful, as I always said it would be," with "men coming down, daily almost now, who have gone up, without a penny, and bring down £500 to £1200, the result of six weeks or two month's work."[29]

Burnaby was not alone in his observations. After considerable assessment of routes, Judge Matthew Begbie observed at the beginning of 1863 how Williams Creek in the Cariboo was "the admitted centre of mining population, energy, and (up to the present time) riches and quantity of diggings." There "houses were rapidly springing up at convenient intervals."[30]

It was also the case that the nature of gold mining in the Cariboo in narrow, steep-sided, and isolated creek beds made it a business requiring extensive financial resources as opposed to mining's earlier dependence on individuals' hard

---

28 Burnaby to his sister Harriet, April 15, 1861, in McLeod and McGeachie, *Land of Promise*, 159–60.

29 Burnaby to his mother, October 6, 1861, in McLeod and McGeachie, *Land of Promise*, 162.

30 "Judge Begbie to Colonial Secretary," January 19, 1863, enclosed in Douglas to Newcastle, No. 9, Miscellaneous, February 2, 1863, CO 60:15.

work and good fortune. The Cariboo would be British Columbia's last great gold rush destination, but of a very different kind than its predecessors.

Minding the gold rush

That the British Columbia gold rush proceeded as well as it did was due in good part to the two men initially in charge, James Douglas on site and Sir Edward Bulwer Lytton in faraway London, acting expeditiously separately and together. When, as described in Chapter 2, Lytton, the secretary of state for the colonies, made the case in the British House of Commons for today's British Columbia mainland being made a new British colony, he drew on information in Douglas's letters, along with his own literary bent, and on the powerful imagery of gold for the taking. Lytton excited the imagination by alluding to "settlers so wild, so miscellaneous, perhaps so transitory" and "persons of foreign nations and unknown character" of whom, he acknowledged, "few, if any, have any intention to become resident colonists and British subjects." Lytton laid down a challenge respecting a new colony "eminently suited for civilized habitation and culture," whose acquisition was too delicious for the Colonial Office to resist.[31]

Douglas was not then, or ever it seems, quite sure what to make of gold miners. His everyday relations seem to have been cordial, yet he repeatedly wrote otherwise in his letters to the Colonial Office, as on December 27, 1858: "I would hardly venture to give a decided opinion on the subject of recruiting a regular military Force, from the Gold Diggers of the Colony, as the men taking service would probably be composed of the idle and worthless classes."[32]

Neither Lytton nor Douglas ventured much beneath the surface of events in respect to gold miners as fellow human beings. Douglas's earlier oversight of the far-flung fur trade contributed to his outlook. When visiting the gold fields extending from today's Fraser Valley through the Cariboo in central British Columbia, Douglas for the most part kept his distance from the miners, though a handful are mentioned by name and possibly engaged with Douglas in casual conversation, mostly because they were British or seemed so.

Likely influenced by Douglas's assessments, the Colonial Office had no more truck with gold miners than was necessary. A minute by long-time clerk Arthur

---

[31] Speech by Sir Edward Bulwer Lytton, July 8, 1858, House of Commons, *Hansard's Parliamentary Debates*, vol. 151, 1090–121.

[32] Douglas to Lytton, No. 56, December 27, 1858, CO 60:1.

CHAPTER 6

Blackwood on a February 2, 1863, letter from Douglas was indicative: "As for the miners they are only fit for digging and washing for gold." They were the antithesis in Blackwood's view to "persons of respectability."[33]

Gold miners had, all the same, to be overseen. Across British Columbia this was done by regional gold commissioners. As defined by the Colonial Office in 1859, "the Gold Commissioner is to be a Justice of the Peace with power to try and settle summarily all mining disputes and abate encroachments." His task was to oversee "the area for each free Miner being a square of one hundred feet," and to "mark out plots of 5 acres for the occupation of the Miners as Gardens or residences, and other plots for the occupation of traders."[34] Commissioners were to report periodically to the governor of British Columbia. Two such reports from the summer of 1866, by which time the practice was firmly in place, are revealing as to what mattered on the ground respecting British Columbia's foundational gold rush.

Peter O'Reilly, who had served in his previous life in the Irish Revenue Police, reported in June 1866 from French Creek in eastern British Columbia that "though the new gold fields have not been extended as much as expected," there has still been "a very marked improvement." The past winter had not treated men well. "No doubt the miners have suffered severely, as few were possessed of means sufficient to enable them to remain in the country, in consequence of the scarcity and high price asked of every article of consumption."[35]

Cariboo gold commissioner William G. Cox, a Dublin banker seduced by the gold rush, described from Richfield, located near the principal Cariboo gold rush town of Barkerville, how its population is "steadily increasing both in white men and in Chinese," the latter "spreading themselves over the country and appear to be doing remarkably well, ... in fact I have not before seen such a general feeling of prosperity and satisfaction since I have been here ... As a general rule the miners have nothing this season to complain of. The water in the creek

---

33 Minute by AB[d] [Blackwood], April 1, 1863, on Douglas to Newcastle, No. 9, Miscellaneous, February 2, 1863, CO 60:15.

34 Rogers to Merivale, November 17, 1859, CO 60:5; report by Peter O'Reilly, gold commissioner, December 4, 1862, enclosed in Douglas to Newcastle, Separate, December 4, 1862, CO 60:13.

35 Report by O'Reilly, June 30, 1866, enclosed in Birch to Cardwell, No. 52, July 10, 1866, CO 60:25.

is abundant without being troublesome. There is no sickness on the Creek and very few patients in the Hospital."[36]

A year earlier, British Columbia's governor Frederick Seymour had taken note on his visit to Williams Creek in the Cariboo of "a very creditable hospital supported by private contributions and a Government allowance of a thousand a year" that is "extremely clean and well managed."[37] Cox was similarly impressed a year later. "Grouse Creek still continues attractive, and is likely to rival Williams Creek in its richness and in their number of claims paying... there are about 400 men on the creek, and a Town is being rapidly built up. All appeared well satisfied and contented."[38]

Estimating numbers of miners

However much we track individual gold miners and sites, it is when we turn to the numbers that we come to realize the British Columbia gold rush was a serious business for a lot of people. It played an important role, whatever the men's origins, in the coming into being of the Canadian province we know today as British Columbia.

Parsing the numbers is also humbling in that they are at best only suggestive, given their limited scope and the toing-and-froing of the two colonies' newcomer populations. Settlement as we have long tended to conceive it was not quick to come into being, except in Victoria, prior to British Columbia becoming a Canadian province in 1871.

Whatever the time period, gold miners came and went for a variety of reasons. Those given by miners departing at the end of the seminal 1858 season were "various, some having families to visit and business to settle in California, others dreading the supposed severity of winter weather, others alleging the scarcity and high price of provisions, none of them assigning as a reason for their departure the want of gold."[39] Writing the next spring, Douglas blamed earlier departures on the lack of an assay office to determine the value of gold that was

---

36 Report by William G. Cox, gold commissioner, July 1, 1866, enclosed in Birch to Cardwell, No. 52, July 10, 1866, CO 60:25.

37 Seymour to Cardwell, No. 33, March 24, 1865, CO 60:21.

38 Report by W.G. Cox, July 1, 1866, enclosed in Birch to Cardwell, No. 52, July 10, 1866, CO 60:25.

39 Douglas to Lytton, No. 40, November 30, 1858, CO 60:1.

mined so that "hundreds of miners worn out with the expense and delay so occasioned, headed in disgust to San Francisco" where their gold could be quickly assayed.[40] Two months later Douglas added to the "various reasons for leaving the country...the high price of provisions, others, a desire to see their friends and to spend a few months comfortably in California; others the irregularity and shallowness of the diggings."[41]

While overall numbers of arrivals in no way approached those of the earlier California and Australia rushes with their hundreds of thousands across a considerable number of years, they mattered, however imprecise the totals, to the course of events in what was until then a wholly Indigenous place apart from a smallish number of fur trade employees.

Population totals are at best suggestive. At the beginning of July 1858, James Douglas informed the Colonial Office that 10,573 passengers had so far arrived by water from San Francisco, which did not include those coming from elsewhere or by land routes.[42] A month later he estimated "about 10,000 foreign miners, in Fraser's River," then the heart of the gold rush.[43] The British consul in San Francisco reported in mid-October 1858 that 24,000 persons had that year left San Francisco for Victoria, with just 2,000 having so far returned.[44]

People moved around the British Columbia colony at will. In early November 1858, as the gold mining season was winding down, Douglas estimated, based on local reports, "the mining population in Fraser's River" was:

From Cornish Bar to Fort Yale	4,000
Fort Yale	1,300
Fort Hope	500
From Fort Yale to Lytton	300
Lytton	900
Fort Lytton to Fountain	3,000
Port Douglas & Harrison River	600
Total	10,600[45]

---

40   Douglas to Lytton, No. 127, Financial, April 8, 1859, CO 60:4.
41   Douglas to Lytton, No. 167, June 8, 1859, CO 60:4.
42   Douglas to Stanley, No. 29, July 1, 1858, 7833, CO 60:1.
43   Douglas to Stanley, No. 34, August 19, 1858, CO 60:1.
44   Edmund Hammond, Foreign Office, to Merivale, October 19, 1858, CO 60:2.
45   Douglas to Lytton, No. 30, November 9, 1858, CO 60:1.

Writing at the end of November Douglas reported that "the exodus from Fraser's River continues at about the rate of 100 persons a week."

In February 1860, based on information received from Douglas and others, the Colonial Office put numbers of miners, probably based on 1859 estimates, as:

Between Hope and Yale	600
Yale and Fountain	800
Fountain and Alexandria	Unknown
Alexandria and Quesnel River	1,000[46]

Two months later, with spring in the air, Douglas described "the constant accession to the population of British Columbia, by the influx of Miners."[47] Newcomers were not necessarily from Britain itself, but very possibly "foreign," to use Douglas's 1860 description as to how "unfortunately the population of this Colony is almost without exception foreign."[48]

From then onward arrivals from China were dominant. Douglas informed the Colonial Office in January 1860 how "a detachment of 30 Chinese miners arrived yesterday, being it is supposed the pioneers of a large immigration of that people for British Columbia."[49] In April, Douglas described how "a great number of Chinese Miners [underlined in original] were...taking up mining claims on the River Bars, in the Lytton district, who are reputed to be remarkably quiet and orderly," and more generally how "British Columbia is becoming highly attractive to the Chinese, who are arriving in great numbers—about 2000 having entered Frasers River since the beginning of the year and many more are expected from California and China." Douglas was ambivalent, given that from his perspective "they are certainly not a desirable class of people, as a permanent population, but are for the present useful as labourers and as consumers, of a revenue paying character."[50] Come July 1860, "about a thousand white miners are working on Fraser's River between Alexandria and Lytton and about four

---

46   Murdoch and Rogers, Colonial Land and Emigration Office, to Merivale, February 7, 1860, CO 60:9.
47   Douglas to Newcastle, No. 39, Financial, April 21, 1860, CO 60:7.
48   Douglas to Newcastle, No. 42, April 23, 1860, CO 60:7.
49   Douglas to Newcastle, No. 8, Miscellaneous, January 24, 1860, CO 60:7.
50   Douglas to Newcastle, No. 42, April 23, 1860, CO 60:7.

CHAPTER 6

thousand Chinese miners are employed in the various districts of the Colony."[51] The Colonial Office reported how "the present fixed population—if so it can be called—of B. Columbia is probably 7000," comprised of "3000 Whites" and "4000 Chinese," while "the population of Vanc. Island in 1859 may be assumed as amounting to 3500."[52]

In February 1861 "about 300 miners were then employed in that vicinity [of Hope], a large proportion of whom were Chinese; and that it was probable there would be a considerable emigration of that class towards Rock Creek and Shimilkomeen [Similkameen] in the course of the spring." In the Yale District,

> the mining claims are with few exceptions in the hands of the Chinese, there being about Two Thousand of this people within the district. As a rule they have been successful and many have returned to their homes the possessors of from Two to Four thousand dollars. There are but few white miners…There are about Two Thousand Chinese in Yale and its environs alone. The cold weather has put a stop to all mining operations.[53]

An internal Colonial Office memorandum in March 1863 estimated the resident population of the mainland colony as:

Scattered—Indians	say 10,000
Chinese	say 5,000
Miners (500 miles from N.West)	5,000
(350 miles from N.West)	500
Totals;	20,500[54]

The calculation excluded "2000 persons scattered along the 500 miles between New Westminster and Cariboo and along the 350 miles between New

---

51   Douglas to Newcastle, Separate, July 6, 1860, CO 60:7.

52   Notes added in the Colonial Office to W. Elmsley to Under-Secretary of State [unnamed], July 21, 1860, CO 60:9, enclosing the original of the petition of May 22, 1860, from Westminster residents to Secretary of State for the Colonies.

53   Douglas to Newcastle, Separate, February 28, 1861, CO 60:10.

54   Newcastle, "British Columbia and Vancouvers Island," memorandum, March 27, 1863, enclosed in Arthur Helps, Whitehall, to Fortescue, June 12, 1863, CO 60:17.

Westminster and Rock Creek, and occupying, besides New Westminster and the Diggings, some half-dozen intermediate villages along these two lines." Nothing was long term, assuredly, given "a find of Gold here or there may at any time change the relative importance of these different clusters of residents." As well, "a few years will make a great difference," given "the progress of the Country is very fast."[55] In July 1863 Douglas commended Chinese miners' utility: "I have lately received intelligence that valuable discoveries of rich mining ground have been made by some Chinese Miners on the Banks and alluvial flats of Bridge River about 20 miles from the Town of Lillooet."[56]

By February 1864 the population of Vancouver Island was estimated at "about 7500 persons exclusive of Indians," which if accurate was likely linked to some one-time gold miners settling down there.[57] Come October, Seymour, the new governor of British Columbia, put its white population at about seven thousand, with the Indigenous population at about sixty thousand.[58]

British Columbia's non-Indigenous population

Whatever their origins and locations, the non-Indigenous population of the British Columbia colony in particular was, consequent on the gold rush, dramatically skewed by sex. A February 1860 British government report, likely based on numbers from James Douglas, noted: "The White population of the Colony amounts to 5000 men with scarcely any Women or Children."[59]

Over the next several years, British Columbia non-Indigenous totals continued to be skewed by gender. According to Douglas, writing in the spring of 1861, "the actual population, Chinamen included, is about 10,000, besides a native Indian population exceeding 20,000," respecting which "it must be remembered that all the white population are male adults,...there being no proportionate number of women or children," by which he meant, and took for granted, white

---

55 Newcastle, "British Columbia and Vancouvers Island," memorandum.
56 Douglas to Newcastle, Separate, July 2, 1863, CO 60:15.
57 Helmcken as Speaker of the Legislative Assembly to Douglas, February 9, 1864, in Douglas to Newcastle, No. 3, Legislative, February 12, 1864, CO 305:32.
58 Seymour to Cardwell, No. 56, October 4, 1864, CO 60:19.
59 Murdoch and Rogers, Colonial Land and Emigration Office, to Merivale, February 7, 1860, CO 60:9.

women and white children.[60] Three years later, in March 1863, the Duke of Newcastle pointed out how "there is comparatively little white population in the Colony."[61] Four months later Douglas described "the immigration of this year so far consists of about four thousand five hundred persons (4,500 persons), chiefly able bodied men, exclusive of women and children, a class of which this Colony is still lamentably deficient."[62]

Everyday consequences of a skewed gender balance in the white population

Male comradery in far distant locations went only so far. Given white women were mostly absent, the alternative for men wanting more was to turn to Indigenous women, with references to their doing so maligning the character of the men directly or by inference. Among early Colonial Office dispatches was an 1849 London newspaper article critiquing the HBC with respect to "the gross immorality which prevails in respect of the Indian women."[63]

However much "white blood" mattered, and it certainly did, the practical option for many, perhaps most, newcomer men on their own and lonely was an Indigenous woman. Men who partnered with Indigenous women did so with differing consequences, depending in part on their placement in the social order, such as it was. While some men escaped scrutiny, others did not, especially if they were named to government positions. Among those "at present unknown to me" who incoming British Columbia governor Frederick Seymour appointed to the Legislative Council at the beginning of 1864 were Henry Maynard Ball of Lytton and John Carmichael Haynes, who had "managed admirably in the establishment of law and order among the miners."[64] Also named were William George Cox and John Boles Gaggin as assistant gold commissioners in the Cariboo.[65]

---

60 Douglas to Newcastle, Separate, April 22, 1861, CO 60:10.
61 Newcastle, "British Columbia and Vancouvers Island," memorandum.
62 Douglas to Newcastle, Separate, July 2, 1863, CO 60:15.
63 *Daily News*, February 17, 1849, CO 305:2.
64 Seymour to Cardwell, No. 59, October 7, 1864, CO 60:19.
65 On Haynes see Seymour to Cardwell, Nos. 71 and 72, November 25 and 26, 1864, CO 60:19; on Cox and Gaggin, Seymour to Cardwell, No. 72, November 26, 1864, CO 60:19; also Margaret A. Ormsby, "John Carmichael Haynes," *Dictionary of Canadian Biography*, vol. 11, http://www.biographi.ca/en/bio/haynes_john_carmichael_11E.html.

A severe shortage of white women in British Columbia meant that partnering with an Indigenous woman was the only option for most miners, like these photographed at the Mucho Oro claim at Stouts Gulch ca. 1868. *Image A-00613 courtesy of the Royal BC Museum.*

What is clear respecting these four men, each of whom merits attention as indicative of a larger phenomenon, is that personal qualities were perceived at least to some extent to override attitudes in the dominant white society that scorned the unions in which they engaged. Some might get a pass, as had James Douglas; others did not.

Two years after his arrival from England in 1859, thirty-six-year-old Henry Maynard Ball described himself as "an officer and gentleman, both civil & military."[66] He was also a married man, with a wife and two young sons back in England. Deemed ideal governance material, Ball was dispatched to Lytton as a justice of the peace and stipendiary magistrate.

By the spring of 1861 Ball's future was, it seems, in shambles. On May 30 almost a hundred "merchants, miners and mechanics of Lytton City and District" petitioned Governor Douglas "that Judge Ball be removed from office

---

66   Henry Maynard Ball, police magistrate, to private secretary of Governor James Douglas, Lytton, June 3, 1861, in CO GR 1372, box 1354, file 1344.

CHAPTER 6

immediately." The first among numerous complaints was his "living with an Indian woman not married to him but keeping her as a public prostitute when he acknowledges that he has a wife & children in London City" to whom he sent support money quarterly.[67]

Ball denied all the complaints except for one: "There is one part of the charges, which I admit is true. I live with an Indian woman, who acts as my housekeeper, and as an excuse for this, I must state that I am isolated here without companions, without society, and have to pass my evenings in a dreary state of solitude—I therefore resorted to the alternative with which I am charged."[68]

Ball's defence had two parts.

First, "I have never allowed this connection to interfere with my public duties, in any way, and I defy any body to assert to the contrary."

Secondly, "His Excellency cannot but observe that the signatories with few exceptions are those of foreigners and Chinamen, many of whom must have been ignorant of what they were signing, and His Excellency must also observe that the signatures of the most respectable portion of the inhabitants are wanting."

A letter of support signed by nine local merchants made the same two points. "Though he like all men may have erred," it had not interfered with "the gentleman's reputation." The ninety-three signatories on the petition represented "the seeming desires of a large portion of the floating population of Lytton."[69]

Ball kept his job. He left Lytton four years later and remained in government service until his retirement in 1881.[70]

The second individual, twenty-eight-year-old Irishman John Carmichael Haynes, had come to British Columbia, like most others, for the gold. He was assisted on his arrival at the beginning of 1859 by his English uncle's acquaintance with Chartres Brew, British Columbia's recently appointed superintendent of police and gold commissioner.[71] This connection got Haynes an almost

---

67   Petition to Governor James Douglas, Lytton, May 30, 1861, in CO, GR 1372, box 1354, file 1344.

68   Ball's response and the petition of support described in the following paragraphs are in CO GR 1372, box 1354, file 1344.

69   Petition to Governor James Douglas, Lytton, June 3, 1861, in Colonial Correspondence, GR 1372, box 1354, file 1344.

70   "Henry Maynard Ball (1825–1897)," typescript in BCA, VF.

71   Hester E [Haynes] White, "John Carmichael Haynes," *British Columbia Historical Quarterly* 4, 3 (1940): 183.

immediate appointment as a constable in the heart of the gold rush.[72] Two years later Haynes settled in Osoyoos in the Okanagan Valley, which would remain his home as he rose through the ranks as a magistrate, government official, and rancher, eventually owning a mighty twenty-two thousand acres of land.[73] It was Haynes's success in collecting customs duties and maintaining law and order that caused the governor to appoint him a member of the newly instituted Legislative Council of British Columbia in 1864.[74]

Haynes had two children with a Colville woman remembered as Julia: Mary Anne, born in 1866; and John Carmichael, born two years later, named after his father. The story long circulating has Haynes continuing to live in the bachelor quarters of the government building at Osoyoos while keeping, just a few yards away, a "separate little log house for his Indian 'wife.'"[75] As to Julia's identity, Christine Quintasket, a Colville woman born about 1885, who published under the pen name "Mourning Dove" to wide acclaim that continues into the present day, is said to have had a white paternal grandfather.[76] In one version of Quintasket's story, he was "an Irishman" who "apparently married her Indian grandmother under the false pretenses of a tribal ceremony. His name was Haynes (or Haines)."[77]

Whatever the particulars, Haynes moved on. The same year his namesake son was born, Haynes, by then aged thirty-seven, married eighteen-year-old Charlotte Moresby, who had come to Victoria with her parents. Her father was a London barrister and younger brother of Sir Fairfax Moresby, admiral of the British Fleet. Charlotte died following the birth of their second child.[78]

---

72 White, "John Carmichael Haynes," 183.

73 Margaret A. Ormsby, ed., *A Pioneer Gentlewoman in British Columbia: The Recollections of Susan Allison* (Vancouver: UBC Press, 1976), 167n.

74 White, "John Carmichael Haynes," 189–90.

75 Conversation of Hamilton Laing with Allan Brooks, recounted by Allan Brooks to Jean Barman, Black Creek, February 23, 1993; Robert M. Hayes, "Pioneer Judge Had Three Families," *Kelowna Daily Courier*, January 8, 1997.

76 Mourning Dove, *Mourning Dove: A Salishan Autobiography* (Lincoln: University of Nebraska Press, 2021), among other editions.

77 Hum-ishu-ma, "Mourning Dove," in *Cogewea, the Half-Blood: A Depiction of the Great Montana Cattle Range* (Lincoln: University of Nebraska Press, 1981), vii; also Ormsby, "John Carmichael Haynes," which ignores this relationship altogether.

78 George J. Fraser, *The Story of Osoyoos, September 1811 to December 1952* (Penticton: Penticton Herald, 1952), 77; White, "John Carmichael Haynes," 198.

CHAPTER 6

Again Haynes moved on. In January 1875 he wed Emily Pittendrigh, who had come to British Columbia three years earlier with her family, her father distinguished by his service in the Crimean War.[79] They would have six children together between 1875 and 1886, the oldest honoured as "the first white child born in Osoyoos."[80]

Born in 1822 in Ireland, the third of the four men, William George Cox, had been a banker in Dublin before deciding he had had enough and moving to New York with his bride. Within the year she returned home, Cox having been enticed west by the British Columbia gold rush. Arriving with a testimonial to colonial surveyor J.D. Pemberton, Cox quickly rose in status...with one wrinkle.[81] His wife tracked him down. Her letters demanded financial support even as he was caught up with an Indigenous woman he described "so sweetly" in a letter to his brother back home in Ireland as "nice & delicate and in native simplicity refined" [underlining in original].[82] However long that relationship lasted, she at some point disappeared from view.

Cox's position as a member of the British Columbia Legislative Assembly in 1867 and 1868 could not shield him from his wife's wrath in the form of letters to all and sundry. As summed up by Helmcken: "Cox was a marked man whether on account of his vote or outside relations I know not. Letters came from his wife anyhow to the Government asserting her destitution. Cox went to California...The further history and end of poor Cox—I do not remember."[83]

The fourth individual, John Boles Gaggin, was yet another Irishman, in his case from a "most respectable" family, who prior to heading to British

79 White, "John Carmichael Haynes," 198.
80 Fraser, *The Story of Osoyoos*, 78.
81 Sue Dahlo, "William Cox: Gold Commissioner," Boundary Historical Society, Report 13 (1995), 31–33; Mrs. W.G. Cox to Governor Seymour, November 5, 1868, and W.A.G. Young to Mrs. W.G. Cox, January 4, 1869, cited in Margaret A. Ormsby, "Some Irish Figures in Colonial Days," *British Columbia Historical Quarterly* 14, 1–2 (1950): 75.
82 Unsigned letter to W.G. Cox, September 21, 1860, reproduced in Ormsby, "Some Irish Figures in Colonial Days," 68.
83 Dorothy Blakey Smith, ed., *The Reminiscences of Doctor John Sebastian Helmcken* (Vancouver: UBC Press, 1975), 234. On Cox, see also G.R. Newell, "William George Cox," *Dictionary of Canadian Biography*, vol. 10, http://www.biographi.ca/en/bio/cox_william_george_10E.html.

Columbia had served in the Royal Cork Artillery Militia. Through family connections, he wrangled a letter from the secretary of state for the colonies, Sir Edward Bulwer Lytton, "in favour of a Mr John Gaggin of the Royal Cork Artillery...to certify that he is a respectable person."[84] Gaggin was thereupon shortly after his arrival in April 1859 appointed chief constable in Yale, becoming in October the magistrate and assistant gold commissioner at Douglas.

Visiting the settlement at Douglas two and a half years later in May 1862, Bishop Hills was in his daily journal not kind to Gaggin. As to the reason:

> Almost every man in Douglas lives with an Indian woman. The Magistrate Mr. Gaggin is not an exception from the immorality. Recently the constable Humphreys was ordered to a distance by the Magistrate. The Indian woman he lived with was named Lucy, by whom he had a child. He proposed to take her with him. The magistrate was for some reason opposed. [The constable asked,] May I depend upon your honour that she shall be safe during my absence. The magistrate promised such should be the case. He violated the promise & induced the woman to come to him.[85]

Gaggin was dismissed from his position when Vancouver Island and British Columbia were united in 1866, which reduced the number of appointed positions.[86]

Indigenous women had not fared well in any of the four cases. They were expendable.

---

84 Quoted in Dorothy Blakey Smith, "John Boles Gaggin," *Dictionary of Canadian Biography*, vol. 9, http://www.biographi.ca/en/bio/gaggin_john_boles_9E.html.

85 May 20, 1862, entry in "The Journal of George Hills," 1862: 50; also Ormsby, "Some Irish Figures in Colonial Days," 63, 69. Humphreys's and Lucy's story is told in depth in Jean Barman, *Invisible Generations: Living between Indigenous and White in the Fraser Valley* (Halfmoon Bay, BC: Caitlin Press, 2019).

86 Ormsby, "Some Irish Figures in Colonial Days," 69; also Michael F.H. Halleran, "Thomas Basil Humphreys," *Dictionary of Canadian Biography*, vol. 11, http://www.biographi.ca/en/bio/humphreys_thomas_basil_11E.html.

CHAPTER 6

Turning to the Cariboo

The Cariboo gold rush beginning in 1861 was an afterthought to the 1858 British Columbia gold rush that had garnered headlines around the world, even though it was distinctive by virtue of its remote location. Compared to the older gold rush, mining in the northerly, increasingly favoured Cariboo was almost wholly seasonal. Douglas reported in February 1863 "the great body of Miners having left the District on the approach of winter, ... causing the suspension of work for nearly seven months in the year." There remained over the winter of 1862–63 at the most 350 men, which Douglas attributed to "the scarcity and high prices of food."[87] The upside was, from Douglas's perspective, twofold: "rendering agriculture a more attractive pursuit and teaching settlers by the inducement of cheap land and high prices to give up the mines for the more certain realization of the farm."[88]

As the next winter approached, Douglas wrote in November 1863 how "it is thought that a considerable number of people will remain here during the winter months—it is generally said 1000, but this I doubt, many who have almost made up their minds to remain will I think fly as soon as the severe weather sets in." Indicative of miners' uncertainty, Douglas added in the same letter, "the miners are now retreating in great numbers from Caribou [sic] and other remote Districts of the Colony on account of the apprehended severity of winter."[89] Writing in May 1865, Douglas's successor as governor of British Columbia, Frederick Seymour, similarly lamented how "the Upper Country is almost deserted in the winter. The Miners have left the Colony. The communications are closed."[90]

Miners thinking of settling down

For many miners, if not all of them, at the time they arrived the British Columbia gold rush was in their heart of hearts a passing fancy. They anticipated returning home richer than when they came, or moving on to some more interesting setting than British Columbia or Vancouver Island, both very much still in the making as opposed to being already made.

---

87   Douglas to Newcastle, No. 11, February 3, 1863, CO 60:15.
88   Douglas to Newcastle, No. 11, February 3, 1863, CO 60:15.
89   Douglas to Newcastle, Separate, November 13, 1863, CO 60:16.
90   Seymour to Cardwell, Separate, May 18, 1865, CO 60:21.

TAKING GOLD MINERS SERIOUSLY (1858–71)

Men from throughout North America and beyond were drawn to the gold fields of British Columbia in hopes of striking it rich. Many returned home, but others, like this miner shown with his horse, dog, and a bag full of gold, chose to remain in BC, where their descendants live to this day. *Photo courtesy of Jolene Cumming.*

Most men soon departed, but others did not. They came for gold, but what they found was a place of being to call their own. The attractions were various, possibly including an Indigenous woman with whom to partner, along with a piece of land to know as their own in a valley, along a plain, or on an island. So it was that the place we know as British Columbia began to come into being.

Miners' transformations were in their essence a matter of individual initiative related to circumstances and possibilities. Some miners were from early on at least thinking of settling down in the interim if not for longer. So gold miners contributed to the well-being of British Columbia for purposes familiar or convenient to them. Douglas reported in June 1859 respecting the completion of "a safe, easy, and comparatively inexpensive route into the interior of British Columbia," how "the people of Port Douglas have expressed their willingness to aid either by their personal labour or by pecuniary contributions in the important work, as however none of them are wealthy, their contributions will not be great but their zeal for the progress and prosperity of the country is encouraging to us and very honorable to themselves."[91] In April 1860, in connection with the construction of a portion of his long-sought road, Douglas described the use of "the larger Lillooet Lake as a water communication," mentioning specifically how "the application of some enterprising settlers to run a Steamer without any special privilege on the larger Lillooet Lake has been granted, and will greatly facilitate transport" given "an excellent mule trail 30 miles in length with substantial bridges over all the rivers [has] connected the larger Lillooet Lake with Lake Anderson."[92]

Travelling in July 1861 from Hope to New Westminster, by which time it was legally possible to take up land, Bishop Hills "observed considerable open land on either side of the Fraser & many cabins as signs of preemption, much land especially near Langley on both sides."[93] Taken "over in Mr Brown's boat" to his farm opposite New Westminster, Hills was so impressed he included the story in his daily journal:

> He began in April, & has now some 13 acres either under cultivation or ready. There are some 5 acres of potatoes, a large portion ready for use, though put in only in May. Swedes turnips who are first coming up also. There are 11 sorts of vegetables also Cucumbers. The land is rich loam with clay bottom & if the water can be kept out must become very valuable. There is about 300 acres of such land. If New Westminster goes on—this will be worth in my opinion a large sum in 5 years.[94]

The non-Indigenous population at New Westminster as elsewhere was sharply differentiated by gender. A census taken a couple of months earlier in April 1861 "found there 290 persons, of these about 30 only are women (not checking female children)."[95]

The passage of time made miners more likely to stick around. According to Vancouver Island governor Arthur Kennedy, over the winter of 1865–66 "a larger number of miners wintered at the mines than theretofore," whereas previously

---

91   Douglas to Lytton, No. 167, June 8, 1859, CO 60:4.
92   Douglas to Newcastle, No. 42, April 23, 1860, CO 60:7.
93   July 16, 1861, entry in "The Journal of George Hills," 1861: 112.
94   July 30, 1861, entry in "The Journal of George Hills," 1861: 114.
95   April 4, 1861, entry in "The Journal of George Hills," 1861: 37.

most miners had retreated over the winter to Victoria or California.[96] A year later British Columbia governor Frederick Seymour wrote in his report of a visit to the gold fields how "the miners are doing well & a population is settling down in Cariboo & its neighbourhood."[97] Judge Begbie was less confident, writing following his own visit a few weeks later as part of his regular circuit: "Not much gold taken out lately—and the prospects of a large out-turn...have quite changed. Many hundreds of men were thrown out of work i.e. one fourth or more of our efficient population" with "a couple of thousand men at work mining."[98] There would be an even greater contraction when on September 16, 1868, Barkerville was destroyed by fire, although rebuilding began almost immediately in what was a tribute to the sturdy way of life that had grown up there.[99]

More than elsewhere, due to distance, Cariboo miners for the most part got on with their lives on their own terms. The Cariboo was British Columbia's last great gold rush destination, and by this time the gaze of the dominant society had lessened. Gold miners had lost much of their initial status as unwanted outsiders.

---

96   Kennedy to Cardwell, No. 48, Separate, June 26, 1866, CO 305:28.

97   Seymour to Buckingham, Private, June 26, 1867, CO 60:28.

98   Matthew Begbie to Thomas Begbie, July 8, 1867, CO 60:31.

99   Granville George Leveson-Gower, 2nd Earl Granville, secretary of state for the colonies, to Seymour, No. 3, December, 29, 1868, NAC RG7:G8C/15.

CHAPTER 7

Crediting Indigenous Women

The tendency during the early years of non-Indigenous men's presence in the future British Columbia to view Indigenous women as lesser persons than their non-Indigenous counterparts was widespread at the time and would long continue to be so. The notion is so engrained, both in everyday life and in the dominant historiography, as needing to be excised not once, but time and again.

Even as Indigenous women could be, and all too often were, stereotyped by virtue of their racial descent and set upon by non-Indigenous men as objects of sexual desire, something else was also happening during the critical quarter century between 1846, when the land base of today's British Columbia was awarded to Britain, and 1871, when that land base became the west coast province of British Columbia.

Indigenous women had their own reasons for accommodating, when they chose to do so, the newcomer men's sexual desires—those reasons, while difficult to intuit given the paucity of first-hand accounts from women's perspectives, are not impossible to imagine. The time is long past when we might deny Indigenous women being determined, tough, and rational persons with minds of their own, who lived in sometimes impossible circumstances during those years when British Columbia hung in the balance.

Indigenous women during the fur trade

The presence of Indigenous women in the lives of non-Indigenous men long preceded the gold rush, being an everyday aspect of the fur trade of the early nineteenth century, which almost inevitably legitimized at least some of their gold-mining successors acting similarly. Prior to Vancouver Island coming into existence as a British possession in 1849, such relationships were commonplace. James Douglas, long before he became governor of the colony of Vancouver

Island, had partnered with the daughter of the fur trader in charge of his first Hudson's Bay Company posting in the Cariboo and of a woman of Cree and French Canadian descent. Despite their wedding in a Christian ceremony as soon as it was possible to do so, unions cutting across white assumptions of acceptability would long be suspect, to some extent continuing to be so into the present day.

Vancouver Island's being made a British colony in 1849 under the aegis of the Colonial Office masked but did not hide its fur trade ambience. Numerous of the men who had a family with an Indigenous woman, or a woman of Indigenous descent, took advantage of the opportunity Vancouver Island gave them to settle down.

Examples abound of men come west with the fur trade who did so. William Henry McNeill and John Lemon are among those recorded as holding twenty or more acres of land on Vancouver Island, with Frederique Minie and Louis Trudelle among those purchasing town lots in Victoria.

Born in Boston in 1801, William Henry McNeill early on commanded vessels along the Pacific coast on behalf of the Hudson's Bay Company. In about 1831 he partnered with Matilda, a chief's daughter who Vancouver Island medical doctor John Sebastian Helmcken recalled as "a very large handsome Kijani woman, with all the dignity and carriage of a chieftainess," which she was, the Kijani being a division of the Haida-language group.[1] The McNeills had nine children together before Matilda, according to Helmcken writing at the end of 1850, "died just before her confinement, attended by Indian women from hemorrhage after twins had been born."[2] In 1866 McNeill turned to a Nass woman named Martha by whom he had no children.[3] McNeill appears to have had divided loyalties, being among the signatories on an 1869 petition to the American president supporting the annexation of British Columbia to the United States.[4]

---

1   Dorothy Blakey Smith, ed., *The Reminiscences of Doctor John Sebastian Helmcken* (Vancouver: UBC Press, 1975), 108; Derek Pethick, *S.S. Beaver: The Ship That Saved the West* (Vancouver: Mitchell Press, 1970), 48, fn3.

2   Smith, *Reminiscences of Doctor John Sebastian Helmcken*, 108.

3   G.R. Newell, "William Henry McNeill," *Dictionary of Canadian Biography,* vol. 10, http://www.biographi.ca/en/bio/mcneill_william_henry_10E.html.

4   Willard E. Ireland, "The Annexation Petition of 1869," *British Columbia Historical Quarterly* 4, 4 (October 1940): 267–87.

Born in about 1815 in rural Quebec, John Lemon joined the HBC in 1833 to be employed variously across the Pacific Northwest. While at Fort McLoughlin on the British Columbia north coast, he lived with a Bella Bella woman. Transferred to Fort Victoria, he and a Saanich woman named Sarah had six children together between 1849 and 1866.[5] Disposing of his Victoria holding, in 1861 Lemon moved his family to Cowichan Bay, where he ran the Cowichan Hotel until his death in 1883.[6]

Born in about 1817 in rural Quebec, Frederique Minie joined the HBC in 1838, to spend a decade between Fort Taku and Fort Stikine in the Alaskan panhandle before being dispatched to Fort Victoria. Between 1853 and 1861 he had four children by a woman described in Catholic Church records as Marguerite Maurice of the "Bibalets" tribe. He then wed Marie Maurice or Morris, identified as a "half breed," "by whom he had two more children."[7]

Born in 1821 in Montreal, Louis Trudelle joined the HBC in 1839 to spend the next eight years on the north coast before being posted in 1851 to Victoria, where he purchased land, soon to decide he preferred Saanich. There he wed a local woman named Julie, who died soon after their first child was born, whereupon he opted for a Cowichan woman named Marie. With Marie or with another woman he had two more children.[8]

Absence of white women

As these examples suggest, white women were a rarity during the British Columbia fur trade and the gold rushes beginning in 1858.[9] Both its distant location and the nature of mining kept away all but a few. Even the handful of "female emigrants" recruited from England in the early 1860s to serve as maids for the handful of white wives in Victoria were possibly lured away, as when a gold miner offered

---

5   Church records, St. Andrew's Catholic Church, Victoria, 1849–1934, in BC Archives, Add. Ms. 1.

6   Bruce McIntyre Watson, *Lives Lived West of the Divide: A Biographical Dictionary of Fur Traders Working West of the Rockies, 1793–1858* (Kelowna, BC: University of British Columbia Okanagan, 2010), 608–9.

7   Church records, St. Andrew's Catholic Church, Victoria, 1849–1934, in BCA, Add. Ms. 1.

8   Watson, *Lives Lived West of the Divide*, 941.

9   For an exception, see Jean Barman, *Constance Lindsay Skinner: Writing on the Frontier* (Toronto: University of Toronto Press, 2002).

Comatatqua Joseph (at right in front row), daughter of Chief Tsil.Ilusalst, married Edmund Shepherd (second from left in front row), originally from New Brunswick, in the early 1860s. Among their children were (back row, left to right) Agnes, Frederick, William, and Cecelia; (front row) Julia and Adelaide. Edmund earned his living through gold mining, working on the Fraser River steamships, and working for the Hudson's Bay Company. He stayed in British Columbia, and the descendants of Edmund and Comatatqua still live in the province. *Photo courtesy of Donna Sweet.*

one of them "2000$ to buy her wedding attire."[10] It is not without reason the two economies have been similarly framed historically as male activities. They were.

Indicative was the experience of thirty-year old Englishman Robert Burnaby, who we met in Chapter 6. Not long after arriving in Victoria at the beginning of 1859, he described in a letter to his older brother back home a ball he attended where "the proportion of ladies to gentlemen was as plums to flour in a workhouse pudding, consequently the Naval and Military men [stationed nearby] had things all their own way." Not only that, but "the majority of the belles are belles sauvages, and you can detect in their black eyes, high cheek bones, and flattened head whence they came."[11] The reference was most

---

10 January 13 15, 1863, entries in "The Journal of George Hills," 1863: 5–6, typescript in Anglican Church, Ecclesiastical Province of British Columbia, Archives.

11 Robert Burnaby to Tom Burnaby, February 22, 1859, in Anne Burnaby McLeod and Pixie McGeachie, *Land of Promise: Robert Burnaby's Letters from Colonial British Columbia* (Burnaby, BC: City of Burnaby, 2002), 65.

likely to their being offspring of HBC personnel and women of Indigenous descent.

The absence of white women was noted and lamented. Governor James Douglas explained to the Colonial Office in October 1859, a year into the gold rush, how "the entire white population of British Columbia does not probably exceed 5,000 men, there being, with the exception of a few white families, neither wives nor children to refine and soften, by their presence, the dreariness and asperity of existence."[12] Even in Victoria numbers were small, an early resident describing as of 1860 "a female" as "a rare object in those days, when women and children were as scarce as hen's teeth and were hardly ever met on the streets."[13]

An internal memo of February 1860 from the British Emigration Office in London to the Colonial Office, based on information received from Douglas, underlines the full extent to which white women were absent, even more so in the mainland colony of British Columbia: "Miners between Forts Hope & Yale are said to be 600, between Yale & the Fountain 800 and about Alexandria and Quesnel River 1000, making in all 2400...The White population of the Colony amounts to 5000 Men, with scarcely any Women or Children."[14] Writing shortly thereafter, the well-travelled Judge Begbie put "the number of Whites in the Colony in July 1860" at three thousand, of whom not more than half was a fixed population, with few women or children.[15]

Indigenous women coming into view

Given newcomer men were, except in rare instances, without a woman of their own kind, so to speak, Indigenous women were even more visible than might otherwise have been the case. The ambivalence of the unwed Bishop Hills, then in his mid-forties, as recorded in his private journal intended for his eyes only, was almost certainly not unlike that of many others. As early as the spring of 1860 Hills could not help but be impressed by how "the young women begin to dress themselves in fashionable attire," taking special note of one who "was washing

---

12 Douglas to Newcastle, No. 224, October 18, 1859, CO 60:5.

13 Edgar Fawcett, *Some Reminiscences of Old Victoria* (Toronto: Walter Briggs, 1912), 264.

14 Murdoch and Rogers, Colonial Land and Emigration Office, to Merivale, February 7, 1860, CO 60:9.

15 Minute by CF [Fortescue], December 15, 1860, on Douglas to Newcastle, No. 58, June 22, 1860, CO 60:7.

her face & really looked pleasing with black sparkling eyes & rosy cheeks."[16] On the other hand, visiting Victoria's "Chympsian [Tsimshian] Village" five days later, Hills did a double take on coming across "two Indian women dressed I may almost say in the latest fashion! Round straw hats with flowing ribbons, & hooped dresses! However, an adornment of their peculiar kind in the shape of red paint purposely daubed upon their faces."[17]

It was not only in Victoria where Indigenous women stood out. On a road trip in July 1860, Hills took note of "two females, very plain young women," riding "as men" into where he and others were camping. "Their dresses were gay—European manufacture—bright colours" and "their horses tore away in like style."[18] Come December 1860 Hills described in his journal how when he entered "an Indian abode," he took note how in the women "there is a grace, a softness of voice, a truly feminine submission, and sometimes even beauty."[19]

It was a fine line for Hills in composing his daily journal entries between being admiring of the women he encountered and lamenting the sharp gender differential and the lack of self-control among white males. Over time Hills became more critical, consequent perhaps on his being caught up in stories respecting white men's intrusion on Indigenous women's bodies. Writing from Cayuse on June 10, 1861, Hills was beside himself:

> The immorality of the whites is almost universal. The poor Indian girls & mothers are all used by them for the worst purposes. They live with these women in the most open manner & put them away for others as their fancy dictates. They can purchase them off their friends. One man makes no secret of having given a large price for his Indian woman—the sum named is $600 £120, but this probably is above the mark. I am glad to say this man is not an Englishman but a Southern American.[20]

Such descriptions were common in Hills's journal. March 13, 1862, "two Xtian Indians" arrived from Fort Simpson explained to Hills how "their friends

---

16   April 23, 1860, entry in "The Journal of George Hills," 1860: 123.
17   April 28, 1860, entry in "The Journal of George Hills," 1860: 15.
18   July 5, 1860, entry in "The Journal of George Hills," 1860: 153.
19   November 23, 1860, entry in "The Journal of George Hills," 1860: 266.
20   June 10, 1861, entry in "The Journal of George Hills," 1861: 73.

have come principally for the purposes of Prostitution." Going to see them, Hills described in his journal what he encountered: "There was much drunkenness going on. Two or three women in particular were in a state of helpless intoxication. Others were busy making up gay dresses."[21]

Indigenous women as objects of sexual desire

The perception of Indigenous women as accessible for sexual purposes, either of their own volition or as persuaded by others, was linked in the non-Indigenous thinking of the day—indeed into the present day—to Indigenous women's long-time characterization as inferior beings intended to service men at their convenience. Viewing Indigenous women in this way validated men's behaving as they would without the women's consent. In the phrase still in use, "she made me do it."

Even among those in charge the language was commonplace, as when British Columbia governor Frederick Seymour described to the Colonial Office in May 1865 how the populations of three towns in the Cariboo, then the centre of a gold rush, "were dressed in flags, and the population turned out into the Streets for it was announced that several sleighs loaded with [derogatory term for Indigenous women] were on the road."[22] Indicative of the perception was a Colonial Office minute tempering an 1851 request from Vancouver Island governor Richard Blanshard to dispatch a garrison of British troops to protect "British subjects" from Indigenous peoples by pointing out how "it is not very uncommon for the Europeans...to be the aggressors by insulting the women of the natives."[23]

The reality was often in plain view. The summer of 1860 witnessed a seasonal migration of "Indian Tribes" numbering upward of four thousand, double the white population, into "the outskirts of the Town of Victoria for the purpose," according to Douglas, of "selling their Furs and other commodities."[24] Douglas thereupon requested as a "moral restraint" a naval vessel, based at nearby Esquimalt, be stationed at the entrance to Victoria harbour, whose officer in charge differently asserted that the Indigenous peoples' "principal object in coming

---

21 March 13, 1862, entry in "The Journal of George Hills," 1861–62: 24.

22 Seymour to Cardwell, No. 38, May 2, 1865, CO 60:21.

23 Minute by G [Grey], November 12, 1851, on Richard Blanshard, governor of Vancouver Island, to Earl Grey, August 11, 1851, CO 305:3.

24 Douglas to Newcastle, No. 39, August 8, 1860, CO 305:14.

here, from what I can collect is the fearfully demoralizing one of trading with the unchastity of the [derogatory term for Indigenous women]."[25]

Indigenous women's sexuality very often trumped other considerations respecting them. Anglican missionary teacher Alexander Garrett was in April 1861 beseeched by "a number of Indians," in Bishop Hills's words, "to free them from the violence of three sailors in one of the Men of War," who "had taken possession of an Indian lodge & were drinking & abusing the poor Indian women." Garrett did so, only to have one of the sailors return the next day with a question: "Can you tell me, says the Sailor, whereabouts is the part of the Camp where I was yesterday?" Not long after, Garrett and his pupils "overheard a quarrel between a drunken Sailor & an Indian woman... abusing him for not paying her the wages in iniquity."[26]

Within this way of thinking, white men's actions toward Indigenous women could have unexpected consequences, as when Chilcotins in May 1864 killed fourteen white men constructing a wagon road from Bute Inlet to the Cariboo, whom they perceived as interfering with their women on their territory. As explained to the Colonial Office by Vancouver Island governor Arthur Kennedy:

> It is known that the Chillcoaten [sic] Tribe are peculiarly jealous of their women and... I would fear that the residence of a number of single white men among the Chilcoatens, and the almost certain results, may be among the causes which have led to the catastrophe.[27]

It was not that Kennedy was himself particularly protective of Indigenous women, asserting to the Colonial Office two months later: "The condition of the Indian population is very lamentable. Drunkenness and prostitution being the prevailing and prominent characteristics."[28]

Two months later Kennedy sought to counter what he now termed "the degraded and drunken habits of the Indians," not by remediation but by separation:

---

25 R. Lambert Baynes, Rear Admiral, to Douglas, August 1, 1860, in Douglas to Newcastle, No. 39, August 8, 1850, CO 305:14.

26 June 10, 1861, entry in "The Journal of George Hills," 1861: 44–46.

27 Kennedy to Newcastle, Separate, May 13, 1864, CO 305:22.

28 Kennedy to Newcastle, No. 40, Separate, July 7, 1864, CO 305:22.

CHAPTER 7

> The present Indian Settlement at Victoria is a disgrace to humanity, and I cannot learn that any effective measures have been taken to prevent the shameless prostitution of women and drunkenness of the men who live mainly by their prostitution. The Indians must be removed from this locality.[29]

In February 1866 Kennedy lamented "prostitution unchecked," which he backed up with letters from the head of the Indian Mission and from Philip Hankin, the superintendent of police. By Hankin's count:

> There are about 200 Indian prostitutes living in Cormorant, Fisgard, and Store Streets in a state of filth, and dirt beyond all description. On entering one of their shanties in the afternoon I have seen 3 or 4 Indian women lying drunk on the floor, nearly naked, covered with blood, and their faces cut with broken bottles with which they had been fighting.
>
> In one place known as the "Gully" between Johnson and Cormorant Streets some of these dens of infamy are two and three stories high, the rooms about eight feet square, and as many as 6 or 8 persons living in each room...
>
> The shanties are principally owned by Chinese, and hired by the Indians at a monthly rental of about 5 dollars...Whiskey sellers, prostitutes and bad characters are to be found in this locality, and unfortunate sailors coming on leave from their ships are allured here by the Indian women, and robbed.
>
> If it were not for the constant supervision of the Police, it would be dangerous for any respectable person to walk through these streets either by day or night. New shanties have lately been erected, and are still increasing in number.[30]

It became a matter of course for officials to demean Indigenous women out of hand without any consideration of newcomer men's roles in the course of events. British Columbia's commissioner of lands and works and surveyor general,

---

29   Kennedy to Cardwell, No. 80, Miscellaneous, October 1, 1864, CO 305:23.

30   Philip Hankin, Superintendent of Police, to Kennedy, February 8, 1866, enclosed in Kennedy to Cardwell, No. 10, Financial, February 13, 1866, CO 305:28.

Joseph Trutch, asserted in early 1870, in a more general report respecting Vancouver Island's Indigenous population, how "prostitution is another acknowledged evil prevailing to an almost unlimited extent among the Indian women in the neighbourhood of Victoria."[31]

Indigenous women used and abused

Many Indigenous women's lives were not pretty. Bishop Hills was repeatedly caught up in cases where they were being used and abused. In the single month of January 1862 in Victoria, he documented five such cases in his journal:

On January 1 he recorded how the wife of "a young man of the Hydah tribe" who "is a Chiefs son," was "led away & is now a Common Prostitute in the town."[32]

On January 19 Hills was beseeched by "an Indian in trouble because his wife had been taken from him by an American," but "on further inquiry it appeared the man was not unwilling to give up his wife if the seducer would give him a good price." It turned out "he wanted 200 Dollars & said a Mexican usually buy the women at such prices."[33]

Later in the same day Hills was asked "to obtain the assistance of Police to fetch back the wife of a young man" associated with the Anglican school Hills oversaw, "who had been abducted by an American."[34]

On January 25 Hills sought to resolve, to no avail, the case of an orphaned Indigenous girl who had run away from a couple who had "endeavoured to force her to prostitute herself," only to have them convince the police to retrieve her. "Afterwards her masters were seen kicking & chasing her down the street."[35]

At the end of the month Hills visited "the Indian Villages," home to groups of Songhees, Fort Rupert, and Haida people in the common Indigenous practice of spending time in Victoria. The Songhees and Fort Rupert villages passed muster from his perspective, but not the Haida village, so Hill evoked in his daily journal: "We visited the Hydah Village also had a talk with various members of

---

31　Joseph W. Trutch, "Memorandum," January 13, 1870, enclosed in Musgrave to Granville, No. 8, January 29, 1870, CO 60:38.

32　January 1, 1862, entry in "The Journal of George Hills," 1861–62: 31.

33　January 19, 1862, entry in "The Journal of George Hills," 1861–62: 5.

34　January 19, 1862, entry in "The Journal of George Hills," 1861–62: 5.

35　January 25, 1862, entry in "The Journal of George Hills," 1861–62: 8–9.

CHAPTER 7

it. There is a boldness & impudence increasingly manifested. The men live upon the iniquitous gains of their wives, daughters, sisters & slaves."[36]

The situation was not limited to Victoria. While taking a walk in June 1862 near where Hills and two others were camping at Boston Bar, he had a similar experience:

> During a stroll from the camp an Indian in wild & disheveled excitement came running through the bushes breathless. He said a man had seized his daughter a young girl & was carrying her off. He had knocked down the mother & threatened to kill her. I soon after met one of my own people who confirmed the account & said the man had refused to listen to their remonstrances. We started in pursuit but could no where discover the party we were in quest of. Such outrages I regret to say are not infrequent. I have had complaints frequently from husbands & fathers of the forcible abduction of their wives & children by the white savage. In the present case the man was either a Frenchman or a Mexican.[37]

So it went time and again.

The dance houses phenomenon

No aspect of the gold rush would be more difficult, even for the zealous Bishop Hills, to eradicate or at the least to moderate than were dance houses. His attention had already turned to them by the end of 1861, as he wrote in his journal on December 22:

> There has lately been opened on a large scale a place of resort called a Dance House. There are two others I understand in the Town. The object of these is to gather together poor Indian women for association with the lower sort of whites. I wrote yesterday to the Chief Commissioner of Police on the subject, expressing the feelings of the Clergy. I was told to day that in America they were not

---

36   January 31, 1862, entry in "The Journal of George Hills," 1861–62: 10–11.
37   June 25, 1862, entry in "The Journal of George Hills," 1861–62: 70.

allowed. Sad indeed if in a British colony evils of this kind should be greater than in a country not noted for its purity.[38]

By the end of January 1862, Hills was becoming even more open in his journal respecting Indigenous women and, more specifically, concerning the purpose and character of dance houses. As noted above, Hills found the situation in the Haida village near Victoria particularly problematic:

> The men live upon the iniquitous gains of their wives, daughters, sisters & slaves. The dance houses which are open every night are great inventories to this kind of wickedness... Dance houses are opened in the Town [Victoria] for the purpose of attracting Indian women. We saw frequent instances of the abduction of wives & children of Indians by dissolute white men & lately several distressing witnesses have come to my notice. They should be protected by which a prohibition sh^d be put to such places. The various tribes need a wise & fine mediator assured with coercive power when necessary. The Indian is like a child & must be treated with kindness yet with firmness.[39]

The next day, visiting "the lodges of the Chmseans [Tsimshian] and Stickeens," Hills came upon "a woman making up a dress" for "the dance house tonight" and lamented in his journal: "Poor creatures they know these things are wrong—but the temptations are too strong. Alas that white men should be the tempters."[40] Hills was almost certainly aware, but conveniently forgot to make visible in his journal, that it was common knowledge dance halls were not only patronized by, but also operated by, white men as profit-making ventures.

The challenge of being perceived as Indigenous

That white women were in very short supply in colonial British Columbia did not make those who were present any less willing to diminish Indigenous women and their daughters, including those making their way in polite

---

38 December 22, 1861, entry in "The Journal of George Hills," 1861–62: 166–67.
39 January 31, 1862, entry in "The Journal of George Hills," 1861–62: 10–11.
40 February 1, 1862, entry in "The Journal of George Hills," 1861–62: 11.

CHAPTER 7

society, such as it was, in a British Columbia in the making. The latter were ever susceptible to being criticized and demeaned, if not to their faces then behind their backs. Such was the case even with James Douglas's five daughters born between 1834 and 1854, who were, in the language of the day, "quarter-breeds" by virtue of their Indigenous maternal grandmother, to which must be added the additional burden of their father's part-Black descent. On the other hand, they were the governor's daughters at a time when even part-white women of any background were desirable by virtue of having some white descent. Douglas was for his part keen to introduce them to desirable unwed men he could envisage as suitable sons-in-law. So it was that when unwed Anglican bishop George Hills arrived in January 1860, he had been in Victoria only a few short months when "he received a note from the Governor asking me to join himself" for a morning ride including, among others, "the two Miss Douglas's."[41]

When Douglas's eldest daughter married, it was not her father's, but rather the couple's doing. John Sebastian Helmcken, a medically trained HBC clerk in his mid-twenties, arrived from London in 1850 and was instantly smitten by Douglas's eldest daughter, Cecilia, whom he described in his memoir:

> I saw Mr. Douglas—he did not impress me very favourably, being of very grave disposition with an air of dignity—cold and unimpassioned... At the windows stood a number of young ladies, hidden behind the curtains, looking at the late important arrivals, for visitors were very scarce here, but we were not introduced. Anyhow before going away, the room of Mr. Douglas, partly an office and partly domestic, stood open, and there I saw Cecilia, his eldest daughter flitting about, active as a little squirrel, and one of the prettiest objects I had ever seen, rather short but with a very pretty graceful figure—of dark complexion and lovely black eyes—petite and nice... I was more or less captivated.[42]

Back in Victoria after a stint in Fort Rupert, Helmcken wrote, "I spent much of my time courting... The courtship was a very simple affair—generally in the

---

41   April 26, 1860, entry in "The Journal of George Hills," 1860: 75.
42   Smith, *Reminiscences of Doctor John Sebastian Helmcken*, 81.

evening, when we had chocolate and singing and what not—early hours kept."[43] Then came Helmcken's next task, set for him by his prospective father-in-law: "I had to build a house. Mr. Douglas gave me a piece of land, an acre, wanted me to build on it, because being close together there would be mutual aid in case of trouble ... It pleased Cecilia—she was near her mother and relatives—no small comfort to her in my absence."[44] They wed on December 27, 1852, and went on to have four sons and three daughters.[45]

Of the other daughters, Jane wed Alexander Dallas, who was her father's successor with the HBC; Agnes wed Arthur Bushby, recruited from England to assist British Columbia Chief Justice Matthew Baillie Begbie; Alice wed Charles Good, a minister's son; and the youngest daughter, Martha, who would in 1901 publish *History and Folklore of the Cowichan Indians*, married Victoria civil engineer Dennis Harris.[46]

That the Douglas daughters wed white men does not mean they were free from being talked about and diminished based on their Indigenous descent. Sophia Cracroft, whom we met in Chapter 5, visited Victoria in the spring of 1861 and described Governor Douglas's wife, Amelia, in a letter home as "a half caste Indian," and their twenty-two-year-old daughter, Jane, as of "the Indian type," even though "two generations removed from it," given "the great width & flatness of the face ... & even her intonation & voice are characteristic (as we now perceive) of her descent."[47]

Returning a decade later, Cracroft had not one bit changed her mind respecting the physical appearance of Amelia Douglas and her family:

> I dare say you may not remember that she was a half caste Indian very shy, awkward, & retiring as much into the background as she

---

43   Smith, *Reminiscences of Doctor John Sebastian Helmcken*, 120.

44   Smith, *Reminiscences of Doctor John Sebastian Helmcken*, 127.

45   Daniel P. Marshall, "John Sebastian Helmcken," *Dictionary of Canadian Biography*, vol. 14, http://www.biographi.ca/en/bio/helmcken_john_sebastian_14E.html.

46   Martha Douglas Harris, *History and Folklore of the Cowichan Indians* (Victoria: Colonist Printing and Publishing Company, 1901).

47   Sophia Cracroft, February 25, 1861, in letter reproduced in Dorothy Blakey Smith, ed., *Lady Franklin Visits the Pacific Northwest: Being Extracts from the Letters of Miss Sophia Cracroft, Sir John Franklin's Niece, February to April 1861 and April to July 1870* (Victoria, BC: Provincial Archives of British Columbia, 1974), 12–13.

can possibly do...She was very cordial...we saw only her grand daughter...who has as much of the Indian features & colouring as her grandmother.[48]

Attitudes even toward otherwise respectable women and their descendants were firmly set in place, as they would long remain.

This white woman's perspective distinguishing persons with Indigenous descent as alien to the way things ought to be would be repeated time and again, almost as a matter of course, by both white women and white men. A well-connected English naval officer who arrived in 1862 to command a Royal Navy gunboat based at Esquimalt near Victoria was vituperative in a letter headed "Private Not to be copied" that he wrote to his well-connected father respecting the "ignorance and barbarism" of James Douglas's family by virtue of "Mrs. Douglas being a half-breed, and her daughter quarter-breeds." Then in his mid-twenties, Edmund Hope Verney described Douglas's wife as "a good creature, but utterly ignorant: she has no language, but jabbers french or english or Indian, as she is half Indian." Douglas's eldest daughter, Cecilia, was "a fine [derogatory term for Indigenous woman]" and his youngest Martha "perhaps the best of the lot: she is a fat s——, but without any pretence to being anything else."[49] Given the "ignorance and barbarism" of Douglas's family, "a refined English gentleman is sadly wanted at the head of affairs."[50] The gulf could not have been greater between the reality of everyday life in British Columbia at the time and elite English assumptions respecting the way they ought as a matter of course to be.

Consequences

Alongside the visible consequences of diminishing Indigenous woman and their male partners, be they white or Indigenous, are the consequences ranging from attitudes to actions for successive generations into the present day. Indigenous women and their offspring by non-Indigenous men were not only encouraged but legally caused to disappear from view with consequences for descendants

---

48   Sophia Cracroft, April 30, 1870, in Smith, *Lady Franklin Visits the Pacific Northwest*, 118.

49   Edmund Hope Verney to Sir Henry Verney, July 20, 1862, in Allan Pritchard, ed., *Vancouver Island Letters of Edmund Hope Verney, 1862–65* (Vancouver: UBC Press, 1996), 74–75.

50   E.H. Verney to Sir H. Verney, August 16, 1862, in Pritchard, *Vancouver Island Letters of Edmund Hope Verney, 1862–65*, 84.

This photograph from the 1930s depicts five generations of a Cariboo family. Helene (Drymouth) Dussault (seated, left) married Joseph Dussault, who was a courier/middleman for the HBC at Thompson's River Post (now Kamloops). Seated at right is her daughter, Angelique (Dussault) Lyne, who married William (Billy) Lyne Jr., son of William Lyne Sr. and Lucy (Tomah/Sklaniuk), a Secwepemc woman of the Williams Lake Band. Standing is Angelique and Billy Lyne's daughter Vivian (Lyne) Pierce; seated on the ground is "Sis" Edith (Pierce) Paxton, Vivian's daughter; and on Granny Lyne's knee is Sis's baby girl, Lois Paxton. *Photo courtesy of Donna Sweet and Dale Benastick.*

and historians alike into the present day. In 1868 the Colonial Office queried Vancouver Island governor Frederick Seymour respecting the establishment of a registry of births, marriages, and deaths. As to his reason for responding in the negative: "The Majority are Indians whom we could hardly expect to register any one of the three great events of life. Many of the white men are living in a state of concubinage with Indian women far in the Interior. They would hardly come forward to register the birth of some half breed bastard."[51]

Not unexpectedly, neither the total numbers of Indigenous people in the future British Columbia, nor the numbers of Indigenous women partnering at least in the moment with non-Indigenous men, are possible to determine in their entirety. In 1861 James Douglas undertook "a census of the Native Tribes" which

---

51   Seymour to Buckingham, No. 100, August 11, 1858, CO 60:33.

counted "25,873 souls" on Vancouver Island, with another eight thousand on "the continental coast of America, immediately opposite Vancouver's Island."[52]

A close reading of contemporary primary and secondary sources, including church and census records, turned up in British Columbia between the beginning of the gold rush in 1858 and 1871, the year it joined Canada, 625 documented unions between named non-Indigenous men and sometimes named Indigenous women. These unions can be variously parsed, but however it be done, the bottom line is that Indigenous women mattered to the future of British Columbia. They not only mattered, they mattered a lot. Just as with gold miners, except for Indigenous women by their actions persuading newcomer men to stay longer, in many cases for a lifetime, there might well have been no British Columbia in the form we know it today.

---

52   Douglas to Labouchere, No. 24, October 20, 1856, 11582, CO 305:7.

CHAPTER 8

Along the Pathway to Canada (1866–71)

The pathway that the Colony of British Columbia took to Confederation with Canada in 1871 was neither even nor straightforward. While the notion of Confederation had been around, there was no guarantee of its success. As the previous chapters have pointed out, the path to Canada was littered with obstacles having to be overcome or bypassed.

Overland dreams

The two far west British colonies of Vancouver Island and British Columbia had, early on, rarely looked beyond their borders. Governor James Douglas had been an exception of sorts with his desire to attract sturdy English folk from wherever they came, albeit with little success given the distance.[1]

The possibility of an overland route across North America was on some minds. As early as 1862, Douglas strategically informed the Colonial Office how he had looked to "overland communication with Canada by a route possessing the peculiar advantages of being secure from Indian aggression, remote from the United States Frontier, and traversing a country exclusively British." Douglas went so far as to cost out the length of time and means of travel across the westernmost sections of such a route as of 1862:

Victoria to Yale or Douglas	2 days	Steamer
On to Lillooet or Lytton	2 days	Stage coach
On to Alexandria	4 days	Stage coach

---

1   As an example, Dr. Archibald Alexander Riddel of Toronto to Earl Carnarvon, under-secretary of state for the colonies, June 9, 1858, CO 305:9.

CHAPTER 8

| On to Fort George | 2 days | Steamer |
| On to Tête Jaune Cache | 5 days | Steamer[2] |

Explaining that parts of the route were already contracted out with "the assistance of a Government loan," Douglas described a "proposed line of intercommunication with Red River and Canada" based on trips he had made in the fur trade.[3] Douglas's ambition generated a range of supportive and not-so-supportive Colonial Office minutes, along with a private company being "formed for the purpose of forwarding Emigrants through Canada overland to British Columbia."[4] Douglas witnessed the latter on his seasonal autumn trip to the mainland colony later in the same year:

> I encountered in the course of my journey a number of overland emigrants from Canada who came through from Red River settlement by the Tête Jaune Cache route... They suffered a good deal of privation, but did not experience any serious difficulties in the route until they had passed Edmonton, from whence to Tête Jaune Cache appears by their representations to be the worst part of the journey, they are, however, of opinion that a good road may be formed between these points at a very moderate cost.[5]

Douglas hoped that "Her Majesty's Government deem it a matter of national importance to open a regular overland communication with Canada."[6] He was not alone in his vision. In May 1862 a resident of New South Wales in Australia enquired hopefully of the Board of Trade in London as to "what progress has been made to connect British Columbia with the Atlantic Ports, through Canada by the Lakes and by Railway."[7] The letter having been forwarded to the Colonial Office, Arthur Blackwood minuted summarily on it: "No real progress:

---

2 Douglas to Newcastle, Separate, April 15, 1862, CO 60:13.
3 Douglas to Newcastle, Separate, April 15, 1862, CO 60:13.
4 Murdoch to Rogers, permanent under-secretary for the colonies, May 20, 1862, May 20, 1862, CO 60:14.
5 Douglas to Newcastle, Separate, October 27, 1862, CO 60:13.
6 Douglas to Newcastle, Separate, October 27, 1862, CO 60:13.
7 A. Brown to Board of Trade, March 21, 1862, enclosed in Sir James Emerson Tennent to Rogers, May 21, 1862, CO 60:14.

only schemes propounded. No attempts at a rail. Most indefinite."[8] What is clear from this exchange is that a rail line, which would win out, was at least in view.

When, during that same autumn of 1862, Anglican bishop George Hills returned from his three-month Cariboo adventure described in Chapter 4, he met on the *Enterprise* on the way from New Westminster to Victoria "a young man who had just come over the Rocky Mountains from Canada with a party of 130." As to how the feat was managed: "they left Fort Garry June 7, each contributed 100$ to the general stock...They brought horses to Tete Jaune Cache, but left them with the Indians who undertook to bring them to Kamloops...They were obliged to make a raft on which they came down the Fraser to Fort Alexandria."[9] While preaching later in the year along the east coast of Vancouver Island, Hills met a "Canadian" who by a combination of roads and water "had come over this autumn by the Rocky Mountains from Canada" with "no real difficulties."[10] Hills was ever more aware of how "by & bye when the railroad sh^d be formed,"[11] immigration to the western colonies would thereby increase.

More concrete steps in that direction followed. A government expedition was, as of March 1866, according to the Colonial Office, exploring "the practicality of a route for Road or Railway, through British Territory from Canada to the Shores of the Pacific."[12]

The dream was becoming a reality, or almost so.

American proximity

Complementing attention to an overland route to Canada was British Columbia's proximity to the United States. No outside factor was more ever-present, due both to that country's location just south of the forty-ninth parallel and to the numbers of Americans arriving with the gold rush or subsequently who, even if they decided to stay, maintained an affinity with their homeland. As early as 1846, American politician William Seward assuredly pronounced in a public

---

8   Minute by AB^d [Blackwood], May 23, 1862, on A. Brown to Board of Trade, enclosed in Tennent to Rogers, May 21, 1862, CO 60:14.

9   October 1, 1862, entry in "The Journal of George Hills," 1861–62: 163, on typescript in Ecclesiastical Province of British Columbia, Archives.

10 November 8, 1862, entry in "The Journal of George Hills," 1861–62: 174.

11 October 24, 1862, entry in "The Journal of George Hills," 1861–62: 174–75.

12 Birch to Cardwell, No. 14, March 2, 1866, CO 60:24.

speech respecting the future British Columbia how "our population is destined to roll its restless waves to the icy barriers of the north."[13]

Among other observers of the course of events was the American consul in Victoria, from 1862, Allen Francis, whose friendship with President Abraham Lincoln had secured him the posting. Francis's dispatches cheerfully tracked, among other topics of interest, what he perceived as Victoria's economic decline, including its non-Indigenous population having more than halved by 1869. His biographer Charles John Fedorak attributes Francis's insights to how his "daily experience put him in contact with many of his compatriots, who had either returned penniless from the gold mines or lost their businesses in Victoria and were returning to the United States."[14]

Francis convinced himself that three-quarters of British Columbia's non-Indigenous population would support joining the United States. "The people, those claiming to be loyal subjects included, are now urging with great unanimity, annexation to the United States," he reported enthusiastically to US Secretary of State Seward in the spring of 1867.[15]

Prospecting annexation

An early, if not the earliest, petition urging British Columbia's annexation may have been influenced by rumblings in the United States that hinted at its annexing most of today's Canada. A bill calling for the annexation of the entirety of British North America was introduced in the US House of Representatives on July 2, 1866, and while never voted on, it signalled to some what might be. The British Columbia petition responded more directly to the two colonies' union in September 1866, which some in Victoria saw as unequal by virtue of, for the first time, the mainland being favoured over themselves. While David Higgins of the *Victoria Chronicle*, a Nova Scotian via the California gold rush, considered annexation "of all the schemes concocted in the brains of political humbugs...

---

13   William Seward, speech at Chautauqua, March 31, 1846, in George E. Baker, ed., *The Works of William Seward* (Boston: Houghton Mifflin, 1884), vol. 5: 320, cited in David E. Shi, "Seward's Attempt to Annex British Columbia, 1865–1869," *Pacific Historical Review* 467, 2 (May 1978): 218.

14   Charles John Fedorak, "The United States Consul in Victoria and the Political Destiny of the Colony of British Columbia, 1862–1870," BC *Studies* 79 (Autumn 1988): 7.

15   Fedorak, "The United States Consul in Victoria," 13.

the wildest and most ridiculous," his competitor, Leonard McClure of the *Victoria Evening Telegraph*, an Irishman who also arrived via California, convinced himself along with some readers that British Columbia's annexation to the United States would have the support of the Queen should a united body of colonists make a formal request for her to allow it.[16] A public meeting held at the end of September attracted, and to some extent coalesced, some three hundred enthusiasts divided between supporters and opponents of annexation. McClure was so disenchanted by the subsequent indecision he returned to California.[17]

Two competing visions of British Columbia's future

Early the next year Britain eclipsed the United States, so it seemed in the moment, with respect to British Columbia's future. On March 29, 1867, the British Parliament passed the British North America Act, joining together the four British colonies of New Brunswick, Nova Scotia, Ontario, and Quebec into a Dominion of Canada under a parliamentary system of governance modelled on the mother country. The act contained a provision for other British possessions to join at a later date.[18]

That was not the only perspective in play. On March 30, 1867, a day after the passage of the British North America Act, US Secretary of State Seward purchased the future Alaska from Russia for US$7.2 million in what he considered to be "a first step in a comprehensive plan to gain control of the entire Pacific Coast" extending south to the border with the United States, and so including

16   David Higgins, *Daily British Colonist and Victoria Chronicle*, September 12, 1866, p. 2, and Leonard McClure, *Victoria Evening Telegraph*, September 10, 1866, p. 2, both cited in Brent Holloway, "'Without Conquest or Purchase': The Annexation Movement in British Columbia, 1866–1871" (master's thesis, University of Ottawa, 2016), 48 and 47.

17   On the meeting and its aftermath through 1871, see Holloway, "'Without Conquest or Purchase'"; and Willard E. Ireland, "The Annexation Petition of 1869," *British Columbia Historical Quarterly* 4, no. 4 (October 1940): 267–87; and Ireland, "Further Note on the Annexation Petition of 1869," *British Columbia Historical Quarterly* 5, no. 1 (January 1941): 67–72.

18   For an accessible overview, see Daniel Heidt, ed., *Reconsidering Confederation: Canada's Founding Debates, 1865–1999* (Calgary: University of Calgary Press, 2018), which includes Patricia E. Roy, "'The Interests of Confederation Demanded It': British Columbia and Confederation," 171–92.

today's British Columbia. Seward anticipated Britain would agree to dispense with the British Columbia colony in settlement of claims for having permitted the US South, during the recently concluded American Civil War, to build ships on British territory.[19]

As described by British Columbia scholar and diplomat Hugh Keenleyside at the annual meeting of the Canadian Historical Association in 1928, when events were still in living memory, or almost so, the toing-and-froing in the two directions got more and more fervent.

> On the whole, English opinion was adverse, rather than favorable to any strong effort to retain British Columbia, and no very grave obstacles would have been opposed to a peaceful transfer to the United States, had this been urged by the colonials themselves. Many considerations of local pride and immediate advantage urged British Columbia towards American annexation. As a state of the Union, local autonomy could be more fully exercised than as a province of the newly formed Dominion of Canada. With the elimination of all trade barriers between British Columbia and the United States, the necessities of life could be obtained more cheaply, trade would be stimulated, and intercourse facilitated. With a population almost equally divided between Americans and British; with Canada far off and little known; with the English homeland unresponsive and apathetic; with a tremendous financial burden and inadequate political institutions; in a physical situation impossible of defence and isolated from the British world; with all these factors urging her forward, the local solution of the difficulties of British Columbia appeared to be found in annexation with her only neighbors—the Western states of the American union.[20]

---

19   Shi, "Seward's Attempt to Annex British Columbia, 1865–1869," 223–25; also John A. Munro, *The Alaska Boundary Dispute* (Toronto: Copp Clark, 1970); David Joseph Mitchell, "The American Purchase of Alaska and Canadian Expansion to the Pacific" (master's thesis, Simon Fraser University, 1976), 59–68, for an excellent overview of contemporary perspectives on the course of events.

20   Hugh L. Keenleyside, "British Columbia—Annexation or Confederation?" Canadian Historical Association, *Report of the Annual Meeting*, 7, no. 1 (1928), 36.

Some aspects of British Columbia were on the other hand deemed to be superior to the United States, as with how Americans "vehemently upheld slavery," considering "the world could not go on without it—the race of [derogatory term for Black people] were fit for nothing else," or so "a talkative neighbour" explained to Anglican bishop George Hills in February 1861, a year after his arrival. So as to convince Hills to her position, she added that she was "really very charitable to others... even to a poor Irishman!"[21] And a Cariboo "storekeeper, a Southern American," told Hills the next year how "he has scarcely met no American in the country who does not sympathize with the South."[22]

By this time self-identifying with British Columbia, Hills was not disposed toward Americans, so he reflected in his daily journal in May 1862, following his seven-hour boat trip between Victoria and New Westminster:

> There were many Canadians & Englishmen on board. It was truly refreshing as a contrast to the sad specimens of fallen men we have had hitherto in miners & adventurers from California & the States. The distance from Canada & England is such that we dared hardly expect to have a British population, but supposed we must be content with a large preponderance of the American element of the Californian stamp, ungodly & vicious.[23]

With the passage of time—and exacerbated by the American Civil War extending from April 1861 to May 1865—numerous persons had crossed the border north into British Columbia because they did not want to be part of the United States. As mentioned in Chapter 3, in May 1861, at Saanich outside of Victoria, Bishop Hills came upon "a party of settlers with cattle, waggons & horses on their way to find a settlement." As to the reason: "They were Englishmen lately arrived from Oregon preferring the old English farmer to the Stars & Stripes. They have been some years in the States, one of them was from Gloucestershire, another from Wales."[24] Early the next year Hills encountered "a family named Tilton who are contemplating residence here" due to his "being a Peace Democrat & of course turned out of office under the new Regime he is regarded

---

21   February 7, 1861, entry in "The Journal of George Hills," 1861: 15
22   August 23, 1862, entry in "The Journal of George Hills," 1861–62: 128.
23   May 14, 1862, entry in "The Journal of George Hills," 1861–62: 47.
24   May 21, 1861, entry in "The Journal of George Hills," 1861: 52.

CHAPTER 8

as a traitor" for "having Southern tendencies."[25]

Hugh Keenleyside, in his address to the Canadian Historical Association, sketched out the position of those in British Columbia who desired union with Canada:

> Not all the settlers in British Columbia, however, were willing to forego their British allegiance, and many there were who preferred union with the Canadian Dominion—could suitable terms be arranged. "No union on account of love need be looked for," wrote one British Columbian. "The only bond of union... will be the material advantage of the country, and the pecuniary benefits of the inhabitants. Love for Canada has to be acquired by the prosperity of the country, and from our children."[26]

In other words, many of the colonists were willing, or desirous, to remain within the Empire if some solution could be found for their economic and political troubles.

Some others individualized their views about Confederation in a form whose first-hand words survive, as was the case with long-time Vancouver Island physician and colonial politician John Sebastian Helmcken. Helmcken began his memoir in 1892 with the words, "Well, here goes—," and continued through five notebooks covering 609 handwritten pages.[27] His position was a quarter of a century later lodged in his memory:

> I came out against Confederation distinctly, chiefly because I thought it premature—partly from prejudice—and because no suitable terms could be proposed...
>
> Our population was too small numerically. Moreover, it would only be a confederation on paper for no means of communication with the Eastern Provinces existed, without which no advantage could possibly ensue. Canada was looked down on as a poor mean

---

25 February 3, 1862, entry in "The Journal of George Hills," 1861–62: 14. The family was living at the time in Olympia, Washington.

26 Keenleyside, "British Columbia—Annexation or Confederation?" 37–38.

27 Dorothy Blakey Smith, ed., *The Reminiscences of Doctor John Sebastian Helmcken* (Vancouver: UBC Press, 1975), xxxciii.

slow people, who had been very commonly designated North American Chinamen. This character they had achieved from their necessarily thrifty condition for long years, and indeed they compared very unfavourably with the Americans and with our American element...Our trade was either with the U.S. or England—with Canada we had nothing to do.[28]

The path to union ran through British Columbia's Legislative Council, created in the merger, in 1867, of the two earlier colonies of Vancouver Island and British Columbia. Legislative Council members were of three kinds. The colony's senior officials, being the colonial secretary, attorney general, treasurer, commissioner of lands and works, and collector of customs, comprised an executive council. The second group consisted of the solicitor general and the eight magistrates posted across the colony at Victoria, Nanaimo, New Westminster, Yale and Lytton, Thompson District, Kootenay West, Kootenay East, Cariboo West, and Cariboo East. The third group was comprised of nine "elected" members, being three from Victoria and one each from Nanaimo, New Westminster, Lillooet, Yale and Lytton, Columbia River and Kootenay, and Cariboo.[29] Support for union or annexation waxed and waned depending on who had been elected or appointed.

In 1868, seeking to break the impasse whereby the Legislative Council, controlled by annexationists, stood firm in opposition to union, the Canadian government took charge, acknowledging how it "desires union with British Columbia and has opened communication with the Imperial government on the subject." The next year the Dominion government took over the rights of the Hudson's Bay Company to the intervening territory between Canada and British Columbia, and the Imperial government appointed a new governor favouring Confederation.[30]

But we are getting ahead of ourselves. There would be a few more bumps and twists in the path before 1869 and the new governor.

---

28   Smith, *Reminiscences of Doctor John Sebastian Helmcken*, 247.

29   G.P.V. Akrigg and Helen B. Akrigg, *British Columbia Chronicle 1847–1871: Gold and Colonists* (Vancouver: Discovery Press, 1977), 340–41.

30   For a succinct summery, Keenleyside, "British Columbia—Annexation or Confederation?" 34–40 with the quotation from 39–40.

CHAPTER 8

Hard economic times

In the short term, the immediate consequence of the US purchase of Alaska in 1867 was to box in British Columbia on the north as well as the south at a time when the colony's economy was floundering. Writing to the Colonial Office in June 1867, Governor Seymour acknowledged a harsh reality: "The finances are, I regret to say, in a deplorable condition...the Colony was, up to the present time kept alive by loans raised in England, on which we have now to pay heavy interest while receiving absolutely no aid of any kind from the Mother country."[31]

Writing a month later, Seymour was so agitated he forgot to sign his letter, to the Colonial Office's righteous indignation. In it Seymour anticipated an annual deficit of £45,000, about which he had "had no idea when in England last year... or else I should have communicated fully with Your Grace's Department on the subject." Seymour aptly observed how "it is now for the first time that the Colony has been thrown on its own resources," having earlier "subsisted to a considerable extent on loans contracted in the Mother Country," as had been the case under James Douglas's watch.[32]

In response to Seymour's unsigned letter, with its harsh reality check respecting British Columbia's state of affairs, the Colonial Office's permanent undersecretary, Frederic Rogers, posed in his minute of September 16, 1867, the fundamental question for the Colonial Office respecting British Columbia's future.

> This only concerns the past. As to the future it is no doubt true that high taxation, distress and want of assistance from home will probably cause the American population of the Colonies to press for annexation—a pressure w^h w^d soon become irresistible... On the other hand if the Colonists once find that the annexation threat [is] satisfactory in extracting money from us they will plunder us indefinitely...
>
> I suppose the question to be (in the long run) is B.C. to form part of the U.S. or of Canada; and if we desire to promote the latter alternative, what form of expenditure or non-expenditure is likely to facilitate or pave the way for it.[33]

---

31   Seymour to Buckingham, Private, June 26, 1867, CO 60:28.

32   Seymour to Buckingham, No. 90, July 15, 1867, CO 60:28.

33   Minute by FR [Rogers], September 16, 1867, on Seymour to Buckingham, No. 90, July 15, 1867, CO 60:28.

Parliamentary Under-Secretary Charles Adderley minuted the next day how British Columbia's future was on the line:

> It seems to me impossible that we should long hold B.C. from its natural annexation. Still we should give & keep for Canada every chance, & if possible get Seymour to bridge over the present difficulties till we see what Canada may do. I think our US Minister should keep his ears open for any overtures of equivalents in exchange of this territory.[34]

Another petition

In July 1867 another petition circulated among dissatisfied Victorians. Intended for Queen Victoria, it gave her a stark choice:

> Either, That Your Majesty's Government may be pleased to relieve us immediately of the expense of our excessive staff of officials, assist the establishment of a British steam-line with Panama, so that immigration from England may reach us, and also assume the debts of the Colony.
> Or, That Your Majesty will graciously permit the Colony to become a portion of the United States.[35]

As with its predecessor, what, if anything, ensued respecting the petition is uncertain.

In his memoir, John Sebastian Helmcken, who was then Speaker of the BC Legislature, recalled about this and subsequent petitions:

> Some Americans privately got up an agitation and tried to persuade the British settlers to petition the President of the United States to use his assistance to have the Island annexed to the

---

[34] Minute by CBA [Adderley], September 17, 1867, on Seymour to Buckingham, No. 90, July 15, 1867, CO 60:28.

[35] Annexation Petition, July 1867, enclosed in Allan Francis to F.H. Seward, July 2, 1867, in *Consular Letters from Victoria, Vancouver Island*, vol. 1 (Washington, DC: Department of State Archives), cited in Ireland, "The Annexation Petition of 1869," 268, fn. 4.

CHAPTER 8

United States. Of course the same arguments and persuasions were used then as since, that it would be for the immediate and permanent benefit of the Island, that all would become rich. They pointed out too the fact that HM Govt cared but little about the Colonies and was willing to let them go, an expense they being at this time of Free Trade agitation and success, an incumbrance of defence, and liable to lead the mother country to war or in case of war the cost of defending them. These doctrines were at this time in the ascendant among the Free Traders—who considered that the Colonies only would stick to England, until they became independent like the United States…

Many talked more or less about annexation—and in press of time when the question of Union with B. Columbia and subsequently Confederation came up, doubtless many debated whether it would not be better to be at once annexed instead of waiting until the whole of Canada had been gobbled up—for I think before this the Americans had bought Alaska…

After the Americans bought it they boasted of Canada being sandwiched—ready to be gobbled up.[36]

Helmcken's biographer points out that, based on his writing, Helmcken was never himself in favour of annexation by the United States, "though for a time he feared that it might be forced upon British Columbia by circumstances," given it "could not continue to exist for long as a separate entity" due to its "financial and commercial problems."[37] British Columbia hung in the balance.

Seymour cast on his own resources

On September 24, 1867, Governor Seymour reported to the Colonial Office "on the desire of the people of this Colony to join the Eastern Confederation," as attested by a resolution "passed by the Legislative Council in favour of negotiations being entered into with a view to a union of all the British Possessions in North America." He was cautious. "Though the motion passed through the Council without opposition, there was but little warmth felt in its favour" owing

---

36 Smith, *Reminiscences of Doctor John Sebastian Helmcken*, 182–83.

37 Smith, *Reminiscences of Doctor John Sebastian Helmcken*, xxii.

to uncertainty as to what benefits would ensue, given "the lands intervening between Canada and our frontier belong to a private Company"—namely, the Hudson's Bay Company."[38]

Seymour speculated on what was feasible given:

> No immigrants from England now resort to this Colony. The only English men who find their way hither filter to us through California, and as adventurous Americans still visit us the population is now becoming alien to a large extent. It is thought by many of those who have made of this their home, that the only chance of its becoming prosperous while a dependency of a very distant Country...is a union with the more developed and apparently more prosperous Colonies on the Atlantic.[39]

Seymour's letter highlights his loneliness and his sense of isolation in his distant location.

The American alternative

In the interim, the American alternative continued to beckon. As economic conditions worsened, talk in British Columbia turned openly and explicitly, including in several local newspapers, to the possibility of the colony joining the United States.[40] The very day after writing his loneliness letter, a distraught Seymour alerted the Colonial Office, in a letter marked "Secret," to "the annexation feeling prevalent in Victoria," to "the absence of all assistance from Home," and to American troops about "to be poured into Alaska" consequent on "their recent purchase to the North of us."[41]

If Seymour was taken up with the American factor, so to a considerable extent was the Colonial Office. A minute of November 6, 1867, on Seymour's September 24 letter respecting the Legislative Council's lukewarm support for Confederation might have changed some minds respecting the Hudson Bay Company's role in the course of events. Frederic Rogers put in its necessary

---

38 Seymour to Buckingham, Separate, September 24, 1867, CO 60:29.
39 Seymour to Buckingham, Separate, September 24, 1867, CO 60:29.
40 Holloway, "'Without Conquest or Purchase,'" 40.
41 Seymour to Buckingham, Secret, September 25, 1867.

order what needed to happen: "It did not appear to H.G. [His Grace, the secretary of state] that any practical steps could be taken in the matter while the Colony was separated from Canada by so large a tract of unoccupied Country, at present in the possession of a private Company."[42]

Seymour continued to update the Colonial Office on what he similarly considered to be a crisis situation. Writing on December 13, 1867, he virtually begged for "a temporary loan from the Mother Country" to offset the need for "$223,000 dollars more than we shall possess to meet existing liabilities." Pointing out how, "with the enormous attractions of California close to us," the colony "cannot greatly increase the taxation without driving out the remaining portion of the population," Seymour reminded the Colonial Office that "when the Gold in Fraser's River was first discovered there was a great rush to the Colony from California and Australia" of "between 12,000 and 13,000 men," whereas currently "between Hope and Yale...not more than half a dozen Chinamen were now the sole workers." Everyone was stretched, including himself. "My own salary is nine months in arrears."[43]

Five days later in faraway London, Colonial Office senior clerk William Robinson, following his close dissection of British Columbia's situation, confirmed to the others that "the finances are in a most embarrassed state, that the Colony is paying heavy interest & sinking fund on Loans contracted in England, that it is largely indebted to the Colonial Bank, to the Crown Agents, to some of its public officers, & that the Salaries of the Public officers are several months in arrears."[44]

Better news at hand

A year later, in August 1868, Seymour permitted himself a touch of optimism. On reading seasonal reports received from the three magistrates under his purview based in the far distant Cariboo, he wrote, "It really seems as if British Columbia is to become a settled Colony at last instead of a mere gold field with an unattached population."[45] Peter O'Reilly had reported from Yale:

---

42   Minute by FR [Rogers], November 6, 1867, on Seymour to Buckingham, Separate, September 24, 1867, CO 60:29.

43   Seymour to Buckingham, No. 162, December 13, 1867, CO 60:29.

44   Minute by WR [Robinson], December 18, 1867, on Seymour to Buckingham, No. 90, July 15, 1867, CO 60:28.

45   Seymour to Buckingham, No. 104, August 22, 1868, CO 60:33.

> The district under my charge is in a very satisfactory state, the best possible proof of which is the increase of permanent settlement and the quantity of land that has been taken up, forty six preemption claims having been recorded by me within the last year.
>
> These farms are not held for the purpose of speculation but have been stocked and put under cultivation, the pre-emptors being stimulated by the success which has attended the older settlers. Crops of all kinds throughout the district are looking remarkably well, and promise large returns. Hitherto the want of a flour mill has been much felt in the neighbourhood of Kamloops, but through the energy of Messrs. Fortune and McIntosh a good mill has been erected at the mouth of Tranquille River, which will prove a great boon to the settlers in that section of Country, and will lead to a much larger extent of Land being put under cultivation than has hitherto been the case.
>
> Cattle have largely increased in numbers, and over four thousand sheep passed through Yale in the last two months, most of which are intended ... for the Bonaparte and Nicola districts.[46]

O'Reilly described how "the banks and bars of the Fraser River continue to be worked by Chinamen, of whom there are about four hundred in the district; their average earnings being from two to four dollars per day to the hand," with the mining population overall "each year being more and more concentrated in Cariboo."[47]

As for access, "the portion of the waggon road now under my supervision extending from Yale to Clinton is in excellent order" so that "large quantities of good have been forwarded over it principally by the Hudson's Bay Company for their posts on Similkameen, Fort Shepherd, and Colville, and also by the settlers from the Southern boundary to the Head of the O'Kanagan Lake."[48]

---

46   Peter O'Reilly, Magistrate, Yale District, to the Colonial Secretary, August 3, 1868, in Seymour to Buckingham, No. 104, August 22, 1868, CO 60:33.

47   O'Reilly to the Colonial Secretary, August 3, 1868, in Seymour to Buckingham, No. 104, August 22, 1868, CO 60:33.

48   O'Reilly to the Colonial Secretary, August 3, 1868, in Seymour to Buckingham, No. 104, August 22, 1868, CO 60:33.

CHAPTER 8

Writing on August 5, 1868, E. Sanders, magistrate of the Lillooet district, described how out of 104 miners at a dozen locations,

> but few are whites, the remainder it is needless to state are Chinese, to these may be added a few Indians, who although not given to mining with persistency, do spasmodically take to gold seeking, more particularly in spring and late in autumn when the waters of the Rivers are at their lowest, thus contributing to some modest extent to the enrichment of the Colony... It is most difficult to ascertain with the least degree of accuracy what amount represents the average earnings of Chinese miners, but I am inclined to think it may be safely estimated at from $4 to $5 a day. Last year the total gain of gold in the district was valued at $50,000^{00}.[49]

Sanders concluded on a note very similar to that of O'Reilly as to how everyday landscapes were changing:

> The settling up of the Land in the district has progressed beyond expectation during the present year. Since January not less than 6080 acres have been taken up and occupied, and I have every reason to believe that the great majority of the preemptors are bonâ fide settlers, men who are likely to till and render their claims productive by the coming spring. The crops everywhere, despite the scarcity of water for the purposes of irrigation are more than usually abundant this year and harvesting in the vicinity of Lillooet at least has been in progress since the 20th of last month. Farmers I am rejoiced to say are as a rule well to do and satisfied, their prospects are not only bright but brilliant, the conviction seems to be gaining ground amongst them that few Countries afford equal, much less superior advantages to the industrious, thrifty, agricultural than this. And the realization of the chief wish of those who have the interests of the Colony at heart, namely that its valleys and broad table lands might be settled up by a permanent white population, seems at last after

---

49   E. Sanders, Magistrate, Lillooet District, to the Colonial Secretary, August 5, 1868, in Seymour to Buckingham, No. 104, August 22, 1868, CO 60:33.

a tedious waiting of many years to be within the range of the possible.[50]

A similar report of August 26, 1868, from Henry Maynard Ball respecting "the state of the New Westminster District, since October 1867," when he took charge of it, reads much the same respecting changing times and growing commitment to the physicality of British Columbia:

> A District possessing such an extent of agriculture and grazing resources has naturally attracted the attention of many who having led a wandering life during the early years of their residence in the Colony are anxious to settle down and carve out for themselves from the waste lands a more permanent home, and numerous preemption claims have been taken up in the District extending from the Chilliwack and Sumas Rivers to the Sea Coast.
>
> The number of new claims preempted, since October amounts to Twenty eight, but I should mention that there are many old established Farms within the limits I mentioned, whose owners are well off and comfortably settled...
>
> The Chilliwhack District possesses by far the finest land and would be more popularly settled were it not cut up and occupied by the Indian reserves. Of them there are fourteen within a circuit of Thirty miles, containing patches of some of the best land. Each Indian tribe has a reserve on which potatoes and other vegetables are grown, and over which their pigs and cattle roam.
>
> It would be impossible and would not be politic to attempt to concentrate them on one large reserve, as the different tribes although speaking the same language are ruled by separate petty chiefs amongst whom much jealousy exists. Up to the present time there has been but little conflict between the White settlers and the Indians, many of the latter being frequently employed as labourers by the farmers.
>
> On the Banks of the North Arm of Fraser River there are about 14 settlements... As a proof that a hard working and industrious

---

50   Sanders to the Colonial Secretary, August 5, 1868, in Seymour to Buckingham, No. 104, August 22, 1868, CO 60:33.

CHAPTER 8

man may in a few years make a comfortable home for himself, I may mention one instance. That of a French Canadian named "Garipee" on the North Arm. In 1864 he preempted a piece of Land, commencing with a sack of potatoes and an axe. He now possesses 18 cows, 2 work oxen, a good house, pigs & chickens with 8 or 10 acres under cultivation & fenced, all acquired through hard work and industrious habits.[51]

Ball went on to describe a steam flour mill at New Westminster that "will now give a new impetus to farming operations in the neighbourhood and offer a good and profitable market for their produce." He added, "The trade of the town of New Westminster is supported partly by the settlers of the neighbourhood, the lumberers at Burrards Inlet, and partly by the Indians who are large consumers of certain articles."[52] As for the site of the future Vancouver: "I must now turn to what I consider the most important portion of the District viz Burrard Inlet and the Lumber Interest. At present there are about 320 men engaged at the two Mills and the different logging camps around the Bay... I have seen as many as 10 ships in the Bay loading and waiting for cargoes at the mill."[53]

What is clear from these observations is that British Columbia was, by the mid-1860s, more energetic and diverse than perceived by the small minority who had arrived in Victoria early on and exercised power at the political level.

The Legislative Council in action

In the spring of that year, April 1868, the Legislative Council passed a resolution favouring "the general principles of the desirability of the Union of this Colony with the Dominion of Canada."[54] In line with the resolution, in September "a

---

51 H.M. Ball, Magistrate, New Westminster District, August 26, 1868, to D. Maunsell, private secretary to Seymour, in Seymour to Buckingham, No. 104, August 22, 1868, CO 60:33.

52 Ball, August 26, 1868, to Maunsell, in Seymour to Buckingham, No. 104, August 22, 1868, CO 60:33.

53 Ball, August 26, 1868, to Maunsell, in Seymour to Buckingham, No. 104, August 22, 1868, CO 60:33.

54 W.A.G. Young, colonial secretary, to Seymour, April 30, 1868, enclosed in Seymour to Buckingham, No. 45, May 14, 1868, CO 60:32; on a subsequent motion that was lost, Seymour to Buckingham, No. 74, July 28, 1868, CO 60:33.

large and respectable Public meeting," sometimes termed a convention, was held at Yale in the Fraser Valley, where those in attendance agreed on "Union or Confederation with the Dominion of Canada," on "Representative Institutions and Responsible Government," on "retrenchment in the Public expenditure," and on "a reciprocal commercial treaty with the United States."[55]

Reporting to the Colonial Office at the end of November, Seymour cautioned that "the proceedings of the Yale Meeting did not meet with universal approval" and that "the more prominent advocates of Confederation were defeated at the last elections in Victoria for members to serve in the Legislative Council." Seymour also pointed out the Yale convention's distinctiveness:

> Local politics have their Head Quarters in Victoria. If one ascends the Fraser but a few miles one finds less excitement and better tempers at New Westminster and so it goes on in proceeding up Country till at Clinton the whole thing is ignored. The miners of Cariboo and Kootenay are in the most profound state of indifference as regards what is passing at Head Quarters.[56]

Taking the Yale proposal seriously as a possible turning point, Frederic Rogers, the permanent under-secretary, was cautiously optimistic in his minute on Seymour's letter:

> It seems to me questionable whether V.C.I. can be conveniently governed from Ottawa. But if the parties concerned think it can, it is certainly not for the British Gov^t (I sh^d say) to stand in their way. Our policy, I should say, was to assist everything w^h tends to make Union practicable, but to discourage that premature & impatient action w^h defeats its own object so far as we can with^t appearing to resist that w^h (I presume) we really wish to see effected.[57]

Rogers was well aware that "the present state of the negotiations with the HBC w^h renders it for the moment absurd to talk of Union bet^n Canada & B.C. is

---

55   Seymour to Buckingham, No. 125, November 30, 1868, CO 60:33.
56   Seymour to Buckingham, No. 125, November 30, 1868, CO 60:33.
57   Minute by FR [Rogers], January 19, 1869, on Seymour to Buckingham, No. 125, November 30, 1868, CO 60:33.

both a real & a producible reason for not entertaining the question now. And I w^d so use it." Rogers set forth some cautions, among them:

1. That formally repres^ve institutions did not answer very well in V.C. Island.
2. That they will almost certainly hasten the course of Anglo-Saxon violence ending in destruction of aborigines. For the purpose of keeping the peace in this respect the American character of the population renders the maintenance of an Executive responsible to an external authority particularly necessary.
3. There is a great practical difficulty in either providing for the representation of aliens & miners (who form a large part of the population) or in leaving them unrepresented…

> In short I submit, that this Colony is not in a state to be relieved from a certain steadying external pressure—& I do not like to relieve it from the pressure of Downing Street [in London] till we can substitute the pressure of Ottawa.[58]

Time would tell, Rogers acknowledged, whether "the 'Convention' is mere empty blast" or something more.[59]

On December 17, 1868, Governor Seymour opened a new legislative session with a sense of optimism, reporting to the Colonial Office: "As far as I can judge I think that the people and their representatives are in a better temper than I have seen them for some years,"[60] adding, in his address to open the session, how "the Public debt has been considerably reduced yet larger sums have been expended on public works of utility."[61] The good mood continued into the new year, and he telegraphed the secretary of state for the colonies on January 20, 1869, as to how "there is an improvement in the Revenue, the Legislative Body is in Session

---

58 Minute by FR [Rogers] January 19, 1869, on Seymour to Buckingham, No. 125, November 30, 1868, CO 60:33.

59 Minute by FR [Rogers] January 19, 1869, on Seymour to Buckingham, No. 125, November 30, 1868, CO 60:33.

60 Seymour to Buckingham, No. 136, December 21, 1868, CO 60:33.

61 Noted in minute by CC [Charles Cox], February 2, 1869, on Seymour to Buckingham, No. 136, December 21, 1868, CO 60:33.

and that everything is tranquil."[62]

A month later Seymour alerted the new secretary of state for the colonies, Granville Leveson-Gower, Earl Granville, as to how "we are anxiously working through a period of intense depression. But I think that when the railroad is made across the continent British Columbia will recover to a certain extent her former prosperity."[63]

The most contentious business of the session came on February 17, 1869, when the Legislative Council passed a resolution reading:

> Resolved
> That this Council impressed with the conviction that under existing circumstances the Confederation of this Colony with the Dominion of Canada would be undesirable, even if practicable, urges Her Majesty's Government not to take any decisive steps towards the present consummation of such Union.
> William A.G. Young
> Presiding Member[64]

Seymour, who was not best pleased by the resolution being "antagonistic to the immediate consummation of such a measure," sent it on to the Colonial Office on March 4, 1869.[65]

However, by the time Seymour closed the session with a speech a week and a half later, he was in high good humour. "I found the Legislative Council in an obliging, conciliatory humour, while disposed to take more of initiation than usual. A good sign, of course, for the working of our present Constitution; I have carried all the Bills to which I attached importance."[66]

Come June 1869 the situation had further improved. The confidential dispatch the secretary of state for the colonies sent Seymour on June 2 speaks for itself:

---

[62] Seymour to Buckingham, telegram, January 20, 1869, CO 60:37.

[63] Seymour to Granville, No. 27, February 23, 1869, CO 60:35.

[64] "Resolution of Legislative Council of 17 February 1869," enclosed in Frederick Seymour to Granville, No. 26, March 4, 1869, CO 60:35.

[65] Seymour to Granville, No. 26, March 4, 1869, CO 60:35.

[66] Seymour to Granville, No. 40, March 17, 1869, CO 60:35.

CHAPTER 8

I have the honor to transmit to you a Copy of a Confidential Dispatch from the Governor General of Canada suggesting at the instance of his Ministers that steps should be taken to forward the incorporation of British Columbia into the Dominion of Canada...

You are aware that the Hudson's Bay Company have accepted the terms recently offered to them for the surrender of their Territorial Rights to the Crown and that in the event of the arrangement being accepted by the Canadian Government there is every prospect of the annexation of the Hudson's Bay Territory to Canada.[67]

Frederick Seymour sadly did not live to read this news. Already in "a delicate state of health, suffering from extreme debility," yet persisting, Seymour died just over a week later, on June 10, 1869, at Bella Coola on board HMS *Sparrowhawk* while on a tour of inspection along the northwest coast of British Columbia.[68] Philip Hankin, the colonial secretary, was sworn in as acting governor.

Hankin was left to reply to a Colonial Office letter asking Seymour for specifics respecting the February 17 resolution against Confederation. "The late Governor left it entirely an open question as to the manner in which each official Member should vote." He explained how "the Majority which passed the Resolution against Union consisted of eleven Members, only five of whom were connected in any way with the Government," whereas "the Minority, in favour of Union, were Mess[rs] Havelock, Humphrey's, Carrall, Robson and Walkem, the last three named Gentlemen natives of the Dominion."[69] Henry Havelock was from Yale; Thomas Humphreys from Lillooet; William Carrall, Cariboo; John Robson, New Westminster; and George Walkem also Cariboo. The first four were among the Legislative Council's eight elected members; Walkem one of the thirteen appointed members. As the Colonial Office may have noted, none of those favouring Confederation were from Vancouver Island. Hankin's concluding sentence took a broader perspective: "It appears to me to be the general opinion that until communication through British Territory is established those who are most interested in the welfare of British Columbia will be opposed to Confederation."[70]

---

67 Granville to Seymour, Confidential, June 2, 1869, CO 398:5.

68 Hankin to Granville, No. 1, June 14, 1869, CO 60: telegram, June 15, 1865, CO 60:36.

69 Hankin to Granville, Confidential, July 19, 1869, CO 60:36.

70 Hankin to Granville, Confidential, July 19, 1869, CO 60:36.

Anthony Musgrave, shown in 1870, was appointed governor of the colony of British Columbia in 1869 and was given the task of arranging the colony's entry into Confederation with Canada. He successfully completed this assignment in 1871. *Image A-01514 courtesy of the Royal BC Museum.*

A new governor

By the time of Frederick Seymour's death in June 1869, the Colonial Office had already laid the groundwork for a successor. Among a host of hopefuls, not surprising in a milieu where Colonial Office appointments were much sought, was the ever-ambitious Colonel Moody, who, writing just a week after Seymour's death, described himself as "entirely unoccupied and free for any duty." His letter was summarily minuted: "Answer already filled up."[71]

A June 16 telegram sent to Philip Hankin read: "Mr. Musgrave is appointed Governor. You may announce that he will proceed to British Columbia immediately."[72]

Anthony Musgrave was, like his predecessors, a career administrator. Born in the West Indies, where his grandfather, father, and then he himself had held office, Musgrave had governed Newfoundland prior to being named to British Columbia on Seymour's death. His crossing to the western colony by rail via New York and San Francisco to take up his new position as of August 23, 1869, abolished any hesitations he might have had about the advantages of that means of transportation.[73]

A critical breakthrough

A critical breakthrough came on August 14, 1869, initiated by a letter from the secretary of state for the colonies, Earl Granville, informing Musgrave that the terms on which the intervening Hudson's Bay Company territory was to be "annexed to the Dominion" had been agreed and the larger decision was now at hand:

> The Queen will probably be advised before long to issue an Order in Council which will incorporate in the Dominion of Canada the whole of the British Possessions on the North American Continent, except the then conterminous Colony of British Columbia. The question therefore presents itself, whether this single Colony should be excluded from the great body politic which is thus forming itself.
>
> On this question the Colony itself does not appear to be unanimous. But as far as I can judge from the Despatches which have reached me, I should conjecture that the prevailing opinion

---

[71] Moody to Granville, June 17, 1869, CO 60:37, with minute by CC [Cox], June 18, 1869.
[72] Granville to Hankin, No. 57, June 16, 1869, NAC RG7:G8C/16.
[73] Kent M. Haworth, "Sir Anthony Musgrave," *Dictionary of Canadian Biography*, vol. 11, http://www.biographi.ca/en/bio/musgrave_anthony_11E.html.

was in favor of union. I have no hesitation in stating that such is, also, the opinion of Her Majesty's Government...

The establishment of a British line of communication between the Atlantic and Pacific Oceans, is far more feasible by the operation of a single Government responsible for the progress of both shores of the Continent than by a bargain negociated between separate, perhaps in some respects, rival Governments and Legislatures.[74]

Not only that but, in what was an interesting acknowledgment from the Colonial Office, Granville wrote:

The constitutional connection of Her Majesty's Government with the Colony of British Columbia is as yet closer than with any other part of North America, and they are bound on an occasion like the present to give, for the consideration of the community and the guidance of Her Majesty's Servants, a more unreserved expression of their wishes and judgment than might be elsewhere fitting.[75]

From the Colonial Office's perspective, British Columbia mattered in a special kind of way, including, as the letter noted "the condition of Indian tribes," making it important that those in charge "take such steps as you properly and constitutionally can, for promoting the favourable consideration of this question."[76]

Governor Musgrave's task was set.

Musgrave in charge

Incoming governor Anthony Musgrave's first order of business, as soon as possible on his arrival in the summer of 1869, was, like his predecessor, to visit the principal settlements, in this case New Westminster, Yale, Lytton, Williams Creek, Cariboo, Clinton, Lightning Creek, and Quesnelmouth. One reason for doing so was to clear up uncertainties left behind by an ailing Seymour; the

---

74   Granville to Musgrave, No. 84, August 14, 1869, NAC RG7:G8C/16.
75   Granville to Musgrave, No. 84, August 14, 1869, NAC RG7:G8C/16.
76   Granville to Musgrave, No. 84, August 14, 1869, NAC RG7.G8C/16.

second to collect "information on the state of feeling with regard to Confederation and other matters."[77]

Musgrave's main task was to convince officials in the localities to support entry into Confederation by assuring them union with Canada would not deprive them of their livelihoods. It was, Musgrave reported to the Colonial Office in August 1869, "the chief topic of interest."[78] Returning to Victoria in mid-October, Musgrave described those he had encountered in his travels as being "almost without exception prosperous," with businesses of all kinds being built on stable foundations, agriculture "being pursued to a greater extent with much success," and stock farming growing in importance.[79]

Writing on October 30, 1869, following his return to Victoria from his trip familiarizing himself with the province, Musgrave laid out for the Colonial Office the potential roadblocks he envisaged on the pathway to Confederation in respect to "the total white population in both sections of the United Colony," which "does not amount to ten thousand," of whom "more than half are resident in Vancouver Island, principally at Victoria." In what had earlier been James Douglas's criteria for belonging or not so, Musgrave differentiated, without explaining why, how "a very large proportion both here and on the Mainland, are not British subjects, and not unnaturally would lean rather towards annexation to the United States," even though "they live contentedly enough under what they admit to be an equitable government, in which the laws are fairly administered."[80]

Respecting the assumption held in Canada that in British Columbia "there is a very general desire for Union, and that opposition is almost entirely confined to Official Members of the Council," seeking "provision for their retirement on suitable Pensions, or at least that they should have the option of so retiring," Musgrave saw no reason not to replicate in that respect in British Columbia what had been "done on the introduction of Responsible Government in the Eastern Provinces" of Canada.[81]

From Musgrave's perspective, "the more prominent of the Agitators for Confederation are a small knot of Canadians who hope that it may be possible

---

77   Musgrave to Granville, No. 7, September 3, 1869, CO 60:36; Granville to Musgrave, No. 105, December 4, 1869, CO, NAC RG7:G8C/16.

78   Musgrave to Granville, No. 1, August 25, 1869, CO 60: 36.

79   Musgrave to Granville, No. 9, October 15, 1869, CO 60:36.

80   Musgrave to Granville, No. 19, October 30, 1869, CO 60:36.

81   Musgrave to Granville, No. 19, October 30, 1869, CO 60:36.

to make fuller representative institutions and Responsible Government part of the new arrangements, and that they may so place themselves in positions of influence and emolument." The "mercantile portion of the Community" sought "to secure in terms with Canada that Victoria should be made a Free Port." In sum, "there is great diversity in the views entertained upon this important question."[82]

Musgrave went on to share his private views on several aspects of Confederation. Respecting the outstanding question of "the introduction of 'Responsible Government' in the local administration after Union," it was Musgrave's "opinion that it would be entirely inapplicable to a Community so small and so constituted as this—a sparse population scattered over a vast area of country." And he fretted over financial matters:

> The liabilities of this Colony are very heavy, and the population is very small...The machinery of government is unavoidably expensive from the great cost of living, which is at least twice as much as in Canada, and the great area over which the action of government must be maintained for a small number of residents...the grant in aid under the British North America Act 1867 to the other Provinces, of 80 cents per head to the population, would amount only to an insignificant sum in our case.[83]

While, as instructed, Musgrave had printed in the Victoria newspaper the government's dispatch "respecting the Union of this Colony with the Dominion of Canada," he was waiting until the Legislative Assembly met in December to lay it before that body.[84]

The Colonial Office minutes on Musgrave's letter of October 30, 1869—which Musgrave of course never saw—bode well for British Columbia's future. Frederic Rogers, the permanent under-secretary of state for the colonies; Earl Granville, secretary of state for the colonies; and William Monsell, parliamentary under-secretary of state for the colonies, decided they would encourage Musgrave "to use his own judgment respecting the mode & time of bringing the question before his Council—and not to suppose himself bound to bring

---

82   Musgrave to Granville, No. 19, October 30, 1869, CO 60:36.
83   Musgrave to Granville, No. 19, October 30, 1869, CO 60:36.
84   Musgrave to Granville, No. 19, October 30, 1869, CO 60:36.

forward any formal proposition, unless he thinks that by so doing he will promote further the acceptance of the Union."[85]

In early 1870 Musgrave managed the feat by, he explained to the Colonial Office, not forcing "Confederation upon the Community without time being afforded for consideration," and "by putting the proposal before the Community in an intelligible form."[86]

A final lunge for British Columbia joining the United States

A final American lunge for British Columbia now came into play, making the rounds of the highest levels of government in Britain and the United States. A petition, prompted by "the avowed intention of Her Majesty's Government to confederate this Colony with the Dominion of Canada," beseeched the American president "to endeavour to induce Her Majesty to *consent to the transfer of this Colony to the United States*" (italics in original).[87] Signed by seventy property holders, businessmen, merchants, and others in Victoria, Nanaimo, and elsewhere on Vancouver Island, "many of us British subjects," the petition was presented to President Ulysses S. Grant on December 29, 1869, by "the special Indian Commissioner for Alaska Tribes," who had been passing through Victoria on his way to Washington, DC, and agreed to take it with him.[88] As indicated by their surnames, and biographical information prepared by historian Willard Ireland, petitioners included numerous shop owners of German or other non-British descent.

On January 3, 1870, Sir Edward Thornton, the British minister to the United States, sent the Earl of Clarendon, secretary of state for foreign affairs, a copy of what he referred to as a "Memorial," which had been brought to Washington "by an American Citizen, Mr. Vincent Colyer," a Quaker who had "recently paid a visit to Alaska for the purpose of inquiring into the condition of the Indians in

---

85   Minutes by FR [Rogers], December 15, 1869, WM [William Monsell], December 18, 1869, and G [Granville], December 24, 1869, on Musgrave to Granville, No. 19, October 30, 1869, CO 60:36.

86   Musgrave to Granville, No. 18, February 21, 1870, CO 60:38.

87   Ireland, "The Annexation Petition of 1869," 270.

88   Ireland, "The Annexation Petition of 1869," 267–87; Ireland "Further Note on the Annexation Petition of 1869," 67–72. For the petition, see 270–73; for information on the signatories, 271–75; and for short biographies of 41 of them, 275–78, all in Ireland, "The Annexation Petition of 1869."

that territory." The memorial had been delivered to the President on December 29, accompanied by a request that he would "not only submit it to his Cabinet but would also send it to the Congress."[89]

Thornton's January 13 letter explained how the memorial delivered by Colyer fit in with larger events in play in Britain's North American colonies. He pointed to an "existing disturbance in the Hudson's Bay settlement, and the asserted disaffection in Nova Scotia," along with "differences arising with [Britain] out of the 'Alabama' affair" consequent on Britain having permitted the South to build merchant ships on its territory during the recently concluded American Civil War. From Thornton's perspective as the British minister to the United States, and on his reading of the American press, these events were "looked upon as the beginning of a Separation of the British Provinces from the Mother Country, and of their early annexation to the U.S." In this view, "England has it in her power, and might not be unwilling, to come to an amicable settlement of these differences on the basis of the cession of our territory on this Continent to the United States."[90]

Events cascaded. Three days earlier, on January 10, 1870, Oregon senator Elijah Corbett, referencing the Colyer memorial, presented a resolution in the United States Senate "that the Secretary of State should inquire into the expediency of including the transfer of British Columbia to the U.S. in any Treaty for the adjustment of all pending differences between the two Countries" related to British actions during the American Civil War.[91]

Events did not play out as former Secretary of State William Seward had predicted. He had assumed Britain would acquiesce to British Columbia's annexation to the United States, thereby getting the Civil War claims off its hands, but not so.[92] The United States pulled back in the face of the Colonial Office's

---

89   Sir Edward Thornton, minister to the United States, to George William Frederick Villiers, Earl Clarendon, secretary of state for foreign affairs, No. 4, January 13, 1870, in Sir Arthur John Otway, under-secretary of state for foreign affairs, to William Monsell, parliamentary under-secretary of state for the colonies, January 17, 1870, CO 60:42.

90   Thornton to Clarendon, No. 4, January 3, 1870, in Otway to Monsell, January 17, 1870, CO 60:42.

91   Thornton to Clarendon, No. 4, January 3, 1870, in Otway to Monsell, January 17, 1870, CO 60:42.

92   See Shi, "Seward's Attempt to Annex British Columbia, 1865–1869," 226–38; Holloway, "'Without Conquest or Purchase,'" 61–62; and Ireland, "The Annexation Petition of 1869,"

support for British Columbia's union with Canada, facilitated by the Hudson's Bay Company's relinquishment of the intervening territory lying between British Columbia and British colonies to the east.

Support and opposition in the Legislative Council

Musgrave was able to forward to the secretary of state for the colonies on February 21, 1870, "Copies of the Resolution which it is proposed to pass embodying the terms on which this Colony would be willing to join the Dominion." As he noted on the letter, "it now remains to be ascertained to what extent the Government of Canada can fulfill the expectations of the Colony."[93] There had been, Musgrave pointed out two days later, trade-offs on the part of British Columbia, with "suffrage limited to British subjects" as opposed to "universal suffrage including foreigners" which "if allowed to continue would very probably defeat Confederation."[94]

The debate of the colony's Legislative Council, which comprised nine elected and six appointed members, on "Confederation with Canada" began on March 9 and ended 100,000 words later on April 6, 1870, with the simple statement in the minutes, "House adopted resolution."[95] Musgrave thereupon reported to London how the Legislative Council had passed all of "the Resolutions which were submitted to them on the subject of Union with the Dominion of Canada," with some suggestions for "modifications in the proposed terms" and "supplementary recommendations" relating to "the peculiar circumstances of this Colony." As requested of him, Musgrave had "succeeded in avoiding the introduction of proposals touching on 'Responsible Government' or the establishment of a Free Port," both potentially contentious issues.[96]

Musgrave was not optimistic about achieving a rail line, and for that reason proposed "to send a delegation to Ottawa to present the proposals," and

---

267–87.

93 Musgrave to Granville, No. 18, February 21, 1870, CO 60:41.

94 Musgrave to Granville, No. 20, February 23, 1870, CO 60:38.

95 British Columbia, Legislative Council, "Debate on the Subject of Confederation with Canada," in James Hendrickson, ed., *Journals of the Colonial Legislatures of the Colonies of Vancouver Island and British Columbia 1851–1871*, vol. 5: *1886–1871* (Victoria, BC: Provincial Archives of British Columbia, 1980).

96 Musgrave to Granville, No. 32, April 5, 1870, CO 60:38.

to discuss and explain them. The delegation comprised "Mʳ Trutch, the Chief Commissioner of Lands and Works," in "whose ability and discretion" Musgrave had "much confidence"; Mr Helmcken, who had "great influence in the Community" despite being "far from...an ardent Confederate"; and "Mʳ Carrall," who was "a Canadian and a zealous advocate of Union," and also "familiar with the wants and views of the people of the Upper Country."[97]

The delegation's negotiations with the federal government were successful, Canada agreeing to build the essential railway linking British Columbia eastward across North America. By November Musgrave was feeling particularly optimistic, daring to close a letter to the new secretary of state for the colonies, John Wodehouse, First Earl of Kimberley: "it seems now probable that very little time will elapse before British Columbia becomes part of the Dominion of Canada."[98]

Public pensions

Before the deal could be signed and delivered, however, agreement also needed to be reached on "the future position of Government Servants as one of those questions requiring some personal care on the part of the Governor."[99] This particularly affected civil servants in Victoria, which continued to see itself as in charge of the order of things. On November 16, 1870, Musgrave reminded the Colonial Office how:

> By the sixth Article of the Scheme of Union agreed upon between the Canadian Ministry and the Delegates from this Government it is stipulated that suitable Pensions such as shall be approved by Her Majesty's Government shall be provided by the Government of the Dominion for those of Her Majesty's Servants in the Colony whose position and emoluments derived therefrom would be affected by political changes on the admission of British Columbia into the Dominion of Canada.[100]

---

97 Musgrave to Granville, No. 32, April 5, 1870, CO 60:38.
98 Musgrave to John Wodehouse, First Earl of Kimberley, secretary of state for the colonies, No. 144, November 16, 1870, CO 60:41.
99 Musgrave to Kimberley, No. 147, November 17, 1870, CO 60:41.
100 Musgrave to Kimberley, No. 147, November 17, 1870, CO 60:41.

CHAPTER 8

Just in case they were not individually known to the Colonial Office, Musgrave shared the names of "those who will be affected injuriously by the change" with their "salaries inserted in the margin":

The Colonial Secretary	Mr Hankin [£800]
The Attorney General	Mr Phillippo [£800]
The Commissioner of Lands and Works	Mr Trutch [£800]
The Collector of Customs	Mr Hamley [£650]
The Auditor General	Mr Ker [£500]
Stipendiary Magistrates	Mr Ball
	M^r O'Reilly
	Mr Sanders
	Mr Bushby
	Mr Pemberton
	Mr Spaulding[101]

These five officers, along with the six magistrates, embodied, on the one hand, the last stand of the colonial establishment's governance of the Island colony and, on the other, the entryway to two stand-alone provinces where political power would be more broadly based. Their stories give a sense of who had mattered, and why they had done so.

Arriving as a Royal Navy officer, Colonial Secretary Philip Hankin had been so enchanted by "the social life of Victoria" he resigned his commission in favour of various civilian appointments, in the course of which his "ability to govern" was called into question, but insufficiently so for him to be denied a lifetime pension that accompanied him to England to become private secretary to the Duke of Buckingham, former secretary of state for the colonies.[102]

Jamaican-born and English-educated Attorney General George Phillippo was appointed attorney general only in 1870, resigning a year later, pension in hand, for a position in British Guinea.

English-born and -educated Commissioner of Lands and Works Joseph Trutch had chased the California gold rush north, reaching British Columbia in 1858, where he worked as a surveyor. He was appointed commissioner of lands

---

101 Musgrave to Kimberley, No. 147, November 17, 1870, CO 60:41.

102 Robert Louis Smith, "The Hankin Appointment, 1868," BC Studies 22 (1974): 26–39 with quotes on 28 and 36.

Securing pensions for British Columbia's many civil servants, including members of the Legislative Assembly, pictured ca. 1870, was one of the preconditions of Confederation. From left to right on porch: W.A. Franklin, house messenger; Henry Holbrook; Wymond Ogilvy Hamley; Edward Graham Alston; Philip J. Hankin; Montague William Tyrwhitt-Drake; Joseph M. Trutch (sitting on porch at top of steps); Thomas L. Wood; Henry Maynard Ball; Edgar Dewdney; Arthur Thomas Bushby. From left to right in foreground: Amor de Cosmos; Henry Pering Pellew Crease; D.B. King (seated on steps, with dog); Thomas B. Humphreys; John Robson. *Image C-06178 courtesy of the Royal BC Museum.*

and works in 1864, even as he established himself as, to quote historian Robin Fisher, among "the people who ran British Columbia and...ran it in their own interests and those of their class," with "anyone who stood in the way...likely to get short shrift from Joseph Trutch and his kind."[103]

Collector of Customs Wymond Ogilvy Hamley followed a distinguished father into the Royal Navy, but resigned to join the Imperial Civil Service, whence he was offered the colonial position.

---

103   Robin Fisher, "Sir Joseph William Trutch," *Dictionary of Canadian Biography*, vol. 13, http://www.biographi.ca/en/bio/trutch_joseph_william_13E.html.

CHAPTER 8

Born into "a family long prominent on the Scottish border," Auditor General Robert Ker came for the gold rush, to be quickly recruited into government service.[104]

Neither were the five stipendiary magistrates everyday arrivals. They each also have their own stories to tell, excepting Spaulding, about whom no information was found. On retiring after fifteen years in the English army, followed by ten years in the Colonial Service in Australia, Henry Maynard Ball had sought a new experience, to have an intermediary successfully recommend him for "an appointment in British Columbia or Vancouver's Island."[105] Born in England and educated in Belgium and Germany, Edward Sanders served in the Crimean War prior to being appointed a gold commissioner in Yale in 1859. The son of a London merchant and of a respected linguist and writer of fiction, Arthur Bushby headed off to the British Columbia gold rush in 1858 with a letter of introduction from the governor of the HBC in London, which got him a job as private secretary to Judge Begbie, who he accompanied on his mainland circuit. He married James Douglas's daughter Agnes and they settled in New Westminster to have five children together.[106] Grandson of a lord mayor of Dublin, Joseph Despard Pemberton became an engineer and surveyor, which skills he transferred in 1851 to Vancouver Island.[107]

In December 1870 Musgrave updated Kimberley respecting the nine members just elected and six appointed to the Legislative Council, whose task Musgrave specified in no uncertain terms: "The business of the Session will be almost entirely limited to completing the proposed Union with Canada...I think that I shall be able to obtain sufficient support even among the elected members to avoid or surmount any complications arising from this cause. All elected Members have been returned in favor of Confederation."[108]

Minutes on Musgrave's letter, all written on the same day by Frederic Rogers; Sir Robert George Wyndham Herbert, assistant under-secretary of state; and Kimberley, retail the Colonial Office's enthusiastic response:

---

104 Dorothy Blakey Smith, "Robert Ker," *Dictionary of Canadian Biography*, vol. 10, http://www.biographi.ca/en/bio/ker_robert_10E.html.

105 Nicholls, Secretary of Greenwich Hospital, to Lytton, February 8, 1859, CO 60:6.

106 Dorothy Blakey Smith, "Arthur Thomas Bushby," *Dictionary of Canadian Biography*, vol. 10, http://www.biographi.ca/en/bio/bushby_arthur_thomas_10E.html.

107 Richard Mackie, "Joseph Despard Pemberton," *Dictionary of Canadian Biography*, vol. 12, http://www.biographi.ca/en/bio/pemberton_joseph_despard_12E.html.

108 Musgrave to Kimberley, No. 163, December 22, 1870, CO 60:41.

He proposes to legislate with the view of paving the way for Responsible Government in the event of, & after, Confederation. RGWH Feb 1/71

I sh^d wholly trust his judgement in the matter, & sh^d leave him discretion. FR 1/2

I agree. K Feb 1/71[109]

From the Colonial Office's perspective, British Columbia was on its way.

Musgrave completing his designated task

Given the obligation Musgrave brought with him to the governorship of British Columbia, it was with obvious relief that he sent a telegram on January 20, 1871, to Kimberley, reading in its entirety:

> Address to Queen for union with Canada on terms agreed upon passed Legislative Council unanimously today.[110]

Senior clerk Charles Cox minuted almost gleefully to the secretary of state on the telegram itself, "This looks like getting to business," whereas others in the office were more cautious: "I fear the Canadian Parliament will demur to the terms, & it is difficult to see how they can carry out the Railway which is the principal inducement to the Columbians."[111]

Two days later Musgrave wrote again, sending printed copies of the address to the Queen in duplicate, one "by the overland route via Olympia in Washington Territory," but "as this mode of transmission is uncertain from the state of the Roads at this time of the year," retaining the original to be sent "by the Mail Steamer next month direct to San Francisco." As well, "Mr Trutch who was one of the Delegates sent to Canada last year for the purpose

---

109 Minutes, February 1, 1871, on Musgrave to Kimberley, No. 163, December 22, 1870, CO 60:41.

110 Musgrave to Kimberley, telegram, January 20, 1871, CO 60:43.

111 Minute by CC [Cox], January 26, 1871, followed by minute by RGWH [Sir Robert George Wyndham Herbert], January 26, 1871; initialled by FR [Rogers], January 27, 1871; EHKH [Edward Hugessen Knatchbull-Hugessen], January 28, 1871; and K [Kimberley], January 29, 1871, on Musgrave to Kimberley, telegram, January 20, 1871, CO 60:43.

of negotiating arrangements for Union" was about to head to Ottawa "with a copy of this Document, by the Mail Steamer for San Francisco about the middle of February," and would bring a copy with him.[112] For all that British Columbia was about to change its status, communication with Britain, or for that matter the rest of the political entity it was about to join, was no more certain than it had been.

Musgrave's task was done, as he wrote the same day, January 22, 1871, to Kimberley:

> This Colony has now finally accepted the terms offered by the Government of Canada for Union with the Dominion, and it only remains to carry out the details of the arrangement, which will probably be completed before the 1st of July next. After that is done my employment here will cease... But, I trust with some confidence in Your Lordship's favorable consideration for further occupation elsewhere.[113]

Life goes on

In the interim, life went on in a British Columbia in the making much as before. Serving members Hankin, Phillippo, Hamley, and Pemberton, along with Edward Graham Alston, were in February 1871 appointed to the new Legislative Council.[114] The same month Musgrave initiated the process of amending the colony's constitution to permit "Responsible Government to come into operation at the first Session of the Legislature subsequently to the Union of the Colony with Canada."[115] Yet even as times were changing, a minute on the letter from Musgrave apologizing for "the irregularity and lateness" of the annual Blue Book acknowledged, a little regretfully perhaps, that "no more Blue Books will be received from B. Columbia as the Colony is about to be merged into the Dominion of Canada."[116]

---

112   Musgrave to Kimberley, No. 3, January 22, 1871, CO 60:43.

113   Musgrave to Kimberley, No. 4, January 22, 1871, CO 60:43.

114   Kimberley to Musgrave, No. 15, February 17, 1871, NAC RG7:G8C/18.

115   Musgrave to Kimberley, No. 13, February 18, 1871, CO 60:43.

116   Minute by WR [Robinson], RM [Robert Henry Meade], and K [Kimberley], May 26, 1871, on Musgrave to Kimberley, No. 49, April 20, 1871, CO 60:43.

The observation was not quite accurate given a final Blue Book was dispatched in June 1871 for the year 1870, about which Musgrave noted cheerfully how "the Year was fairly prosperous in respect of the material interests of the Colony."[117] British Columbia's final Blue Book described in upbeat fashion how "the explanation of the diminution of Import Duties is to be found...in the increased production of articles of food and general consumption within our own borders"; "Agriculture, Stockraising and the minor operations of Husbandry have been much and successfully extended both on the Mainland and on Vancouver Island"; and "applications for land for settlement have been numerous." Gold mining was ongoing, and Vancouver Island coal deposits were further developed. The Blue Book not unexpectedly took special pleasure in noting how "the public debt will be assumed by Canada," and work would soon be "commenced for the construction of the proposed Railway."[118] The future was in view.

British Columbia becoming Canadian

The work of unification was underway. Writing to Musgrave on May 27, 1871, Kimberley, as he signed himself, had "the honor to transmit from Her Majesty an Order in Council dated 16th May uniting British Columbia to the Dominion of Canada," for which "I caused the 20th of July to be fixed for this Union."[119] Whether the letter was the usual format or related in particular to British Columbia, the next paragraph must have struck a chord:

> It gives me much satisfaction to express to you how fully sensible Her Majesty's Government are of the energy zeal and ability with which you and the Officers of your government have laboured to effect this Union, which it is confidently anticipated will confer important and lasting benefits in British Columbia and by the consolidation of Her Majesty's possessions in North America will greatly promote their progress in the career of prosperity of which they seem destined by their natural resources.[120]

---

117   Musgrave to Kimberley, No. 66, June 21, 1871, CO 60:44.
118   Musgrave to Kimberley, No. 66, June 21, 1871, CO 60:44.
119   Kimberley to Musgrave, No. 52, May 27, 1871, NAC RG7:G8C/18.
120   Kimberley to Musgrave, No. 52, May 27, 1871, NAC RG7:G8C/18.

CHAPTER 8

Responding on July 12, 1871, Musgrave described how "I have given due publicity to the Order in Council, and have proclaimed the 20th of July to be observed as a Public Holiday in honor of the occasion." He was optimistic about the future: "On that day this Province will quickly become a part of the Dominion, and so far as the future can be foreseen, there is now no reason to apprehend any reaction of public feeling adverse to the Union, or any difficulty in arrangement of the several Departments of public business." Musgrave went on to detail with a sense of relief how, very importantly, "arrangements have been completed for payment of the floating Public Debt by the Canadian authorities through the Bank of British Columbia on the 15th instant," and how longtime public figure Joseph Trutch, who had been appointed lieutenant governor, would be "on his way to Victoria at the end of this month," allowing Musgrave to be on his way.[121]

As for the Colonial Office, it quite literally cleaned house in respect to its one-time colony, requesting the following of Musgrave in a June 28, 1871, letter:

> You will select from the Records of the Colony all Despatches from the Secretary of State to the Governor which are marked as confidential or secret, and also similar Despatches from the Governor to the Secretaries of State and cause them to be packed in packing cases and transmitted to me at this office. If it should be found that such Despatches have been bound up with public Despatches, I shall wish you to send them all to me. If on the other hand the public Despatches have been kept separately you will cause them to be packed in cases to await any directions...as to their ultimate disposal.[122]

In case that letter did not arrive, Kimberley alerted Musgrave in a letter of July 5, 1871, how: "I sent to you this day at 3.5 P.M. a telegraphic Despatch in the following words 'Pack up and send home all Confidential and Secret Despatches.'"[123] Just like that, in the blink of an eye, British Columbia was shorn of a critical aspect of its history as a colonial possession by a Colonial

---

121   Musgrave to Kimberley, No. 68, July 12, 1871, CO 60:44.

122   Kimberley to Musgrave, No. 65, June 28, 1871, NAC RG7:G8C/18.

123   Kimberley to Musgrave, No. 67, July 5, 1871, NAC RG7:G8C/18.

Office now shifting its attention to its myriad other British colonies around the world.

Musgrave on his way

As for the indispensable Musgrave, he had been preparing his exit for some time, energized by the need for surgery in London to repair a problem with his leg prior to his next appointment. In January 1871 he had alerted the Colonial Office, as it obviously already knew, that "the Governments of Ceylon and Hong Kong will both become vacant some time during this year by expiration of the usual term of service," and he was hopeful.[124] Musgrave departed British Columbia on July 25, 1871, for London, where he would "report in person the satisfactory completion of the Union of this Colony with Canada."[125] He would go on to important postings as governor of Natal (1872-73), South Australia (1873-77), Jamaica (1877-83), and Queensland (1885-88). As Musgrave had found out time and again, to be in British Columbia was to be alone and lonely, and it can only be hoped his next postings were more agreeable.

British Columbia saved for Canada

As explained in the annual *Colonial Office List* enumerating the "Colonial Dependencies of Great Britain," British Columbia was by virtue of having been "admitted into Union with the Dominion of Canada on the 20th July 1871" no longer present as a colonial possession.[126]

British Columbia had been saved for Canada. The deed was done just a quarter of a century after Britain and the United States had in 1846 divided the almost wholly Indigenous Pacific Northwest between them. More so than with any other constituency, Indigenous women had been used and abused in the process, but, while victimized, had not faltered, descendants into the present day testifying along with their male Indigenous counterparts to their strength of character in the face of adversity. What would otherwise have been the case, it is

---

124 Musgrave to Kimberley, No. 4, January 22, 1871, CO 60:43.

125 Musgrave to Kimberley, No. 75, July 24, 1871, CO 60:44.

126 Arthur N. Birch and William Robinson, *The Colonial Office List of 1873* (London: Harrison, 1873), 30.

CHAPTER 8

impossible to know in retrospect, just as it is respecting other aspects of a British Columbia in the making.

There had not been perfection but there had been survival, and the newly minted province of British Columbia set in place in 1871 was now on its own to prove itself in a Canada that was itself in the making.[127]

---

127   Among numerous histories of the later time period in British Columbia, see Jean Barman, *The West beyond the West: A History of British Columbia*, 3rd edition (Toronto: University of Toronto Press, 2007).

APPENDIX

Members of the Colonial Office during the time covered by
British Columbia in the Balance

Secretary of State for War and the Colonies	
Henry George Grey, 3rd Earl Grey	July 1846–February 1852
John Pakington, 1st Baron Hampton	February 1852–December 1852
Henry Pelham-Clinton, 5th Duke of Newcastle	December 1852–June 1854

Secretary of State for the Colonies	
Sir George Grey	June 1854–February 1855
Sidney Herbert	February 1855
Lord John Russell	February 1855–July 1855
Sir William Molesworth	July 1855–November 1855
Henry Labouchere	November 1855–February 1858
Edward Stanley, Lord Stanley	February 1858–June 1858

APPENDIX

Sir Edward George Earle Bulwer Lytton	June 1858–June 1859
Henry Pelham-Clinton, 5th Duke of Newcastle	June 1859–April 1864
Edward Cardwell	April 1864–June 1866
Henry Howard Molyneux Herbert, 4th Earl of Carnarvon	July 1866–March 1867
Richard Temple-Grenville, 3rd Duke of Buckingham and Chandos	March 1867–December 1868
Granville Leveson-Gower, 2nd Earl Granville	December 1868–July 1870
John Wodehouse, 1st Earl of Kimberley	July 1870–February 1874

People who wrote or received letters

Charles Adderley, 1st Baron Norton	Parliamentary under-secretary for the colonies, 1866–1868
John Ball	Permanent under-secretary for the colonies, 1836–1848
H.H. Berens	HBC governor, 1858–1863
Arthur Birch	Colonial secretary of British Columbia 1864–1866; acting governor of British Columbia, 1866–1867
Arthur Johnstone Blackwood	Senior clerk in the Colonial Office, 1840–1867
Richard Blanshard	Governor of Vancouver Island, 1849–1851
Edward Cardwell	Secretary of state for the colonies, 1864–1866
Andrew Colvile	Deputy governor of the HBC, 1839–1852; governor of the HBC, 1852–1856

APPENDIX

Charles Cox	Senior clerk in the Colonial Office, 1860–1871
John Otway O'Connor Cuffe, 3rd Earl of Desart	Under-secretary for the colonies, 1852
Sir James Douglas	Governor of Vancouver Island, 1851–1864; Governor of British Columbia, 1858–1864
Thomas F. Elliot	Assistant under-secretary in the Colonial Office, 1847–1868
William Edward Forster	Parliamentary under-secretary for the colonies, 1865–1866
Chichester Fortescue	Parliamentary under-secretary for the colonies, 1857–1866
J.R. Godley	Assistant under-secretary, War Office, 1855
Henry George Grey, 3rd Earl Grey	Secretary of state for the colonies, 1846–1852
Sir George Grey	Secretary of state for the colonies, 1854–1855
Edmund Hammond	Permanent under-secretary of the British Foreign Office, 1854–1873
Philip Hankin	Superintendent of police for Victoria, 1864–1866; colonial secretary for British Columbia, 1869–1871; acting governor of British Columbia, 1869
Benjamin Hawes	Permanent under-secretary for the colonies, 1846–1851
Henry Howard Molyneux Herbert, 4th Earl of Carnarvon	Parliamentary under-secretary for the colonies, 1858–1859; secretary of state for the colonies, 1866–1867, 1874–1878
Sir Robert George Wyndham Herbert	Assistant under-secretary for the colonies, 1870; permanent under-secretary, 1871–1892
Sidney Herbert	Secretary of state for the colonies, 1855

APPENDIX

Henry Turner Irving	Junior clerk in the Colonial Office, 1858–1863
Vane Jadis	Assistant clerk in the Colonial Office, 1846–1867
Sir Arthur Kennedy	Governor of Vancouver Island, 1864–1866
Henry Labouchere, Baron Taunton	Secretary of state for the colonies, 1855–1858
Granville George Leveson-Gower, 2nd Earl Granville	Secretary of state for the colonies, 1868–1870
Sir Edward George Earle Bulwer Lytton	Secretary of state for the colonies, 1858–1859
Herman Merivale	Permanent under-secretary for the colonies, 1848–1859
Sir William Molesworth	Secretary of state for the colonies, 1855
William Monsell	Parliamentary under-secretary for the colonies, 1868–1870
T.W.C. Murdoch	Chairman of the Colonial Land and Emigration Commission, 1847–1876
Sir Anthony Musgrave	Governor of British Columbia, 1869–1871
Henry Charles Norris	Clerk in the Colonial Office, 1841–1879
John Pakington, 1st Baron Hampton	Secretary of state for war and the colonies, 1852
Sir Frederick Peel	Under-secretary for the colonies, 1851–1855; financial secretary to the Treasury, 1860–1865
Henry Pelham-Clinton, 5th Duke of Newcastle	Secretary of state for the colonies, 1852–1854, 1859–1864
Sir John Henry Pelly	Governor of the HBC, 1822–1852

APPENDIX

Frederic Rogers	Assistant under-secretary for the colonies, 1846–1847; permanent under-secretary, 1859–1871
Lord John Russell	Secretary of state for the colonies, 1855
Frederick Seymour	Governor of British Columbia, 1864–1868; governor of united colony, 1868–1869
John Shepherd	Deputy governor of the HBC, 1852–1856; governor of the HBC, 1856–1858
W.G. Smith	Secretary for the HBC, 1843–1871
Edward Stanley, Lord Stanley	Secretary of state for the colonies, 1858
Sir James Stephen	Permanent under-secretary for the colonies, 1836–1848
H.K. Storks	Secretary for military correspondence, War Office, 1857–1859
Richard Temple-Grenville, 3rd Duke of Buckingham and Chandos	Secretary of state for the colonies, 1867–1868
Stephen Walcott	Secretary to the Colonial Land and Emigration Commission, 1840–1869
John Wodehouse, 1st Earl of Kimberley	Secretary of state for the colonies, 1870–1874

Colonial Office staff whose initialled minutes are referenced in notes

AB[d]	Arthur Johnstone Blackwood	Senior clerk in the Colonial Office, 1840–1867
BH	Benjamin Hawes	Permanent under-secretary for the colonies, 1846–1851

APPENDIX

C	Henry Howard Molyneux Herbert, 4th Earl of Carnarvon Eton and Oxford University	Parliamentary under-secretary for the colonies, 1858–1859; secretary of state for the colonies, 1866–1867, 1874–1878
CBA	Charles Adderley, 1st Baron Norton Oxford University	Parliamentary under-secretary for the colonies, 1866–1868
CC	Charles Cox Eton	Senior clerk in the Colonial Office, 1860–1871
CF	Chichester Fortescue, 2nd Baron Clermont, 1st Baron Carlingford, Lord Carlingford Oxford University	Parliamentary under-secretary for the colonies, 1857–1866
D	John Otway O'Connor Cuffe, 3rd Earl of Desart	Under-secretary for the colonies, 1852
EBL	Sir Edward George Earle Bulwer Lytton Cambridge University	Secretary of state for the colonies, 1858–1859
EC	Edward Cardwell Winchester and Balliol College	Secretary of state for the colonies, 1864–1866
EHKH	Edward Hugessen Knatchbull-Hugessen, 1st Baron Brabourne Eton and Oxford University	Under-secretary of state for the colonies, 1871–1874
FR	Frederic Rogers Eton and Oxford University	Assistant under-secretary for the colonies, 1846–1847; permanent under-secretary, 1859–1871
G	Henry George Grey, 3rd Earl Grey Cambridge University	Secretary of state for the colonies, 1846–1852
G	Granville George Leveson-Gower, 2nd Earl Granville Eton and Oxford University	Secretary of state for the colonies, 1868–1870
HCN	Henry Charles Norris	Clerk in the Colonial Office, 1841–1879

APPENDIX

HL	Henry Labouchere, Baron Taunton Winchester College and Cambridge University	Secretary of state for the colonies, 1855–1858
HM	Herman Merivale Harrow and Oxford University	Permanent under-secretary for the colonies, 1848–1859
HTI	Henry Turner Irving	Junior clerk in the Colonial Office, 1858–1863
JB	John Ball Oscott College and Cambridge University	Permanent under-secretary for the colonies, 1836–1848
JS	Sir James Stephen Cambridge University	Permanent under-secretary for the colonies, 1836–1848
K	John Wodehouse, 1st Earl of Kimberley Eton and Oxford University	Secretary of state for the colonies, 1870–1874
N	Henry Pelham-Clinton, 5th Duke of Newcastle Eton and Oxford University	Secretary of state for the colonies, 1852–1854, 1859–1864
RGWH	Sir Robert George Wyndham Herbert Eton and Oxford University	Assistant under-secretary for the colonies, 1870; permanent under-secretary, 1871–1892
RM	Sir Robert Henry Meade Harrow and Cambridge University	Under-secretary for the colonies, 1871–1892
SJB	Samuel Jasper Blunt	Senior clerk, 1839–1866
TFE	Thomas Frederick Elliot Harrow	Assistant under-secretary in the Colonial Office, 1847–1868
VJ	Vane Jadis	Assistant clerk in the Colonial Office, 1846–1867

APPENDIX

WD	William Dealtry Eton and Cambridge University	Clerk, 1837–1879
WEF	William Edward Forster Grove House School	Parliamentary under-secretary for the colonies, 1865–1866
WM	William Monsell Winchester College	Parliamentary under-secretary for the colonies, 1868–1870
WR	William Robinson	Assistant senior clerk, 1862–1870; Senior clerk, 1870–1871

INDEX

Adams, John, 24
Adderley, Charles, 165, 263
Admiral Island. *See* Saltspring Island
Alaska, 14, 24, 170, 208, 257–58, 262, 264, 265, 280
Alexandra Bridge, 133
Alexandria
    Bishop Hills visit, 203
    HBC fort, 28
    population, 223, 240
    roads, 108, 119–20, 121–22, 129, 133, 253, 255
Alston, Edward Graham, **285**, 288
American Civil War. *See under* United States
Anderson Lake, 200, 234
Anglican Church. *See* Church of England
Antler Creek mines, 101, 132
Australia
    British colonies, 22, 55, 77, 163, 291
    gold rush, 38, 42, 77, 210, 222
    miners inquire about BC, 254

Ball, Henry Maynard, 132–33, 226, 227–28, 269–70, 284, **285**, 286
Barkerville, **157**, 235
Barman, Jean, and BC history, 11–13
Begbie, Matthew Baillie, 74–75, 82, 86–87, 102, 125, 218, 235, 240, 249, 286
Birch, Arthur, 147
Black people
    in BC, 181

    and Church of England, 170–71, 174
    experience racism, 175–76, 185, 188, 191–92, 198
    and Lady Franklin, 189, 191–93
    rifle corps, 44, 191, 192
    on Saltspring Island, 184
    in Victoria, 43–44, 174–76, 187
    view of American prejudice, 176
Blackwood, Arthur
    American element in BC, 142, 153, 162
    British element in BC, 215
    cross-Canada railway, 254–55
    loan to BC, 106–7, 119, 131, 134
    representative government in BC, 125
    Royal Engineers, 81, 104, 114
    Vancouver Island Legislative Assembly, 142, 158–60, 162
    Victoria's economic downturn, 159–60
    view of miners, 219–20
Blanshard, Richard, 23, 242
Blue Book, 85–86, 140–41, 146–50, 288–89
Boston Bar, 87, 89, 96–97, 108, 180, 200, 246
Brew, Chartres, 75n85, 228
Bridge Creek, 123
Bridge River, 97, 225
Bridgman, Samuel and Jane, 169
British Columbia
    becomes Canadian province, 11, 14–15, 166, 291–92

history, 11–12, 13
history as colony (1846–1871), 12–16
and Hudson's Bay Company, 18–19
as Indigenous place, 18
and United States, 12, 16
See also Colony of British Columbia; United Colony of British Columbia
British Columbia Loan Act 1864, 134
British North America Act 1867, 94, 257, 279
Brown, Robert Lundin, 179
Burdett-Coutts, Angela, 167, 186, 187
Burnaby, Robert, 212, 217–18, 239
Burrard Inlet, 108, 147, 157, 173, 270
Bushby, Agnes (née Douglas), 191, 249, 286
Bushby, Arthur Thomas, 87, 249, 284, **285**, 286
Bute Inlet, 145, 243

California
acquired by US, 35
Black migrants, 43, 174–75
gold rush, 14, 32, 35, 38, 41, 42, 94, 180, 210, 217, 222
Mexican possession, 24, 35
miners from, 48, 65, 87, 130, 132, 155, 159, 180, 211, 213, 223, 256–57, 259, 265, 266
threat to BC, 45
trade with Victoria, 33
winter retreat for miners, 72, 88, 221–22, 235
See also San Francisco
Canada
creation, 94, 257
cross-country railway, 57, 254–55, 273, 282–83, 287, 289
purchases Rupert's Land from HBC, 261, 271, 274, 276, 282
road link to BC, 118–19, 122, 129–30, 253–55
threat of annexation by US, 256, 264, 281
union with BC, 260–61, 262–63, 264–66, 270–72, 274, 277–80, 281–83, 286–88, 289–90
Canada Flat. *See* Lillooet
Cann, George, 99, 100
Cardwell, Edward, 142, 158
Cariboo gold rush
beginning, 100–103
Bishop Hills visits, 202–3
British media coverage, 122
decline, 156, 160, 161–62
depletes Fraser River settlements, 101, 118, 218, 267
described by Begbie, 218, 235
described by Burnaby, 218
described by gold commissioners, 220–21
described by justices of the peace, 132
described by Seymour, 155–56, **157**, 221, 235
difference from Fraser rush, 101, **101**, 155, 218–19, 232
justices of the peace, 132 (*see also* gold commissioners)
mining population, 130–31, 132, 224–25
production, 124
richness, 124, 155
roadbuilding, 122, 129–30, 133, 146, 157, 243
winter departures, 102, 124, 141, 155, 156, 220, 232, 234–35
See also Douglas, James; Seymour, Frederick
Cariboo region
about, 100

INDEX

Hudson's Bay Company, 237
Indigenous-white families, **251**
magistrates, 261, 266–67
Musgrave's visit, 277
name, 100n46
political representation, 261, 274
settlement, 221, 235
Carnarvon, Earl of (Herbert, Henry Howard Molyneux), 76, 81, 82, 94, 159
Carrall, William, 274, 283
Cayoosh. *See* Lillooet
Cayuse, 200, 241
Chemainus, 141
Chilcotin people, 145, 243
Chilliwack, 269
Chinese people
  in BC, 65, 149, 171, 203
  and Church of England, 171, 203
  equal treatment, 180, 183, 186, 207
  miners, 65, 89, 171, 180, 195, 220, 223–25
  remain on Fraser River, 155, 195, 217, 223–25, 266, 267, 268
  on Vancouver Island, 86, 141, 153, 171, 196–97
  in Victoria, 196–97, 244
Chinook jargon, 172, 173
Christ Church (Victoria), 172, 193
Christy, Samuel, 58n38
Church of England
  based in Victoria, 27, 164
  in BC, 167, 199–200, 202
  Black worshippers, 170–71, 174, 175–76, 192–93
  Chinese worshippers, 171, 203
  Indigenous worshippers, 170–71, 181–82, 198–201, 203
  iron church, 167, 178, 187
  racial mixing, 170–71, 174, 176, 184, 192, 193, 199, 200

See also Hills, George
Clarendon, 4th Earl of (George William Frederick Villiers), 280
Clinton, 267, 277
coal mining, on Vancouver Island, 29, 33–34, 140, 289
Colonial Office
  about, 16, 20, 22, 25
  BC debt, 59–60, 76–78, 81–82, 106–8, 109–11, 130–32
  BC union with Canada, 262–63, 265–66, 271–72, 274, 279–80, 281–82, 286–87, 289
  Colony of British Columbia, 39, 40, 52–60
  Colony of Vancouver Island, 22–26
  correspondence, 11–12, 16, 20, 25, 290
  correspondence, speed of, 24–25, 52, 66, 138, 287–88
  Fraser River gold rush, 40, 52–54
  Hudson's Bay Company, 18n1, 20–22, 23, 37–38, 72–73
  Indigenous peoples, 37, 63, 132, 242, 277
  James Douglas, 16, 47, 66–67, 72, 76–77, 87–88, 94–95, 107, 127, 134–37, 139, 159–60
  letters from miners' families, 217
  loses interest in BC, 85
  overland link to Canada, 254–55
  Queen Charlotte Islands gold, 35–36
  representative government in BC, 125–29, 135–36, 142–43
  Richard Moody, 92–93, 115, 116–17, 275–76
  Royal Engineers, 60–62, 64, 80–82, 90–91, 103–5, 131–32
  threat of US annexation, 53–54, 65, 265–66
  uniting colonies, 150–51, 161–65

305

INDEX

Vancouver Island Legislative
Assembly, 153, 158–59, 160
view of miners, 53–54, 63, 128, 132, 210, 219–20
See also Blackwood, Arthur; Blue Book; Elliot, Thomas Frederick; Fortescue, Chichester; Granville, 2nd Earl of (Granville Leveson-Gower); Lytton, Edward Bulwer; Newcastle, 5th Duke of (Henry Pelham-Clinton); Rogers, Frederic, Baron Blachford
Colony of British Columbia
absence of white women, 225–27, 240
accuses Douglas of favouring Vancouver Island, 124, 127, 128
agriculture, 87, 116, 118, 123, 148–49, 174, 202, 232
allows non-British political participation, 214
American influence, 63, 147
Blue Book, 146–50
British media coverage, 122
British population, 259–60
capital city, 75 (*see also* New Westminster)
commissioner of lands and works, 112, 117, 261, 284–85 (*see also* Moody, Richard Clement; Trutch, Joseph)
communication with outside, 215
creation, 14, 39, 40, 52–60
deemed superior to US, 259
Douglas replaced as governor, 138–39 (*see also* Seymour, Frederick)
economic development, 59, 87, 147, 155, 156–57, 160
established, 14
falls out of favour with Colonial Office, 85
finances, 59–60, 63–64, 67, 73–74, 94–95, 106–8, 109, 262
gold rushes, 102–3 (*see also* Cariboo gold rush; Fraser River gold rush)
Hudson's Bay Company, 72–73
Indigenous peoples, 129, 145, 147–48, 151, 224, 225, 243
Indigenous population, 149, 224, 225, 251–52
Indigenous-white relationships, 226–31, 233, **251**
law and order, 12–13, 50, 71, 75n85, 132, 180, 227–29, 231, 261
legislative creation, 55–58, 66
name, 57, 58, 59
need for military force, 91, 93, 94–95, 103, 105
overland link to Canada, 118, 122, 129–30, 253–55
population, 50, 71–72, 124–25, 129, 149, 151, 214, 222–26, 240
ranching, 216, 229
religious diversity, 182–83
representative government, 60, 124–29, 135, 136, 151, 226, 229, 230
rivalry with Vancouver Island, 150, 171, 196
roads, 65, 66, 68, 72, 87, 103, 106–8, 119–22, 123, 156–57, 202, 233–34
Royal Engineers, 61, 64, 67–68, 78, 80–81, 89–91, 93–95, 104, 105, 110, 111–15, 117, 130–32
settlement, 50, 58, 69, 75–76, 103–4, 118, 123–24, 148, 156, 221, 232, 234, 235
sources of revenue, 59, 66, 78, 98, 130
subsidizes Vancouver Island, 83, 147, 152–53, 154–55, 159–60, 208
support for British rule, 259–60
threat of US annexation, 105, 106, 110, 208, 237, 255–58

306

INDEX

transportation costs, 99, 119–20, 122, 123, 130–31
union with Vancouver Island, 14, 57, 152, 155, 158, 162–63, 231, 256
winter departures, 149, 208
See also New Caledonia; United Colony of British Columbia

Colony of Vancouver Island (VI)
absence of white women, 239–40
agriculture, 33, 123, 140–41, 259
American influence, 141–44
benefits from mainland gold rushes, 45, 83, 147, 152–53, 154–55, 159–60, 208
British influence, 205
British population, 153
coal mining, 29, 33–34, 140, 289
and Colonial Office, 22
colonization, 14–15, 22, 23, 26–27, 29–32
communication with outside, 24–25
cost of land, 26–27, 31, 58
creation, 14, 20–26
economy, 33–34, 143
fear of Russian invasion, 35
finances, 158
foreign trade, 33
governing structures, 30, 141, 142–44
governor, 23, 138 (*see also* Douglas, James; Kennedy, Arthur)
Hudson's Bay Company, 20–22, 23, 24–26, 28–34, 237
Indigenous population, 29–30, 86, 141, 251–52
Legislative Assembly, 31–33, 125, 142–43, 152–53, 158–59, 160, 162
magistrates, 30n42, 172, 185–86, 213–14, 261
population, 27, 29–30, 86, 123, 140, 141–42, 153, 224, 225
proposal to give non-British vote, 142–43

proximity of US, 27, 31, 33, 34, 35
racial mixing, 170–71
representative government, 30, 31–32, 136, 141 (*see also* Legislative Assembly subentry)
sawmills, 204
settlement, 118, 123, 214, 221
terms of HBC grant, 28, 31
treaties with Indigenous peoples, 26
union with Colony of BC, 14, 57, 161–63, 231, 356
vital statistics, 251
See also United Colony of British Columbia

Columbia River and Kootenay district, 261
Colvile, Andrew, 32
Colyer, Vincent, 280–81
Comox, 203–4
Connolly, Amelia. *See* Douglas, Amelia
Cooper, James, 75n85
Corbett, Elijah, 281
Cotsford, Betsy, 170
Cotsford, Harriet, 170
Cotsford, Thomas, 169–70
Cowichan, 205
Cowichan Bay, 238
Cox, Charles, 287
Cox, William G., 220–21, 226, 230
Cracroft, Sophia, 186–98, 205, 212–13, 249–50
Crease, Henry Pering Pellew, **285**
Crickmer, William Burton, 196
Cridge, Edward, 172, 193
Crimean War, 35, 230, 286
Crossley, Francis, 58n38

Dallas, Alexander, 193, 194, 249
Dallas, Jane (née Douglas), 188–89, 193, 249
Dally, Frederick, 101

dance houses, 246–47
de Cosmos, Amor, **285**
Dewdney, Edgar, **285**
Disraeli, Benjamin, 62
Dog Creek, 203
Douglas (town). *See* Port Douglas
Douglas, Amelia, 24, **25**, 169, 188, 191, 237, 249–50
Douglas, James
  about, 24, 52
  and Bishop Hills, 86, 169, 174, 188, 248
  Cariboo gold rush, 100–101, 123–24, 129–30, 132–33, 232
  class assumptions, 213–14
  conflict of interest as governor, 24, 26, 32–33, 37, 53, 72–73
  correspondence with Colonial Office, 16, 24–25, 166
  correspondence with Lytton, 52–54, 59–64, 68–70, 72–74, 82–83
  criticized, 109, 111, 124–29, 250
  described by Sophia Cracroft, 196
  family, 32, 47, 188–89, 191, 236–37, 248–49, 250, 286
  fear of US annexation, 34–37
  Fraser River gold rush, 38–39, 41–43, 44–51, 64–66, 69, 70–72, 88–89, 219, 221–23
  governor of BC, 14, 40, 59, 70, 85, 117–18, 134–37, 138, 151
  governor of Vancouver Island, 14, 23, 24–26, 33–34, 85, 134–37, 138, 140, 151
  HBC employee, 14, 15, 23–24, 32–33, 39, 53, 59, 63, 86, 209, 236–37
  Indigenous census, 251–52
  and Indigenous peoples, 26, 42–43, 48–50, 63, 102n52, 145, 242
  linking BC with Canada, 118–19, 129–30, 253–54
  Order of the Bath, 84, 137
  photo, **25**
  preference for British colonists, 66, 118, 126–27, 213–14, 253
  preference for Victoria, 83, 124, 127, 128, 135, 153–54, 159–61, 164
  at Prince of Wales celebratory dinner, 205–6
  relationship with Colonial Office, 47, 66–67, 72, 76–77, 87–88, 94–95, 107, 127, 134–37, 139, 159–60
  representative government, 30–32, 124–29
  requests loan, 74, 76–79, 81, 106–8, 119, 120–21, 262
  roadbuilding, 75–76, 94, 96–100, 117–22, 129–30, 135, 233–34
  Royal Engineers, 89, 90–92, 93, 94–95, 96–97, 98, 99, 103, 104, 105, 111–14, 117, 130–32, 138
  significance in BC becoming province, 12, 15–16, 24, 137, 139
  union of colonies, 137, 159
  urges settlement of mainland, 50–51, 103, 232
  in Victoria, 27, 64, 160, 163, 191
  view of Americans, 44–45, 70, 71, 82
  view of Chinese people, 223, 225
  view of miners, 46, 71, 88, 117–18, 209–10, 213, 214, 219
Douglas, Jim, 199
Douglas treaties, 26
Duncan, Eric, 204
Dunn, John Thompson, 170
Dussault, Helene (née Drymouth), **251**
Dussault, Joseph, 251

Edenshaw, 190
Edward VII, 205
Ellice, Edward, 58n38

INDEX

Elliot, Thomas Frederick
- about, 120, 132, 139, 150
- BC finances, 108, 109–10, 120, 132
- Colony of BC Blue Book, 150
- representative government in BC, 126–27, 128
- roadbuilding, 109–10, 120
- Royal Engineers, 98, 114–15
- Vancouver Island Assembly, 142, 153, 158–59
- Victoria vs New Westminster, 128, 139

Elwyn, Thomas, 132

Esquimalt, 24, 35, 45, 47, 83, 141. *See also* Royal Navy

Fedorak, Charles John, 256
Fisher, Robin, 285
fisheries, 147
flour mills, 149, 267, 270
Forster, William Edward, 142–43, 161
Fort George, 28, 254
Fort Hope. *See* Hope
Fort Langley, 28, 47, 78–79, 82, 104, 108, 195, 234
Fort McLoughlin, 238
Fort Rupert people, 245
Fort Shepherd, 267
Fort Simpson, 28, 241, 273
Fort St. James (BC), 24, 28
Fort Stikine, 28, 238
Fort Taku, 238
Fort Victoria, 23, 24, 28, 33, 170, 238. *See also* Victoria
Fort Yale. *See* Yale

Fortescue, Chichester
- about, 107
- BC finances, 107, 108, 109, 120–21
- recommends Douglas's removal, 135
- representative government in BC, 125
- roadbuilding, 120–21
- Royal Engineers, 98, 105, 114–15

view of Arthur Kennedy, 140

Fountain, 222, 223, 240
Francis, Allen, 256
Francis, Jacob, 176
Franklin, Jane, 186–98
Franklin, John, 186
Franklin, W.A., **285**
Fraser, Donald, 210–11

Fraser River
- North Arm, 269–70
- steamships, 72, 121–22, 182, 195, 239, 253–54
- transportation route, 44–45, 47, 75, 119, 121–22

Fraser River gold rush
- abandoned for Cariboo, 101, 118, 218, 267
- benefits to Victoria, 45, 83
- British media coverage, 210–11, 212
- described by Europeans, 56, 155, 194–95, 217
- first year, 38–39, 41, 47–51, 72, 210–11
- gold exports to US, 79
- Hudson's Bay Company, 79–80
- law and order, 47, 48–51, 56–57, 64–66, 69–70, 71, 82, 83, 87, 94–95, 99, 226–29 (*see also* gold commissioners)
- licences, 38–39, 40, 66
- miners, American, 41–42, 43–45, 47, 48, 65, 79, 87
- miners, described, 43, 44–45, 47–48, 64–65
- miners, Indigenous, 39, 42–43, 268
- miners, killed, 65, 68
- miners, numbers, 71, 221–25, 266
- oversight (*see* gold commissioners)
- process, 49, 213
- roadbuilding, 65, 66
- significance in BC becoming province, 12

309

INDEX

steamer travel, 194–95
winter, 77, 88, 211, 218, 221–22, 223
See also Douglas, James; miners, gold
Fraser Valley, 148, 219.
 See also Hope; Yale
Freezy, Chief, 172
French Creek, 220
Friesen, Jean, 167

Gaggin, John Boles, 12, 226, 230–31
Ganges Harbour Settlement, 184.
 See also Saltspring Island
Garrett, Alexander, 171, 199, 243
Gibbon, Edward, 213
Gibbs, Mifflin, 176, **177**, 191
gold
 annual production in BC, 79, 124, 268
 early rushes, 38, 217
 exported from BC, 78, 79
 mining process, 48, **49**, **101**, 101–2, 155, 215, 218–19, 227
 Queen Charlotte Islands/Haida Gwaii, 34, 35–36
 Similkameen, 106
 See also Australia; California gold rush; Cariboo gold rush; Fraser River gold rush; miners, gold
gold commissioners, 220, 226, 228, 231.
 See also Cox, William G.; Gaggin, John Boles; O'Reilly, Peter
Good, Alice (née Douglas), 249
Good, Charles, 249
Gottfried, Frank, 179
Gottfriedson, Frank, 179
Grant, John Marshall, 99–100
Grant, Ulysses S., 280
Granville, 2nd Earl of (Granville Leveson-Gower), 273, 276–77, 279–80
Great Britain
 Imperial project, 54–55

and Pacific Northwest, 14, 16, 19–20
self-supporting colonies, 77
Union Bill (1866), 162–63
unites BC with Canada, 289
US Civil War, 137, 208, 258, 281
US threatens to annex BC, 103, 258
War Office, 62, 80
See also Colonial Office; Royal Engineers
Grey, 3rd Earl of (Henry George Grey), 20–21, 22
Grouse Creek, 132, 221

Haida Gwaii. *See* Queen Charlotte Islands
Haida people, 31–32, 35–36, 173, 184, 190, 237, 245–46, 247
Hamley, Wymond Ogilvy, 284, 285, **285**, 288
Hankin, Philip J., 189, 244, 274, 276, 284, **285**, 288
Hanley, Wymond, 75n85
Hard Curry gold mine, 133
Harris, Dennis, 249
Harris, Martha (née Douglas), 249, 250
Harris, Thomas, 189, 205–6
Harrison Lake, 65
Harrison Lillooet Road, 97
Harrison River, 96, 104, 222
Hart, John, 170
Havelock, Henry, 274
Haynes, John Carmichael, 226, 228–30
Helmcken, Cecilia (née Douglas), 32, 191, 248–49, 250
Helmcken, John Sebastian
 about, 15, 33
 arrives in Victoria, 29
 ensures Victoria is capital of united colony, 164
 marriage, 248–49
 on Matilda McNeill, 237

310

memoir, 15, 260
on petition for annexation, 263–64
proposal to give "aliens" the vote, 142–43
Speaker of Assembly, 32–33, 142
union with Canada, 260–61, 283
on William Cox, 230
Hendrickson, James, 12, 23
Herbert, Robert George Wyndham, 286–87
Higgins, D.W., 209n1, 256–57
Hills, George
  about, 167
  accepts diversity, 171, 173, 174–76, 180–81, 182–83, 186, 192
  appointed bishop of BC, 167–68, **168**
  based in Victoria, 164, 171
  Black people, 174–76, 178, 185, 188, 192
  dance houses, 246–47
  described by Sophia Cracroft, 187, 188
  Indigenous languages, 180, 181–82
  Indigenous people, 170–71, 172–73, 174, 181, 184–85, 202
  Indigenous women, 181, 184, 185–86, 240–42, 245–47
  Indigenous-white relationships, 12–13, 169–70, 178–79, 183, 201, 204–5, 231
  and James Douglas, 86, 169, 174, 188, 248
  and Jane, Lady Franklin, 186
  later career, 206–7
  marriage and sexual relations, 178–79
  middle way, 171, 173, 176, 182–83, 186, 188, 192, 206–7
  nuanced view of colonies, 166
  private journal, 12–13, 15, 86, 166–67
  racial mixing, 169–71, 174–75, 183
  Roman Catholics, 171, 174, 184, 207
  servants, 169
  travels in BC, 12–13, 99, 171, 173–74, 178–83, 198–203, 213, 215–17, 231, 234, 241, 255
  travels on Vancouver Island, 203–5
  view of Americans, 183, 259
  view of miners, 212, 213, 215
  view of religion in BC, 182–83
  views on women, 201
  See also Church of England
Hill's Bar, 50, 217
Holbrook, Henry, **285**
Hope
  Bishop Hills visits, 178, 181–82, 200
  calls for representative government, 125–26, 127
  Fraser gold rush, 47, 70–71, 118, 195, 211
  HBC post, 28, 178
  Indigenous-white relationships, 178–79
  population, 126, 222, 223, 224, 240
  roadbuilding, 89, 96, 99–100, 108, 129
hospitals, 95, 127, 221
Hudson's Bay Company (HBC)
  about, 18–19
  in British Columbia, 18–19, 28, 72–73
  in Cariboo region, 237
  coal mining, 29, 34
  and Colonial Office, 18n1, 20–22, 23, 37–38, 72–73
  Colony of Vancouver Island, 20–22, 23, 24–26, 28–34, 237
  effects of colonization, 72–73
  employee relationships with Indigenous women, 19, 32, 216, 226, 236–38, **239**, **251** (*see also* Douglas, Amelia)
  employees remain in BC, 19, 216, 237–38
  employees settle on Vancouver Island, 29, 30, 32

311

Fraser River gold rush, 79–80
in Pacific Northwest, 20, 24
Rupert's Land, 18n, 261, 265–66, 271–72, 274, 276, 282
trading posts, 28
on Vancouver Island, 14, 20, 33
in Victoria, 193
See also Douglas, James; specific forts
Humphreys, Thomas B., 12–13, 231, 274, **285**

Indigenous peoples
on BC mainland, 14–15, 16, 18, 41–42, 224, 251–52
Bute Inlet massacre, 145, 243
Church of England, 170–71, 181–82, 198–201, 203
in colonial government service, 48, 50
and Colonial Office, 37, 63, 132, 242, 277
in Colony of BC, 129, 144–45, 147–48, 149, 151, 224, 225, 243
death rituals, 148, 169, 195
employed by white farmers, 269
Fraser River gold rush, 36, 39, 42–43, 48–50, 57, 65, 68, 70, 211
liquor regulation, 70, 148
mine for gold, 39, 42–43, 47–48, 268
reserves, 145, 189, 269
Roman Catholic church, 145, 184
vaccination, 132, 202
on Vancouver Island, 29–30, 86, 140, 141, 251–52
Vancouver Island treaties, 26
in Victoria, 172–73, 184, 185–86, 189–90, 196, 239, 241, 242–47
winter habitations, 195–96
See also under Douglas, James; Hills, George

Indigenous women
accusations of profligacy, 185, 242–44
children from relationships with white men, 201, 216, **239**, **251**, 291
(*see also* Douglas, James: family)
clothing style, 181, 184, 190, 200, 240–41
mistreatment by white men, 185–86, 211, 241–47
prostitution, 185, 242, 243–45
relationships with HBC employees, 19, 32, 216, 226, 236–38, **239**, **251**
(*see also* Douglas, Amelia)
relationships with prospectors, 12, 16, 216, 233
relationships with white men, 12–13, 167–70, 178–79, 183, 201, 204–5, 216, 226–31, 233, 236, 249, 252
significance in BC becoming province, 12, 252
sold by Indigenous men, 245, 246, 247
viewed as lesser persons, 178–79, 201, 204–5, 207, 216, 231, 236, 242, 247–48
See also under Hills, George
Invisible Generations (Barman), 13
Ireland, Willard, 280
Irving, Henry Turner, 90, 103

Jewish people, 188, 197, 203
Joseph, Comatatqua, **239**
Julia (Colville woman), 229
Julie (Saanich woman), 238

Kamloops, 28, 216, 251, 255, 267
Keenleyside, Hugh, 258, 260
Kekachunchalee, 179
Kennedy, Arthur
about, 140

governor of Vancouver Island, 86, 138–39, 140–44, 152–54, 158, 160, 161–62, 163
   Indigenous peoples, 140, 243–44
   later career, 163
   supports union of colonies, 153–54
   view of Americans, 141, 143–44, 153
Ker, Robert, 284, 286
Killian, Crawford, 184
Kimberley, 1st Earl of (John Wodehouse), 283, 286–87, 289, 290
King, D.B., **285**
Kootenays, 28, 156, 261, 271

Labouchere, Henry, 42, 52, 57
land pre-emption, 104, 184, 234, 267, 268, 269–70
Lemon, John, 237, 238
Lester, Peter, 185, 192
Lightning Creek, 277
Lillooet
   Anglican priest, 179
   Bishop Hills visits, 200, 202, 215
   English settlers, 213, 215
   magistrate, 268
   miners, 215, 268
   political representatives, 261, 274
   roads, 97, 108, 202, 253
   settlement, 123, 268–69
   transportation charges, 119
Lillooet Lake, 99, 234
Lillooet people, 179, 182, 198–99
Lincoln, Abraham, 256
logging, 59, 147, 148, 270
London Times, 92n16, 122, 144, 210–11
Loring, James, 133
Lowe, Robert, 58n38
Lucy. *See* Semo, Lucy
Lyne, Angelique (née Dussault), **251**
Lyne, William (Billy), Jr., 251

Lyne, William Sr., 251
Lytton (town)
   Bishop Hills visits, 179, 200, 202
   Chinese miners, 223
   government representatives, 226, 261
   Indigenous-white relationships, 178–79, 228
   magistrate, 180, 226, 227–28, 261
   Musgrave visits, 277
   photo, **73**
   population, 72, 214, 222, 223
   roads, 72, 96, 108, 253
Lytton, Edward Bulwer
   about, 52
   Colony of BC, 55–57, 66–69, 76–77, 219
   committed to "Imperial project," 54–55
   correspondence with Douglas, 52–54, 59–64, 68–69, 72–74, 82–83
   demands colonial self-sufficiency, 94–95
   letters of introduction, 217, 231
   relationship with Douglas, 69–70, 94–95
   Royal Engineers, 60–61, 67, 80–81, 114
   secretary of state for the colonies, 52, 55, 58, 68, 85
   vision of cross-Canada railway, 57

Macaulay, Thomas Babington, 213
Marie (Cowichan woman), 238
Martha (Nass woman), 237
Matilda (Haida woman), 237
Maurice, Marguerite, 238
Mayne, Richard Charles, 193
McCall, William, 99, 100
McClure, Leonard, 257
McKay, Donald, 170

McLean, Donald, 216
McNeill, William Henry, 237
Merivale, Herman, 39, 61–62, 65, 77, 91
Metchosin, 141
Methodists, 203
miners, gold
American, 41–42, 43, 45–46, 48, 53–54, 63, 65, 69–70, 79, 87, 128, 180, 183, 217, 255
from Australia and New Zealand, 202
British, 43, 65, 87, 213–14, 215, 216–17
and British authority, 46, 48–50, 54, 64, 69–70, 71, 87, 94, 180
Chinese, 65, 89, 155, 171, 180, 195, 217, 220, 223–25, 266, 267, 268
described by Robert Burnaby, 212
described by Sophia Cracroft, 194, 195, 212–13
described in *London Times*, 211
diet, 203, 211
independence, 209–10, 211–12, 215
Indigenous, 39, 42–43, 47–48, 268
and Indigenous peoples, 42, 48–50, 70, 211
leave BC, 72, 78, 88, 221–22, 256
migratory, 149, 217–18, 221–23, 225, 232
numbers, 64–65, 71, 101, 221–25
photographs, **227**
prefer Victoria to New Westminster, 128, 139, 152
relationships with Indigenous women, 12, 16, 216, 233, **239**
relationships with white women, 238–39
remain in BC, 69, 72, 88, 101–2, 218, 232, **233**, 233–35
roadbuilding, 65, 66, 68
significance in BC becoming province, 12, 208–9, 221, 233–35

in winter, 77, 88, 149, 208, 211, 218, 221–22, 223, 234
See also California; Cariboo gold rush; Fraser River gold rush; Oregon; San Francisco; Victoria
Minie, Frederique, 237, 238
Monsell, William, 279
Moody, Mary, 92
Moody, Richard Clement
angles for governorship, 91–92, 115, 116–17, 275–76
criticized by Colonial Office, 92–93, 115, 116–17
criticized by Douglas, 98, 103
endless demands, 89–90, 92–93, 95–96, 111–14, 117
leads Royal Engineers in BC, 83, 94
leaves BC, 116–17
refuses to account for expenses, 113–14, 117
salary, 91, 112
tension with Douglas, 93, 96, 98, 105, 111–12, 117, 132, 138
See also Royal Engineers
Moresby, Charlotte, 229
Moresby, Fairfax, 26, 229
Morris (Maurice), Mary, 238
Moses, Mr., 187
Mucho Oro gold claim, **227**
Murderer's Bar, 211
Musgrave, Anthony
about, 276
achieves union with Canada, 287–88, 289–90
appointed governor of BC, 275–76
builds support for union with Canada, 277–80, 282–83, 286–87
later career, 291
photo, **275**
public pensions, 278, 283–84
visits mainland, 277–78

INDEX

Nanaimo
   Bishop Hills visits, 205
   coal mining, 29, 34
   government representation, 261
   population, 29, 140, 141
   support for annexation, 280
   support for union of colonies, 158
New Caledonia, 24, 28, 56, 57, 58.
   See also Colony of British Columbia
New Westminster
   Bishop Hills visits, 173, 198, 234
   Black people, 198
   calls for representative government, 124–26, 128
   capital of Colony of BC, 75, 92
   celebrates Queen's birthday, 99, 145
   Church of England, 171
   economic development, 147, 156, 157, 269–70
   government representatives, 261, 274
   under Governor Seymour, 144, 145, 146, 156–57, 163–64, **165**
   land sold at auction, 104
   Musgrave's visit, 277
   name, 75
   population, 126, 224–25, 234
   proposed as capital of united colonies, 163–64
   roads, 108, 122, 146, 157
   Royal Engineers, 95, 104, 115–16, 163
   schools, 147, 198
   settlement, 147, 234, 269–70
   subordinate to Victoria, 128, 139, 152, 159, 163
Newcastle, 5th Duke of (Henry Pelham-Clinton)
   advocates land pre-emption, 104
   BC finances, 108, 109, 111, 119, 120–21, 133
   replaces Douglas as governor, 85, 136–37

   on representative government, 129, 151
   on Richard Moody, 116
   Royal Engineers, 98, 104, 105, 111, 114
   San Juan Islands, 105–6
   secretary of state, 85, 150, 158
   uniting colonies, 150–51, 158
Nicol, Charles, 87
Norman Morison (ship), 29

Okanagan, 28, 229, 267
Oregon
   acquired by US, 19, 35
   BC gold rushes, 39, 47, 72, 106, 155, 159
   British settlers, 118, 259
   fur trade, 20
   threat to Vancouver Island, 31, 37, 45, 91
   war with Indigenous peoples, 36–37, 50, 91
   winter retreat for miners, 72
O'Reilly, Peter, 123, 132, 220, 266–67, 284
Ormsby, Margaret, 27, 116, 142
Osoyoos, 229–30

Pacific Northwest
   about, 19
   divided between UK and US, 14, 19–20, 35
   HBC activities, 24
   See also British Columbia; Colony of British Columbia; Colony of Vancouver Island; Hudson's Bay Company; Oregon; Vancouver Island; Washington state
Papeus, Mr., 175
Paxton, Edith (neé Pierce) "Sis," 251
Paxton, Lois, **251**
Pelly, John Henry, 18n1, 20–22, 26
Pemberton (town), 108, 200

INDEX

Pemberton, Joseph Despard, 172, 230, 284, 286, 288
Perry, Adele, 24
Phillippo, George, 284, 288
Pidcock, Reginald, 204
Pierce, Vivian (née Lyne), **251**
Pittendrigh, Emily, 230
Plutarch, 213
Port Douglas
    Bishop Hills visits, 12–13, 198–99, 231
    calls for representative government, 125–26
    gold commissioners, 231
    Indigenous peoples, 198–99
    Indigenous-white relationships, 12–13, 231
    population, 89, 97, 99, 126, 199, 222
    roads, 89, 97, 99, 119–20, 129, 233–34, 253
    school, 147
    served by steamers, 72
Port Townsend, 79–80

Queen Charlotte Islands, 31, 34, 35–36
Queensborough. *See* New Westminster
Quesnel(le), 122, 132, 133, 214, 223, 240, 277
Quintasket, Christine, 229

railway, cross-Canada, 57, 254–55, 273, 282–83, 287, 289
Red River Settlement, 129, 254
Reeve, Henry, 203
Richards, G.H., 205–6
Richardson, Mr., 184
Richfield, 122, 220
roadbuilding
    Bute Inlet, 145, 243
    Cariboo Road, **97**, 146
    by civilian labour, 96, 98, 100, 130, 233–34

    in Colony of BC, 65, 66, 68, 72, 87, 89, 94, 103, 117–22, 129–31, 133, 135, 156–57, 202
    link to Canada, 118, 122, 129–30, 253–55
    loans, 106–8, 109–10, 111, 119–21, 134, 146
    lower freight costs, 99, 119–20, 122, 123, 130–31
    by Royal Engineers, 96–100, 104, 105, 111, 112
    size of task, 75–76
    by volunteers, 65, 66, 68, 233
    in Yale District, 267
Robinson, William, 266
Robson, John, 274, **285**
Rock Creek, 224, 225
Roebuck, John Arthur, 58n38
Rogers, Frederic
    BC union with Canada, 262, 271–72, 279–80, 286–87
    capital of united colonies, 164
    on James Douglas, 160
    Rupert's Land, 265–66, 271–72
    threat of US annexation, 262, 265–66
    union of colonies, 162
Roman Catholics
    ethnicity, 182
    and Indigenous people, 145, 174, 184
    segregate schools, 175, 188, 198
    in Victoria society, 205
    won't serve Anglican bishop, 171
Royal Engineers
    costs imposed on BC, 89–91, 93–94, 95, 105, 110, 111–15, 117
    funding, 61, 64, 67–68, 78, 80–81, 90, 130–32
    leave BC, 114–15
    roadbuilding, 89, 93–94, 96–100
    seen as failure, 103, 104, 105
    sent to BC, 60–62, 64, 80, 83

INDEX

settle in BC, 100, 105, 115–16
threat from US, 91
See also Moody, Richard Clement
Royal Navy, 35, 36, 45, 47, 52–53, 239, 242–43
See also Esquimalt
Royle, Stephen, 27
Rupert's Land, 18, 21–22
Russia, 24, 35, 257
Russian America, 14, 24, 170
See also Alaska

Saanich, 118, 238, 259
Saltspring Island, 141, 184, 213–14
San Francisco
  news of Fraser gold rush, 210–11
  racism, 192
  source of miners, 43, 44, 142, 210–11, 222
  transfer point for Victoria shipping, 138
  waypoint for mail from BC, 287–88
  winter destination of miners, 78, 149, 152, 156, 221–22
San Juan Islands, 37, 80, 103, 105–6, 192, 194
Sanders, Edward, 268–69, 284, 286
Sandon, Viscount, 58n38
Sapperton, 95–96, 181, 194
Satellite (ship), 47, 51, 65, 70
sawmills, 147, 204, 270
Semo, Lucy, 12–13, 231
Seton Lake, 200
Seward, William, 255–56, 257–58, 281
Seymour, Frederick
  about, 144
  death, 274
  governor of Colony of BC, 138–39, 144–46, 226
  governor of united colony, **157**, 163, 165, 262–63, 266, 272–73

and Indigenous peoples, 144–46
and New Westminster, 152, 163–64
population of BC in winter, 232
population of Colony of BC, 214, 225
threat of annexation by US, 265–66
view of Indigenous women, 242
view of Indigenous-white relationships, 251
views on union of colonies, 152, 153–58
views on union with Canada, 264–65, 271
visits Cariboo, 146, 221, 235
Shakespeare, William, 213
Shepherd, Edmund, **239**
Similkameen, 100, 106, 108, 224, 267
Sisters of St. Ann, 198
Skinner, Thomas, 32
smallpox, 202
Smith, Robert L., 152–53
Soda Creek, 122
Songhees people, 172, 190, 245
Spaulding, Mr., 284, 286
Spuzzum, 87, 99, 108, 133, 200
Staines, Robert John, 27
Stephen, James, 18n1
Steptoe, Edward, 50
Stikine people, 247
Stouts Gulch (BC), **101**, 227

Taschelak, 181
telegraph, 147, 157, 215
Tête Jaune Cache, 254
The Times (London), 92n16, 122, 144, 210–11
Thompson's River Post, 28, 251.
  See also Kamloops
Thornton, Edward, 280–81
Tomah/Sklaniuk, Lucy, 251
Trinity Anglican Church (New Westminster), 171

INDEX

Trudelle, Louis, 237, 238
Trutch, Joseph, 119, 133–34, 175, 244–45, 283, 284–85, **285**, 290
Tschymānā, Chief, 174
Tsilhqot'in people, 145, 243
Tsimshian people, 173, 184, 241, 247
Tyrwhitt-Drake, Montague William, **285**

United Colony of British Columbia
  agriculture, 267, 268–70, 289
  arguments pro/con annexation by US, 258, 259–60, 262–63, 264, 278
  arguments pro/con union with Canada, 260–61, 264–65
  becomes Canadian province, 208, 253, 289, 290, 291–92
  Blue Book, 288–89
  British immigrants, 265
  capital city, 163–65
  communication with outside, 287–88
  debt, 262–63, 266, 272, 289, 290
  Legislative Council, 261, 264–65, 270–71, 273, 274, 282, 286–87, 288
  magistrates, 261, 266–70
  negotiations with Canada, 282–83
  obstacles to union with Canada, 265, 266, 271–72, 274, 278–79
  petition to Queen Victoria, 263–64
  petition to US president, 263–64
  population, 278
  public pensions, 278, 283–84
  representative government, 261, 271, 272, 278–79, 282, 288
  support for British rule, 259–60
  threat of US annexation, 262–63, 280–81
  united colony proclaimed, 162–63
  See also Musgrave, Anthony; Seymour, Frederick

United States
  Black people, 43, 176
  as British colony, 77–78
  Civil War, 137, 201, 205–6, 208, 258, 281
  demands reparations from Britain, 137, 208, 258, 281
  English immigrants leave for Canada, 118
  faster settlement of Pacific Northwest, 27
  land pre-emption, 27, 104
  Queen Charlotte Islands gold, 35–36
  racism, 174–76, 188, 192, 259
  threatens to annex BC, 31, 34–36, 45, 57–58, 103, 208, 237, 255–58, 280–81
  threatens to annex Canada, 256, 264, 281
  See also California; Oregon; San Francisco; San Juan Islands; Washington state

Vancouver (BC), 173, 270
Vancouver Island
  coal mining, 29, 33–34, 140, 289
  population, 278
  support for US annexation, 280
  against union with Canada, 260–61, 274
  See also Colony of Vancouver Island; United Colony of British Columbia
Verney, Edmund Hope, 250
Victoria
  absence of white women, 239–40
  benefits from mainland gold rushes, 45, 83, 152, 154–55, 159–60, 164
  capital of united colony, 164–65
  Church of England, 27, 164, 167, 172, 178, 187, 193 (*see also* Hills, George)

dance houses, 246–47
desire to unite with Colony of BC, 158
display of Secessionist sentiment, 205–6
free port, 147, 162, 279, 282
HBC employees, 193
liquor licences, 141, 143
members of Legislative Council, 261
police, 44, 244, 246
population, 29
preferred to New Westminster, 128, 139, 152, 159, 163
prostitution, 241–42, 243, 244–45
schools, 27, 175, 188, 189–90, 192, 194, 198, 245
shopping, 193, 196
suffers from decline in Cariboo business, 156, 160, 161–62
support for annexation by US, 265, 280
winter refuge for miners, 141, 155, 156, 208, 218, 234–35
See also under Black people; Douglas, James; Fort Victoria; Indigenous peoples
Victoria, Queen, 58, 59, 71, 84, 99

Walkem, George, 274
War of 1812, 19
Washington, Mrs., 176
Washington state, 19, 35, 39, 47, 106, 287
Wells Fargo, 79n95
Wentworth-Fitzwilliam, Charles William, 58n38
White, James, 58n38
Williams Creek, 132, 157, 218, 221, 277
Williams Lake, 123, 129, 133, 203
women, European
arrive with Royal Engineers, 95, 113–14, 117

in Colony of BC, 12, 16, 123–24, 125, 225–26, 234, 238, 240
in Colony of VI, 27, 197, 204–5, 238–40
servants, 204, 238–39
See also Cracroft, Sophia
Wood, Thomas L., **285**
Wyld, James, 58n39

Yale
Bishops Hills visits, 200, 202, 203
Chinese miners, 224, 266
Church of England, 196, 203
convention on union with Canada, 270–71
government representatives, 71, 125, 231, 261, 274
Indigenous habitation, 195–96
Musgrave's visit, 277
population, 71, 203, 222, 223, 240, 266
roads, 98–99, 121, 129, 156, 253, 267
schools, 147
settlement, 266–67
steamboats, 195
Young, William A.G., 75n87, 273